baker's
bible atlas

baker's bible atlas

CHARLES F. PFEIFFER

CONSULTING EDITORS
E. Leslie Carlson, Old Testament
Martin H. Scharlemann, New Testament

REVISED EDITION

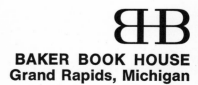

BAKER BOOK HOUSE
Grand Rapids, Michigan

Baker's BIBLE ATLAS
Copyright © 1961, 1973, 1979 by
Baker Book House Company

4211-29
ISBN: 0-8054-1129-1

Library of Congress Catalog Card Number: 60-15536

First Printing, June, 1961
Second Printing, September, 1961
Third Printing, February, 1962
Fourth Printing, June, 1962
Fifth Printing, January, 1964
Sixth Printing, October, 1965
Seventh Printing, December, 1966
Eighth Printing, September, 1969
Ninth Printing, March, 1971
Tenth Printing, January, 1972
Eleventh Printing (Revised), January, 1973
Twelfth Printing, April, 1974
Thirteenth Printing, March, 1975
Fourteenth Printing, April, 1976
Fifteenth Printing, September, 1977
Sixteenth Printing (Revised), August, 1979
Seventeenth Printing, July, 1980
Eighteenth Printing, February, 1982

Printed in the United States of America

PREFACE

Western man looks to the lands surrounding the eastern Mediterranean for the origins of his spiritual and cultural heritage. Here, in the Tigris-Euphrates and the Nile river valleys man's earliest civilizations developed. Here, too, transpired the events recorded in the Bible—events of profound importance to the spiritual life of men in every age.

Much of the Bible is a record of history—the history of God's dealings with His people Israel. The events it records took place in a specific geographical environment. Although in some respects separated by God from the idolatries of her neighbors, Israel never lived in isolation. Ur of the Chaldees, Canaan, Egypt, Moab, the Philistines, the Aramaeans, Assyria, Babylonia—these and many more places and peoples constantly meet the reader of the Bible. To understand our Bible we must be able to visualize the dealings of Israel with her neighbors, and to observe the bearing of geography on the history of Israel. The modern westerner may have difficulty in reconstructing the scenes removed from him by thousands of miles as well as by thousands of years. The gap may be bridged in part by an atlas, and the maps, illustrations, and text of *Baker's Bible Atlas* are designed to help the reader to understand his Bible.

The text of this atlas is closely related to the Biblical narrative. Although some attention is given to the Near Eastern backgrounds of Biblical history, the Bible itself is the focus of attention. Our concluding chapters seek to trace the continuing history of Bible lands, emphasizing the work of modern archaeologists who have provided so much that is of value to the Bible student. The Bible lands are very much in the news today, and the careful student will want to gain some understanding of modern developments.

An atlas must, of necessity, be the result of the labors of many individuals. It is a pleasure to acknowledge the gracious assistance given by the consulting editors, Dr. E. Leslie Carlson of Southwestern Baptist Theological Seminary, Ft. Worth, and Dr. Martin Scharlemann of Concordia Seminary, St. Louis. These men have given freely of their time and labors and should be considered in large measure responsible for the excellencies of the Atlas. Final decisions were made by the editor, however, and he alone must accept responsibility for errors of fact or judgment.

*　　*　　*　　*　　*

For the use of the photographs, which enhance the value of the Atlas, we express thanks to Professor Jack Finegan of the Pacific School of Religion and to President Nelson Glueck of Hebrew Union College — Jewish Institute of Religion who has provided photographs of his explorations. Organizations that have generously given access to their collections are acknowledged elsewhere.

We wish to acknowledge the work of the C. S. Hammond Company in providing maps which embody the latest advances in cartography even as they reflect the current state of knowledge in the area of Biblical geography. The maps of the Modern Near East and Excavated Sites in Bible Lands are reproduced through the courtesy of *The Christian Science Monitor*.

The co-operation and counsel of Mr. Cornelius Zylstra of the Baker Book House has marked every step in the production of the Atlas. The burden of detail has fallen on his shoulders, and he has cheerfully seen the project through to completion.

Charles F. Pfeiffer

Beverly Farms, Mass.
March 3, 1961.

PUBLISHER'S PREFACE TO THE ELEVENTH PRINTING

The widespread use of this atlas has not decreased since it was first published in 1961. In this span of time eleven printings were made, and nearly 100,000 copies of *Baker's Bible Atlas* are now in print.

The eleventh printing of this atlas has been revised to reflect the most recent developments in the political scene of the Near East and to present the latest research in the field of archaeology. In addition, new photos that more effectively and attractively illustrate the text are included.

The author, Charles F. Pfeiffer, has painstakingly updated the text. With this textual revision, along with the graphic improvements, we are happy to continue making this atlas available to Bible students everywhere.

CONTENTS

I.	World of the Old Testament	11
II.	The Land of Palestine	23
III.	The Table of the Nations	35
IV.	The Empires of the Fertile Crescent	45
V.	The Journeys of the Patriarchs	53
VI.	Lands of the Sojourn and Wandering	63
VII.	The Exodus and Wilderness Wandering	71
VIII.	Palestine before the Conquest	77
IX.	The Conquest of Canaan	85
X.	Palestine Divided among the Twelve Tribes	93
XI.	Palestine under the Judges	99
XII.	The Kingdom of Saul	121
XIII.	The Empire of David and Solomon	129
XIV.	The City of Jerusalem	139
XV.	The Divided Kingdom	147
XVI.	Judah Alone	155
XVII.	Exile and Restoration	161
XVIII.	The Hellenistic Age	169
XIX.	The Roman Empire	175
XX.	New Testament Palestine	181
XXI.	The Life of Christ	189
XXII.	Early Apostolic History	199
XXIII.	Journeys of the Apostle Paul	205
XXIV.	Geography of the Book of Revelation	223
XXV.	The Centuries Between	229
XXVI.	Bible Lands Today	237
XXVII.	Biblical Archaeology in the Twentieth Century	249
	Time Line of Bible History	271
	Gazetteer	275
	Index of Modern Place Names	325
	Index	331

Colored Maps

Pages 105-120

1. Physical Map of Palestine.............................105
2. The Ancient World at the Time of the Patriarchs.......106-107
3. The Exodus 108
4. The Empire of David and Solomon....................109
5. The Kingdoms of Israel and Judah....................110
6. Medo-Babylonian Realms 111
7. The Persian Empire 112
8. Jerusalem of David and Solomon.....................113
9. Jerusalem in the Late Monarchy.....................113
10. Jerusalem in Jesus' Time 113
11. Palestine in New Testament Times..................114
12. The Roman World 115
13. Journeys of the Apostles 116
14. Paul's First Missionary Journey.....................116
15. Paul's Second Missionary Journey...................117
16. Paul's Third Missionary Journey....................117
17. Paul's Journey to Rome............................118
18. The Spread of Christianity.........................119
19. Archaeological Sites in Israel and Jordan.............120

Black and White Maps

Ancient Semitic World 12
Mountains and Rivers of the Old Testament World 17
Natural Divisions of Palestine 24
Bodies of Water of Palestine 28
Mountains of Palestine 31
The Nations According to Genesis 10 36
The Fertile Crescent 46
The Route of the Exodus and the Conquest of Canaan 64
Canaan before the Conquest 78
Canaan as Divided among the Twelve Tribes 94
The Kingdom of Saul 122
Outline Map of Ancient Jerusalem 140
The Kingdoms of Israel and Judah 148
The Roman World in the Time of Caesar 176
Palestine in the Time of Christ 182
Early Journeys of Christ, Galilean Ministry and Later Ministry of Christ 190
The Spread of Christianity 230
The Modern Near East 238
Excavated Sites in Bible Lands 250

Illustrations

Overlooking the Mediterranean 15
A Cedar of Lebanon 18
Ur of the Chaldees 21
The Nile River 22
The River Jordan 27
The Mound of Megiddo from the Air . . 34
Ziggurat at Ur 48
The Stele of Hammurabi 49
Ishtar Gate, Babylon 51
Beer-sheba 54
Sodom 57
Underground Silos 58
Shechem 61
Hebron 62
The Sphinx and the Pyramids 66
The Way to Elath 68
The Traditional Mount Sinai 72
View from Mount Nebo 76
Ruins of Byblos 81
The Sea of Galilee 83

Amman, Jordan 84
Jericho 86
Hazor Excavations 88
Valley of Ajalon 91
Huleh Valley 92
The Mound of Beth-shan (Beit Shean) . . 97
Mount Tabor 100
Ashkelon 103
Nob, the City of Priests 124
Wilderness of Judaea 127
Gibeah of Benjamin 130
Pool at Gibeon 132
Megiddo, Model of
    "Solomon's Stables" 135
Copper Mining in the Negeb 137
Ezion-geber 138
Aerial View of Jerusalem 143
Jerusalem 144
Hill of Ophel, Jerusalem 146
Moabite Stone 150

Shrine at Megiddo 152
Black Obelisk of Shalmaneser 153
A Judaean Landscape 156
Mound of Megiddo 159
Air View of Susa (Biblical Shushan) ... 162
Stairway from Darius' Palace,
    Persepolis 165
Gate of Xerxes, Persepolis 166
Persepolis 168
Ancient Greek Theatre, Epidaurus ... 170
The Erechtheum, Athens 174
Pisidia 179
Gerasa 180
Tiberias on the Sea of Galilee 185
The Treasury at Petra 187
Petra 188
Road from Nazareth 192
Synagogue at Capernaum 193
Jacob's Well 194
The Village of Sychar 195
Antioch-on-the-Orontes 200
Harbor of Caesarea 203
The Appian Way 206
The Ruins at Ephesus 208

Ancient Aqueduct, Pisidia 211
Neapolis 213
Areopagus 215
Steps to the Areopagus 216
Antioch-on-the-Orontes 217
The Taurus Mountains 224
Ephesus Today 226
Pergamum 227
Patmos 228
Air View of Dura-Europus 232
Crusader Castle at Sidon 235
At the Mount of Olives 236
Tiberias on the Sea of Galilee 241
Bay of Haifa 243
Hebron 244
Scene in Modern Jordan 246
Near Jerusalem 248
Step-Trench, *Tell Jeheidah*, Syria 250
Gulf of Aqaba 253
Caves overlooking Wadi Qumran 255
Sargon's Palace at Khorsabad 264
Pergamum 267
Athens 268
Corinth Canal 269

Acknowledgments of Illustrations

Christian Science Monitor, The, pages 238, 250

Consulate General of Israel, pages 68, 88, 241

Finegan, Jack, page 86

Galloway, Ewing, pages 170, 269

Glueck, Nelson, page 257

Gökberg, H., pages 208, 226, 227, 267

Hayesod, Keren, page 27

Israel Government Tourist Office, pages 15, 184

Israel Office of Information, pages 58, 100, 137, 192, 203, 243

Jordan Tourist Department, pages 187, 244

Kelsey Museum of Archaeology, University of Michigan, pages 179, 211

Levant Photo Service, pages 62, 84, 92, 97, 127, 138, 144, 146, 180, 188, 195, 236

Matson Photo Service, pages 21, 72, 76, 91, 124, 130, 142, 156, 194, 200, 246, 258

Oriental Institute, University of Chicago, pages 34, 49, 50, 135, 150, 152, 153, 159, 162, 165, 166, 168, 252, 264

Palphot, page 103

Pfeiffer, Charles F., page 57

Pritchard, James B., page 132

Religious News Service, pages 18, 54, 101, 217, 228, 248

Royal Greek Embassy, pages 213, 215, 216, 268

Stewart, James P., page 61

Three Lions, Inc., page 83

Trans World Airlines, pages 66, 174, 206

Turkish Information Service, page 224

UNESCO, page 22

Yale University, page 233

Zion Research Library, pages 48, 235

The World of the Old Testament

ANCIENT SEMITIC WORLD

Copyright by C. S. HAMMOND & Co., N. Y.

Scale of Miles

0   100   200   300   400

The World of the Old Testament

In a spiritual sense, Palestine (or Canaan) is the homeland of Christian as well as Jew. The events of Biblical history took place at the very heart of the ancient world—and that history continues to challenge man with its God-given message.

Man is a creature of space as well as time, so that geography must be added to history if we are to gain an adequate concept of his varied activities. This is also true of our study of the Bible. Palestine (Canaan) is located along the eastern coast of the Mediterranean—with trade routes leading to Europe and Africa. There are direct roads northwest into Asia Minor and northeast into the Tigris-Euphrates Valley. Palestine itself frequently served as a buffer state between rival nations of the ancient world.

The position of Palestine is not less strategic today than in ancient times, however. In part this is due to the oil deposits which have been found there. Rivalries among Arab states, and the bitter controversies between Israeli and Arab make for increasing tensions. With many problems still unsettled, the modern states of the Middle East are seeking to rebuild and irrigate barren lands which once were described as "flowing with milk and honey."

The events of Old Testament history took place in the territory which is bounded by four great bodies of water—the Mediterranean (or the Great Sea), the Black Sea, the Caspian Sea, and the Persian Gulf. This territory extends eastward as far as Iran (ancient Persia)

and westward to Egypt. The mountains of Ararat in Armenia and Mount Sinai in the Sinai Peninsula mark its northern and southern limits. This territory extends about fourteen hundred miles from east to west, and nine hundred miles from north to south. In area it is equal in size to about one-third the land area of continental United States or about 1,110,000 square miles.

A large part of the area included in the Old Testament world is desert. A glance at the map will confirm this. The desert occupying the southern part of the Old Testament world is actually an extension of the Sahara Desert which extends across northern Africa and which is interrupted only by the Nile River and the Red Sea. East of the Red Sea it continues in the land now known as Saudi Arabia.

North of the desert, however, is a cresent-shaped strip of territory to which the Egyptologist, J. H. Breasted, gave the name, "the Fertile Crescent." Beginning at the head of the Persian Gulf, the Fertile Crescent extends northwestward through the Tigris-Euphrates Valley to the region of Haran and Carchemish—the Padan-aram of the Bible. It then moves southwestward along the Mediterranean, through Syria and Palestine to the borders of Egypt.

The great civilizations of history have developed along waterways and in terrain which could be profitably cultivated. Egypt, at the western end of the Old Testament world, has been appropriately called "the gift of the Nile." At the other end of the Fertile Crescent, Sumerians and their Babylonian and Assyrian successors developed a high culture in the land of Mesopotamia. Other parts of the Fertile Crescent were settled by Aramaeans, Canaanites, Phoenicians, Philistines, and—of course—Israelites. Part of the history of Israel took place at each end of the Fertile Crescent—in Egypt and Babylon—but the greater part of her history was spent in the land known as Canaan, or Palestine. Except for a brief period during the reigns of David and Solomon, Israel was not a world power. Instead, she served as a buffer state between the conflicting interests of Egypt and a succession of great powers in the East—Assyria, Babylonia, and Persia.

LARGE BODIES OF WATER

Mediterranean Sea. The most important waterway of classical antiquity, the Mediterranean, borders Palestine on the west. There are few harbors along the Palestinian coast of the Mediterranean, with the result that Israel made little use of the sea. Joppa (modern Jaffa) served as a port during Old Testament times, and Caesarea became the major Palestinian port under Roman rule (*see* Map 1). Haifa, at the foot of Mount Carmel, is the principal Mediterranean port for modern Israel.

The Phoenicians of Tyre were the great sea-going people of the Bible world. They engaged in trade and established colonies throughout the eastern Mediterranean and North Africa. Phoenician traders first introduced the alphabet to their Greek counterparts. Hiram, king of the Phoenician city-state of Tyre, assisted David and Solomon in their building projects.

The Mediterranean was mentioned as the western boundary of the territory promised to Israel. It is called "the Great Sea toward the going down of the sun" (Josh. 1:4).

Persian Gulf. East of the Arabian peninsula, forming the western border of Persia, is the Persian Gulf which connects the Tigris-Euphrates Valley with the Arabian Sea and, ultimately, with the Indian Ocean. Many writers suggest that alluvial deposits brought downstream by the Tigris and Euphrates rivers have caused the Persian Gulf gradually to recede. The city of Ur, the ruins of which are now one hundred and fifty miles from the head of the Persian Gulf, is thought by some scholars to have been on the Gulf in ancient times. Recent geological studies, however, suggest that the coastline of the Persian Gulf has not changed appreciably since the days of the Sumerians.

Caspian Sea. The largest inland body of water in the world, the Caspian Sea is a salt lake, about 169,000 square miles in extent at the northeastern extremity of the Bible world. It is about 730 miles long from north to south, and varies in width from 130 to 270 miles. It forms the natural boundary between the continents of Europe and Asia, and is nearly surrounded by Russian territory today. Bordering the Caspian Sea on the south is modern Iran.

Red Sea. The fifteen hundred mile length of the Red Sea forms a natural division between Africa and the Arabian Peninsula. Through the Gulf of Aden and the Arabian Sea it empties into the Indian Ocean. This body of water averages about 180 miles in width, diminishing gradually at its northern and southern extremities. Since the building of the Suez Canal, ships pass through the Red Sea en route from the Mediterranean to India and the East. The Red Sea has

Overlooking the Mediterranean from Haifa. From the slopes of Mount Carmel the city of Haifa can be seen in the foreground. The Bay of Acre (Accho) and the Mediterranean appear in the background.   *Courtesy, Israel Government Tourist Office*

two northern arms: on the west the two hundred mile long **Gulf of Suez** which separates Arabia from Egypt and leads into the Suez Canal, and on the east the hundred mile long **Gulf of Aqaba** which separates the Sinai Peninsula from Arabia (*see* Map 3).

Black Sea. North of Asia Minor, and forming a natural boundary between Europe and Asia, is the Black Sea. This body of water covers about 168,500 square miles, and is about 750 miles in length and 385 miles in breadth. The Black Sea is not mentioned in the Old Testament.

There are two other bodies of water which merit mention. They are the Dead Sea and the Sea of Galilee. Since these lie within the borders of Palestine proper they will receive attention in Chapter 2.

IMPORTANT RIVERS

Tigris. Rising in the highlands of Armenia in Asia Minor, the Tigris River flows about 1,150 miles southeastward to join the Euphrates. The combined stream, known as the *Shatt al Arab*, flows into the Persian Gulf about one hundred miles farther downstream. In ancient times the important Assyrian cities of Ashur and Nineveh were on the banks of the Tigris. This river is the Hiddekel of Genesis 2:14 and Daniel 10:4.

During the days of the Assyrian kings the Tigris was an important means of transportation, and its importance has been revived during the twentieth century. Mosul, in northern Iraq, the center of extensive oil deposits, and Baghdad the city of the medieval caliphs and the capital of modern Iraq, are both situated along its banks. Modern irrigation projects of the Iraqi government include the rebuilding of canals first built over three thousand years ago to connect the Tigris and Euphrates rivers.

Euphrates. The Euphrates has its source in the Anti-Taurus range of eastern Turkey not far from the Black Sea, and flows through Syria in a southeasterly direction toward southern Mesopotamia where it joins the Tigris to form the *Shatt al Arab.* About 1,675 miles in length, the Euphrates is first mentioned in Genesis 2:14. It was "the river" (Exod. 23:31; Deut. 11:24) or "the great river" (Gen. 15:18; Deut. 1:7) of the Old Testament. At one time the northern boundary of the Hebrew monarchy (II Sam. 8:3; 10:16; I Kings 4:24), the Euphrates served as the dividing line between spheres of Babylonian and Egyptian influence during the reign of Jehoiachin of Judah (II Kings 24:7).

Orontes. From the Beqa'a Valley in Lebanon, the Orontes flows about two hundred and fifty miles northward between the Lebanon and Anti-Lebanon Mountains through northwestern Syria, after which it turns westward, flowing into the Mediterranean at Seleucia Pieria, the port city of ancient Antioch-on-the-Orontes. The early Christian center of Antioch, as well as the Old Testament cities of Riblah, Hamath, and Kadesh were located in the Orontes valley. At Kadesh-on-the-Orontes, a historic battle was fought between the Hittites and the forces of Rameses II (*ca.* 1285 B.C.), during which the Egyptian Pharaoh had to cut his way out of an ambush to save himself and most of the Egyptian army. The non-aggression pact which was subsequently signed between the Pharaoh of Egypt and the king of the Hittites was the first of its kind in history.

Nile. The lakes of equatorial Africa and the mountains of Ethiopia produce the streams known as the White and the Blue Nile which converge about 1,625 miles north of Lake Victoria, at Khartoum, the capital of the Sudan. Another stream, the Atbara, adds its silt-laden water at Atbara, about two hundred miles northeast of Khartoum. The result is the Nile, the river which made Egyptian civilization possible. Ancient historians did not exaggerate when they called Egypt "the gift of the Nile." Without the Nile, Egypt would be part of the great desert which crosses northern Africa and the Arabian peninsula.

From its ultimate headstream, the Kagera, the Nile flows about four thousand miles northward to the Mediterranean to form the longest river system in the world. From Khartoum to its principal mouths at the Delta, it traverses about eighteen hundred miles of country which is completely barren except for the fertility produced by the annual flooding of the Nile River supplemented from early times by irrigation. The modern Egyptians conserve the waters of the Nile by means of a dam at Aswan which provides the means for irrigation of land which would otherwise be useless. In antiquity, Egypt comprised the Nile valley north of the first cataract at Aswan (ancient Syene), opposite the island of Elephantine. The Nile valley from the first cataract to the head of the Delta was known as Upper Egypt, and the Delta was termed Lower Egypt.

The Nile is said to have had seven mouths in ancient times, two of which were of particular significance. The Pelusiac, or eastern branch, was nearest Canaan and was most familiar to the peoples of the Fertile Crescent. The

WORLD OF THE OLD TESTAMENT

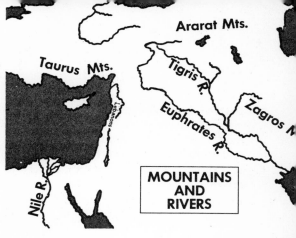

Canopic, or western branch, was used in trade with Greece, the Mediterranean islands and, later, with Phoenicia.

The predictability of the Nile floods formed the basis for the economy and, ultimately, the wealth of Egypt. Each year the flood begins in June at the head of the Delta (modern Cairo). It reaches its height in October, after which it recedes until April. As the flood waters recede, crops are sown on the moist fertile soil. An inadequate inundation spells famine for Egypt. At Thebes in Upper Egypt (*see* Map 6) the Nile at flood stage should reach thirty-six feet above its ordinary level. By the time it reaches the head of the Delta it has diminished to twenty-five feet above normal. Flowing through the Delta the waters disperse until they are but four feet above normal as they enter the Mediterranean.

MOUNTAIN RANGES

Ararat. The mountains of Ararat, the landing place of Noah's ark (Gen. 8:4), are located in eastern Armenia about midway between the Caspian and Black Seas. Tradition states that Noah's ark landed on the twin-peaked mountain known to the Turks as *Agri Dagh* ("the painful mountain") which rises seventeen thousand feet from the Plain of Aras, itself nearly three thousand feet above sea level. The Kurds call the traditional Ararat *Koh-i-Nu* ("mountain of Noah"). The surrounding area consists of lava-formed terrain which is for the most part uninhabited.

Zagros. The Zagros Mountains, east of the Tigris River, run from northwest to southeast paralleling ancient Assyria and Elam. They reach an elevation averaging nine thousand feet and form the traditional boundary between Assyria and Media.

Taurus. Along the southern coast of Asia Minor, the Taurus (or Silver) Mountains reach as high as 12,250 feet above sea level. North of Tarsus (*see* Map 15), the birthplace of Paul, the Taurus range may be crossed through the Cilician Gates, an important pass leading to the heart of Asia Minor. The range has important mineral deposits, including silver for which the mountains are named. Northeast of the main Taurus range is the Anti-Taurus range, including the Amanus mountains of northern Syria.

Lebanons. The Lebanons, forming a continuation of the Taurus range of Asia Minor, are, in reality, two roughly parallel ranges, the Lebanons on the west and the Anti-Lebanons on the east. After extending one hundred miles through Syria and Palestine, they lead into the Palestine ranges and ultimately end at the Gulf of Suez. Between the two Lebanon ranges is the fertile valley known in antiquity as Coele Syria ("hollow Syria"), a name loosely applied at times to all of southern Syria and to Palestine with the exception of Phoenicia. In Joshua 11:17 the valley proper is called *Biq'ath ha-Lebanon* ("Valley of the Lebanon"). It is sometimes referred to as the Beqa 'a ("the valley").

Mount Hermon (*see* Map 1), with its snow-covered peaks which dominate the landscape of northern Israel, is a spur of the Anti-Lebanons reaching a height of over nine thousand feet. The cedars of Lebanon were esteemed by the inhabitants of ancient Egypt and Mesopotamia, as well as by David and Solomon who used them in their building projects. Some may still be seen on *Jebel Makmal*, one of the highest points in the Lebanons (*ca.* 10,200 feet).

The Lebanon Range continues southward where it becomes the plateau of Upper Galilee and the "hill country" of Lower Galilee (*see* Map 1). A branch south of the Plain of Jezreel is known as the Carmel ridge (*see* Map 1). The central mountain range extending through Samaria and Judaea (*see* Map 1) is a continuation of the Lebanons, and mountains east of the Jordan are similarly extensions of the Anti-Lebanon range, with the Jordan valley forming an extension of the Beqa'a valley.

A Cedar of Lebanon. Choice wood from the cedar forests was exported to Egypt and the Fertile Crescent nations. Hiram of Tyre provided cedar wood for Solomon's Temple in Jerusalem. The great forests of antiquity are now greatly diminished in size.

Religious News Service Photo

LANDS

During the course of Old Testament history many changes took place in the political, social, and economic life of the Fertile Crescent. Boundaries were frequently shifted and strong peoples were made tributary to conquering nations. The locations of the lands on the maps are therefore largely approximate.

North and east of the Fertile Crescent there were three lands which played a part in Old Testament history:

Armenia. The high plateau and mountain region southeast of the Black Sea, north of Assyria, was the land of the Armenians. Assyrian inscriptions speak of the land as *Urartu* (Ararat) (*see* Map 2). Here Noah and his sons left the ark; and to this region the sons of Sennacherib, the Assyrians who besieged Jerusalem, fled after having killed their father (II Kings 19:37).

Media. The Medes, or Medians, inhabited the region northeast of Babylon between the Caspian Sea and the Zagros Mountains (*see* Map 2). Madai, a son of Japheth (Gen. 10:2), appears in Scripture as the ancestor of the Median people.

Persia. Southeast of Media and north of the Persian Gulf in the western part of the Iranian plateau, the ancient Persians made their first historical appearance (*see* Map 6). Under King Cyrus, Persia became a world power conquering the neighboring Medes, the Lydians of Asia Minor, and the Babylonian Empire. The Persians under Cambyses gained control of Egypt, but Greece resisted successfully and ultimately, under Alexander of Macedon, brought about the defeat of Persia.

The most highly developed civilizations of antiquity developed in the lands of the Fertile Crescent:

Sumer. The land at the head of the Persian Gulf became the center of the oldest civilization of the Fertile Crescent. Our earliest written documents, inscribed with a stylus on clay tablets, come from the city-states of Sumer where civilization was flourishing as early as the fourth millennium B.C.

Babylonia. Babylon proper was a city-state on the lower Euphrates. During its long history it was ruled by kings from various lands—Sumerians, Akkadians, Amorites, Assyrians, and Chaldeans. Hammurabi, the Amorite lawgiver, and Nebuchadnezzar, the greatest king of the Neo-Babylonian Empire, are familiar figures in ancient history. Under Nebuchadnezzar, Babylonia became master of the Fertile Crescent and Jerusalem itself was destroyed (587 B.C.).

Assyria. Assyria proper was the land bounded by the mountains of Armenia on the north, the Median highlands on the east, and the lower Zab River on the south. It extended a short distance west of the Tigris into Mesopotamia. During the time of its greatest extent—the eighth century B.C.—the Assyrians controlled territory from the Persian Gulf to the Mediterranean. The combined forces of Media and Babylon brought about the destruction of Nineveh (612 B.C.), the Assyrian capital. The empire itself came to an end shortly after this decisive battle.

Elam. The land between the Zagros Mountains and the lower Tigris River, east of Babylonia, was occupied by a people known as Elamites. As early as the days of Abraham, we read of a "King of Elam" named Chedorlaomer (Gen.

14:1-11). During the eighth and seventh centuries B.C. the Elamites were persistent foes of the Assyrians, but the Elamite capital at Susa (Biblical Shushan) fell about 645 B.C. Elamites later served with Assyrian forces in the invasion of Palestine (cf. Isa. 22:6). After the fall of Nineveh (612 B.C.) they enjoyed a brief period of independence before being incorporated into the Babylonian Empire of Nebuchadnezzar. Cyrus, the founder of the Persian Empire, began his career as prince of Anshan, the province of Elam south of Susa. Elam became a part of the Persian Empire, with Susa serving as one of its capitals. Elamite Jews were present at Pentecost, according to Acts 2.

Mesopotamia. The Hebrew Bible uses the term *Aram Naharaim* ("Aram of the Two Rivers") for the district where Abraham and his family sojourned en route to Canaan. This territory, generally referred to as *Mesopotamia* ("between the rivers"), includes the land east of the Middle Euphrates, as far north as the River Habor. In Greek usage the term Mesopotamia signified the Tigris-Euphrates valley, including the southern sector once occupied by Sumerians and Babylonians.

Lands surrounding the eastern Mediterranean are frequently mentioned in the Biblical records.

Lands of the Hittites. The center of Hittite power was in Asia Minor along the Halys River although Hittite peoples also settled in Syria and Palestine. Carchemish, on the Euphrates River at the arch of the Fertile Crescent, was the wealthy eastern center of Hittite power. Israelite contacts with Hittites date from patriarchal times (Gen. 15:20) to the days of the monarchy (II Chron. 8:7).

Syria. The region along the eastern coast of the Mediterranean from the Anti-Taurus Range southward to Bashan is commonly known as Syria, a term used by the Greeks for the tribes ruled by the Assyrians. The Biblical name for the country is Aram (*see* Map 5), and the people, Aramaeans. From Padan-aram ("Plain of Aram") came Rebekah to be the wife of Isaac. Although a part of David's empire, the Aramaeans formed independent city-states in subsequent years. The most important of these had its capital at Damascus.

Phoenicia. Phoenician territory was the narrow strip of land between the Mediterranean and the Lebanon Mountains, north of Palestine and south of the Orontes River (*see* Map 1). From their port cities of Tyre and Sidon, the Phoenicians colonized the islands of the Mediterranean and northern Africa. The Tyrian colony of Carthage challenged Rome in its bid for domination of the western Mediterranean.

Canaan. The name Canaan is used in the early books of the Bible to designate Palestine west of the Jordan. The term appears in the Amarna tablets (14th century B.C.) in referring to the Phoenician coast. All of western Syria was called Canaan by the Egyptians. Usually, however, the terms Canaan and Palestine are synonymous. Before its conquest by Joshua, Canaan comprised a large number of city-states which were nominally subject to Egypt.

Philistia. Non-semitic Philistines migrated from the Aegean region, particularly Crete (Biblical Caphtor), to the coastal plain of Palestine between Joppa and Gaza (cf. Amos 9:7) (*see* Map 4). Though there were Philistines in Canaan during patriarchal times, they arrived in

Ur of the Chaldees. This is a general view of the ruins of that ancient city in present day Iraq.

Courtesy, Matson Photo Service

The Nile River. To the right in the photo, on the facade of an ancient temple, four colossi representing Rameses II (1290-1224 B.C.) stand about sixty-seven feet high.

Courtesy, UNESCO

force about the first quarter of the twelfth century B.C. and became one of the chief rivals of the Israelites. They had a high culture and had learned the use of iron before it was known in Israel (cf. I Sam. 13:19-22) .

It is ironical that the Philistines should give their name to the land historically associated with Israel. Roman writers called it *Palestina*, a shortened form of the Greek *Syria Palaistine*, the name used by the Greeks for southern Syria, including Judaea.

Egypt. Egypt is the name of the country along the Nile River in Africa where a highly diversified culture developed a thousand years before the days of Abraham. Bordering Canaan, Egypt had significant contacts with Israel from the days of the patriarchs until the end of Biblical history. This country will be discussed in more detail in Chapter 6.

The Land of Palestine

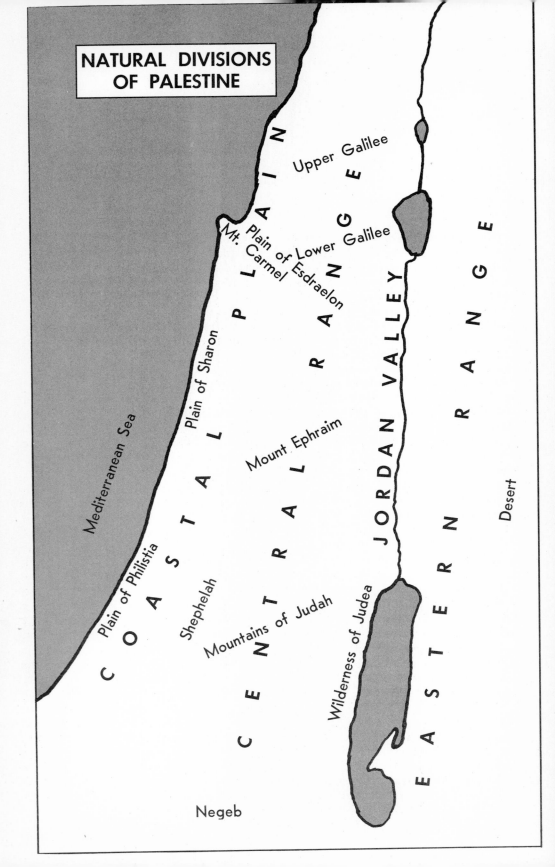

NATURAL DIVISIONS OF PALESTINE

Upper Galilee

Plain of Lower Galilee

Plain of Esdraelon

Mt. Carmel

Plain of Sharon

Mediterranean Sea

Mount Ephraim

JORDAN VALLEY

EASTERN RANGE

Desert

Plain of Philistia

Shephelah

Mountains of Judah

Wilderness of Judea

COASTAL PLAIN

CENTRAL RANGE

Negeb

The Land of Palestine

The name Canaan was used in the Old Testament for the land between the Jordan and the Mediterranean, bounded on the north by the Lebanon Mountains and on the south by the desert.

Palestine, strictly speaking "Philistine land," came to be applied to the land occupied by the twelve tribes of Israel. This included both Canaan and the region east of the Jordan known as Gilead. Palestine proper is bounded on the north by the Leontes River, Mount Lebanon and Mount Hermon, on the east by the Syrian Desert, and on the south by the River of Egypt (*Wadi el-Arish*) and the Negeb. The Mediterranean is its western boundary. This includes a territory of about 12,000 square miles, roughly equivalent to the combined area of Massachusetts and Connecticut.

NATURAL DIVISIONS

Palestine includes a series of clearly defined topographical features running north and south between the Mediterranean and the desert. These are, in order from west to east: the Coastal Plain, the Central Range, the Jordan Valley, and the Eastern Range. Beyond the Eastern Range is the desert.

Coastal Plain. The narrow Coastal Plain extends with varying widths along the entire western coast of Palestine except where Mount Carmel projects out into the Mediterranean. Immediately north of Carmel is the small but very fertile Plain of Accho, and then the narrow plain which served as the home of sea-going Phoenicians in ancient times. South of Carmel is the Plain of Sharon, extending southward to Joppa with a width varying from six to twelve miles. In ancient times Sharon was largely wooded. It is one of the most fruitful areas of the modern state of Israel which takes pride in the famous Jaffa (i.e. Joppa) oranges.

From Joppa to the borders of Egypt the Coastal Plain widens still farther to a width of twenty miles. This section is called the Plain of Philistia, for here the ancient foes of Israel maintained their strongholds.

An important spur of the Coastal Plain directly east of Mount Carmel links the coastal area with the Jordan Valley. This Plain of Esdraelon, or Valley of Jezreel, is the strategic key to Damascus and the Tigris-Euphrates Valley on the one hand, and Syria-Palestine and Egypt on the other. The fortress city of Megiddo, overlooking Esdraelon, has a history going back to 3500 B.C. It was captured by the Egyptian Pharaoh Thutmose III (*ca.* 1468 B.C.). Canaanites controlled the city during the time of Joshua, but the destruction of Sisera's army (Judg. 4) gave the Israelites control of Esdraelon and its cities. Napoleon campaigned there (1799) as did the British general Allenby, Viscount of Megiddo (1917).

Between the Coastal Plain and the Central Range in the area from Gaza to Jaffa is a series of foothills called by their Hebrew name, the Shephelah. They are semidetached from the main hill country by several connected cross valleys running north and south. As George Adam Smith puts it, "The mountains look on the Shephelah, and the Shephelah looks on the sea—across the Philistine Plain. It curves round this plain from Gaza to Jaffa like an amphitheatre." The Shephelah served as a buffer between Israel and her Philistine enemies. In times of strength, the Israelites occupied the towns of the Shephelah. In times of weakness, the Philistines pushed the Israelites back into the mountains.

Central Range. The area most commonly associated with the Israelites is the "hill country" or mountainous region between the Shephelah and the Jordan Valley, actually an extension of the Lebanons. It extends southward as far as the desert, which begins near Hebron. The Central Range may be divided into subsections corresponding to the mountains of Galilee, Samaria, and Judaea.

In rugged Upper Galilee, the mountains average about 2,800 feet above sea level. Mount Meiron *(Jebel Yarmuk),* the highest point in the state of Israel, is located near the village of Meiron. The altitude here is almost 4,000 feet.

Lower Galilee has hills about 1,800 feet high. In this section lies the fertile Plain of Jezreel extending about twenty miles in a northwest to southeast direction, and fourteen miles northeast to southwest.

The hill country of Samaria is called "Mount Ephraim," while the Judaean highlands are known as "The mountains of Judah." The altitude varies from 2,000 to 3,000 feet. Immediately north and west of the Dead Sea is the Wilderness of Judaea, called Jeshimon, "desolation" in the Old Testament—an area of limestone, flint, and marl about thirty-five miles by fifteen. Here David fled from Saul. Here, too, the Qumran Community settled in the second century B.C., producing Biblical and sectarian texts which were preserved for two thousand years in caves near the Dead Sea.

South of Hebron is the area known as the Negeb, or Negev. Because of its geographical location in relation to Judaea, the term Negeb was translated "south" in earlier versions of the Old Testament (cf. Gen. 13:1 A.V.). Actually it means "dry" and refers to the semi-arid territory which extends as far south as Elath on the Gulf of Aqaba. Vegetation is abundant in the Negeb immediately after the winter rains, but the land is as barren as the desert during the hot summer. The Biblical patriarchs sojourned there, but they lived in tents and took their flocks to better pasture land when the need arose. Beer-sheba, in the heart of the Negeb, served as the southern boundary of Israel ("from Dan to Beer-sheba") and was a place of importance because of its wells. It is still the market center of the Israeli Negeb under its modern name *Beer-sheva.*

Jordan Valley. The Jordan depression is one of the most remarkable geological phenomena on the earth's surface. The sources of the Jordan at Banias (Phoenician Panias), near Caesarea Philippi are 1,200 feet above the Mediterranean. The river drops to 1,292 feet below sea level at the delta where it enters the Dead Sea, the bottom of which is another 1,300 feet lower.

From the point where the Jordan leaves the Sea of Galilee to the place where it enters the Dead Sea is sixty-five miles. The Jordan has a barrier of cliffs on either side from two to fifteen miles apart. The plain of Jericho, immediately north of the Dead Sea, is fourteen miles wide.

The ground that lies between the normal channel of the Jordan and the level reached during the floods of March and

The River Jordan. Between the Sea of Galilee and the Dead Sea, the Jordan flows through a deep depression (the *Ghor*), three miles wide at its northern end, and twelve miles wide in the region of Jericho. The Jordan bed itself (the *Zor*) varies in width from ¼ mile to two miles. Along its banks is a jungle of semi-tropical vegetation known as the "Pride of Jordan." From the air the Jordan looks like a gigantic twisting serpent between green thickets or white marl hills. It is not navigable, and even canoe travel is hazardous.

Courtesy, Keren Hayesod, Jerusalem

April is a jungle of tropical vegetation. The Jordan curves and twists through this thick growth of trees and scrub known in the Old Testament as "the Swelling," or more accurately, "the pride of Jordan." Lions and other beasts lurked there and became the terror of settlers (cf. Jer. 12:5; 49:19).

The land of Palestine is actually cut into two parts by the deep valley, known as *el Ghor,* which extends southward from the area between the Lebanons and Anti-Lebanons of Syria, and includes the Sea of Galilee, the Jordan Valley, and the Dead Sea and continues southward as the Arabah. The geological fault which produced *el Ghor* may be traced for 3,000 miles to Lake Nyasa in southern Africa.

Eastern Range. The mountains east of the Jordan rift are higher and steeper than those to the west. The northern section, extending from Damascus to the Yarmuk River, which enters the Jordan just below the Sea of Galilee, is known as Bashan. This plateau area, about 2,000 feet above sea level, was known for its productivity in Old Testament times (cf. Ps. 22:12; Jer. 50:19).

Between the Yarmuk Valley and Moab lies the land of Gilead, the well-watered tableland where the Gadites and the Reubenites settled (Josh. 13:8-12). The hills of Gilead were covered with trees, and the land was famous for its medicinal balm (Jer. 8:22; 46:11). Mount Nebo, reaching a height of 2,631 feet, was in Gilead. From the summit of Nebo, Moses looked westward to view the Promised Land which he did not enter.

The Mountains of Moab stretch like a wall, 3,000 feet high, along the eastern rim of the Dead Sea. There is no natural boundary between Gilead and Moab. At times Moab occupied the entire eastern shore of the Dead Sea. More frequently, however, the River Arnon, which enters the Dead Sea at about the central point

of its eastern shore, was the northern boundary of Moab (cf. Num. 21:13). The Zered River (*Wadi el-Hasa*) formed the southern boundary of Moab, separating it from Edom.

BODIES OF WATER

Palestine's history has been largely conditioned by its waterways. These may be classified as follows:

The Jordan River. The sources of the Jordan are four, three from the east and

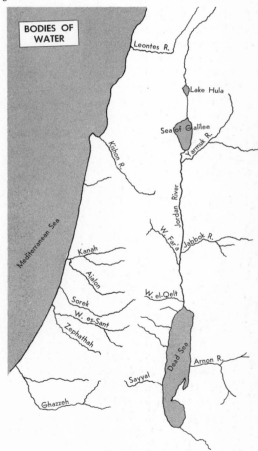

one from the west. These are: (1) The *Nahr Bâniyâs*, which drains the south side of Mt. Hermon and also receives water from the cave springs once dedicated to the Greek god Pan at Caesarea Philippi, 1,000 feet above sea level; (2) The *Nahr el-Liddâni*, which gushes from a fountain at Dan *(Tell el-Qâdî)* and joins the Banias about five miles from their points of origin; (3) The *Nahr Hasbâni* which runs a course of twenty-four miles due north roughly in line with the Jordan River itself; and (4) The *Nahr Bereighith*, which is the westernmost source.

From the *Nahr Hasbâni* source of the Jordan to Lake Hula is a distance of about forty miles; from Hula to the Sea of Galilee, fifteen miles; and from the Sea of Galilee to the Dead Sea, sixty-five miles. By its windings, however, the Jordan is about two hundred miles long. It varies in width from eighty to one hundred and eighty feet. Its depth is from five to twelve feet. During its course it falls over three thousand feet, an average of twenty-two feet to the mile.

The Lakes. There were three lakes in Palestine:

Lake Hula was a triangular sheet of water, about four and one-half miles long and three and one-half miles wide, located in the swampland of Upper Galilee. Some scholars suggest that Hula was the ancient Merom where Joshua defeated the Hazor confederacy (cf. Josh. 11:5 ff.). A location at Meiron southwest of Hula is favored by more recent scholarship. The state of Israel completed a program of land reclamation by draining the Hula swamps. Two deep canals were dug across the marshes from the north to south. The water now flows on to the Jordan, the bed of which was straightened and deepened to facilitate the flow to the Sea of Galilee.

The Sea of Galilee, called Chinnereth ("Harp") in the Old Testament, is twelve and one-half miles long, and seven and one-half miles wide at its greatest breadth, and seven hundred feet below sea level. Its shape has been likened to a harp (hence Chinnereth), or a pear.

The Dead Sea, also known as the Salt Sea and Lake Asphaltitis, is forty-eight miles long and has a maximum width of ten miles. Its surface is 1,292 feet below the level of the Mediterranean, and it reaches a depth of 1,300 feet. It has been calculated that six and one-half million tons of water flow into the Dead Sea daily. Because of the extraordinary evaporation caused by the intense heat of the area, the water left in the sea contains about 25 per cent of solid substance. Salt, potash, and bromine are currently extracted commercially from the sea at the Israeli city of Sedom (the site of Biblical Sodom according to one tradition).

The Brooks or Wadis. Wadi is an Arabic word used to designate the channel of a watercourse which is usually dry. During and after the rainy season the wadi is a river or stream, frequently large and rapid. Important wadis of Palestine are:

From east of the Jordan:

The Yarmuk flows from the highlands of Bashan and enters the Jordan south of the Sea of Galilee. The Land of Gilead forms the southern border of the Yarmuk and its tributaries.

The Jabbok, now known as the *Nahr ez-Zarqâ,* flows through the heart of the tableland of Gilead and enters the Jordan a little south of midway between the Sea of Galilee and the Dead Sea. It was the place where Jacob wrestled with the mysterious "man" (cf. Gen. 32:24) who humbled him and blessed him.

The Arnon, now known as the *Wadi el-Mûjib,* enters the Dead Sea about the middle of its eastern shore. It was crossed by the Israelites (Deut. 2:24) and frequently served as northern border of Moab (Judg. 11:18).

The Zered, now known as the *Wadi el-Hasā,* enters the Dead Sea at its southeastern corner. It served as the natural boundary between Edom and Moab and was crossed by the Israelites enroute to Canaan.

Flowing into the Jordan from the west:

The Wadi Far'ā flows from the mountains of Samaria, entering the Jordan south of its junction with the Jabbok.

The Wadie Qelt runs eastward from the Judaean highlands, entering the Jordan just north of the Dead Sea. Jericho obtains water from Wadi Qelt.

The Wadi Qumrân extends from the Judaean wilderness to the northwest corner of the Dead Sea. From the second century before Christ until about A.D. 70, a monastic sect usually identified with the Essenes had a settlement near the mouth of the *Wadi Qumrân.* Scholars of ancient history and Biblical scholars have found the leather scrolls found in caves near the Qumran community center a valuable source of information.

The Kidron separates the eastern slope of Jerusalem from the Mount of Olives. It flows southward, joining the Valley of Hinnom (Gehenna) which bends around the western and southern borders of the old city of Jerusalem. After the Kidron and Hinnom valleys join at the southeast of Jerusalem, they continue toward the Dead Sea under the name of *Wadi en-Nar* ("Valley of Fire"), which enters the sea south of Qumran.

The Wadi Murabba'ât has its source in the Judaean highlands and empties into the Dead Sea about one-quarter the way down its western shore. Scrolls of a period later than those discovered at Qumran have been found in the *Wadī Murabba'ât.*

The Wadi Sayyal also flows from the Judaean wilderness to the Dead Sea, which it enters about two-thirds the way down its western shore.

Flowing into the Mediterranean:

The Leontes, or Litani, flows southward between the Lebanon and the Anti-Lebanon ranges, thence westward to enter the Mediterranean north of Tyre. The Leontes and the Orontes are the only two rivers of Syria which reach the Mediterranean. The Orontes is in the far north of Syria. Its chief city, Antioch, was important in New Testament times.

The Kishon is formed by branches from Mount Tabor and Mount Gilboa which meet in the Plain of Jezreel at the foot of Megiddo. It then flows westward, entering the Bay of Acre north of modern Haifa. The victory of Israel over the Canaanite forces of Sisera was attributed to a storm during which the Kishon overflowed its banks. The Canaanite chariots sank in the mire and Sisera, the Canaanite captain, met his death in the tent of Jael.

The Crocodile River, or *Nahr ez-Zerqā,* flows westward from the Carmel ridge into the fertile Plain of Sharon, entering the Mediterranean north of Caesarea. It marks the southern limit of Phoenician penetration.

The Kanah, now known as the Yarkon, enters the Mediterranean north of Tel Aviv after winding westward from the mountains of Samaria. A few miles east of its mouth it is joined by the Ajalon which has its source in the mountains north of Jerusalem. In Biblical times the Kanah served as the southern boundary of Manasseh, with Dan and Ephraim sharing the territory immediately to the south. The Yarkon, the name by which the stream is known in modern Israel, has been connected by a pipe line with the Negeb where it serves as the principal source of water for irrigation.

The Sorek flows westward from Jerusalem, entering the Mediterranean about ten miles south of Joppa. Here, centuries ago, Samson performed his heroic exploits and fell under the charms of the Philistine girls. In 1889 a railroad to Jerusalem was built in the Valley of Sorek. Trains between Tel Aviv and Jerusalem follow this route today.

The Wadi es-Sant, or Valley of Elah ("Vale of the Terebinths") connects Hebron with the Philistine territory. Above Socoh a branch from the south divides the Shephelah lowlands from the highlands of Judah. The Elah enters the Mediterranean about ten miles south of the Sorek.

The Valley of Zephathah is south of Elah, which it joins near the city of Ashdod. Mareshah, the birthplace of Micah, was in the Valley of Zephathah. In the same valley the armies of Asa defeated Zerah, the Ethiopian (II Chron. 14:9-15).

The Wadi Ghazzeh flows in a northwestward direction from the Negeb, south of Beer-sheba. It is probably to be identified with the Brook Besor. The *Ghazzeh* enters the Mediterranean south of Gaza.

The Wadi el-'Arish, known as the "River of Egypt," formed the southern boundary of the tribe of Judah, as it did earlier of the Philistine territory. It drains the seasonal surplus water from the Wilderness of Paran into the Mediterranean. South of the *Wadi el-'Arish* was territory controlled by Egypt.

MOUNTAINS

The mountains of Palestine fall into two distinct groups, divided by the Jordan rift. West of the Jordan the mountains are all a part of the central range. The mountains and plateaus east of the Jordan are similarly related.

Mountains West of the Jordan:

From north to south in the land of Palestine we note a series of mountains:

The Lebanon range, already discussed in Chapter 1, stretches northward in a line parallel to the coast of the Mediterranean. The Anti-Lebanons form a par-

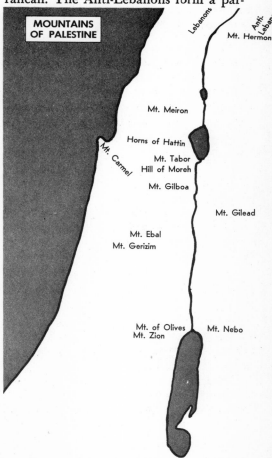

allel range east of the Beqa'a Valley. The hundred mile ranges of the Lebanons and the Anti-Lebanons average heights of 6,500 to 7,000 feet for long distances. The two highest peaks in the Lebanons, *Jebel Makmal* and *Kurnat es-Sauda,* rise to 10,200 feet.

Mount Meiron (Jebel Yarmuk) in Upper Galilee is almost four thousand feet high. This is the highest point in the mountainous region of Galilee.

The Horns of Hattin, near traditional "Mount of Beatitudes," is a twin-peaked elevation 1,200 feet high. From Hattin a panoramic view extends northward to Mount Hermon and eastward, across the Plain of Genessaret to the Sea of Galilee.

Mount Tabor, at the northeast corner of the Plain of Jezreel, reaches an altitude of 1,843 feet. It is five miles east of Nazareth and twelve miles west of the southern end of the Sea of Galilee. Here Deborah and Barak mustered the armies of Israel to meet the Canaanite threat.

The Hill of Moreh, popularly known as Little Hermon, south of Tabor, is 1,815 feet high. The Midianites assembled at the Hill of Moreh when Gideon assembled his small Israelite army at the nearby Spring of Harod. Moreh is four miles northwest of Mount Gilboa.

Mount Gilboa guards a key pass from the Plain of Jezreel to the Jordan Valley. At its highest point it has an altitude of 1,696 feet above sea level. Here Saul and Jonathan died in battle with the Philistines (I Sam. 28:4; 31:1-8).

Mount Carmel, south of the Plain of Jezreel, juts into the Mediterranean. It is 1,732 feet high at its highest point and 500 feet high where it meets the sea. On one of the peaks of Mount Carmel, Elijah challenged the priests of Baal and demonstrated the power of the God of Israel. Modern Haifa is built on the slopes and at the foot of Mount Carmel.

Ebal and *Gerizim,* the twin mountains of Samaria form the narrow mouths of a pass through which traffic of all kinds has passed since the most ancient times. The city of Shechem, south of Ebal, stands guard over the pass. The mountains, 3,084 and 2,890 feet high, afford a vantage point from which the whole of Palestine may be viewed. Here, after the conquest of Canaan, Joshua assembled the tribes of Israel to rehearse in their hearing the Mosaic Law. The blessings were pronounced from Mount Gerizim, and the curses from Mount Ebal (Deut. 11:29; Josh. 8:33-35).

Mount Zion was originally the scarp of rock on the southern tip of the ridge between the Kidron and the Tyropoeon valleys of Jerusalem. After the construction of the Temple on the northeastern hill (commonly called Mount Moriah), the term Zion was applied to that hill also. In subsequent years as the city of Jerusalem grew the name Zion became a synonym for the Holy City. East of Jerusalem, across the Kidron Valley, is Mount Olivet, or the Mount of Olives.

The tableland east of the Jordan includes:

Mount Hermon, the southern end of the Anti-Lebanon range, was the northern limit of Israel's conquest. The principal peak of the twenty mile long mountain is divided into three summits, the highest of which is 9,232 feet above sea level. Hermon is covered with snow throughout the year, and its snow-capped peaks can be seen from the Dead Sea, 120 miles away.

Mount Gilead is mentioned as a place where Gideon assembled his army and dismissed those who were fearful (Judg. 7:3). The location is not certain but would presumably be in the Gilead region, south of the Yarmuk and east of the Jordan. Mountains reach heights of about 3,000 feet in this area.

Mount Nebo (Jebel en-Neba), twelve miles east of the point where the Jordan empties into the Dead Sea, was the place from which Moses viewed the Promised Land before his death in the land of Moab. Some authorities suggest that Pisgah was the name of the range of which Mount Nebo (2,631 feet) was the summit.

THE PLAINS

The Aramaeans had good reason to think that the God of Israel was a "god of the hills" (I Kings 20:23). It was in the hill country that Israel was firmly established. The plains were conquered slowly, and they were an easy prey to Israel's warlike neighbors.

The Coastal Plain, as already noted, runs along the Mediterranean coast of Palestine. The lower part of the Coastal Plain was the home of the ancient Philistines, and its northern sector was Phoenician territory. Solomon maintained a seaport at Joppa in the Plain of Sharon through which trade with the Phoenicians of Tyre was maintained.

The Plain of Esdraelon, north of Mount Carmel, provided the means of access from the Coastal Plain to the Jordan Valley. In the Old Testament it is frequently called "the Valley of Jezreel" from the city at its eastern end. An alternate name, "the Valley of Megiddo" comes from the famous fortress guarding Esdraelon from the west.

The Negeb, the dry south country, may be regarded as a plain. It is actually hilly terrain, but the hills are not as high as in the north. The Negeb extends southward from Hebron; Beersheba serves as its prin-

cipal oasis and market city. Although not a desert, the Negeb is dry and unproductive apart from irrigation. Israel has been active in developing the Negeb, with modern cities such as Arad developing rapidly.

The Plain of Jericho is the name sometimes applied to territory north of the Dead Sea where the Jordan Valley is at its widest. East of the Dead Sea in the same general area is *the Plain of Moab,* where Elimelech and Naomi sojourned during a time of famine in Bethlehem-Judah.

Bashan contains a vast highland known as the Hauran, drained by the Yarmuk River. The Bashan Plateau is comparable in productivity with the plains west of the Jordan. It is excellent grazing land so that the "bulls of Bashan" became proverbial.

HIGHWAYS (*See* Map 3)

Ancient Palestine had few harbors, and the Israelites were not a sea-going people. Solomon engaged in some maritime trade (I Kings 10:22), and Jehoshaphat ran into difficulties at the Red Sea port of Ezion-geber (Elath) at the head of the Gulf of Aqaba (I Kings 22:48). Most of the communication between Israel and her neighbors, near and far, was by land. The great highways which joined the ancient civilizations along the Nile with those along the Tigris and Euphrates passed through Palestine.

The Coastal Route. The principal trade route crossing Palestine came northward from Egypt and ran along the Mediterranean Coast as far as Mount Carmel. The southern part of this route was known as "the Way of the Land of the Philistines." It was this well-traveled route which Israel avoided at the time of the Exodus (Exod. 13:17).

At Carmel the road divided into two sectors, one of which continued northward to Phoenicia, and the other turned eastward across the Plain of Esdraelon to the Jordan Valley. Here the route divided again, one part going northward into Northern Syria, and the other reaching northeastward toward Damascus.

The Crusaders spoke of the coastal route as the "Via Maris"—the way of the sea. The prophet Isaiah spoke of the "way of the sea" (Isa. 9:1—English text) but it is probable that he was there referring to the Sea of Galilee. Recent writers on Biblical geography avoid the term "Via Maris."

The Water-parting Route. A second important route follows the hill country along the relatively flat terrain of central Palestine. Beginning with Beersheba in the Negeb the road goes northward through Hebron, Bethlehem, Jerusalem, Bethel and Shechem. It then passes through Megiddo where it crosses the branch of the coastal route which runs through the Plain of Jezreel This junction served to accent the importance of Megiddo as a military stronghold to be taken or defended in time of crisis.

Josiah of Judah died at Megiddo in an attempt to stop 'Pharaoh Necho from joining forces with the Assyrians.

From the junction at Megiddo, the water-parting route heads northwestward. It joins the coastal route and connects Acre, Tyre, and Sidon with the cities of central Palestine.

The King's Highway. The most important road of the Transjordan country in ancient times was the King's Highway. From Elath on the Gulf of Aqaba, it went northward through Petra, Kirhareseth, and Karnaim to Damascus. This road was evidently used during the invasion of the four kings from the east described in Genesis 14. Israel requested permission to use the King's Highway following their wilderness wandering, but Edom threatened to battle them in the event they attempted to do so (Num. 20:17-18).

From the King's Highway branch roads led to the country west of the Jordan. One of these crossed the Jordan at Jericho with additional branches going to Judaea and Samaria. Another unrelated route came from the Gulf of Aqaba to Hebron, in southern Judaea where it met a route coming from the Nile Delta.

The Mound of Megiddo from the Air. The citadel of Megiddo has been located at *Tell el-Mutesellim* which was purchased and excavated by the Oriental Institute of the University of Chicago.

Courtesy, Oriental Institute

CHAPTER III

The Table of the Nations

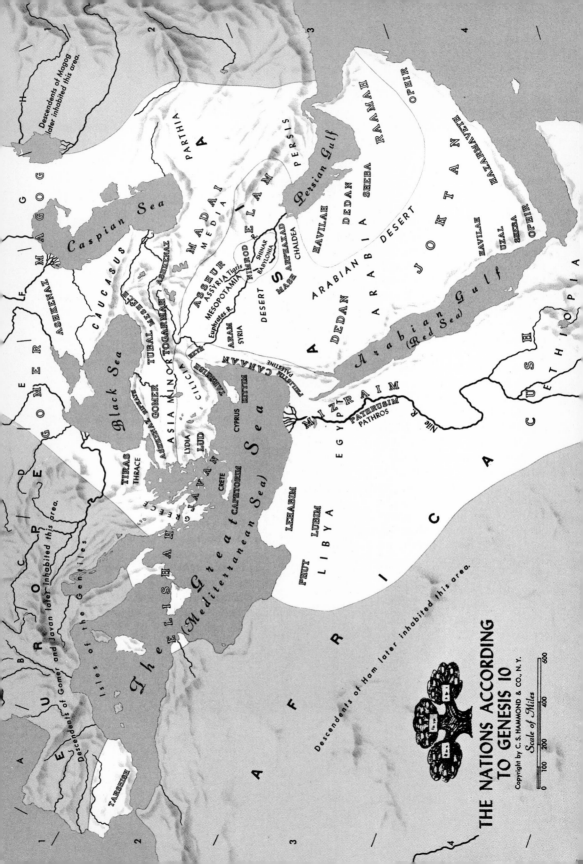

Descendents of Magog later inhabited this area.

MAGOG

ASHKENAZ

GOMER

EUROPE

Caspian Sea

CAUCASUS

Black Sea

TUBAL

MESHECH

TOGARMAH

ASHKENAZ

GREECE

TIRAS
THRACE

ASIA MINOR

ASHKENAZ

LYDIA

LUD

CRETE

CAPHTORIM

JAVAN

ELISHAH

The Great
(Mediterranean Sea)
Sea

CYPRUS

HITTITE

CILICIA

TARSHISH

TARSHISH

Isles of the Gentiles

Descendents of Gomer and Javan later inhabited this area.

PARTHIA

MADAI
MEDIA

ELAM

ASSHUR
ASSYRIA
MESOPOTAMIA
Tigris
Euphrates R.

ARAM
SYRIA

PALESTINE

CANAAN

PHILISTIM PALESTINE

NIMROD
SHINAR
BABYLONIA

MASH
ARPHAXAD
CHALDEA

PERSIS

Persian Gulf

HAVILAH

DEDAN

DEDAN

ARABIA

DESERT

ARABIA DESERT

ARABIAN
DESERT

SHEBA

RAAMAH

OPHIR

JOKTAN

HAZARMAVETH

HAVILAH

UZAL

SHEBA

OPHIR

Arabian Gulf
(Red Sea)

MIZRAIM
EGYPT

PATHRUSIM
PATHROS

Nile R.

CUSH
ETHIOPIA

LEHABIM

LUBIM

LIBYA

PHUT

A F R I C A

Descendents of Ham later inhabited this area.

THE NATIONS ACCORDING
TO GENESIS 10

Copyright by C. S. HAMMOND & CO., N.Y.

Scale of Miles

0   100   200   400   600

The Table of the Nations
(Genesis 10)

The ancient Israelites had more than an academic interest in the nations which surrounded them. Some of Israel's neighbors were bitter foes, while others had proved themselves friends and allies. Remote peoples were known to live on the fringes of the Old Testament world, and the Biblical writers were interested in tracing their relationship to the Israelites.

The Table of Nations is not, of course, all-inclusive. Nations which had no dealings with ancient Israel are not mentioned. The focus of attention is the Mediterranean region. Nations of southern Europe, northern Africa and, in particular, western Asia formed the Biblical world, and it is those nations that are listed in the genealogies of Genesis 10.

At first glance the records appear to be personal rather than national. Men such as Nimrod, Terah, and Abraham do occupy important places in the lists. On the other hand we read of nations or peoples such as "the Jebusite, the Amorite, and the Girgasite" (Gen. 10:16). In some instances we are not certain whether a name is to be taken in a personal or tribal sense. The statement that "Canaan begat Sidon his firstborn" (Gen. 10:15) appears to be a simple genealogical statement, but four verses later (Gen. 10:19) it is clear that Sidon was a city marking one of the borders of the Canaanites. Historically Sidon was the "firstborn" of the Canaanite cities, although her sister city of Tyre later took the dominant position.

The Table is arranged in climactic form. The first reference is to the Japhetic peoples who occupied Europe and parts of Asia. These were the people most remote from Biblical Israel. The Hamitic peoples of Asia and Africa are given second place. Many of these had close contacts with the Israelites. Semitic history, of which the family of Abraham is a conspicuous part, is presented last.

In studying this chapter and when examining the map the reader must remember that the exact location of these nations is in many cases indefinite and conjectural.

THE JAPHETIC NATIONS

Seven families of "sons of Japheth" (Gen. 10:2) are named: Gomer, Magog, Madai, Javan, Tubal, Meshech, and Tiras. Seven other described as his grandsons (Gen. 10:3-4) appear in the line of Japheth. In modern usage the terms Aryan or Indo-European are used to describe these peoples.

GOMER. First mentioned of the "sons of Japheth" is Gomer. The Assyrian monuments speak of the *Gimirrai*, a people known to the Greeks as the *Kimmerioi*. According to Homer they lived north of the Black Sea on the fringes of the world known to the Greeks. At a later time they moved southward from their homes north of the Caucasus Mountains, invaded Asia and threatened the Assyrian Empire. Defeated by Esarhaddon of Assyria, they turned westward and overran parts of Asia Minor, maintaining a foothold in Cappadocia. The

Lydian king Gyges was killed in battle with the *Kimmerioi,* but his successor, Alyattes, succeeded in driving them out of Asia Minor.

Three sons of Gomer are mentioned as separate tribes in the Table of Nations: Ashkenaz, Riphath, and Togarmah (Gen. 10:3). When we think of their possible location, we turn our thought toward Asia Minor.

Ashkenaz. A people known to the Assyrians as the *Ashguzai* or *Ishkuzai* may be the Biblical Ashkenaz. Jeremiah speaks of Ashkenaz as a people allied with Armenia (Ararat, Jer. 51:27). A prince of Mysia and Phrygia appears in the writings of Homer with the name *Ascanios.* From present knowledge, however, we cannot reconstruct the history of Ashkenaz or assign to it any specific location.

Riphath. The Jewish historian Josephus located Riphath in Paphlagonia, an ancient Roman province in Asia Minor on the south coast of the Black Sea, and some recent scholars have suggested a possible relationship to the 'Rebas River in Bithynia. Greek writers spoke of Riphaean Mountains skirting the northern shore of the world. Neither the Bible nor secular literature affords a definite clue to the identity of Riphath.

Togarmah. Josephus identified Togarmah with the Phrygians, who were famous for their horses (cf. Ezek. 27:14). Other writers point to the Armenians who claim Haik son of Thorgom as their ancestor. Assyrian monuments speak of a *Til-garimmu* (Hittite, *Tegarama*) which may be related to Togarmah. Aside from the fact that war horses from Togarmah in "the uttermost parts of the north" were traded for the luxury wares of Tyre (Ezek. 38:6; 27:14), Togarmah has left no impress on subsequent history.

MAGOG. The Amarna Tablets from Egypt (14th century B.C.) mention a people called *Gagaia* who may be related to the Gog associated with Magog (Ezek. 38; 39). Josephus equated Magog with the Scythians who inhabited the area north and east of the Caspian Sea, and who invaded Palestine during the seventh century B.C. The Israelites probably thought of Magog as a northern nomadic people.

MADAI. The word Madai is uniformly translated, "Medes," a people who lived south of the Caspian Sea. By 700 B.C. Media was a prosperous kingdom. Shalmaneser III fought the *Amadai* ("Medes") in the Zagros Mountains and forced them to pay tribute to Assyria (ca. 386 B.C.). Subsequently, however, the Medes joined Nabopolassar of Babylon in bringing about the defeat and destruction of the Assyrian capital at Nineveh (612 B.C.). The Medes formed an important part of the empire of Cyrus, but their history was soon absorbed into that of Persia.

JAVAN. Javan is the Hebrew name for the Ionians or, more generally, the Greeks. Cuneiform inscriptions of Sargon (722-705 B.C.) speak of "the Javanites who are in the midst of the sea." The first contacts of Israel with Greeks was with the Ionians of Asia Minor and adjacent islands who, like the ancient Phoenicians, were noted for their trade and commerce.

Four subdivisions of Javan are noted: Elishah, Tarshish, Kittim, and Dodanim (Gen. 10:4).

Elishah. The name Elishah usually occurs with the Hebrew word for islands, or coastlands. Purple and scarlet are said to have been important products exported by Elishah (Ezek. 27:7). Some scholars identify Elishah with Carthage in North Africa on the basis of the leg-

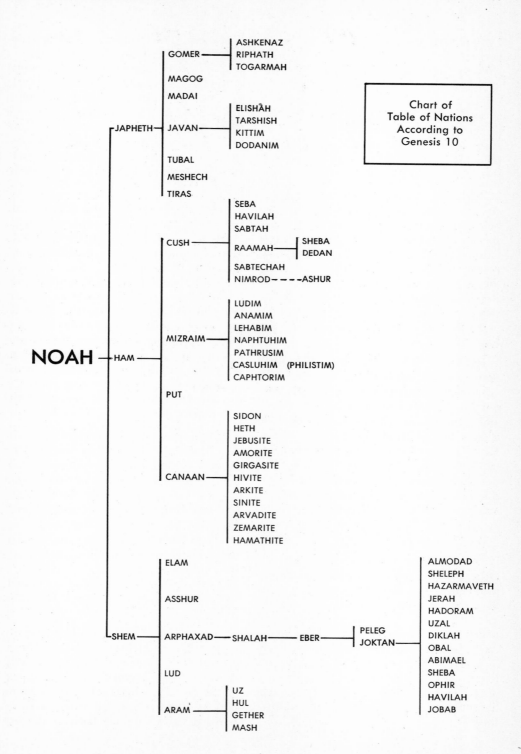

Chart of
Table of Nations
According to
Genesis 10

end that it was founded by Elissa, a princess of Tyre. Traditionally, however, Elishah has been associated with the Greek colonies of southern Italy and Sicily.

Tarshish. A *tarshish* is a smelting plant, or refinery, and numerous places have borne that name. Paul's birthplace, Tarsus in Asia Minor, and a Tarshish in Sardinia have similar names. The most remote goal of Mediterranean commerce in both classical and Old Testament times was Tartessus in southern Spain, declared by Herodotus to be beyond the Pillars of Hercules. Actually Tartessus was not far from Gibraltar. The Greek writers Strabo and Diodorus speak of silver, iron, tin, and lead as products of Tartessus, which many writers identify with Biblical Tarshish.

Kittim. Kittim (sometimes spelled Chittim) is, strictly speaking, the Island of Cyprus, one of whose cities is named Kition. In later usage Kittim seems to have become a term for islanders in general. The author of the apocryphal book of I Maccabees uses it to identify the Macedonians (I Macc. 1:1), and it is used in Daniel (11:30) and in post-Biblical Jewish literature in referring to the Romans. The Habakkuk Commentary found at Qumran mentions Israel's enemies as the Kittim.

Dodanim (or *Rodanim*). The letters "d" and "r" are very similar in Hebrew and there is some question concerning the correct reading of this word. Dodanim appears in Genesis 10:4, but Rodanim in I Chronicles 1:7 (Hebrew text). If the term Dodanim is original, the reference may be to the Danunim people of Cilicia, mentioned in the Phoenician Karatepe Inscription. Earlier writers noted the similarity between Dodanim and the Dardanians, the name used of the people of Troy in Homer's *Iliad*. Rodanim would suggest the Isle of Rhodes in the Aegean Sea with the many islands in its vicinity. No definite location can be assigned.

TUBAL and MESHECH. Scripture usually associates the two names, Tubal and Meshech (Ezek. 27:13; 32:26; 38:2, 3; 39:1). Assyrian texts mention the *Tabali* of Asia Minor who gave "great horses" as tribute to Ashurbanipal. Their territory was close to Cilicia, a land famed for its horses (I Kings 10:28). Meshech, in eastern Phrygia, was Assyrian *Mushki*, Greek *Moschi*.

TIRAS. Probably identical with the Tyrsenoi of classical tradition and the Turusha of earlier Egyptian texts, the people known as Tiras occupied islands and coast lands of the Aegean. These islanders are doubtless the piratical sea people known as *Turusha* who invaded Syria and Egypt during the thirteenth century before Christ. They are also said to have been the ancestors of the Etruscans.

THE HAMITIC NATIONS

The peoples designated in Scripture as Hamites rose to prominence early in history. Israel had closer contacts with the Hamites than with the more remote Japhetic peoples. The Hamites settled in northern Africa and western Asia.

Four "sons of Ham" are mentioned: Cush, Mizraim, Phut, and Canaan (Gen. 10:6).

CUSH. Traditionally Cush has been translated "Ethiopia" following the usage of the ancient Greeks. The territory would better be designated as Nubia, the region south of the First Cataract of the Nile.

The descendants of Cush represent six other peoples: Seba, Havilah, Sabtah, Raamah and Sabtechah (Gen: 10:7), and Nimrod (Gen. 10:8).

Seba. Seba appears to have been located in Africa, presumably near Cush. Their location remains highly indefinite. The name should be distinguished from the Sheba in southwestern Arabia.

Havilah. Havilah is thought to have been located in central Arabia bordering the coast of the Persian Gulf. The name also occurs among the descendants of Shem.

Sabtah (or Sabatah). The Greek geographer, Pliny, speaks of Sabota, a name corresponding to the Shabwat of the South Arabic inscriptions. It was the capital of Hadramaut, a district on the southern   coast of Arabia famed for trade in incense. No definite location can be assigned.

Raamah. Raamah has not been identified, but it is believed to have been located in southeastern Arabia near Ma'an. Two subdivisions of Raamah are mentioned. Sheba was the land of the Sabaeans in Yemen, also mentioned in the genealogy of Shem, and Dedan, a people of northwestern Arabia along the Red Sea.

Sabtechah. The area of Sabtechah is uncertain. It was probably in southeastern Arabia.

Nimrod. Nimrod is named as the founder of an early empire in Babylon. The cities mentioned as comprising his empire (Gen. 10:10) are in the territory which was subject to Babylon at an early period. Nimrod is said to have extended his conquests northward to include Assyria (Gen. 10:11). His reputation as a cruel conqueror has given rise to many legends. Jewish Aggada made him the founder of the Tower of Babel. A ziggurat near Babylon is known by the Arabs as *Birs Nimrûd*. All this points to a location in lower Mesopotamia.

MIZRAIM. The Hebrew word for Egypt is *Mizraim,* a dual form based on the historical division of Egypt into two sections: Lower Egypt, comprising the Nile Delta, and Upper Egypt, the Nile Valley southward from the head of the Delta to the First Cataract. Israel had frequent contacts with Egypt throughout Biblical history.

The family of Mizraim had several branches: Ludim, Anamim, Lehabim, Naphtuhim, Pathrusim, Casluhim, and Caphtorim (Gen. 10:13, 14).

Ludim. The Hamitic Ludim of North Africa served as bowmen in the armies of Egypt and Tyre (Isa. 66:19; Ezek. 27:10; 30:5). They are probably to be distinguished from the Ludim, or Lydians, mentioned among the descendants of Shem.

Anamim. Nothing is known about the Anamim.

Lehabim, or *Lubim.* A people known as Libyans dwelt on the southern shore of the Mediterranean, west of Egypt. The Twenty-second Dynasty of Egypt was Libyan in origin. Its founder was Sheshonk, Biblical Shishak, who invaded Jerusalem and Judah during the reign of Rehoboam (II Chron. 12:2-9).

Naphtuhim. Identification of the Naphtuhim is uncertain. Some have derived the name from the Egyptian *Na Ptah,* "the (people) of Ptah," and associated Naphtuhim with the district around Memphis, the center of Ptah worship. A more probable suggestion relates Naphtuhim to "northern land," i.e. the Egyptian Delta.

Pathrusim. The term Pathrusim is used of the people of Pathros (Jer. 44:15), a name based on the Egyptian word for the south. Southern or Upper Egypt included the narrow valley of the Nile from the First Cataract at Aswan (Elephantine) to the head of the Delta. Ezekiel (29:14) calls Pathros the land of the origin of the Egyptians. This agrees with Egyptological studies which note the earliest Egyptian civilization in Upper Egypt.

Casluhim. We have no hint concerning the home or history of the Casluhim except for the note that they were ancestors of the Philistines.

Caphtorim. Caphtor is usually identified with the island of Crete, known as *Keftiu* in Egyptian sources. The Philistines are said to have come from Caphtor (Amos 9:7). The translators of the Greek Septuagint, however, translated Caphtor by the Greek name, Cappadocia, a section of Asia Minor. Possibly the *Keftiu* occupied not only the island of Crete but also surrounding islands and coastlands.

PHUT, PUT. Old Persian inscriptions mention *Putaya,* a district in North Africa west of the Nile Delta. Another identification suggested for Phut is ancient Punt, modern Somaliland in East Africa.

CANAAN. The land of the Phoenicians and the Canaanites of Syria and Palestine was called Canaan during Israel's early history. Important Canaanite groups include: Sidon, Heth, Jebusites, Amorites, Girgasites, Hivites, Arkites, Sinites, Arvadites, Zemarites, and Hamathites (Gen. 10:15-18).

Sidon. The Phoenician city of Sidon is termed the "firstborn" of Canaan. It is mentioned in the Amarna Tablets (*ca.* 1400 B.C.) and appears to have been the greatest of the Phoenician coastal cities until outstripped by its "daughter" Tyre.

Heth. The "sons of Heth" are the Hittites whose ancient political and cultural center was at the bend of the Halys River in Asia Minor. In the day of Abraham, Hittites were settled in the Hebron area (*see* Map 2). After the Conquest under Joshua they continued to live among the Israelites. Ephron, a

Hittite soldier in David's army, was judicially murdered by the king.

Jebusites. The Jebusites maintained their stronghold in the city of Jebus, the name which they gave to the city of Jerusalem (*see* Map 2). They resisted Israelite strength until the time of David when Jebus was captured and, under the name of Jerusalem, made capital of united Israel. Remnants of the Jebusites were subjected to bond service by Solomon (I Kings 9:20).

Amorites. Amorites were among the primitive inhabitants of Canaan encountered by Abraham. They are described as inhabiting the west shore of the Dead Sea and the nearby mountains (Gen. 14:7, 13). At the time of the Exodus the Amorites dwelt in mountainous territory (Deut. 1:44). Two Amorite kingdoms occupied the area from the Arnon River to Mount Hermon (Deut. 3:8), and their rulers, Sihon and Og, were defeated in their battle against Joshua (Num. 21:34-35) (*see* Map 3). Amorites moved into western Palestine and their name there became practically synonymous with the Canaanites. Amorite tribes also settled in Mesopotamia where one of their number, Hammurabi, became famous as an able king and lawgiver.

Girgasites. Aside from the fact that they are a Canaanite tribe we know nothing of the Girgasites.

Hivites. Tribes known as Hivites dwelt at Shechem during the time of Jacob (Gen. 33:18; 34:2) (*see* Map 2). Joshua entered an alliance with the Hivites of Gibeon (Josh. 9). Further settlements are described as being at the foot of Mount Hermon (Josh. 11:3) and extending northward in the direction of Hamath (Judg. 3:3). They were forced to render bond service to Solomon as a means of advancing his building program (I Kings 9:20-22). The Hivites seem to have been closely related to the

Horites. Some scholars suggest that Hivite is but a variant form of the word Horite.

Arkites. Arkites were inhabitants of the Phoenician city of Arqa, twelve and one-half miles north of Tripolis at the northwestern foot of the Lebanons.

Sinites. The annals of the Assyrian monarch Tiglath-pileser III mention the people of *Siannu* "on the shore of the sea" (i.e. the Mediterranean), along with the cities of Arqa and Simirra.

Arvadites. Arvad, the most northerly of the Phoenician cities, was located 125 miles north of Tyre (*see* Map 2). Built on an island about two miles from the mainland, Arvad was able to resist Pharaoh Thutmose III when most of the other Phoenician cities surrendered to Egypt. Tiglath-pileser I tells how he embarked in ships of Arvad and sailed on the Great Sea (i.e. the Mediterranean). During the time of Sargon the leading Phoenician cities were Arvad, Tyre, and Gebal.

Zemarites. Mention is frequently made of *Simirra* in the Assyrian annals of Tiglath-pileser III and his successors. The earlier Amarna letters mention the city of *Sumur.* Its location has not been established.

Hamathites. Hamath was an influential city on the Orontes River in Syria (*see* Map 2). Under David, Solomon, and Jeroboam II, the city of Hamath formed the northern boundary of Israel (II Sam. 8:9; I Kings 8:65; II Kings 14:25).

THE SEMITIC NATIONS

The writer of Genesis arranged his genealogies in such a way that the reader is prepared for the elaboration of the line of Shem through Terah and Abraham.

Five major branches of the Semitic family are discussed: Elam, Asshur, Arphaxad, Lud, and Aram (Gen. 10:22).

ELAM. The province beyond the Tigris River, north of the Persian Gulf and east of Babylon was known as Elam. Periodically the warlike Elamites invaded the Fertile Crescent and secured control of southern Mesopotamia. The Semitic conqueror Sargon of Akkad called himself "conqueror of Elam" (2400 B.C.) and his successors kept the Elamites subjugated for three centuries. Later, however, an Elamite conqueror sacked Babylon and carried the famous stele bearing the Code of Hammurabi to his capital at Susa. Elam subsequently became a province of the Persian Empire and is now a part of Iran.

ASSHUR. North of Babylon in the Tigris-Euphrates Valley, Asshur, or Assyria, grew into one of the great powers of antiquity. From its capital at Nineveh, on the Tigris River, Assyria ruled a territory which extended westward to the Mediterranean. Samaria, the capital of Israel, fell to the Assyrians in 722 B.C., and Jerusalem barely escaped capture by Sennacherib two decades later.

ARPHAXAD (or *Arpachshad*). Ptolemy, the Greek geographer, mentions an Arrapachitis on the Great Zab River, northeast of Nineveh, which some students identify with Biblical Arphaxad. Others consider the word a compound of Arpak and Chesed, i.e., Arpak of the Chesdim (Biblical Chaldaeans). Kraeling prefers Arap of Chesed, suggesting Arappa as a variant pronunciation for Arrapakha, modern Kirkuk in Iraq. From the family of Arphaxad came Eber (Gen. 10:24), the patronymic ancestor of the Hebrews. The line of Abraham is traced through Eber (Gen. 11:11-26). Another branch of the Arphaxad line was that of Joktan, from whom arose thirteen Arabian tribes that dwelt in the southeastern and southern sections of the Arabian Peninsula. In some instances names appear here which also occur in the genealogy of Ham. Among these, mention may be made of: Hazarmaveth, Sheba, Ophir, and Havilah.

Hazarmaveth. The name is known elsewhere as Hadramaut, the narrow, arid coastal plain and the broad plateau of South Arabia.

Sheba. The south Arabian kingdom of Sheba, or Seba, had a high culture. The visit of the Queen of Sheba to Solomon was doubtless concerned, in part, with trade arrangements. Archaeological work in Sheba has produced significant remains dating to the eighth century B.C.

Ophir. The exact location of Ophir is not known. Many think it to have been located on the Red Sea, adjacent to Yemen. Ophir was noted for its fine gold (I Kings 10:11). Solomon's navy sailed from Ezion-geber on the Gulf of Aqaba down the Red Sea to Ophir. In exchange for copper, produced in the Israelite refineries at Ezion-geber, Solomon's ships brought back silver, gold, apes, ivories and peacocks (or baboons, according to another translation) (I Kings 10:22).

Havilah. Havilah is thought to have been located north of Sheba in Arabia, between Ophir and Hazarmaveth. Nomadic Ishmaelites and Amalekites lived in the area of Havilah (Gen. 25:18; I Sam. 15:7). The name Havilah is also used of the gold-producing region through which the Pishon, one of the rivers flowing out of Eden (Gen. 2:11, 12), passed.

LUD. The term Lud is probably a reference to the Lydians of Asia Minor. Tradition states that a man named Atys was the father of three sons, Lydus, Mysus, and Car. These sons gave their names to the nations of Asia Minor known as the Lydians, Mysians, and Carians. Although looked upon as barbarians by the Greeks, they were highly civilized peoples. Egyptian monuments locate the *Luden* near Mesopotamia. It has been conjectured that they were displaced by the Assyrians, after which they migrated to Asia Minor. When the fabulously rich Croesus was defeated by Cyrus the Great (*ca.* 540 B.C.), Lydian independence came to an end. Under the Romans Lydia was part of the Province of Asia.

ARAM. The region known as Aram, or Syria, was inhabited by people known as Aramaeans. *Aram-naharaim,* "Aram of the Two Rivers," translated "Mesopotamia" in the Authorized Version of the Bible, was the name given to the region around Haran in northern Mesopotamia where Laban, "the Aramaean," and other members of Abraham's family settled. Aramaic states centering in Zobah, Maachah, Geshur, and, most important of all, Damascus, played an important role in later Biblical history.

The Empires of the Fertile Crescent

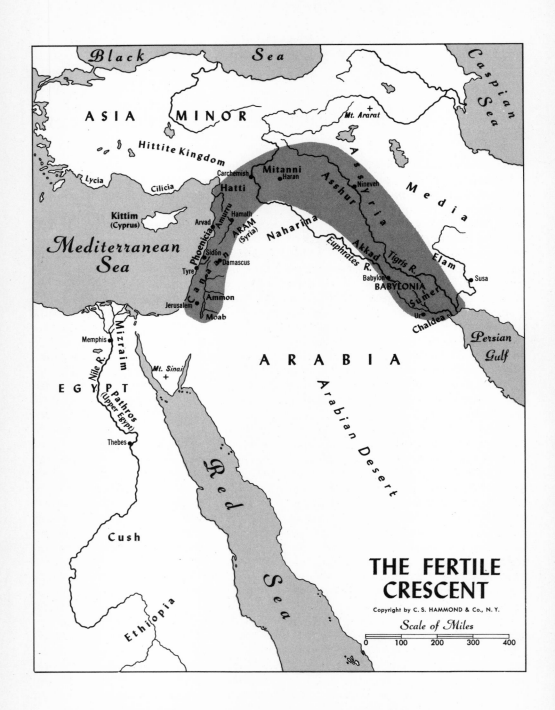

Black *Sea*

Caspian *Sea*

ASIA MINOR

Mt. Ararat +

Hittite Kingdom

Lycia

Cilicia

Carchemish

Mitanni
Haran

Assyria

Nineveh

Media

Hatti

Kittim
(Cyprus)

Arvad

Hamath

Amurru

ARAM
(Syria)

Naharina

Asshur

Akkad

Tigris R.

Elam

Mediterranean
Sea

Phoenicia

Sidon

Damascus

Euphrates R.

Tyre

Canaan

Babylon
BABYLONIA

Susa

Jerusalem

Ammon

Sumer

Moab

Ur

Chaldea

Persian
Gulf

Memphis

Mizraim

ARABIA

Mt. Sinai
+

EGYPT

Nile R.

Pathros
(Upper Egypt)

Arabian Desert

Thebes

Red
Sea

Cush

Ethiopia

THE FERTILE CRESCENT

Copyright by C. S. HAMMOND & Co., N. Y.

Scale of Miles

0   100   200   300   400

The Empires of the Fertile Crescent

No history takes place in a vacuum. Consciously or unconsciously cultural and political developments in one land have their effect on neighboring lands. The Bible makes it abundantly clear that the history of Israel was influenced by its neighbors. Canaanite Baal-worship was a constant attraction and source of temptation. The institution of kingship in other nations influenced the Israelite desire for a king. Invasions by Assyrians and Babylonians form the background against which the records of the captivities of both Israel and Judah took place. The Fertile Crescent bristled with activity, and a basic understanding of that activity forms the background for Biblical studies.

Sumer. At the head of the Persian Gulf, in the southern part of the alluvial plain between the Tigris and Euphrates Rivers, we find at the dawn of recorded history (*ca.* 3000 B.C.) the land of Sumer. It was the pictographic writing of the Sumerians, later developed into Akkadian cuneiform, which marked the beginning of writing at the eastern extremity of the Fertile Crescent. About the same period Egyptian hieroglyphics developed, but there is no evidence of a connection between the two most ancient methods of writing.

Sumer, strictly speaking, was not an empire. Sumerian units of government were city-states, including the Biblical Ur and Erech (Uruk or Warka), fifty miles northwest of Ur (Gen. 10:9-10). Other important Sumerian cities were Calneh (Nimrûd) "in the land of Shinar" (Gen. 10:10), Lagash, and Eridu.

The fertility of the land in southern Mesopotamia and commerce on the Persian Gulf permitted the attainment of a high degree of culture among the Sumerians. Irrigation was provided and floods controlled by means of a system of canals connecting the Tigris and the Euphrates river valleys. The Sumerians produced the sexagesimal system—the method of numbering by sixties—which is still used in reckoning time and in measurements of the circle. Our oldest law codes, those of Eshnunna (in Akkadian), Lipit Ishtar and Ur-Nammu (in Sumerian) are Sumerian in origin. Business life in ancient Sumer was developed to the point where standard weights and measures were employed.

The characteristic form of Sumerian religious architecture was the *ziggurat,* an artificial mountain built in the form of a step pyramid serving as the platform for a temple. It is thought that these ziggurats reflect an earlier period of Sumerian history when the gods were worshiped in the mountains. To many of the peoples of the Fertile Crescent the proper place for worship was a "high place."

Sumerian literature, preserved on cuneiform clay tablets, includes a flood story which in many ways parallels the Biblical account of Noah and the ark. A Sumerian "King List" records the names of eight sovereigns who reigned for fabulously long periods of time before the flood. The First Dynasty of Kish

Ziggurat at Ur. Ziggurats were artificial mountains on the top of which a temple was built. The ziggurat at Ur was begun by Ur-nammu (ca. 2350 B.C.) and restored by Nabonidus (ca. 550 B.C.). It was a solid mass, two hundred by one hundred feet in length and breadth, and seventy feet high.
Courtesy, A Marguerite Smith Collection, Zion Research Library

contained twenty-three kings whose total reign amounted to 24,510 years! As the list progresses to the later kings the lengths of the reigns are drastically reduced.

Akkad (or *Accad*). In Gen. 10:10 the founding of Akkad is attributed to Nimrod "the mighty hunter." Sumerian power was challenged, around 2400 B.C., by a Semite of humble birth named Sargon, who made Akkad his capital. Akkad is thought to have been located on the Euphrates River, a short distance southwest of modern Baghdad. From the name of its capital city, northern Mesopotamia was called Akkad, as southern Mesopotamia was known as Sumer. The Akkadian language was a Semitic tongue, related to Hebrew, Aramaic, and Arabic, whereas the Sumerian language was non-Semitic.

Sargon of Akkad built a mighty empire extending as far west as the Mediterranean, and including the city-states of Sumer in southern Mesopotamia. At the close of the Akkadian Dynasty the Sumerians enjoyed a brief period of revival before both groups passed forever from the historical scene.

Kingdom of Mari. Like many peoples of antiquity, the Semitic Amorites

moved about a great deal and it is difficult to pinpoint them geographically. During the third millennium B.C. the Sumerians spoke of Syria and Palestine as "the land of the Amorites." An important Amorite Empire, the Kingdom of Mari, during the second millennium B.C. had its center at the city of Mari on the middle Euphrates, south of its junction with the Habor.

Invading Amorites from Mari wrought havoc among the Sumerians, although Sumerian culture continued as the heritage of its rivals. Excavations of Mari, directed by André Parrot of the Louvre, have brought to light significant buildings, including a palace complex covering fifteen acres. The twenty thousand clay tablets from Mari contain material of interest both to the historian and to the Biblical scholar. These tablets include correspondence between Zimri-Lim, the last king of Mari, and Hammurabi, the famous Babylonian lawgiver, to whom the city of Mari fell.

Babylon. The term Babylon, or Babylonia, is sometimes used of the southern part of Mesopotamia—the Tigris-Euphrates River Valley. Babylon was the important city on the Euphrates River which gave its name to the empire which was built by its ambitious rulers. Babylon is associated in the Bible with a tower which was expressive of man's self-sufficient rebellion against God (Gen. 11:9).

Under the rule of an Amorite king, Hammurabi, Babylon reached its first period of brilliance as a world power. Hammurabi planned Babylon as a model city with streets built in a straight line, intersecting at right angles. The city, however, was but the hub of a mighty empire. Hammurabi also beautified the cities of Ashur and Nineveh, later to serve as important centers in the Assyrian Empire. Ancient Babylon produced a group of scholars whose treatises on astronomy, philology, lexicography, mathematics, and magic were standard for centuries. Practical matters such as canals, river navigation, and wage scales were not neglected.

Numerous cuneiform classics from Hammurabi's time have been discovered. Of particular interest to the Bible student are the Babylonian Creation Story, and the Gilgamesh Epic with its Babylonian form of the earlier Sumerian flood story. Best known, however, is the famous law code which illustrates the complex nature of life in Hammurabi's Babylon. A diorite stele of the Code of Hammurabi was discovered in 1901 by de Morgan at Susa where it had been taken by raiding Elamites.

The Hittite Empire. Although the center of the Hittite Empire, Hattushash (the modern Bogaskoy), was in Asia Minor northwest of the Fertile Crescent, the Hittites had continuous contacts with the Israelites and the nations of the Tigris-Euphrates Valley. The Hittites spoke an Indo-European language and formed a cultural bridge between the Semites and the Greek world.

Two Hittite kingdoms are known. The Old or Proto-Hittite Kingdom lasted from about 1740 B.C. to about 1460 B.C. Little has been discovered of this period of Hittite history which roughly parallels the Biblical patriarchal age. From about 1460 B.C. to about 1200

B.C. the New Kingdom Hittites developed both culturally and politically. Several Hittite states are known to have existed in Asia Minor during this period. Hittite borders were extended to Syria and Mesopotamia where Mitanni served as a buffer state around 1370 B.C. Hammurabi's Babylon was destroyed by Hittites about 1530 B.C.

The Stele of Hammurabi. This diorite shaft inscribed with the Code of Hammurabi dating from ca. 1700 B.C. was found at Susa in 1901.
Courtesy, Oriental Institute

Although at one time victorious over the Egyptian Pharaoh Rameses II, invasion by Aegean peoples brought about the overthrow of the Hittite Empire during the thirteenth century B.C. Hittite states continued in Syria, however, where the city of Carchemish on the Euphrates served as the last outpost of Hittite power. When it fell to Sargon II during the eighth century B.C., Hittite history came to an end.

Mitanni. About the time of Hammurabi, non-Semitic Hurrians from the Median highlands invaded northern Mesopotamia and dominated the region between the Mediterranean and Media. This territory, known as Mitanni, included the Biblical city of Haran, where Abraham sojourned on his way to Canaan. Although never powerful in their own right, the Mitannians held a balance of power between the Hittites and Egypt, with whose royal family they intermarried for political purposes. The Mitannians were the first people of the Fertile Crescent to domesticate the horse. They wrote treatises on horses in Hittite cuneiform. From Mitanni, horses were introduced into Asia Minor and, at the time of the Hyksos dynasty, into Egypt.

The Hittites reduced Mitanni's power to the position of a buffer state between Assyria and Asia Minor (*ca.* 1365 B.C.). A century later Mitanni was incorporated into the rising Assyrian Empire.

Assyria. Assyria had its center on the upper Tigris. With a culture dating to the third millennium B.C., Assyria had a long and significant history. It reached its greatest geographical extent during the lifetime of Isaiah (*ca.* 700 B.C.), when Assyrian territory extended from the Mediterranean to the Persian Gulf.

With the downfall of the Hammurabi Dynasty in the sixteenth century B.C., Babylon was in a state of decline. The more rugged Assyrians to the north embarked on a policy of empire which made them feared throughout the Fertile

Crescent. Under Tiglath-pileser I (1118-1078 B.C.) Assyrian forces took Urartu (Armenia) to the north, Babylon to the south, and went westward through Syria to the Mediterranean. Although this success was ephemeral, it was typical of what would take place two centuries later. During the ninth century Ashurnasirpal II not only conquered vast territories but also installed Assyrian governors and thus guaranteed the implementation of Assyrian goals.

Shalmaneser III continued the policy of empire. In his famous Black Obelisk, now at the British Museum, he boasts of the tribute which he received, including that of "Jehu the son (!) of Omri." Tiglath-pileser III furthered Assyrian power by establishing control over Syria. Ahaz of Judah served as his vassal, thus indirectly aiding the Assyrian conquest of Damascus. Assyria continued to expand under Shalmaneser V and Sargon. Samaria fell in 722 B.C. and the Kingdom of Israel was absorbed into Assyria. Sennacherib, Sargon's son, sought to bring the remainder of western Palestine under Assyrian control, but he was stopped at Jerusalem. His successor Esarhaddon defeated the Chaldeans, who threatened Assyria, and succeeded in deposing the Egyptian Pharaoh Tirhakah and establishing Necho on the throne of Egypt.

Under Ashurbanipal (*ca.* 650 B.C.) Assyria reached its zenith. Nineveh was at the height of her glory as the capital of the empire. Ashurbanipal amassed a great library of cuneiform tablets which have been the delight of archaeologists since their discovery in the nineteenth century. Revolts in Egypt during the reign of Ashurbanipal presaged the end, however. Shortly after his death, Cyaxeres the Mede and Nabopolassar, the Chaldean governor of Babylon, combined forces to bring about the destruction of Nineveh (612 B.C.). With Nin-

Ishtar Gate, Babylon. This reconstruction of ancient Babylon in the time of Nebuchadnezzar ...ows a royal procession passing through the gate on its way to the palace. The "Hanging ...ardens" appear in the upper right, with the ziggurat in the distant background.

eveh fallen, it was but a short time before the Assyrians passed from the historical scene.

The Neo-Babylonian, or *Chaldean Empire*. (*See* Map 6.) After the fall of Assyria most of the tributary peoples claimed their independence. It then became necessary for Nebuchadnezzar, the son of Nabopolassar, to conquer Syria and Palestine for Babylon.

After a victory over the Egyptian Pharaoh Necho and the remnants of the Assyrian army at Carchemish (605 B.C.), Nebuchadnezzar received news of his father's death, and hastened home to claim the throne. He subsequently returned to Palestine and did what the Assyrians had never been able to accomplish. Jerusalem fell to Nebuchadnezzar (587 B.C.)!

The Neo-Babylonian Empire was short-lived, however. No really brilliant ruler succeeded Nebuchadnezzar. Under Nabonidus and Belshazzar popular discontent grew until a change in government was inevitable. In the meantime Cyrus, the young ruler of the obscure Persian province of Anshan, began his brilliant conquests. Babylon fell to Cyrus in 539 B.C., and the Neo-Babylonian Empire came to an inglorious end.

The Persian Empire. Cyrus of Anshan made rapid conquest of surrounding territories. After uniting his own Persians he conquered the neighboring Medes and then moved northwest into Asia Minor where he conquered the gold-rich Lydian Empire. In 539 B.C. he entered Babylon and made it a province of the Persian Empire.

To the Jews, Cyrus was the king who made possible a second Exodus. His decree permitted Jews taken captive by Nebuchadnezzar to return to Jerusalem and rebuild their Temple.

Under Cambyses the Persians conquered Egypt, bringing to an end the rule of the Pharaohs. Darius the Great, of Persia, attempted to conquer Greece, but suffered a decisive defeat at Marathon (490 B.C.). He permitted the Jews to continue their work on the Temple, however, and it was dedicated during his reign.

Darius, Xerxes, and Artaxerxes organized the Persian government and extended its borders from central Asia to Libya. Greece, however, had successfully resisted the Persian invasions. Ultimately Greek culture was destined to supplant that of Persia.

The Persian Empire maintained its independence for two hundred years before it fell to the youthful Alexander of Macedon. The tide of empire moved out of the Fertile Crescent, and Europe for the first time controlled the East.

CHAPTER V

The Journeys of the Patriarchs

Beer-sheba. This photo overlooking the modern city of Beer-sheba gives a panoramic view of the countryside where the patriarchs wandered. Each of the patriarchs—Abraham, Isaac, and Jacob—temporarily dwelt at Beer-sheba. This town was significant in the history of Israel.

Religious News Service Photo

Use Map 2

CHAPTER V

The Journeys of the Patriarchs

The earliest records of the Bible are concerned with the entire human race. The very name, Adam, means "man." The stories of creation, the fall, and the flood are presented in terms of mankind as a whole. With the call of Abraham, however, the attention becomes focused upon a particular family which subsequently developed into the nation of Israel. Abraham and his "seed," or descendants, are the covenant people throughout the Old Testament. Promises of a universal nature continue, and mercy is shown, among others, to Rahab, Ruth, and the men of Nineveh, but God's revelation was given to the people of Israel. It was only after the advent of Christ that a self-conscious missionary program was carried out and even then considerable reluctance was shown in its earliest stages.

THE JOURNEYS OF ABRAHAM

The history of Israel properly begins with Abraham. Esteemed "the father of the faithful," he left Ur of the Chaldees, the city of his birth, journeyed as a pilgrim through the Fertile Crescent and after an eventful life passed on his faith and promises to his son, Isaac.

Ur of the Chaldees (Gen. 11:27-32). The Sumerian city of Ur, on the lower Euphrates River, was rediscovered by J. E. Taylor and exploratory excavations were made in 1854. During the years 1922 to 1934 large-scale excavations were carried out under the sponsorship of the British Museum and the Museum of the University of Pennsylvania by Sir Leonard Woolley. Spectacular discoveries of Sumerian history and culture reflect life during a period long before the time of Abraham. It is now evident that Ur was not a primitive city in the days of the patriarchs. As one of the important Sumerian cities it possessed an elaborate system of writing, advanced means of mathematical calculations, religious records, refined specimens of art, a school system, and much else that modern man equates with civilization and refinement.

Haran (Gen. 11:27—12:4). From Ur, Abraham journeyed northward through the Fertile Crescent until he reached Haran, an important trading city on the Balikh River, a tributary to the Euphrates, in the territory subsequently known as Padan-aram ("The Fields of Aram").

Northern Mesopotamia was regarded as the proper ancestral home of Abraham's family. Cyrus H. Gordon suggests that the Ur of the book of Genesis was not the famous city of that name in southern Mesopotamia, but another in the north, not far from Haran. Emil G. Kraeling reminds us that a southward movement of tribesmen from northern Mesopotamia takes place annually to this day. When the central government was weak, Bedouin tribesmen were free to settle permanently in the fertile territory of southern Mesopotamia. It is possible that Terah or his forefathers originated in northern Mesopotamia and migrated to the south.

The trek to Haran may then have been a return to familiar territory. Religiously, Ur and Haran had much in common. Both communities had shrines to the moon god. The descendants of Nahor, Abraham's brother, settled permanently in Haran. To this territory, known also as Aram Naharaim ("Aram of the two Rivers"), or Mesopotamia ("between the Rivers"), Abraham later sent his servant to seek a bride for his son Isaac. Thence also Jacob fled from the wrath of his brother Esau, and married Leah and Rachel, the daughters of Laban, "the Aramaean."

Canaan (Gen. 12:5-9). Abraham and his wife Sarah set out from Haran for Canaan accompanied by Lot, Abraham's nephew. Canaan was controlled by Egypt during the Twelfth Dynasty (1991-1786 B.C.). It was occupied by tribes collectively known as Canaanites whose worship of Baal included fertility rites which caused them to be denounced by a later generation of spiritual leaders in Israel. In patriarchal times, however, "the iniquity of the Amorites" was not yet full. The patriarchs sought to dwell in peace among their neighbors in Canaan.

Although a man of wealth and influence, Abraham lived a semi-nomadic life. His wealth was not in real estate, but in movable property. Herds and flocks were particularly important, although Abraham also possessed silver and gold and numerous household servants. His first stopping place in Canaan was at Shechem in the narrow pass between the twin mountains, Ebal and Gerizim, in what later became the district of Samaria. Next Abraham and his company moved twenty miles southward to Bethel.

Egypt (Gen. 12:10-20). Because Palestine depends on adequate rainfall during the rainy season to provide sustenance throughout the year, the threat of famine is a continuing one. Egypt, fertilized and irrigated by the annual inundation of the Nile River supplemented by irrigation could frequently provide food when Canaan was famine stricken. On one such occasion, Abraham found it necessary to journey to Egypt to seek grain. Fearing that the reigning Pharaoh might become infatuated with Sarah, and seek to kill her husband, Abraham tried to pass his wife off as his sister. Pharaoh, however, upon learning the truth, forced Abraham to leave the country. Abraham and his family returned to Bethel.

Hebron (Gen. 13:5-18). Scarcity of pasture land for their herds and flocks caused Abraham and his nephew Lot to separate. Lot chose the area near Sodom, which was very fertile before the catastrophe which brought about the destruction of Sodom and Gomorrah. Abraham took the highlands around Hebron, a city particularly associated with the patriarch's later years. There Sarah died, and a family burial lot was purchased from Ephron the Hittite. David first reigned as king in Hebron, and here, too, Absalom began his tragic revolt. The Arabs call Hebron *El Khalil*, "the friend," a reference to Abraham's reputation as the "friend of God" (Jas. 2:23).

The Battle of the Kings (Gen. 14). Lot, who first settled in the neighborhood of Sodom, later moved into the city itself and became involved in its problems. These became acute when a coalition of four kings from city-states in southern Mesopotamia demanded tribute of the five "cities of the plain" including Sodom. The cities of Sodom, Gomorrah, Admah, Zeboiim, and Zoar were located in what is now the southern portion of

Sodom. A mountain known as *Jebel Usdum* marks the traditional locale of Sodom, thought to be buried under the waters of the southern sector of the Dead Sea. Potash works and a salt mine are currently in operation at the foot of *Jebel Usdum.*   Photograph by Charles F. Pfeiffer

the Dead Sea below the tongue of land known as the Lisan which protrudes from its eastern shore. Fresh water streams flowing from the mountains of Moab made possible a rich culture in this area in the days of Lot. In subsequent years, however, a great change took place. Evidence indicates that an earthquake struck the area about 1900 B.C. The petroleum and the gases of the region helped produce a conflagration which totally obliterated the cities of the plain. The Sodom which Lot knew, however, was one of wealth and luxury which seemed to be excellent prey for an army bent on plunder. Copper mining was carried on in the area between the Dead Sea and the Gulf of Aqaba in ancient times, and the cities of the plain may have controlled these mines. The invaders from the East were initially successful in securing tribute from this wealthy area.

After paying tribute for twelve years, however, the cities rebelled. The rulers from the East attacked the following year. They came through Gilead down the King's Highway to Moab and Edom where a number of cities were subdued. These included the twin cities of Ashtaroth and Karnaim, east of the Sea of Galilee, and Ham, farther south. They continued east of the Dead Sea where victories were scored at Shaveh Kiriathaim, probably to be rendered "the plain

of Kiriathaim." Villages in the plain were conquered by the invaders from the East.

Journeying farther south the invaders came to Mount Seir, or Edom, and continued their conquests. They then went on to El-Paran, "on the border of the wilderness," probably to be identified with Elath on the Gulf of Aqaba. From El-Paran they turned northwestward to En-mishpat, identified as Kadesh-barnea. Then they traveled in a northeasterly direction to Hazezon-tamar, also known as En-gedi, on the western shore of the Dead Sea. After the battle with the Amalekites at Hazezon-tamar, the king of Sodom and his allies attacked the Eastern Confederacy and a battle was fought in the Valley of Siddim, apparently the name of a district at the southern end of the Dead Sea.

An escapee from the battle brought word to Abraham at Hebron that the kings from the East had conquered the king of Sodom and his allies, and that Lot had been taken captive. Abraham thereupon gathered a personal army of 318 men and pursued Lot's captors to Laish, the town at the foot of Mount Hermon which was later captured by the Danites and renamed Dan. Gaining the initiative, Abraham continued his attack until he gained a victory at Hobah, north of Damascus.

On his return from the campaign with

both the spoils of battle and the men he had rescued, Abraham stopped at Salem where he met and was blessed by a priest-king named Melchizedek. Salem is usually identified with Jerusalem, which did not become an Israelite city until the reign of David. It was known as *Urusalim* in the Amarna Letters of the fourteenth century B. C.

Although Abraham had journeyed

Underground Silos. Archaeologists have discovered in the vicinity of Beer-sheba, in the Negeb, underground silos for the storage of agricultural produce. Calcinated grains of wheat, barley, lentils, and grapes were found inside. *Courtesy, Israel Office of Information*

through much of this territory in his earlier years, his expedition against the kings of the East was a major undertaking. The fact that he could gather together an army and defeat a coalition of kings is a witness to the wealth and power of the patriarch.

Beer-sheba (Gen. 20—25). After the destruction of Sodom and Gomorrah (Gen. 18—19), Abraham moved southward and spent some time at Beer-sheba, the principal oasis of the Negeb. Beer-sheba is twenty-seven miles southwest of Hebron and formed the southern border of the land of Israel in later years (cf. I Chron. 21:2). It was famous for the wells which gave the community its name. Proximity to water was a necessity to the patriarchs with their herds and flocks. At Beer-sheba, Abraham made an alliance with Abimelech of Gerar (Gen. 26:26-33). During the days of Ahab and Jezebel, the prophet Elijah found a place of sanctuary in the Beer-sheba area after his victory over the prophets of Baal (I Kings 19:3-4).

Moriah (Gen. 22). Conscious of God's guidance, Abraham journeyed northward from Beer-sheba, taking his son to "the land of Moriah" where Isaac was to be offered as a sacrifice. The term, Moriah, was later used of the mountain on which Solomon's Temple was built (cf. II Chron. 3:1) and tradition associates the place of Abraham's great trial with the Temple Mount. There are serious objections to this identification, however. Jerusalem, or Salem, was a settled community in Abraham's day. The patriarch paid tithes to Melchizedek, its priest-king. Moriah, on the other hand, appears to have been a quiet place removed from the normal activities of men.

Traditions, moreover, concerning the location of Abraham's "land of Moriah" vary. The Samaritans, evidently for partisan reasons, identify Moriah with Shechem. Some recent scholars suggest a reading of "land of the Amorite" instead of "land of Moriah," which would be so general a term as to allow for any solitary district in Canaan. No suggestion is without difficulty, and it seems best to regard the Moriah of the patriarchal record as a lonely land, far removed from the usual haunts of men, where Abraham had his most trying encounter with God.

THE JOURNEYS OF ISAAC

The Biblical account of the life of Isaac is quite brief. His earlier life is a part of the history of his father, Abraham, and the biography of his later years is incorporated into the story of Jacob. Isaac lived in a comparatively small range of territory:

Beer-lahai-roi (Gen. 16:7, 13, 14; 24:62; 25:11). The Angel of the Lord appeared to Hagar at Beer-lahai-roi when she was fleeing from her mistress, Sarah. Subsequently, Isaac dwelt there. Scripture locates it in the wilderness of Beersheba "between Kadesh and Bered" (Gen. 16:7, 14). The exact location is unknown, although the work of Nelson Glueck has greatly increased our knowledge of the Negeb where Beer-lahai-roi was certainly located.

Gerar (Gen. 26:1-16). For a time Isaac enjoyed the hospitality of Abimelech, king of Gerar. The mound of *Tell Jemmeh*, partially excavated by Sir Flinders Petrie, is usually identified with ancient Gerar. It is located southeast of Gaza on the border between Palestine and Egypt. Petrie's excavations lead us to believe that Gerar controlled a rich caravan trade. Incense altars which date from the sixth to the fourth centuries

B.C. indicate that Gerar was on the spice and incense routes from Arabia to Palestine and the West.

Rehoboth (Gen. 26:22). When Isaac found it necessary to leave Gerar he moved farther up the wadi in which Gerar was located. After a series of disappointments there, he dug a well at Rehoboth which was not disturbed by Abimelech's herdsmen. Rehoboth is probably to be identified with *er-Ruhaibeh*, the name given to the ruins of a town located in a wadi of the same name about eighteen miles southwest of Beersheba, at the point from which the road which crosses the desert branches toward Gaza and Hebron. The city seems to be mentioned in the Amarna tablets under the name *Rubuta*.

Beer-sheba (Gen. 26:23-33). Here Isaac made a treaty of peace with the Philistine ruler, as his father had done some years before, and determined to settle there. In patriarchal fashion he first built an altar for the worship of God, and then pitched his tent.

Hebron (Gen. 35:27). Isaac's last days were spent in Hebron where Abraham had settled after parting from Lot (Gen. 13:5-18). There Isaac died and was buried by his sons, Jacob and Esau, in the cave which Abraham had purchased from Ephron the Hittite.

THE JOURNEYS OF JACOB

Jacob, subsequently named Israel, was the father of the twelve Israelite tribes. His life may be outlined as follows:

Beer-sheba (Gen. 26:33—27:46). Here Jacob and his twin brother, Esau, were born and lived their earliest years. After cheating Esau of his birthright and deceiving his father, Isaac, Jacob found it necessary to flee northward to Haran, the home of his uncle, Laban.

Bethel (Gen. 28). Fleeing the vengeance of Esau, Jacob passed the night at Bethel about twelve miles north of Jerusalem on the road to Shechem. There he received the divine promise of a safe return to the land of his birth. The vision of the heavenly ladder reminded Jacob that the God of his fathers would not forsake him in his journeys. Bethel later became an important shrine. Golden calves were placed there by Jeroboam I to dissuade his people from going to the Temple at Jerusalem.

Haran (Gen. 29; 30). Jacob spent a much longer time in Haran than he had anticipated. He worked seven years for the beautiful Rachel, only to be given her unattractive sister, Leah, instead. He labored seven more years for Rachel, and then remained and acquired considerable property. About twenty years of Jacob's life were spent with Laban.

Return to Canaan (Gen. 31—33). Sensing hostility among the sons of Laban, Jacob determined to take his household and possessions back to Canaan. Without telling Laban, he and his family fled. At Mizpeh ("watchtower"), somewhere in the northern highlands of Transjordan, Laban overtook Jacob and reprimanded him for his hasty departure. Jacob protested innocence of any wrong-doing and an amicable agreement was reached. An altar was built, named by Laban "Jegarsahadutha," the Aramaic equivalent of the Hebrew *Gal 'ed*, meaning "heap of witness." It served as a visible reminder that Jacob and Laban had covenanted to go their separate ways in peace and good will.

Mahanaim (Gen. 32:1). After the treaty with Laban, Jacob journeyed on to Mahanaim ("two camps"), probably located north of the Jabbok at the mound known as *Khirbet Mahneh*. There, fearful of an encounter with the brother he had wronged twenty years earlier, Jacob was encouraged by a vision of angels. In later years, Ish-bosheth, the son of Saul, reigned at Mahanaim while David ruled Judah from Hebron. Absalom, David's son, suffered his tragic death in a wooded area in the vicinity of Mahanaim.

Penuel (or Peniel) (Gen. 32:22-32). On a lonely spot along the north shore of the Jabbok, Jacob had his mysterious encounter with the angel who both made him lame and gave him a blessing. Peniel ("the face of God") cannot be located with certainty but it was in the vicinity of Succoth, east of the Jordan.

Succoth (Gen. 33:17). The sixty-foot mound, *Tell Deir 'Alla*, probably the site of Succoth, is located on a magnificent highland site near the Jabbok in the Jordan Valley east of Shechem. Here Jacob built shelters for his family and booths for his cattle after the happy reconciliation with Esau.

Residence in Canaan (Gen. 34—45). Crossing the Jordan, Jacob was back in Canaan for the first time in over twenty years. Like Abraham, he settled first in Shechem and later moved on to other communities.

Shechem (Gen. 33:18—34:31). Shechem, now identified with *Tell-Balatah*, was located between Mount Gerizim and Mount Ebal in the area later known as Samaria. It occupied a strategic site, dominating the pass between the two mountains. Excavations indicate that Shechem was settled as early as 2000 B.C., at which time it was subject to

Shechem. Remains of the East Gate indicate that rebuilding from time to time eventually raised the passageway within the gate to a level five steps above the inner street. Walls of large bricks interlaced with wooden beams once stood on the foundations visible here.

Photograph by James T. Stewart

Egypt. Jacob's sojourn there was interrupted by the slaughter of the Shechemites by his sons, Simeon and Levi.

Bethel (Gen. 35:1-15). Leaving Shechem, Jacob journeyed southward to Bethel, where Abraham had earlier sojourned and where Jacob himself had seen the vision of the ladder from heaven. There Jacob renewed his covenant with God. Excavations of the mound, known as *Beitin,* were begun in 1934 by an expedition sponsored by the Pittsburgh-Xenia Theological Seminary and the American School of Oriental Research.

Ephrath (Bethlehem) Gen. 35:16-21). Five miles south of Jerusalem, on the main highway to Hebron, is Bethlehem, or Ephrath. Here Rachel died in giving birth to Benjamin, Jacob's youngest son. The traditional tomb of Rachel on the side of the road from Jerusalem to Bethlehem dates back to the fifteenth century A.D. The grave is known to have been marked, however, in the sixth century A.D. when the pilgrim Arculf visited there.

Hebron (Gen. 35:27). A journey of fifteen miles southward from Bethlehem brought Jacob to Hebron, where Abraham and Isaac had both settled. There Jacob was reunited with Isaac. During Jacob's sojourn in Hebron his favorite son, Joseph, was sold into slavery by his brothers who were tending their flocks at Dothan, a town about eleven miles north of Samaria on the main caravan route between Damascus and Egypt (Gen. 37:1-36).

In Egypt (Gen. 45—49). At the invitation of Joseph, who had become vizier (prime minister) of Egypt, Jacob and his family left Hebron and settled in Goshen, a small but fertile district between the eastern channel of the Nile and the desert. The valley of Goshen centered in the *Wadi Tumilat* and extended from Lake Timsah to the Nile. It was from thirty to forty miles long and was the part of Egypt closest to Palestine.

Jacob's Burial Procession (Gen. 50:1-14). The embalmed body of Jacob was taken from Egypt to Hebron for burial. Probably due to the hostility of Philis-tine and Amorite tribes, the direct route was avoided. The funeral procession passed around the southern end of the Dead Sea, through the land of Moab, and crossed the Jordan at Abel-mizraim opposite Jericho. The term, Abel-mizraim, may mean either "meadow" or "mourning" of Egypt. E. G. Kraeling suggests that the name reflects a time when an Egyptian garrison was settled at a place called Abel-mizraim. The peculiar circumstance of Jacob's funeral procession gave to the place a new significance and it became associated with the mourning of the Egyptians.

Hebron.   Prominent in the narratives of the patriarchs, Hebron is located in the Judaean highlands, fifteen miles southward of Bethlehem.   *Copyright, Levant Photo Service*

CHAPTER VI

Lands of the Sojourn and Wandering

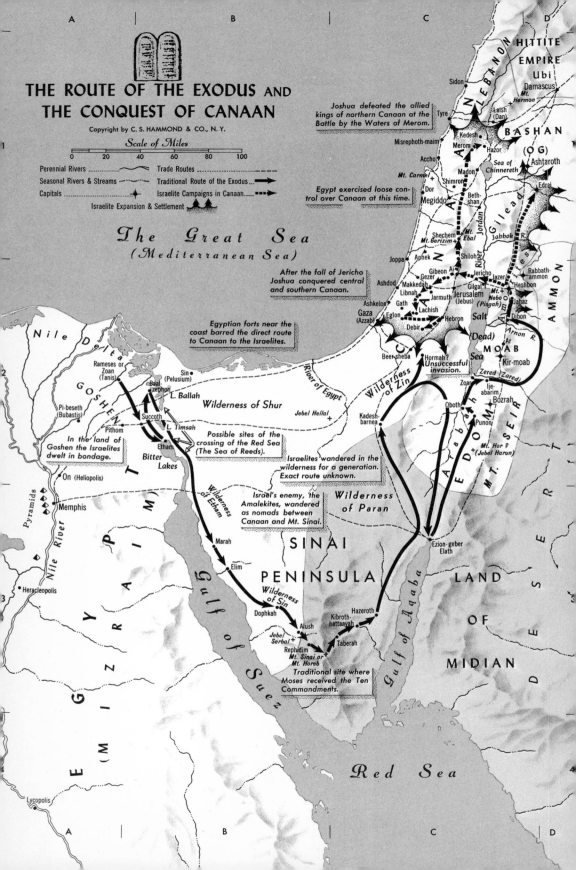

THE ROUTE OF THE EXODUS AND THE CONQUEST OF CANAAN

Copyright by C. S. HAMMOND & CO., N.Y.

Scale of Miles

0 20 40 60 80 100

Perennial Rivers ....
Seasonal Rivers & Streams ....
Capitals ....

Trade Routes ....
Traditional Route of the Exodus ...→
Israelite Campaigns in Canaan.....▪▸

Israelite Expansion & Settlement

The Great Sea
(Mediterranean Sea)

Joshua defeated the allied kings of northern Canaan at the Battle by the Waters of Merom.

Egypt exercised loose control over Canaan at this time.

After the fall of Jericho Joshua conquered central and southern Canaan.

Egyptian forts near the coast barred the direct route to Canaan to the Israelites.

In the land of Goshen the Israelites dwelt in bondage.

Possible sites of the crossing of the Red Sea (The Sea of Reeds).

Israelites wandered in the wilderness for a generation. Exact route unknown.

Israel's enemy, the Amalekites, wandered as nomads between Canaan and Mt. Sinai.

Hormah? Unsuccessful invasion.

Traditional site where Moses received the Ten Commandments.

HITTITE EMPIRE

Ubi

Damascus

Mt. Hermon

BASHAN

(OG)

Ashtaroth

Edrei

Sidon

Tyre

Laish (Dan)

Kedesh

Merom

Hazor

Misrephoth-maim

Accho

Sea of Chinnereth

Madon

Mt. Carmel

Shimron

Dor

Megiddo

Beth-shan

Gilead

Jabbok R.

Shechem
Mt. Gerizim Mt. Ebal

Jordan River

Joppa

Aphek

Shiloh

Jazer

Rabbath-ammon

Gezer

Jericho

Ashdod

Makkedah

Gibeon Ai

Gilgal

Heshbon

Ammon

Libnah

Jarmuth

Jerusalem (Jebus)

Mt. Nebo (Pisgah)

Ashkelon

Gath

Lachish

Jahaz

Gaza (Azzah)

Eglon

Debir

Hebron

Salt (Dead) Sea

MOAB

Kir-moab

Ar

Dibon

Arnon R.

Beer-sheba

Zered Zared

Zoar

Ije-abarim

Bozrah

Wilderness of Zin

Oboth

EDOM

MT. SEIR

Punon

Mt. Hor? (Jebel Harun)

Kadesh-barnea

Wilderness of Paran

Arabah

Ezion-geber Elath

LAND OF MIDIAN

Nile Delta

Rameses or Zoan (Tanis)

Sin (Pelusium)

Baal-zephon

L. Ballah

GOSHEN

Pi-beseth (Bubastis)

Succoth

Wilderness of Shur

River of Egypt

Jebel Hellal

Pithom

L. Timsah

Etham

Bitter Lakes

On (Heliopolis)

Pyramids

Memphis

Nile River

Heracleopolis

Wilderness of Etham

Marah

Elim

SINAI PENINSULA

Wilderness of Sin

Dophkah

Alush

Jebel Serbal

Rephidim
Mt. Sinai or Mt. Horeb

Kibroth-hattaavah

Taberah

Hazeroth

Gulf of Aqaba

Gulf of Suez

DESERT

Lycopolis

Red Sea

Lands of the Sojourn and Wandering

THE LAND OF EGYPT

Location. Ancient Egypt, the scene of one of the oldest of civilizations, consisted of the valley and Delta of the Nile. It extended from the first cataract of the Nile River northward to the Mediterranean. South of the first cataract was the land of Nubia. The desert bordered the Nile Valley on both east and west. East of the Delta was the Wilderness of Shur which extended to southern Palestine. The Wadi el-Arish, known in the Old Testament as the River or Brook of Egypt, was the border between the two nations. Ancient Egypt comprised a territory of about 9,600 square miles, a little larger than the state of New Hampshire.

Divisions. Throughout ancient history two Egypts were recognized as separate entities. Northern, or Lower Egypt as it is properly called, is the triangular Delta of the Nile between the eastern or Pelusiac branch and the western or Canopic branch. The Nile is one of the few rivers in the world that flow from south to north, hence the apparent contradiction that Lower Egypt is north of Upper Egypt. Rich soil brought by the Nile from equatorial Africa makes the Delta particularly fertile. In Roman times it provided much of the grain needed by the Empire. Southeast of the Pelusiac branch of the Nile lay the land of Goshen, the home of Israel during the sojourn in Egypt.

Southern, or Upper Egypt, is a narrow valley, varying in width from two to ten miles as it follows the course of the Nile. Our knowledge of ancient Egypt comes, not from the ruins of ancient cities but from the tombs, pyramids, and temples built in the desert which stretches interminably on either side of the Nile Valley.

The history of Egypt began when Upper and Lower Egypt were united under Nar-Mer, or Menes, the founder of the First Dynasty. Subsequent kings wore a double crown indicating that they ruled "the two Egypts."

The People of Egypt. Mizraim, the Hebrew name for Egypt, is listed as a son of Ham in the Table of the Nations (Gen. 10). The Egyptian people developed one of the earliest of civilizations. At about the same time as the Sumerians (ca. 3000 B.C.), Egypt emerged from pre-history. The development of the hieroglyphic system of writing made possible records which enable us to trace the development of Egyptian life and thought.

From paintings and statues left by Egyptian artists before 2500 B.C. we gather that Egyptians were short of stature. They possessed deep-set eyes, large cheek bones, fairly thick lips, and a comparatively short nose. Their hair seems to have been black and straight. Unlike the Semites, they were clean shaven. The Egyptian language is described as Hamito-Semitic, for it has many points in common with the Semitic tongues. Egyptian mechanical genius is exhibited in the structure of the pyramids and tombs built in the desert adjacent to the Nile. Both the artistic and literary materials buried with the dead help us to reconstruct life in ancient Egypt. Desert burial has preserved materials which would perish in moist regions.

History of Egypt. The history of united Egypt begins with Menes, the first Pharaoh of the First Dynasty, according to Manetho, an Egyptian historian who wrote during the Hellenistic period. Old Kingdom Egypt (*ca.* 2700-2200 B.C.), known as the Pyramid Age, was an era when the arts and sciences flourished. Both civil and religious functions were centered in the Pharaoh who was regarded as a god. The Old Kingdom was followed by a period of anarchy and chaos, called the First Intermediate Period (*ca.* 2200-1991 B.C.), when the central government was weakened and local nobles were able to assert their

power. The strong Twelfth Dynasty, however, marked the beginning of the classical Egyptian period, the Middle Kingdom (*ca.* 1991-1786 B.C.). Although the Pharaoh regained control he ruled over a feudal society through the local princes ("nomarchs" or rulers of Egyptian states known as nomes). Middle Kingdom Egypt produced some of the great literary masterpieces of the ancient world such as *Sinuhe*, one of the first secular stories for reading enjoyment.

Middle Kingdom Egypt came to an end in the middle of the eighteenth century B.C. with the invasion of the Asiatic Hyksos ("rulers of foreign lands"). From their capital city of Avaris in the Nile Delta they ruled parts of Western Asia as well as Egypt. The introduction of the horse and chariot and the concept of Empire were important Hyksos contributions to Egyptian culture.

The hated Hyksos were ultimately expelled by a native Egyptian dynasty which inaugurated the New Kingdom or

Egypt: The Sphinx and the Pyramids. Built during the Old Kingdom (twenty-seventh to the twenty-second centuries B.C.) the pyramids bear mute witness to the splendor that once belonged to Egypt. The sphinx contains the head of Pharaoh Khafre on the body of a lion. Khafre's body was placed in a nearby pyramid.   *Courtesy, Trans World Airlines*

Empire period (*ca.* 1570-1065 B.C.). Following the expulsion of the Hyksos, the Egyptians advanced into Palestine and Syria, reaching as far as the Euphrates River. Strong Egyptian garrisons were maintained at crucial points and Egyptian isolationism was forever at an end. Although Bible scholars differ concerning the date of the Exodus (dates from 1225 to 1447 B.C. are suggested), it certainly took place during the New Kingdom.

Egypt continued as an important power until conquered in 525 B.C. and annexed to the Persian Empire, but it never regained the strength and prestige it enjoyed during the days of Rameses II (1290-1224 B.C.) when Egypt ruled the East. It vied first with Assyria and later with Babylonia for control over Syria and Palestine. A pro-Egyptian party encouraged the Israelite kings in Samaria to rebel against Assyria, bringing on the destruction of the Northern Kingdom in 722 B.C. History repeated itself in 587 B.C. when the pro-Egyptian party in Judah urged Zedekiah to defy Nebuchadnezzar, king of Babylon. In both instances there was no effective aid from the Nile Valley. Egypt proved to be a broken reed. Although once the greatest of nations, her glory had departed.

Important Places in Lower and Upper Egypt.

Memphis, on the Nile ten miles south of modern Cairo, was the ancient capital of Egypt. Imhotep, the architect-physician of Djoser, a Third Dynasty Pharaoh, erected a terraced step pyramid in the Memphis necropolis at Sakkarah. This is the oldest stone structure in Egypt.

Heliopolis, Biblical "On" (Gen. 46: 20), nineteen miles north of Memphis, was the religious center of early Egypt.

As its name implies, Heliopolis ("city of the sun") was dedicated to the Egyptian sun god, Re.

Raamses, or *Rameses,* an Egyptian store-city, was located in Goshen and built by Hebrew slave labor. It served as the capital of the Nineteenth Dynasty (1310-1200 B.C.) and was the starting-point for Israel's journey to Canaan (Exod. 12:37).

Alexandria, founded by Alexander the Great (332 B.C.), was located on the Mediterranean fourteen miles west of the Canopic branch of the Nile (*see* Map 12). The large Greek-speaking Jewish colony in Alexandria produced the Greek translation of the Old Testament known as the Septuagint.

Thebes (*see* Map 12), *No,* or *No-Amon,* was capital of the Eighteenth Dynasty. Homer describes it in glowing terms as the city of one hundred gates. In the days of Herodotus the voyage up the river (i.e. south) from Heliopolis to Thebes, in Upper Egypt, required nine days. The famous Temple of Amon at Karnak, opposite Thebes, is considered the finest example of New Kingdom religious architecture. Thebes declined after assaults by the Assyrians Esarhaddon and Ashurbanipal, and was finally crushed by Rome (30-29 B.C.). Cf. Nahum 3:8; Jer. 46:25; Ezek. 30:14-16.

THE WILDERNESS OF THE WANDERING

The Sinai Peninsula, where Israel spent most of her forty-year period of wandering, is located between the Gulf of Suez and the Gulf of Aqaba, the two northern arms of the Red Sea.

The term "wilderness" aptly describes the Sinai Peninsula and the lands north

The Way to Elath. This is a scene in the Arabah. Eziongeber (Elath) was an important center for the smelting of copper and iron which were mined in the Arabah.

Courtesy, Consulate General of Israel

of it. Five areas on the route of the Exodus are designated as wildernesses (Shur, Etham, Sin, Paran, and Zin). These are, for the most part, in the northern and central sections of the peninsula. The region is a tableland of limestone from 2,000 to 2,500 feet high. There are few springs and even the *Wadi el-Arish* ("the River of Egypt") is dry most of the year.

The Wilderness of Shur. The land immediately east of Goshen was called "the Wilderness of Shur." The term Shur, meaning "wall," is reminiscent of the fact that a wall had been erected at the western border of Egypt to keep out the "sandfarers," i.e. the desert Bedouins. Hagar, the Egyptian, had headed in the direction of Shur when fleeing the wrath of Sarah.

Wilderness of Etham. Etham, "on the edge of the wilderness" (Exod. 13:20), appears to have been an Egyptian stronghold located between Lake Timsah and the Bitter Lakes. The portion of the Sinai Peninsula south of the Wilderness of Shur is known as the Wilderness of Etham.

The Wilderness of Sin. This wilderness should be distinguished from the Wilderness of Zin, another section of the Sinai Peninsula. The Wilderness of Sin was located between Elim and Mount Sinai, in the western part of the peninsula. The oasis of Dophkah, the last stopping place before Sinai, was in this area. Dophkah has been identified by some scholars with Serabit el-Khadim, an important mining center where one of the most ancient types of alphabetic writing was discovered.

The Wilderness of Paran. In the east central region of the Sinai Peninsula, bordering the Arabah and the Gulf of Aqaba, lay the Wilderness of Paran, "the great and terrible wilderness" (Deut. 1:19). Here the Israelites wandered for thirty-eight years after accepting the pessimistic majority report of the spies sent from Kadesh-barnea to determine the feasibility of entering the Promised Land.

The Wilderness of Zin. Southwest of the Dead Sea, across the Arabah from Edom, lay the Wilderness of Zin. From Kadesh-barnea on its southern border the spies entered Canaan (Num. 13:21).

In this wilderness Israel was guilty of the sin of murmuring against the Lord (Num. 27:14).

Mount Sinai. The mountain range associated with the names of Sinai and Horeb is located in the southern part of the Sinai Peninsula. Most scholars identify the mount where the law was given with a peak called, in Arabic, *Jebel Musa*, "Mount Moses." This mountain reaches an altitude of 7,519 feet. The famous Monastery of St. Catherine, located here, has a valuable library of ancient manuscripts.

Scholars do not all agree concerning the true site of Sinai. Some have placed it in the land of Midian, because of apparent references to volcanic action which is foreign to the Sinai Peninsula. Others have suggested locations near Kadesh or Petra. The traditional Mount Sinai, however, seems to accord best with the available data.

The Arabah. The gorge extending from the southern end of the Dead Sea to the Gulf of Aqaba is known as the Arabah, a part of the geological "fault" which includes the Jordan Valley. Immediately south of the Dead Sea, the Arabah is 1,275 feet below sea level. It rises to 300 feet above sea level farther south in the area west of Sela (Petra), the Edomite city which controlled caravan trade between the desert and Gaza. Iron and copper mines in the Arabah (Deut. 8:9) are the largest found anywhere in the ancient Near East.

Inhabitants. The Biblical account of the Exodus mentions the Amalekites as an enemy which attacked Israel (Deut. 25:17-19; Exod. 17:8-16). In Abraham's time Amalekites were in the area southwest of the Dead Sea (Gen. 14:7). A son of Esau also bore the name Amalek (Gen. 36:12, 16) and we read of a "mount of the Amalekites" in Ephraim (Judg. 12:15). Archaeology has thrown no light on this nomadic people.

THE LAND OF EDOM

Boundaries. On the southeast border of Palestine in the region south of the Dead Sea, between the Zered River and the Gulf of Aqaba lay the ancient land of Edom. The mountainous nature of the country east of the Arabah gives it its alternate Biblical name, Mount Seir. In secular records Edom first appears in the stele of the Egyptian Pharaoh Merneptah (1224-1216 B.C.).

Names. Esau, or Edom ("red"), settled in the area of Mount Seir ("hairy") (cf. Gen. 36:8). Both Seir and Edom are frequently used in Scripture to describe this mountainous territory. In Hellenistic times the term Idumaea is used of the land of the ancient Edomites. The territory of Idumaea differed from that of Edom, however, because the Nabataean Arabs pushed the Edomites, or Idumaeans, out of their ancestral home into the territory west of the Dead Sea as far north as Hebron.

Natural Features. Seir or Edom is usually described as mountainous territory. West of the mountains is a line of low limestone hills which are followed by higher, igneous rocks, chiefly porphyry. Red and variegated sandstone rises to a height of two thousand feet with abrupt cliffs and deep ravines. The eastern side of the mountain consists of an almost unbroken limestone ridge which slopes gently away into the desert. Although he was not the chief heir of Isaac, the inheritance of Esau was a rich one, for he was blessed "with" (not "from" as in most translations) "the fatness of the earth and the dew of heaven" (Gen. 27:39, 40). Terraced hillsides yielded abundant vegetation, and Edom became a prosperous nation.

Chief Cities. The capital and northern metropolis of Edom in Old Testament times was Bozrah (Gen. 36:33; I Chron. 1:44), modern Buseirah. Ancient Bozrah was internationally famous for its weaving industry and the dyed garments, which it exported. Part of its wealth was expended in the building of ornate palaces (Amos 1:12).

After the Nabataean Arabs displaced the Edomites (*ca.* 300 B.C.) the city of Sela (Isa. 16:1), called Petra ("rock") (*see* Map 3) by the Greeks, served as the capital of an extensive empire. Petra was a caravan city high in the Ash-Shara mountain chain in which many of the buildings were literally hewn out of the natural rock. It was located about sixty miles south of the Dead Sea.

On the Gulf of Aqaba at the southern extremity of Edom lay Ezion-geber, an important port with access to the Red Sea. In the days of Israelite dominance Ezion-geber, later called Elath, was the important commercial city of Israel. Through Ezion-geber passed the trade route known as the King's Highway.

Trade routes from Egypt reached Ezion-geber where they joined this important highway and continued north through the heart of Edom. Joining other routes they provided communication between Egypt and the Euphrates Valley. The King's Highway was used in patriarchal times (Gen. 14), and Moses requested permission to use it during the Exodus (Num. 20:17; 21:22).

Copper from nearby mines was smelted in refineries at Ezion-geber. Ruins of these refineries, dating to the time of Solomon, were discovered by Nelson Glueck, an archaeologist who has done much work in the Negeb.

History. Our earliest references suggest that Mount Seir was early occupied by Hurrians, or Horites. During the patriarchal age it was conquered and settled by Esau, brother of Jacob, whose descendants are known as Edomites. Refusal of the Edomites to permit Israel to use the King's Highway through the center of their land made it necessary for the Israelites to detour around the country en route from Egypt to Canaan. In the days of the monarchy both Saul and David defeated the Edomites, and Edom was incorporated into the kingdom of Israel. With the division of the kingdom, Edom became a part of Judah, the Southern Kingdom. Edom rebelled, however, regaining her independence in the days of Jehoram, the idolatrous son of Jehoshaphat. At the time of Nebuchadnezzar's invasion of Palestine, Edom joined the Babylonians against Judah and Jerusalem, a fact which evoked the condemnation of the prophet Obadiah. During Maccabean times the Idumaeans were forcibly incorporated into the Jewish state and made to conform to the Jewish laws. They lost their national identity after the destruction of Jerusalem (A.D. 70).

The Exodus and Wilderness Wandering

The Traditional Mount Sinai. Known in Arabic as *Jubel Musa,* the traditional Mount Sinai towers above the plain of *er-Râha,* probably to be identified with the "desert of Sinai" where the Israelites encamped.   *Copyright, The Matson Photo Service*

The Exodus and Wilderness Wandering

A theological reason is given in Scripture for the circuitous route taken by the Israelites on their journey to Canaan. God, we are told, "did not lead them by way of the land of the Philistines, although that was near," but rather led them "by the way of the wilderness" (Exod. 13:17-18). The coastal road, known by the Egyptians as the "Way of Horus," was a busy one constantly garrisoned by Pharaoh's armies. The path of God's direction had its own perils, but they were of a different variety. The wilderness provided a training ground on which the Lord revealed Himself to Israel and prepared His people for entrance into Canaan. Although a generation perished in the wilderness, under Joshua a new generation entered the land of promise.

The route of the Exodus itself may be divided into several stages.

From the Land of Goshen to the Sea of Reeds (Exod. 12—14; Num. 33:5-8). After the solemn Passover ceremony the Israelites, directed by Moses, left their homes in Goshen and headed eastward. The city of Rameses, rebuilt by a Pharaoh of that name and named Per-Rameses, "house of Rameses," was the starting point of the Exodus (Exod. 12:37). Rameses was contiguous with the Delta city of Zoan or Tanis, a royal store city on the eastern shore of the Tanitic branch of the Nile, at the center of the eastern Delta. The Hyksos rulers of Egypt established their capital there, giving it the **name of Avaris**. It con-

tinued to be an important metropolis although it was later overshadowed by Alexandria, built by the Macedonian ruler, Alexander the Great, in the western Delta (332 B.C.). From Rameses the Israelites moved southeastward to Succoth ("booths"), the first encampment after leaving Egypt. Here Israel halted to organize before moving eastward toward Sinai. From Succoth they continued to Etham, "on the edge of the wilderness." An Egyptian fortress north of the Bitter Lakes was known as Hetém ("fort"). This may be the Etham of the Exodus. It is conceivable that an Egyptian garrison at Etham threatened Israel, with the result that they turned back toward Pi-hahiroth near Baal-zephon (Exod. 14:2; cf. Num. 33:7). The name Baal-zephon suggests the sanctuary of a well-known Canaanite deity, the "Baal-of-the-North," or "Hidden Place." The fact that Baal had a shrine in Egypt is indicative of the extent of Canaanite religious influence.

The Egyptian armies pursued the Israelites to the area of Pi-hahireth (Exod. 14:9). By means of a "strong east wind" the waters of the sea were parted, and Israel was able to cross over into the Sinai Peninsula "on dry land" (Exod. 14:21-22).

The exact place of the crossing is unknown. Many scholars place it north of the Bitter Lakes and the town of Suez along the present Suez Canal. Simons suggests the southern marshes of the Bitter Lakes as the place of crossing. The Biblical term for the sea which was opened before the Israelites is *Yam Suph*, literally the "Sea of Reeds" (Exod. 13:18). The area now known as the Bitter Lakes may have been connected with the Red Sea in ancient times, thus accounting for the traditional rendering of "Reed Sea" by "Red Sea." There are numerous theories of the exact spot of crossing but none has gained unqualified acceptance.

From the Sea of Reeds to Sinai (Exod. 15—40; Num. 33:8-15). Crossing the Sea of Reeds, Moses led the Israelites into the Wilderness of Shur, the northwestern part of the Sinai Peninsula. After a journey of three days, Israel reached Marah, the place of bitter waters (Exod. 15:22-23; Num. 33:8). The bitterness of the desert springs contrasted unfavorably with the sweet waters of the Nile Valley. The oasis of Marah has been tentatively identified as *Ain Hawara*, a few miles inland from the gulf and about forty-seven miles from the town of Suez on the ancient road south to the turquoise mines.

Seven miles south of Marah was the *Wadi Gharandel*, the possible location of Elim, with its seventy palm trees and twelve wells (Exod. 15:27; Num. 33:9). Upon leaving the oasis of Elim, Israel entered the Wilderness of Sin, the desert plain at the foot of the Sinai Plateau (Exod. 16:1). Here the people murmured because of lack of food, and God miraculously provided quails and manna (Exod. 16).

The site of Rephidim ("plains"), somewhere between the Wilderness of Sin and Mount Sinai, has not been identified. Here, after Israel protested because of lack of water, Moses was instructed to strike the rock to provide for the people's thirst. Moses called the place Massah ("testing") and Meribah ("contention") because of the murmuring of the Israelites (Exod. 17:1-7). At

Rephidim a battle was fought with Israel's enemies, the Amalekites. Moses, strengthened by Aaron and Hur, prayed on a nearby hill, while Joshua fought in the valley below (Exod. 17:8-16).

Mount Sinai (or Horeb, its alternate name) is sacred to Israel as the place where God gave his law to Moses and entered into covenant with his people. The etymology of the word Sinai is uncertain. It may refer to *seneh*, the thorn bush, or it may be derived from the name of Sin, the ancient Semitic moon god. The word Horeb means "the desolate place."

A tradition, dating to early Christian times, suggests the peak known as *Jebel Musa* ("Mount Moses") as the Sinai of the Biblical narrative. *Jebel Musa* is part of a short ridge extending about two miles. Of its two peaks, *Ras es-Safsafeh* has an altitude of 6,540 feet and *Jebel Musa* 7,519 feet. The plain of *Er-Râha*, the foot of *Jebel Musa*, has sufficient water for an encampment of some duration.

While Israel was encamped at the foot of Mount Sinai, Moses ascended into the mountain to receive the Law (Exod. 19—31). The people, however, desirous of having visible gods, made a golden calf as an object of worship. When Moses saw what was taking place he cast the tablets of the Law to the ground, breaking them. He then destroyed the golden calf and prayed that God might forgive the people (Exod. 32).

Subsequently the Law was again given to Moses, who communicated it to the people (Exod. 34) and directed the building of the Tabernacle as the meeting place between God and Israel (Exod. 35—40). Before leaving Sinai the people were numbered and organized according to their tribal responsibilities (Num. 1—2).

From Sinai to Kadesh-barnea. After spending about a year at Sinai the camp of Israel was directed to march north-eastward toward the land of Canaan. At Taberah ("burning") some who murmured against the Lord were consumed by "the fire of the Lord" (Num. 11:1-3). Kibroth-hattaavah ("graves of lust") was the place of burial of the Israelites who had met divine judgment as a result of lusting after the delicacies of Egypt (Num. 11:4-35). At Hazeroth, Miriam and Aaron criticized Moses for his marriage to an Ethiopian (Cushite) woman. Miriam was stricken with a form of leprosy which lasted for one week, during which time she was isolated from the camp of Israel (Num. 12). Hazeroth ("enclosures"—probably for flocks) is possibly the modern 'Ain Khudra. The locations of Taberah and Kibroth-hattaavah are uncertain.

From Hazeroth the Israelites marched through the Wilderness of Paran, encamping for a time at Kadesh-barnea, about seventy miles south of Hebron. The exact location of Kadesh-barnea has long been debated. The Arabic site known as 'Ain Qadeis may still be regarded as the best tentative location. Kadesh-barnea became the center of Israelite life during thirty-eight years of wandering. From Kadesh the twelve spies were sent northward into Canaan, and the adverse report of ten of them struck such terror in the hearts of the Israelites that they refused to enter the land. God declared that the generation that lacked faith at Kadesh-barnea would perish in the wilderness (Num. 14).

Early in their wilderness experience the Israelites made an abortive attempt to press into southern Canaan, contrary to the command of Moses. They sought to take the region near Hormah, a town in the rugged hill country of southern Judaea, thought to have been near Beersheba. The Amalekites and Canaanites defeated the Israelites and pursued them to Hormah (Num. 14:39-45).

From Kadesh-barnea to the Plains of Moab (Num. 13—36). The longest period (thirty-eight years) of the wilderness wandering is one of which we know little. The pilgrims who left Egypt became wanderers in the wilderness. At the beginning and at the end of the period we find Israel at Kadesh, which seems to have served as their headquarters. In the interval they traveled extensively in the Negeb and in the Wilderness of Paran. Mention is made of the death of Aaron and his burial on Mount Hor (Num. 20:23-29), but the location of Mount Hor is uncertain.

At the close of the thirty-eight year period in the neighborhood of Kadesh, the Israelites asked permission of the Edomites to cross through their country en route to Canaan. When Edom refused to grant this permission Israel was forced to take a circuitous route. They traveled south as far as Ezion-geber on the Gulf of Aqaba. Then they turned northward again and passed Mount Seir in Edom. At the Zered River, Israel entered Moab without incident. Crossing the Arnon they went into the country of Sihon, king of the Amorites, who sought to prevent them from passing through his land. At Jahaz, Sihon was defeated in a battle, the report of which struck terror in the hearts of the inhabitants of Canaan (Num. 21:21-31; cf. Josh. 2:10). A further battle with Og, king of Bashan, at Edrei, established the military position of Israel east of the Jordan (Num. 21:33-35).

The story of Balaam (Num. 22—24) illustrates the hopelessness of the situation from the standpoint of the Moabites and their allies. A soothsayer, or "magician," was imported from Pethor (Assyrian, *Pitru*, tentatively identified with *Tell Ahmar*, south of Carchemish) to place a curse on Israel and so bring about their defeat. Unable to do this, Balaam actually pronounced blessings upon Israel (Num. 24:5-9). Later, however, Balaam suggested that the Moabites invite the Israelites to take part in their fertility cult worship at Baal-peor. This orgy of licentiousness brought about a divine judgment on Israel, although God did not blot out His people as Balaam desired (Num. 31:15-16).

The tribes of Reuben, Gad, and half the tribe of Manasseh looked upon the rich Transjordanian pastureland as suit-able for their herds and flocks. They requested permission to settle there (Num. 32). Moses granted this permission on condition that the men cross with the other tribes and take part in the conquest of Canaan before returning to their inheritance.

From Mount Nebo (*Jebel en-Neba*) in the Abarim range in Moab, Moses viewed the Promised Land which he was not permitted to enter. Somewhere in this majestic hill country he was buried, bringing to an end the period of the wilderness wandering.

Bethlehem

Jerusalem

Dead Sea

Jordan River

View from Mount Nebo. This unusual infra red telephoto picture of "The Promised Land" from Mount Nebo shows the Dead Sea with the Jordan River flowing into it. Traces of Jerusalem and Bethlehem are visible on the horizon.

Courtesy, Matson Photo Service.

Palestine before the Conquest

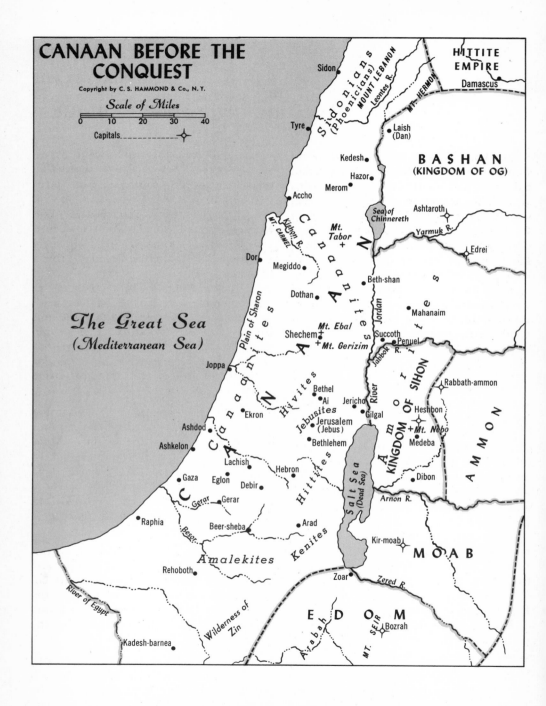

CANAAN BEFORE THE CONQUEST

Copyright by C. S. HAMMOND & Co., N. Y.

Scale of Miles

0   10   20   30   40

Capitals ------------ ✦

HITTITE EMPIRE

Sidon

Damascus

Tyre

Laish (Dan)

Kedesh

BASHAN (KINGDOM OF OG)

Hazor

Merom

Accho

Ashtaroth

Sea of Chinnereth

Yarmuk R.

Edrei

Mt. Tabor +

Dor

Megiddo

Beth-shan

Dothan

Mahanaim

Jordan

Shechem

Mt. Ebal +
+ Mt. Gerizim

Succoth

Penuel

Jabbok R.

Joppa

River

Rabbath-ammon

Bethel

Ai

Jericho

Gilgal

Ekron

Jebusites

Jerusalem (Jebus)

Heshbon

Ashdod

Bethlehem

+ Mt. Nebo

Ashkelon

Medeba

KINGDOM OF SIHON

Lachish

Hebron

Gaza

Eglon

Debir

Dibon

AMMON

Gerar

Gerar

Arnon R.

Raphia

Besor

Beer-sheba

Arad

Kir-moab

MOAB

Rehoboth

Zoar

Zered R.

River of Egypt

Wilderness of Zin

Arabah

MT. SEIR

Bozrah

EDOM

Kadesh-barnea

The Great Sea
(Mediterranean Sea)

Sidonians (Phoenicians)

MOUNT LEBANON

Leontes R.

MT. HERMON

Canaanites

MT. CARMEL

Kishon R.

Plain of Sharon

Canaanites

Hivites

Jebusites

Hittites

Kenites

Amalekites

Canaanites

Amorites

Salt Sea (Dead Sea)

Palestine before the Conquest

Our knowledge of life in Palestine before its occupation by the Israelite tribes has increased markedly during recent years. The excavation of important cities, such as Hazor and Jericho, has helped fill the gaps in our knowledge of early Canaanite culture and history. Clay tablets from Ras Shamra (ancient Ugarit) have provided valuable information concerning the nature of the religion and social structure of an important Canaanite community of the fifteenth and fourteenth centuries before Christ.

THE EARLIEST INHABITANTS

Some of the earliest human remains yet discovered come from caves excavated at Mount Carmel overlooking the Coastal Plain and the Mediterranean at *Wadi el-Mughârah*. Thirteen cultural levels have been traced, affording the anthropologist abundant material for a study of Stone Age civilization. In the absence of writing, however, we cannot piece together the details of these prehistoric settlers, and many conclusions are necessarily tentative. The location of the tribes is further complicated by the fact that they were highly nomadic. The maps referring to this period are therefore suggestive rather than definitive.

The Bible has numerous references to early inhabitants of Palestine. These include:

Rephaim. The Rephaim were aboriginal giants who lived in Canaan, Edom, Moab, and Ammon. Og, king of Bashan at the time of the Exodus, was "of the remnant of the Rephaim" (Deut. 3:11). The name Rephaim is also used of a fertile valley running southwest from Jerusalem to Bethlehem. Danel, the hero of the Ugaritic tablets is described as "The Man of Repha," an apparent reference to his tribe. Rephaim are frequently mentioned in the administrative tablets of ancient Ugarit.

The term Rephaim may mean either "strong ones" or "spirits of the deceased." It occurs in both senses in the Bible and in the Ugaritic literature. The people known as Rephaim have left no written records, but there can be no doubt of their important place in the primitive history of Palestine.

Zuzim (or *Zamzummim*) occupied the eastern plateau south of Bashan and Gilead. Their capital at the time of Abraham (Gen. 14:5) was Ham, located in Trans-Jordan east of Beth-shan, thought by some to be Rabbath-ammon (modern Amman). After Ammonites pushed into Zuzim territory, the Zuzim lost their tribal identity.

The *Emim* were located south of the Zuzim in the area east of the Dead Sea. During the Battle of the Kings (Gen. 14), both Zuzim and Emim were defeated by Chedorlaomer and his allies. Their land was later occupied by the Moabites.

The *Horim* (also known as Horites, or Hurrians) lived on Mount Seir in Edom before they were dispossessed by Esau (Gen. 36:21-30). Many scholars identify the Biblical Horim with the

Hurrians, a non-Semitic people who entered northern Mesopotamia and the eastern highlands from an Indo-Iranian locale. By the second millennium before Christ they were spread over much of the Middle East. W. F. Albright concluded that the Hurrians originated south of the Caucasus Mountains, and appeared in the region of the Zagros Mountains about 2400 B.C. They spread over a wide area, including the city of Nuzi, east of the Tigris. Excavations of Nuzi have revealed a number of their customs, some of which are strikingly similar to those of the Hebrews during patriarchal times. The Hurrians were conquered by the Hittites (*ca.* 1370 B.C.), and their land subsequently fell to Assyria (*ca.* 1250 B.C.).

The *Avim* lived in the Shephelah between the Philistine Plain and the mountains of Judaea (Deut. 2:23; Josh. 13:2, 3). They were conquered by the Caphtorim, or Cretans, whose Palestinian descendants are known as Philistines.

The *Anakim.* Hebron was the home of the Anakim, who called it Kirjath-arba. The gigantic stature of the Anakim terrified the spies who felt that Israel could not hope to conquer them (Num. 13). Although defeated by Caleb (Josh. 14) during the conquest of Canaan, remnants of the Anakim mingled with the Philistines of the Coastal Plain. Goliath and his brothers, although Philistine by nationality, may have been descendants of the Anakim (I Sam. 17:4; II Sam. 21:15-22).

TRIBES OF THE PATRIARCHAL ERA

The aboriginal tribes were either extinct or were in a minority in patriarchal times. Important peoples in the land when Israel entered Canaan were:

Canaanites. All of the tribes of Canaan are sometimes collectively called Canaanites. Specialized terms came to be used, however, to distinguish groups of Canaanites who settled in specific regions. These tribes are thought to have come from the northeastern part of Arabia before 3000 B.C. By that date there had already been built a number of important Canaanite cities, including Jebus (Jerusalem), Megiddo, Byblos (Gebal), Gezer, Hamath, and Beth-shan. The Israelite spies reported, "The people be strong that dwell in the land, and the cities are walled and very great" (Num. 13:28). After the conquest of Canaan by Israel and the arrival of Philistine invaders in southwestern Palestine, the Canaanites were restricted to the coastal strip of northern Palestine and southern Syria called Phoenicia, the Greek equivalent of Canaan. The Phoenician Canaanites settled numerous Mediterranean islands, and Carthage in North Africa. Their fertility cult and human (particularly infant) sacrifice, were denounced by the prophets of Israel. Some Canaanites, notably Rahab and her household were incorporated into the people of Israel.

Philistines. Emigrating from the Aegean region, particularly Crete (Amos 9:7), Philistines had settled in southern Palestine before the Patriarchal Age. Gerar was the principal Philistine city at this early period. It appears to have controlled a rich caravan route and to have enjoyed a comfortable standard of living. During the twelfth century B.C. a body of Philistines bound for Egypt was repulsed by Pharaoh Rameses III. They settled instead in what became the land of Philistia—the southern part of the Coastal Plain extending from Joppa to Gaza. The Philistines were non-Semitic, hence "uncircumcised." They had a monopoly of iron in Palestine until the

This is a newer
ed of both
of the ones
we have
1 Ref
1 Circ

Ruins of Byblos (Gebal). This is all that remains of the once-great Phoenician city of Byblos. A Canaanite town was already located at this place when Israel invaded Palestine.

Religious News Service Photo

time of David (I Sam. 13:19-22). Led
by the "lords" of their five cities—Ashdod, Ashkelon, Ekron, Gath, and Gaza—
they oppressed Israel during the time of
the Judges, and probably spurred the
desire of many Israelites for a king. Under David and Solomon the Philistines
were made tributary to Israel, but they
were never permanently subjugated.
They maintained their individuality until Hellenistic times. Gaza, after a long
siege, fell to Alexander the Great (332
B.C.), and the Philistines subsequently
were absorbed by other peoples and
passed from history.

Hittites. The Biblical "sons of Heth"
(Gen. 10:15) were related to the Anatolian Hittites whose cultural center
was in Asia Minor at the bend of the
Halys River. It is not known whether
the Palestinian Hittites were immi-
grants from the Anatolian plateau or
remnants of an earlier Palestinian
people who were not displaced when
Semitic and Hurrian peoples invaded
Canaan at the end of the third millennium. Anatolian Hittities are known to
have had dealings with Egypt at an
early date.
Hittites are frequently mentioned in
the Old Testament narrative. Genesis
23 records the dealings of Abraham with
Ephron the Hittite in the Hebron area.
Esau married Hittite wives (Gen. 26:34)
and Israelite spies found Hittites living
in the mountains of Canaan (Num. 13:
29). A Hittite, Uriah, was a warrior in
David's army (II Sam. 11:1-27).

Girgasites. Little is known of the Girgasites, who seem to have lived in the
region west of the Sea of Galilee (Josh.
24:11). They were probably absorbed
by the surrounding tribes.

Hivites. In the time of Jacob, Shechem
was a principal Hivite city (cf. Gen.
34:2). Early in Joshua's conquest of Ca-

naan several Hivite towns north of Jerusalem, including the city of Gibeon,
made a peace treaty with him (Josh.
9:3-15). The term "Hivite" may be a
variant of the Horites, or Hurrian
people.

Perizzites. Nothing is definitely known
concerning the Perizzites. Their name implies that they were villagers. It is believed that they were Hittite ironworkers
living in towns of Canaan. Others suggest
that they were villagers from southern
Palestine. As late as the return from
Babylonian captivity the Perizzites appear in the Biblical records (Ezra 9:1).

Jebusites. The term Jebusite is used
of the Canaanites who dwelt in Jerusalem, which bore the name Jebus during
the period of their occupation. A Jebusite king was slain by Joshua (Josh. 9:1;
10:26) but the Jebusites continued to
occupy Jerusalem until the time of
David (II Sam. 5:6-9).

Amorites. (*See also* Map 1.) Among the
most powerful of the peoples of Canaan
were the Amorites, a Semitic people
called "Westerners" by the civilized
peoples of Mesopotamia. This name is
occasionally used in the Old Testament
as a synonym for the Canaanites (cf.
Gen. 15:16). When the two are distinguished, the Amorite is described as inhabiting the "hill country" and the Canaanite is located on the Mediterranean
coastal plain and in the Jordan Valley
(Num. 13:29).
In the third millennium B.C. Syria
and Palestine were called by the Sumerians, "the land of the Amorites."
Early in the second millennium B.C. ag-
gressive Amorites conquered most of
Mesopotamia. The Amorite capital at
Mari, on the middle Euphrates, has
yielded some 20,000 cuneiform tablets
from patriarchal times. These tablets
deal with military, diplomatic, and ad-

The Sea of Galilee. In this productive region the Jordan River leaves the southern end of the lake. Canaanite tribes living near the Sea of Galilee had this same magnificent view that we so much admire today.

ministrative affairs. Hammurabi, the famous Babylonian lawgiver, was an Amorite.

Before crossing into Canaan, the Israelite armies fought an Amorite king, Sihon, whose headquarters were at Heshbon, east of the Jordan near Mount Nebo. When Sihon refused to allow the Israelites to pass through his territory, the Israelites clashed with the Amorites at Jahaz (Num. 21:21-23). Centuries later Israelites commemorated in song their victory over Sihon and his allies (Ps. 135:11; 136:19).

TRIBES AT THE TIME OF THE CONQUEST

In addition to the tribes that were in Palestine during the Patriarchal Age we meet two new peoples, closely related to the Israelites.

Moabites. The narrative of Genesis 19:30-37 indicates that Lot was the progenitor of the Moabites. Their early history is unknown, but in language and general background Moab had much in common with Israel. Spiritually, however, she was on a considerably lower plane. She worshiped Chemosh by burning living children in sacrifice. Her religious life also included the fertility cult with its religious prostitution. The fertile land of Moab, east of the Dead Sea, provided a haven for Elimelech and Naomi when famine struck Bethlehemjudah. Ruth, the Moabitess, returned to Bethlehem with Naomi and became an ancestress of David.

Ammonites. The Moabites and the Ammonites are both described as descendants of Lot, Abraham's nephew (Gen. 19:30-38). The territory of the Ammonites was north of Moab on the edge of the desert. Their god Molech (or Milcom) to whom human sacrifices were offered, was the "abomination of the Ammonites" (cf. I Kings 11:5, 7). At the time of the conquest, the kingdom of Sihon lay between Ammon and the Jordan. The Ammonite capital, Rabbathammon, situated along the Jabbok (cf. Deut. 3:11), continues to bear its historical name, Amman, and is now the capital of the state of Jordan.

Amman, Jordan. This historic city was the Old Testament Ammonite capital. Today, this restored ancient theatre demonstrates the city's significance in the days of the Roman Empire, including the time of Christ. *Courtesy, Levant Photo Service*

The Conquest of Canaan

Jericho. The city of Jericho was located 825 feet below sea level about eight miles northwest of the point where the Jordan enters the Dead Sea. From time to time the city of Jericho has shifted sites because of sieges, earthquakes, and other catastrophies.

Courtesy, Jack Finegan

CHAPTER IX

The Conquest of Canaan

After a generation of wandering in the wilderness, Israel entered the Promised Land. The Book of Joshua records the events associated with the conquest of the land of Canaan and the division of the land among the tribes. In a wider sense, the conquest began with the victories of Moses in the territory east of the Jordan and was not completed until the capture of Jerusalem during David's reign. The period of the conquest, however, is usually defined as the period during which the land of Canaan was being occupied by the Israelites.

THE TRANSJORDAN TERRITORY

At the time of the arrival of the Israelites, eastern Palestine between the Zered and Arnon Rivers was occupied by the Moabites, and that section north of the Arnon was inhabited by the Amorites. The Amorites were divided into two kingdoms. Gilead was ruled by Sihon, whose capital was at Heshbon, and the northern tableland of Bashan was ruled by Og. On the borders of the Arabian Desert, and tributary to Sihon, were the Midianites (Josh. 13:21). Near the Moabites were their nomadic kinsmen, the Ammonites.

Gilead (Num. 21:21-31). Shortly before Israel reached eastern Palestine, the Amorites had wrested from the Moabites the land between the Arnon and the Jabbok. Moses sent messengers to these Amorites requesting permission to journey through their land. Permission was refused, and a battle was fought at Jahaz, a city mentioned in the Moabite Stone which may be the modern *Khirbet Umm el-Idhâm*. Israel decisively defeated the Amorites at Jahaz, and took their entire land. This conquest gave Israel a foothold in eastern Palestine. Included in this territory was the rich tableland from the Arnon to the Jabbok.

Bashan (Num. 21:32-35). North of the Yarmuk River was the rich land of Bashan ruled by Og, who was said to be "of the remnant of the Rephidim." At the battle of Edrei (modern *Der'a*), Og was slain and his kingdom passed into the possession of Israel.

The *Midianites* (Num. 25, 31). The Midianites were a Bedouin people who lived in the Arabian Desert east of the Gulf of Aqaba. Their nomadic habits brought them west into the Sinai Peninsula and north into the Jordan Valley and Canaan. Midianites joined the Moabites in seeking the aid of Balaam in cursing Israel, but he uttered a blessing instead. Under Phinehas the priest, grandson of Aaron, the Midianites east of the Jordan were annihilated (Num. 31:6-8).

Before the death of Moses, the entire country east of the Jordan and north of the Arnon was conquered by Israel. This territory was assigned to the tribes of Reuben, Gad, and the half tribe of Manasseh under condition that their warriors assist the other tribes in the conquest of western Palestine before returning to their inheritance.

Hazor Excavations. At the time of Joshua, Hazor was described as "the head of those kingdoms" (Josh. 11:10). Excavations directed by Yigael Yadin (standing, second from left, foreground) indicate that the city once had a population of 50,000. Joshua defeated a confederacy of kings headed by Jabin of Hazor. *Courtesy, Consolate General of Israel*

PALESTINE

Following the death of Moses, Joshua led the people across the Jordan into the land of Canaan. Three major campaigns which brought much of Canaan into Israelite possession and made possible the division of the land among the tribes, are described in the Book of Joshua. It should be remembered, however, that important pockets of resistance continued for several centuries after the time of Joshua. The Book of Judges reminds us of the strength of Canaanites and others who were not subdued by Joshua and continually harassed the Israelites. It was not until David's reign that Jerusalem itself was incorporated into Israelite territory. Gezer was given as a wedding present to Solomon by the Pharaoh of Egypt.

Central Palestine (Josh. 3—9). After crossing the Jordan, Joshua established his camp at Gilgal, east of Jericho (Josh. 4:19; 5:10). Although several locations have been suggested for Gilgal, includ-

ing *Khirbet el-Etheleh* and *Khirbet en-Nitla,* no positive identification is possible. From Shittim spies were dispatched to the strategic, fortified city of Jericho. They returned with reports which suggested the wisdom of prompt attack. Jericho ("moon city," i.e., a city where the moon god was worshiped) is one of the oldest occupied sites in the Middle East. It is about seventeen miles northeast of Jerusalem and five miles west of the Jordan. The location, about 825 feet below sea level, near the *Wadi Qelt.* Known as the "city of palm trees" (Deut. 34:3), Jericho was also famous for such subtropical fruits as dates and figs. The Jericho oasis was on a main caravan route from eastern Palestine to Ammon.

The record of the conquest of Jericho makes it clear that God gave the city into the hands of the Israelites (Josh. 6). The contents of Jericho were burned as a kind of "first fruits" offering in which everything was devoted to the Lord.

Following the victory at Jericho, the key city to central Palestine, a small Israelite army marched upon Ai ("the ruin") northwest of Jericho, about one and one-half miles from Bethel. Some scholars believe that Ai was a military outpost of the city of Bethel. This would resolve the problem of the omission of Bethel in the record of the conquest and the inconclusive archaeological results from Ai itself.

An initial defeat at Ai, occasioned by Achan's sin, was turned into victory after the sin was punished. By stratagem and ambush Ai was taken and the victorious march of Israel continued. Moving northward Israel assembled in solemn convocation in the vale of Shechem, between Mount Ebal and Mount Gerizim. There the Law was read and a copy of the Mosaic Law was inscribed on stone (Josh. 8:32).

The town of Gibeon, on a terraced hill about six miles north of Jerusalem, was the most important member of a Hivite tetrapolis (others: Beeroth, Chephirah, and Kirjath-jearim). The Hivites may be identified with the Horites or Hurrians. The Gibeonites dressed themselves in rags and brought along stale bread, pretending that they had come from a great distance and thus tricked Joshua into making a protective treaty (Josh. 9). By doing this they sought to avoid war with the Israelite invaders and protect their own land. Although their deceit was soon discovered, Joshua kept his word. The Gibeonites and their allies were not destroyed. Instead they became "hewers of wood and drawers of water," i.e., they were assigned menial labor among the Israelites.

Southern Palestine (Josh. 10). Joshua's occupation of central Palestine, by conquest and by treaty, was tactically the most effective way to gain possession of the whole land. A union of the Canaanite city-states might have made things much more difficult. If Joshua could divide the country and subjugate the cities one by one, the task would be much simpler.

The destruction of Jericho and Ai, and the defection of Gibeon, served as a warning to the Canaanite kings cf the south. Under the leadership of Adoni-zedek, king of the city-state of Jerusalem (Jebus), an alliance was formed in which the rulers of Hebron, Jarmuth, Lachish, and Eglon agreed to join in resisting Israelite encroachments. The kings attacked Gibeon, perhaps as an object lesson to others who might wish to make a separate peace with Israel. When Joshua received word of the attack he assembled his warriors at Gilgal, made a swift night march, attacked the enemy and then pursued them through the mountain passes guarded by the two Beth-horons in the Valley of Ajalon. After relieving the Gibeonites, he chased the enemy from Upper Beth-horon (1730 feet above sea level) to Lower Beth-horon, one and three-quarters miles down the valley, where a providential hailstorm contributed to the disastrous defeat of Israel's foes (Josh. 10:8-11). The fleeing kings were pursued to Makkedah, in the Shephelah north of Lachish, where they were slain. Joshua followed up his victory with the capture, in succession, of the strongholds of Libnah, Lachish, Eglon, Hebron, and Debir. The battle at Beth-horon had been decisive. The sacred writer summarized it in the words, "the Lord fought for Israel" (Josh. 10:14).

Northern Palestine (Josh. 11). A confederacy of the city-states of northern Palestine under the leadership of Jabin, the powerful king of Hazor, attempted to resist the armies of Joshua in that part of the country. In a swift march up the Jordan Valley, Joshua attacked the Northern Confederacy at the Waters of Merom, on older maps identified with Lake Hula, but now generally located at the town of Meiron, southwest of Hazor. A plain is located at Meiron and abundant water is provided by a spring that flows through a valley of that name (*Wadi Meirôn*) to the Sea of Galilee. These are thought to be "the waters of Merom."

After defeating the Northern Confederacy at Merom, Joshua burned Hazor (Josh. 11:11), but spared the other cities, converting them into centers of Israelite life. The Northern Campaign closed the war of conquest, although strife continued between Israel and her neighbors for several centuries.

SUPPLEMENTARY CONQUESTS

Although much was accomplished, the conquest of Canaan was not completed in Joshua's day, and many victories were short lived. The Coastal Plain remained in Philistine hands. In most of the tribes strong pockets of resistance continued and in some instances cities occupied by Joshua were subsequently recaptured by their original inhabitants. The Book of Judges records three campaigns which occurred after the conquest:

Campaign of Judah and Simeon (Judg. 1:1-19). The tribes of Judah and Simeon agreed to assist each other in fighting the Canaanites in their respective territories. Simeon joined Judah in a campaign against a particularly cruel Canaanite king, Adoni-bezek, the ruler of Bezek, thought to be the modern *Khirbet Ibzîq*, south of Mount Gilboa. Adoni-bezek was captured and his thumbs and big toes were cut off—the type of mutilation he had practiced. Mutilation generally disqualified a person from holding office according to ancient standards. Such acts became a means of insuring that an unwanted ruler could not gain power again. After the victory over Adoni-bezek,

Judah continued the attack upon her enemies "who dwelt in the hill country, in the Negeb, and in the lowland" (Judg. 1:9). The Biblical record indicates that these campaigns were successful, but the enemy usually retained sufficient strength to fight back at a later time. A campaign in the Negeb resulted in the destruction of Zephath, or Hormah, as it was also called (Judg. 1:17).

Campaign of Caleb and Othniel (Josh. 15:13-19; Judg. 1:10-15). For his faithfulness in a time of general unbelief, Caleb was rewarded by having the city of Hebron assigned to him. Although it had been taken by Joshua (Josh. 10:36-37), it was reoccupied soon afterward by its earlier inhabitants. Caleb, however, led an army against the city and took it for his allotment. He promised his daughter, Achsah, to the warrior who would take Debir, also called Kirjath-sepher, twelve miles southwest of Hebron. Debir is usually identified as *Tell Beit Mirsim*, excavated by W. F. Albright and M. G. Kyle from 1926-32. Others locate Biblical Debir at *Khirbet Rabud*, five and three-quarter miles southwest of Hebron on the way to Beer-sheba.

Othniel, described as the younger brother (perhaps half-brother, or nephew) of Caleb, captured Debir and won his bride. She requested of her father *Gulloth-mayim*, perhaps a place name meaning "spring of waters," as her dowry. In the barren Negeb it would be particularly necessary to have access to water. Caleb thereupon gave his daughter *Gulloth-illith* and *Gulloth-tachtith*, probably place names which mean "upper springs" and "nether springs." Some scholars identify these wells with the springs above and below the road at *Seil ed-Dilbeh*, five and three-quarters miles southwest of Hebron on the road to Beer-sheba, one of the best-watered

Valley of Ajalon at Lower Beth-horon. Here, following the miracle of Joshua's long day (Josh. 10), the Israelite armies defeated a coalition of kings from southern Canaan.

Huleh Valley. This view looks across a man-made pond at the north end of the valley. In the time of the judges, some Danites traveled to this region and relocated a little farther north, near one of the sources of the Jordan River. *Courtesy, Levant Photo Service*

valleys in southern Palestine. J. Simons rejects the identification of *Tell Beit Mirsim* with Biblical Debir, suggesting instead *Khirbet Terrameh* because of its proximity to these wells.

The Danite Campaign (Judg. 18). The tribe of Dan was unable to possess its allotment because of the Philistine power on the Coastal Plain. A group of Danites searched for a new home, traveling as far north as Laish, or Leshem, near one of the sources of the Jordan. When the spies brought back their report to Zorah and Eshtaol in Danite territory, a part of the tribe agreed to migrate to the north. Their first encampment was called Mahaneh-Dan ("camp of Dan"), thought to have been located west of Kirjath-jearim, slightly west of Jerusalem. At a village in Mount Ephraim they robbed a man named Micah of the cult objects from his private chapel and took along his Levite priest, in order to establish their own religious institutions (Judg. 18:30). At Laish the Danites fell upon the Phoenician occupants, destroyed their city, and built in its place the city of Dan. This city, now identified with the mound *el-Qadi*, became the northernmost settlement of Israel, as Beer-sheba was its southern limit. The entire Israelite territory was frequently described as the country "from Dan to Beer-sheba."

Palestine Divided among the Twelve Tribes

CANAAN AS DIVIDED AMONG THE TWELVE TRIBES

c. 1200-1020 B.C.

Copyright by C. S. HAMMOND & Co., N. Y.

Scale of Miles

0 10 20 30 40

The Great Sea
(Mediterranean Sea)

Sidon

Zarephath

Damascus

Tyre

Kanah

Sidonians (Phoenicians)

MOUNT LEBANON

Leontes R.

MT. HERMON

DAN
Laish (Dan)

A S H E R

N A P H T A L I

Kedesh

B a s h a n

Hazor

MANASSEH

Accho

Cabul

Ashtaroth

Sea of Chinnereth

Aphek

Hammath

ZEBULUN

Mt. Tabor

Kishon R.

MT. CARMEL

Dor

Megiddo

Shunem

ISSACHAR

Yarmuk R.

Edrei

Jezreel

Taanach

Beth-shan

Ramoth-gilead

Mahanaim

MANASSEH

G i l e a d

A M M O N

Plain of Sharon

Mt. Ebal
Shechem
Mt. Gerizim

Jordan

Succoth

Jabbok R.

Penuel

Kanah

Shiloh

EPHRAIM

Jazer

Rabbath-ammon

Joppa (Japho)

Ajalon

Beth-horon

Bethel

Jericho

River Jordan

Gilgal

Jabneel

D A N

Gezer

Gibeon

BENJAMIN

Heshbon

Mt. Nebo

Ashdod

Libnah

Jerusalem (Jebus)

Medeba

Beth-shemesh

Bethlehem

Ashkelon

Philistines

J U D A H

R E U B E N

Gaza

Lachish

Caleb

Hebron

Salt Sea (Dead Sea)

Gerar

Ziklag

En-gedi

Aroer

Arnon R.

Raphia

Cherethites

Kenites

Beer-sheba

M O A B

Hormah

SIMEON

Rehoboth

Zered R.

River of Egypt

Wilderness of Zin

E D O M

Palestine Divided
among the Twelve Tribes

The Book of Joshua records the territories and towns allotted to each of the twelve tribes. An inheritance in Transjordan had earlier been assigned to Reuben, Gad, and half the tribe of Manasseh (Num. 32; Josh. 13). Following the conquest of Western Palestine, Judah and the descendants of Joseph (Ephraim, and the other half of the Manasseh tribe) cast lots at Gilgal for their portions. Judah received the south portion of the land, Ephraim was assigned a small but choice portion in the center, and Manasseh the land immediately to the north (Josh. 15—17). The remaining seven tribes waited a long time before obtaining their tribal inheritance. After a rebuke by Joshua for their slowness, they assembled at Shiloh and divided the unassigned portions of the land by lot (Josh. 18—19). The Cities of Refuge and the cities allotted to the Levites were assigned late in the life of Joshua (Josh. 20—21). The body of information serves as a national register of the lands assigned to the tribes, although in some cases the tribes never occupied the whole of their assigned areas.

EAST OF THE JORDAN

The tribes of Reuben and Gad occupied land which had once been the territory of Sihon, the Amorite ruler whose capital was at Heshbon.

Reuben was situated north of Moab, the river Arnon serving as the south-

ern boundary line. Reuben's northern boundary was the *Wadi Hesban,* a valley leading to the Jordan from Heshbon.

Gad occupied the territory extending from north of the Hesban to a point north of the Yarmuk.

The proximity of Moab to the south and Ammon to the east made life precarious for the tribes of Reuben and Gad. Reuben disappeared from history during the eleventh century B.C. when its territory was occupied by Moab. The Ammonites oppressed Israel as early as the eleventh century. Jephthah "the Gileadite" (Judg. 11) delivered his people from the Ammonite oppression. After the division of the kingdom, Gad became a part of the Northern Kingdom. Jeroboam established a capital at Peniel in Gad (I Kings 12:25). In 734 B. C., following a series of Assyrian raids, the tribe was deported by Tiglath-pileser III.

The half tribe of Manasseh east of the Jordan occupied the land of Bashan, once the kingdom of Og. It extended from the Yarmuk northward to Mount Hermon. Its eastern border was the undefined edge of the desert. With the rise of the Aramaean kingdom of Damascus during the ninth and eighth centuries, Manasseh became a battle ground of conflicting Israelite-Aramaean interests. Ammonites also pressed upon Manasseh from the southeast. Men of Manasseh were carried into captivity by Tiglath-pileser III (I Chron. 5:18-26). Others were deported after the fall of Samaria (722 B.C.).

WEST OF THE JORDAN

Palestine proper, "the Promised Land," was west of the Jordan. This area may be divided into three sections for ease in classification.

The Southern Tribes:

Judah was assigned the territory westward from the Dead Sea, extending (ideally) to the Mediterranean. Until the days of David, Judah's territory was restricted to the hill country south of Jerusalem. Bethlehem, Hebron, and later, Jerusalem were important Judaean cities. During the days of the Judges and often in subsequent history, the Coastal Plain was in the hands of the Philistines. The low hills known as the Shephelah, between the Philistine Plain and the Judaean Mountains, frequently shifted back and forth from Israel to the Philistines. The Negeb ("southland") was also a part of the territory assigned to Judah.

Simeon did not have an inheritance of its own. In the blessing of Jacob, the aged patriarch said of Simeon and Levi, "I will divide them in Jacob, and scatter them in Israel" (Gen. 49:7). Simeon was assigned the southwestern portion of Judah's allotment (Josh. 19:1-9). The boundary was indeterminate, but it included Beer-sheba, Gerar, Arad, Hormah, and Ziklag. Most of these cities were in Philistine hands until the time of David. Simeon early lost its individuality and its territory was incorporated into the tribe of Judah.

Benjamin was assigned the territory north of Judah and east of Dan. The country was only twenty-five miles from east to west and about fifteen at its widest extent from north to south, yet it included many cities important in Biblical history: Jericho, Bethel, Gibeon, Mizpeh, and Ramah. Jerusalem was on the border between Judah and Benjamin. Saul, Israel's first king, was a Benjamite, a choice which minimized the incipient rivalry between Judah and Ephraim. Although Benjamin's loyalty to David sometimes wavered, it remained true to Judah when Jeroboam led away the ten tribes to form the Northern Kingdom.

Dan was assigned the land west of Benjamin, extending to the Mediterranean. Since most of this area was occupied by the Philistines, the Danites were forced to find other territory. This was done when a portion of the tribe migrated northward and took Laish, at the foot of Mount Hermon near the headwaters of the Jordan, which they renamed Dan. This northern Dan was considered the northern boundary of Israel.

The Central Tribes:

Ephraim, and *the half tribe of Manasseh* which settled west of the Jordan, was given the land north of Benjamin. This territory is very fertile compared with the rocky terrain of Judah. The western part of Manasseh, along the Mediterranean, is known as the Plain of Sharon, a particularly fruitful area. Northern Manasseh included the Plain of Esdraelon, or Jezreel. The sacred city of Shiloh, where the ark was kept in the days of Eli and Samuel, was in Ephraimite territory. Shechem, where Abraham pitched his tent upon entering Canaan, was located in Manasseh between Mount Ebal and Mount Gerizim. There Joshua assembled the tribes to renew their covenant with God (Josh. 24). The term Mount Ephraim is used for the central mountain range in the area later known as Samaria. In times of battle Israelite armies frequently assembled at Mount Ephraim. There Deborah lived and encouraged Barak to defend Israel when Sisera and the Canaanites threatened her very existence. Ephraim and Manasseh were closely related historically and geographically. They are frequently described as "Joseph tribes" because of their relationship to the patriarch Joseph. Jacob adopted the two sons of Joseph, the beloved son of his favored wife Rachel, thus giving them tribal status.

Manasseh was unable to subdue a string of Canaanite fortresses in the Valley of Esdraelon along her northern boundary: Beth-shan, Ibleam, Taanach, and Megiddo (Josh. 17:11). Enemy occupation of these strategic fortresses posed a threat to the Israelite tribes and hindered communications with the four tribes farther north. At a later period Solomon made Megiddo a center of chariotry installations.

Issachar occupied territory north of Manasseh and south of Zebulun and

The Mound of Beth-shan (Beit Shean). This mighty mound once supported the ancient city of Beth-shan overlooking the Valley of the Jordan River. *Copyright, Levant Photo Service*

Naphtali. A ten-mile stretch of the Jordan immediately south of the Sea of Galilee formed her eastern border. Mount Tabor, where Barak assembled his forces to fight Sisera, was on the northwestern border, between Issachar and Zebulun. En-dor, where Saul found the woman with the familiar spirit, Shunem, where Elisha performed one of his miracles, and Jezreel, where Israelite kings had a palace (II Sam. 2:9) and where Jezebel met her death, are among the better known places in Issachar. As in other tribes, Israelite occupation of Issachar was largely limited to the mountain district until the time of David.

The Northern Tribes:

The tribes of Zebulun, Asher, and Naphtali, with the city of Laish conquered by and renamed Dan, occupied the northern part of Canaan.

Asher was located along the Mediterranean Sea coast between the Plain of Sharon and Phoenicia. Nominally Asher occupied much of the territory of southern Phoenicia, including Tyre, but this land was never actually incorporated into Israel. Both David and Solomon recognized Hiram of Tyre as king of the land and had commercial dealings with him. Already by the time of David, Asher had become so insignificant a tribe that it is omitted in the list of chief rulers (I Chron. 27:16-22). Remnants from Asher in the mountainous part of the territory did preserve their identity, however. In the New Testament, Anna, the prophetess, is described as a woman of Asher (Luke 2:36-38).

Naphtali was allotted the territory between Asher and the northern section of the Jordan River, and the western shore of the Sea of Galilee. Kedesh (Naphtali) and Hazor were among its important towns. In the time of Joshua,

Hazor led a strong confederacy against Israel. Like the other northern tribes, Naphtali was exposed to attack from powerful neighbors. The Aramaean Kingdom of Damascus made inroads into Naphtali. It further suffered at the hands of the Assyrians when Tiglath-pileser III took many of its citizens captive (733 B.C.), about a decade before the fall of Samaria.

Zebulun occupied a smaller area than Asher and Naphtali but its history is somewhat parallel. The territory included a small portion of the fertile Plain of Jezreel and the rich farm land of the present Nazareth region. Although cut off from the Mediterranean by Asher, and from the Sea of Galilee by Naphtali, Zebulun had ready access to the sea through the Plain of Jezreel and could easily reach such rich markets as Sidon. The important trade route between Egypt and Damascus passed through Zebulun. She suffered the same perils as her neighboring tribes, however, and many Zebulunites were taken captive by Tiglath-pileser.

THE TRIBE OF LEVI

Levi, the priestly tribe, received no tribal territory but was allotted certain cities among the other tribes. In all there were forty-eight Levitical cities, an average of four cities to each tribe. Six of these cities were assigned as Cities of Refuge where the innocent manslayer might be granted asylum (Josh. 20). Cities were chosen on each side of the Jordan in the south, center, and north of the land. These east of the Jordan were: Bezer in Reuben, Ramoth-gilead in Gad, and Golan in Manasseh. Hebron in Judah, Shechem in Manesseh, and Kadesh in Naphtali were the Cities of Refuge west of the Jordan.

CHAPTER XI

Palestine under the Judges

Mount Tabor. Here, in the northeast part of the Jezreel Plain, Hebrew soldiers under Deborah and Barak gathered before advancing against the Canaanites who were camped on the plain below.

Courtesy, Israel Office of Information

CHAPTER XI
Palestine under the Judges

After the death of Joshua there was a tendency on the part of the Israelites to lapse into idolatry, worshiping the gods and engaging in the cult practices of their idolatrous neighbors. We learn from the history recorded in the Book of Judges that God delivered His people into the hands of their enemies during periods of apostasy until they turned from their sin and prayed for deliverance. When this took place, God raised up spiritually endowed leaders to deliver them from their oppressors. These leaders, known as Judges, differed greatly in function from the later kings. Kings pass their right of rule on to their sons in dynastic succession. Judges, however, were individually raised up of God in times of crisis and endowed with spiritual gifts to meet those crises. Usually they acted as leaders of their people until death but no principle of succession was recognized. It is thought that many of the judges ruled over limited regions, and more than one may have been in authority at the same time in different parts of the land. The period of the Judges is one of tribal, rather than national, emphasis.

The Mesopotamian Oppression (Judg. 3:5-11)

A king from "Mesopotamia" (Hebrew *Aram-naharaim,* "Aram of the two rivers"), oppressed Israel shortly after the death of Joshua. Cushan-rishathaim ("doubly wicked Cushan"), who sent his armies through Syria into Canaan, is the first recorded enemy from a distance to invade Canaan after the Israel-ite settlement. During the time of the Judges, Canaan was nominally subject to Egypt. The Hittites overran Mitanni, the state which served as a buffer in northern Mesopotamia between the Hittite and Assyrian kingdoms. Cushan was probably an obscure Hittite prince who wished to challenge Egyptian power in Canaan. The real suffering, however, took place among the Israelites.

An alternate view suggests that Cushan was from Edom, rather than Aram. The two words look very much alike in Hebrew and the proximity of Edom to the tribe of Judah is a point in favor of this interpretation.

Extensive military campaigns were carried on throughout the Fertile Crescent as early as the time of Sargon of Akkad (*ca.* 2360 B.C.) so that a Mesopotamian origin for Cushan cannot be dismissed on *a priori* grounds. Neither Biblical nor extra-Biblical sources throw further light upon the person of Cushan.

Othniel, the son of Kenaz (cf. Josh. 15:16-19), was raised up of God to deliver His people from the oppressions of Cushan. The Biblical record preserves no details, but it states the fact of Othniel's victory over Cushan and the period of "rest" or peace which followed.

Moabite Oppression (Judg. 3:12-30)

Eglon of Moab, the area east of the Dead Sea and south of the Arnon, joined forces with Ammonites and Bedouin Amalekites to attack the Israelite tribes. He was evidently able to subdue the tribes east of the Jordan, after which he crossed into Benjamin. Jericho, known as "the city of palm trees" (Judg. 3:13), was occupied by Eglon. The curse pronounced by Joshua on any who would rebuild Jericho (Josh. 6:26) may have referred only to the building of a fortified city there. From Jericho, Eglon, like Joshua before him, acquired a foothold in all of Palestine.

Deliverance came to Israel, however, when Ehud, a Benjamite, while delivering tribute to Eglon, plunged his sword into the king's abdomen. Ehud then mustered the armies of Israel and slew most of the Moabites who were in Israelite territory west of the Jordan.

Early Philistine Oppression (Judg. 3:31)

Brief mention is made of a Philistine raid upon the hill country of Judaea. Shamgar, the son of Anath, with no other weapons but an oxgoad, repelled the Philistines. The exact place of this battle is not mentioned, but it must have been somewhere on the frontier between Judah and the Philistine country. Six hundred of the Philistines were slain. Shamgar is a Hurrian name, and Anath is the name of the Canaanite goddess of sex and war. These names indicate the variety of contacts between Israel and her neighbors during the time of the Judges.

The Canaanite Oppression (Judg. 4—5)

The Israelite conquest of Canaan produced resentment among the remaining natives of the land. When opportunity came, they struck back. From strategic points in the Jezreel Valley, the Canaanites were able to expand their holdings until they threatened the whole of the nation. Their leader was Jabin, who, like an earlier Jabin (Josh. 11:1), ruled the powerful city-state of Hazor. Sisera, Jabin's general, dwelt at Harosheth, present-day *Tell 'Amar,* at the place where the Kishon passes through a narrow gorge to enter the Plain of Accho. It is about sixteen miles northwest of Megiddo.

Deborah, the only woman judge, called upon Barak of Naphtali to aid in gathering an army from the northern tribes of Issachar, Zebulun, and Naphtali. The fighters gathered at Mount Tabor in the northeastern part of the Plain of Jezreel and advanced in force against the Canaanites who were encamped on the plain below. Sisera and his army were thrown into a rout when the very stars in their courses seemed to fight against them. A storm caused the River Kishon to overflow its banks, and Sisera's chariots became a liability instead of an asset. Sisera, himself, fled on foot to the tent of Jael, the wife of Heber, the Kenite, where he was made welcome. After the Canaanite general had fallen asleep, however, Jael drove a tent pin through his head. With the defeat of Sisera and of Jabin, his king, large scale Canaanite resistance was ended. Although there were pockets of resistance until the time of David, victories during the judgeship of Deborah and Barak made it possible for the Israelites to settle in the Plain of Jezreel without fear of Canaanite molestation.

Midianite Oppression (Judg. 6—8)

The nomadic Midianites joined with Amalekite Bedouins in a series of invasions which devastated central Palestine. Raids were made at harvest time, when the invaders would steal and destroy crops, forcing the Israelites to seek refuge in mountain caves. The man endowed of God to deliver Israel from Midianite oppression came from "Ophrah of the Abi-Ezrites" (Judg. 6:11) thought to have been a town fifteen miles northwest of Beth-shan, now known as *et-Taiyibeh.* Gideon summoned his countrymen to Mount Gilboa while the enemy was encamped at the foot of the Hill of Moreh, six miles to the north, across the Valley of Jezreel. Staging a night attack, Gideon, with three hundred chosen men, defeated the Midianite hosts.

The defeated Midianites fled down the ravine past the ancient fortress city of Beth-shan at the point where the Valley of Jezreel connects with the Jordan Valley. They continued down the Jordan Valley through Abel-meholah, located at about the mid-point between the Sea of Galilee and the Dead Sea. At Beth-barah ("house of crossing"), an unidentified location, the men of Ephraim captured and slew the two Midianite princes, Oreb and Zeeb. East of the Jordan the Israelites faced opposition at Succoth and Peniel in the Jabbok Valley. Gideon continued pursuit, however, threatening punishment on his return. At Karkar, doubtless on the lower Jabbok, he encountered the remainder of the Midianite army. The kings of the Midianites, Zebah and Zal-

munna, were captured and subsequently put to death.

Ammonite Oppression (Judg. 10—11)

The tribes east of the Jordan were oppressed by their Ammonite neighbors for a period of eighteen years. The Israelites rallied at Mizpeh of Gilead, the place where Jacob and Laban had made their covenant many years before (Gen. 31:49). Needing leadership they turned to Jephthah, the son of a prostitute, who had fled from his father's house amidst the taunts of his half-brothers. The Gileadites sent to Tob, on the fringes of civilization, where Jephthah had become leader of a band of outlaws. On condition that he be acknowledged leader of his people, Jephthah agreed to lead the Gileadites against Ammon. The Gileadites had no choice, and Jephthah became their leader. He fought the Ammonites at Aroer, on the north bank of the Arnon, and drove them northward devastating their territory as far as Minnith. This

Ashkelon. The ancient Philistine city of Ashkelon was rebuilt by Herod the Great whose sister, Salome, resided there. Ruins from the Roman period are illustrated.
Courtesy, Palphot, Israel

was possibly *Khirbet Hamzeh,* four miles northeast of Heshbon. The fruits of victory brought sorrow to Jephthah, however, for he had foolishly vowed to offer to God as a sacrifice the one whom he would first see on returning after a victorious battle. It was his own daughter who rushed out to meet him.

Following his victory over the Ammonites, Jephthah was involved in a civil war with the Ephraimites who resented the fact that they had not been called to participate in the battle— and, of course, the spoils! The Ephraimites were defeated. Thereupon they fled toward the fords of the Jordan (perhaps Beth-barah), where many were slain while attempting to cross. To distinguish Ephraimites from Gileadites they were asked to pronounce the password, "Shibboleth." Because of dialectical differences, the Ephraimites said "Sibboleth" and thus betrayed the fact that they were not Gileadites.

The Philistine Oppression (Judg. 13—16)

With the exception of the Philistines, the nations which threatened Israel during the time of the Judges were effectively subdued. Sporadic attacks upon Israel took place over a period of years, but only the Philistines posed a continuing challenge to Israelite sovereignty. As late as the time of Saul we read of Philistine garrisons at Bethel (I Sam. 10:3-5) and at Geba (I Sam. 13:3).

The exploits of Samson were of a personal nature. He led no armies and performed his deeds of valor without help. His foes, the Philistines, occupied the coastal plain from Gaza northward toward Mount Carmel. They kept strong garrison posts, and by their monopoly of iron prevented the Israelites from making weapons (I Sam. 13:19 ff.).

Much of Samson's life was lived in the Valley of Sorek, the most direct route from the hill country near Jerusalem to the Philistine plain. Zorah, where Samson was born (Judg. 13:2 ff.), was situated on a hillside overlooking the Sorek. Here also was Timnah, or Timnath, where Samson first sought a wife (Judg. 14:1), and where he performed deeds of strength (Judg. 14:6); and Eshtaol near which he was buried (Judg. 16:31).

During the time of the Judges we read of the migration of Danites from their territory along the Mediterranean to the city which bears their name in northern Palestine. The city of Laish, or Leshem, was in the Sidonian (i.e. Phoenician) sphere of influence when it was conquered by the Danites and renamed Dan.

At Aphek in Ephraim, probably *Râs el-'Ain,* about eleven miles northeast of Joppa, Israel suffered a humiliating defeat early in the career of Samuel. To insure victory over the Philistines, Israel made a fetish of the ark, bringing it to the battlefield. Instead of bringing victory to Israel, however, the ark itself was taken, and the Philistines gained a major victory. It did not prove helpful to the Philistines, however. When taken to their temple at Ashdod the image of Dagon fell before the ark. Later a plague broke out among the people. Successively the ark was sent from Ashdod to Gath, to Ekron, and then to Beth-shemesh in the Sorek Valley at the border between Israel and the Philistines. Men of Beth-shemesh irreverently peered into the ark, and, as a result, many died (I Sam. 6:19). Then it was sent to Kirjath-jearim ("city of forests"), modern *Tell el-Azhar,* on the border between Judah and Benjamin in territory which was indisputably Israelite. There the ark remained until it was taken to Jerusalem during the reign of David.

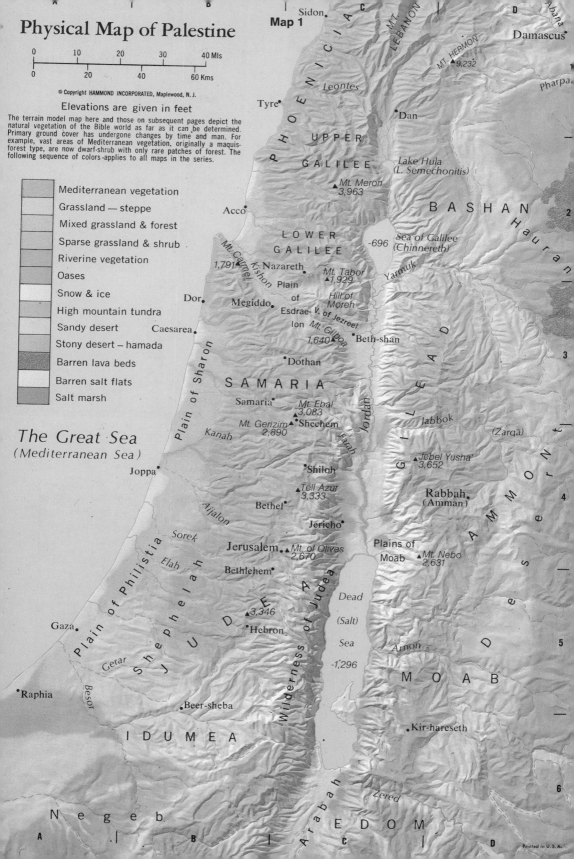

Physical Map of Palestine

Map 1

© Copyright HAMMOND INCORPORATED, Maplewood, N.J.

Elevations are given in feet

The terrain model map here and those on subsequent pages depict the natural vegetation of the Bible world as far as it can be determined. Primary ground cover has undergone changes by time and man. For example, vast areas of Mediterranean vegetation, originally a maquis-forest type, are now dwarf-shrub with only rare patches of forest. The following sequence of colors applies to all maps in the series.

- Mediterranean vegetation
- Grassland — steppe
- Mixed grassland & forest
- Sparse grassland & shrub
- Riverine vegetation
- Oases
- Snow & ice
- High mountain tundra
- Sandy desert
- Stony desert — hamada
- Barren lava beds
- Barren salt flats
- Salt marsh

The Great Sea
(Mediterranean Sea)

Sidon
MT. LEBANON
Abana
Damascus
PHOENICIA
MT. HERMON ▲ 9,232
Pharpa
Leontes
Tyre
Dan
UPPER GALILEE
Lake Hula (L. Semechonitis)
BASHAN
Hauran
Acco
Mt. Meron 3,963
LOWER GALILEE
-696
Sea of Galilee (Chinnereth)
Mt. Carmel 1,791
K. Kishon
Nazareth
Mt. Tabor 1,929
Yarmuk
Dor
Megiddo
Plain of Esdrae- lon
Hill of Moreh
V. of Jezreel
Mt. Gilboa 1,640
Beth-shan
Caesarea
Dothan
G I L E A D
SAMARIA
Samaria
Mt. Ebal 3,083
Mt. Gerizim 2,890
Shechem
Jabbok
(Zarqā)
Plain of Sharon
Kanah
Jordan
Farah
Jebel Yusha 3,652
A M M O N
Joppa
Shiloh
Tell Azur 3,333
Bethel
Rabbah (Amman)
Aijalon
Sorek
Jericho
Jerusalem
Mt. of Olives 2,670
Plains of Moab
Mt. Nebo 2,631
Elah
Bethlehem
Plain of Philistia
Shephelah
JUDEA
Wilderness of Judea
Dead (Salt) Sea -1,296
Gaza
Gerar
Hebron ▲ 3,346
Arnon
M O A B
Besor
Raphia
Beer-sheba
Kir-haresheth
I D U M E A
N e g e b
Arabah
Zered
E D O M

Printed in U.S.A.

The geographical setting for much of the Biblical narrative is within that half circle of arable land known as the Fertile Crescent. In the east the arc follows the alluvial plains of the Euphrates and Tigris rivers. It widens as one moves northwest through grassland and steppe, then it turns southwest at the Mediterranean coast and continues as a narrow belt through Phoenicia and Palestine. The arc ends in the green ribbon of the Nile. Rainfall, always scant and seasonal in the Middle East, has changed little since the beginning of the Biblical era. Cropland and grassland areas remain much as they were in Abraham's day and the extent of desert is unchanged. Forests, however, have been slowly cut back by man so that today large expanses of mountain forest or wooded areas of the Mediterranean type are scarce.

Deciduous & coniferous forest

Mediterranean vegetation

Grassland — steppe

Mixed grassland & forest

Sparse grassland & shrub

Riverine vegetation

Oases

Snow & ice

High mountain tundra

Sandy desert

Stony desert — hamada

Barren lava beds

Barren salt flats

Salt marsh

Salt desert

Black

Troy
ASSUWA
Sangarius

Hermes
Karabel
Maeander   Beycesultan
ARZAWA

LUKKA

M I N O A N
Rhodes
ALASHIY
KITTIM
(Cyprus)
CAPHTOR
(Crete)

M Y C E N A E A N   D O M A I N

M e d i t e r r a n e a n   S e a
(Great or Upper Sea)

Avaris
(Zoan)
Lower
Egypt
On
Memphis
(Noph)
Heracleopolis

L i b y a n
Hermopolis
Akhetaton
(Tell el-Amarna)

D e s e r t
Nile
Upper
Abydos
Egypt
(T

NUB

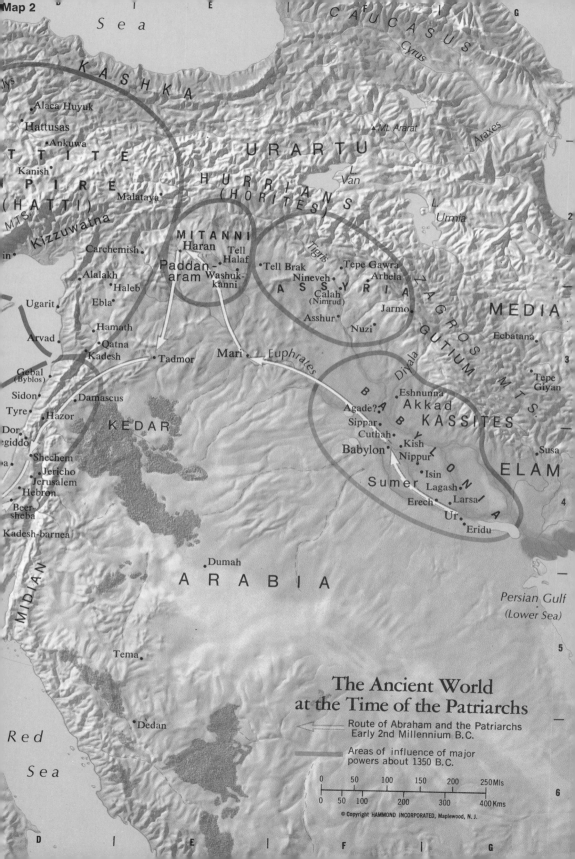

Map 2

Sea

CAUCASUS

Cyrus

KASHKA

Alaca Huyuk
Hattusas
Ankuwa

Kanish

TTITE
PIRE
(HATTI)

Malataya

MTS.

Kizzuwatna

in

Mt. Ararat

URARTU

HURRIANS
(HORITES)

L. Van

L. Urmia

Araxes

Carchemish

Alalakh
Haleb

Ugarit

Ebla

Hamath

Qatna
Kadesh

Arvad

Gebal
(Byblos)

Sidon
Tyre

Dor
giddo

a

Hazor

Damascus

KEDAR

Shechem
Jericho
Jerusalem
Hebron

Beer-
sheba

Kadesh-barnea

MIDIAN

Red

Sea

MITANNI

Haran
Paddan-
aram

Tell
Halaf

Washuk-
kanni

Tell Brak

Tigris

Tepe Gawra
Nineveh   Arbela
Calah
(Nimrud)

ASSYRIA

Asshur

Jarmo

Nuzi

ZAGROS

GUTIUM

MTS.

MEDIA

Ecbatana

Tepe
Giyan

Mari

Euphrates

Tadmor

Diyala

B A B Y

Eshnunna

Agade?

Sippar

Cuthah

Babylon

Kish

Nippur

Akkad

KASSITES

L O N I A

Isin

Susa

ELAM

Sumer

Lagash

Larsa

Erech

Ur

Eridu

Dumah

A R A B I A

Persian Gulf
(Lower Sea)

Tema

The Ancient World
at the Time of the Patriarchs

← Route of Abraham and the Patriarchs
Early 2nd Millennium B.C.

Areas of influence of major
powers about 1350 B.C.

Dedan

0   50   100   150   200   250 Mls
0   50 100   200   300   400 Kms

© Copyright HAMMOND INCORPORATED, Maplewood, N.J.

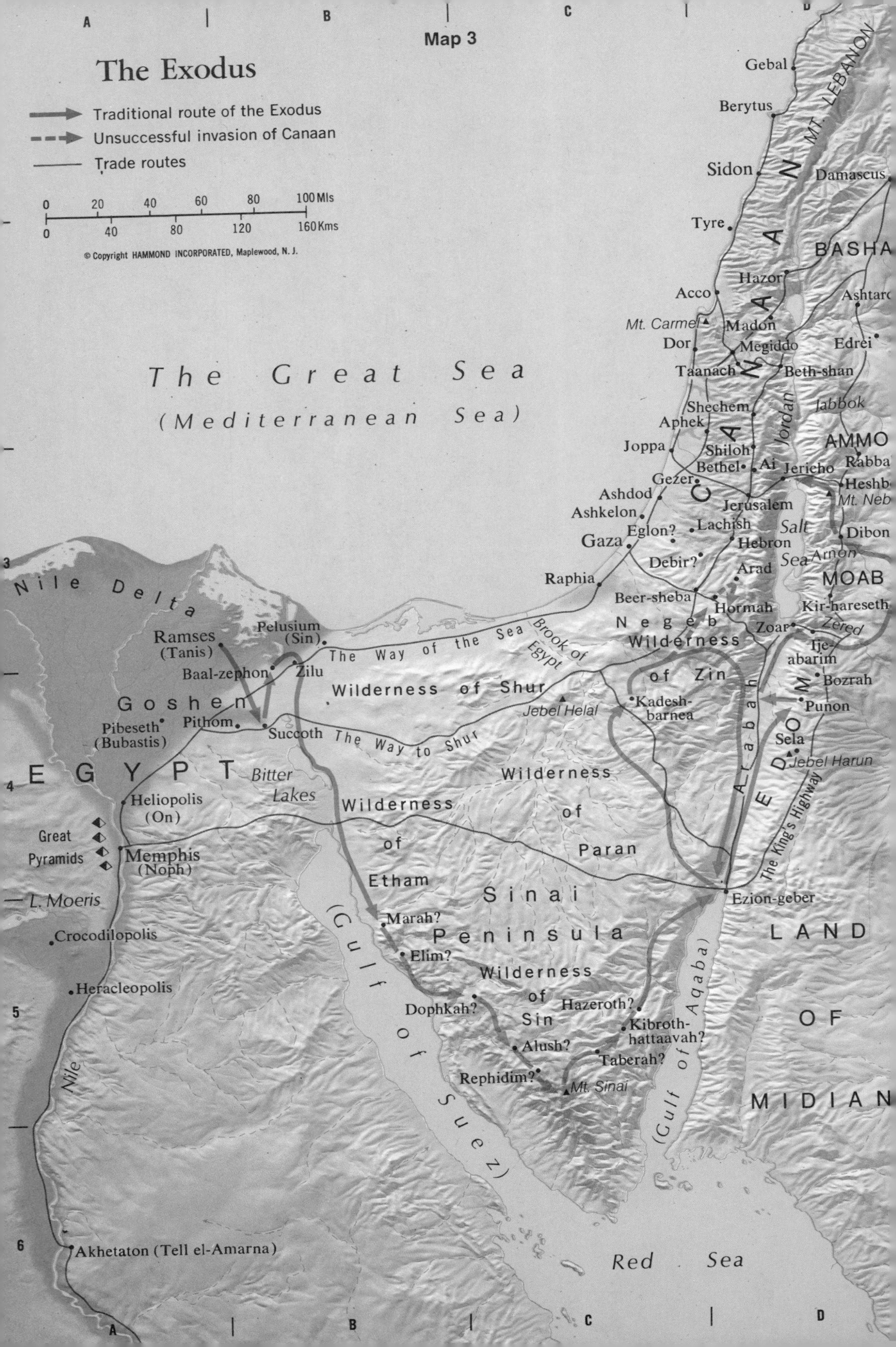

Map 3
The Exodus
Traditional route of the Exodus
Unsuccessful invasion of Canaan
Trade routes
0 20 40 60 80 100 Mls
0 40 80 120 160 Kms
© Copyright HAMMOND INCORPORATED, Maplewood, N. J.
A
B
C
D
3
4
5
6
The Great Sea
(Mediterranean Sea)
Gebal
Berytus
MT. LEBANON
Sidon
Damascus
Tyre
CANAAN
BASHA
Hazor
Acco
Ashtaro
Mt. Carmel
Madon
Dor
Megiddo
Edrei
Taanach
Beth-shan
Shechem
Jordan
Jabbok
Aphek
Joppa
Shiloh
AMMO
Bethel
Ai
Jericho
Rabba
Gezer
Heshb
Ashdod
Mt. Neb
Jerusalem
Ashkelon
Lachish
Salt Sea
Eglon?
Dibon
Gaza
Hebron
Arnon
Debir?
Arad
MOAB
Raphia
Beer-sheba
Hormah
Kir-hareseth
Negeb
Zoar
Zered
Nile Delta
Pelusium (Sin)
Ramses (Tanis)
The Way of the Sea
Brook of Egypt
Wilderness of Zin
Ije-abarim
Baal-zephon
Zilu
Wilderness of Shur
Bozrah
Goshen
Kadesh-barnea
Jebel Helal
EDOM
Punon
Pibeseth (Bubastis)
Pithom
Succoth
The Way to Shur
Arabah
Sela
Jebel Harun
EGYPT
Bitter Lakes
Wilderness of Paran
Heliopolis (On)
Wilderness of Etham
The King's Highway
Great Pyramids
Memphis (Noph)
L. Moeris
Sinai Peninsula
Ezion-geber
Marah?
LAND OF MIDIAN
Crocodilopolis
Elim?
(Gulf of Suez)
(Gulf of Aqaba)
Wilderness of Sin
Heracleopolis
Dophkah?
Hazeroth?
Kibroth-hattaavah?
Alush?
Taberah?
Rephidim?
Mt. Sinai
Nile
Akhetaton (Tell el-Amarna)
Red Sea

A | B | C | D

Map 4

HITTITES

Ugarit

Tiphsah

Euphrates

HAMATH

Orontes

Hamath

1

Arvad

KITTIM
(CYPRUS)

Tadmor

The Great Sea

Kadesh

Zedad

(Mediterranean Sea)

ARAM—

2

Lebo-hamath

Hazar-enan

ZOBAH

Gebal

Berothai

S y r i a n

Berytus

BETH-REHOB

ARAM—

Sidon

MT. HERMON

Damascus

D e s e r t

3

Tyre

Abel

Dan

DAMASCUS

Kedesh

Hazor

MAACAH

ARGOB

Acco

Cabul

Ashtaroth

GESHUR

Mt. Carmel

Edrei

Dor

TOB

Megiddo

Jezreel

Ramoth-gilead

Salecah

Taanach

Mt. Gilboa

Beth-shan

Hepher

Mahanaim

Jordan

Shechem

Succoth

Joppa

ISRAEL

Rabbah

Gezer

Beth-horon

AMMON

Bethel

PHILISTIA

Gibeah

Jericho

Ashdod

Jerusalem

Heshbon

Beth-shemesh

Ashkelon

Gath?

Medeba

Gaza

Lachish

Hebron

Salt

Ziklag?

Sea

Aroer

Raphia

Gerar

Arad

Beer-sheba

MOAB

4

Tamar

Kir-hareseth

AMALEK

Kadesh-barnea

Bozrah

River of Egypt

Punon

EDOM

5

The Empire of David and Solomon

——— Boundary of the empire
at its greatest extent

⬚ Territory conquered by David

⬚ Territory in the far north under
economic influence of Solomon

⊡ Fortified places of Solomon

✕ Copper mining centers

Sela

Arabah

0 10 25   50   75   100 Mls

0 20 40 60 80 100 120 140 160 Kms

✕ Ezion-geber

© Copyright HAMMOND INCORPORATED, Maplewood, N.J.

6

A | B | C | D

The Kingdoms of Israel and Judah

Map 5

Approximate frontiers
ISRAEL — Hebrew kingdoms
AMMON — Foreign kingdoms

10 20 30 40 Mls
20 40 60 Kms

© Copyright HAMMOND INCORPORATED, Maplewood, N.J.

The Great Sea
(Mediterranean Sea)

PHOENICIA

Sidon
Tyre
Leontes
Ijon
Abel-beth-maachah
Dan
Kedesh
Hazor
Merom
Galilee
Acco
Chinnereth
Cabul
Rumah
Hammath
Plain of
Mt. Tabor
Shunem
Dor
Esdraelon
Megiddo
Jezreel
Taanach
Mt. Gilboa
Ibleam
Dothan
Jabesh-gilead
Socoh
Tirzah
Samaria
Mt. Ebal
Mt. Gerizim
Shechem
Succoth
Aphek
Shiloh
Joppa

Mt. Carmel
Kishon
Plain of Sharon
Kanah

SYRIA
(ARAM)
Damascus
MT. HERMON
Bashan
Sea of Chinnereth
Aphek
Karnaim
Ashtaroth
Yarmuk
Havvoth-jair
Edrei
Ramoth-gilead
Beth-shan
Abel-meholah
Tishbe
Penuel
Mahanaim
Jabbok

I S R A E L
Gilead
AMMON

Lod
Gath
Jabneel
Gezer
Gibbethon
Ekron
Aijalon
Zorah
Ashdod
Beth-shemesh
Ashkelon
Adullam
Mareshah
Lachish
Adoraim
Debir?
Ziph
Ziklag?
Gaza
Gerar
Raphia
Sharuhen
Arad
Beer-sheba

Bethel
Mizpah
Gibeon
Ramah
Geba
Zemaraim
Gilgal
Jericho
Jerusalem
Bethlehem
Tekoa
Beth-zur
Hebron
En-gedi

J U D A H
Wilderness of Judah

Jazer
Rabbah
Shittim?
Heshbon
Mt. Nebo
Medeba
Jahaz
Ataroth
Dibon
Aroer
Arnon
Ar?
M O A B
Kir-hareseth

Salt Sea

PHILISTIA

Besor

Negeb
Ascent of Akrabbim
Zoar
Tamar
Zered
E D O M

Map 6

Medo-Babylonian Realms

Political boundaries of major
powers about 560 B.C.

500 MIs
800 Kms
400
600
300
200
400
100
200
0
0

© Copyright HAMMOND INCORPORATED, Maplewood, N.J.

Jaxartes
Oxus
Aral Sea
Caspian Sea
Erythraean Sea
PARTHIA
EMPIRE
HYRCANIA
MEDIAN
MEDIA
Ecbatana
PERSIA
ELAM
Susa
BABYLONIA
Nippur
Erech
Ur
Persian Gulf
CAUCASUS
SCYTHIANS
URARTU
Tigris
Opis
Sippar
Babylon
ASSYRIA
Harran
Nisibis
Nineveh
Euphrates
NEW
Anat
BABYLONIAN
EMPIRE
IZALLA
Carchemish
SYRIA
Riblah
ARABS
Dumah
KINGDOM
CAPPADOCIA
Halys
KUE
Tarsus
Damascus
Tyre
Megiddo
JUDAH
Jerusalem
Tema
Dedan
Sinope
Black Sea
LYDIA
Sardis
OF
Lycia
Cyprus
trib. to Egypt
Mediterranean Sea
Red Sea
THRACIANS
GREEKS
Aegean
Sea
Athens
Sparta
Crete
(Danube)
Sais
Memphis
KINGDOM
OF
EGYPT
Nile
Thebes
Syene
(Elephantine)
LIBYANS
Temple of
Amon
ETHIOPIA

Map 7

The Persian Empire

Limits of the Persian empire c.500 B.C.
Persian royal road
Royal residences
Red Sea-Nile canal built by Darius I

0   100   200   300   400   500 Mls
0   200   400   600   800 Kms

MASSAGETAE

SCYTHIANS
(SAKA)

Aral
Sea

CHORASMIA

Jaxartes

Oxus

SOGDIANA

•Cyropolis

•Bactra

BACTRIA

•Margiana

MARGUS

Caspian Sea

HYRCANIA

•Zadrakarta

PARTHIA

•Daunghan

ARIA

PERSIAN

•Rhagae
•Ecbatana

MEDIA

•Dumgham

EMPIRE

DRANGIANA

•Yazd

•Gabae

PERSIS

Persepolis
(Parsa)•
•Pasargadae

Lower
Sea

CARMANIA

•Pura

GEDROSIA
(MAKA)

HINDU KUSH

•Taxila
(Kabul)•
•Cophen

GANDARA

ARACHOSIA

Indus

Probable
ancient
coastline

HINDUSH
(INDIA)

•Pattala

Erythraean

Sea

•Gerrha

ARMENIA

CAUCASUS

•Cyrus
Araxes

•Van
Urmia

•Arbela

•Opis •Babylon
•Sippar •Nippur
BABYLONIA
•Ashur •Erech
•Asshur
Tigris
•Harran
Euphrates
•Tadmor

SUSIANA
•Susa
Ulai

Behistun•

THRACE
•Apollonia

•Phasis

MOSCHI

•Melitene

•Trapezus

CILICIA
•Tarsus
•Assus
•Thapsacus
•Damascus

•Hamath
•Arvad
•Gebal
•Tyre

JUDAH
•Jerusalem
•Gaza

•Blath

•Dumah

ARABIA

•Dedan

•Tema

Red

Sea

•Panticapaeum

Black Sea

•Chersonesus
•Sinope

•Byzantium

MACEDONIA

LYDIA
•Sardis
•Gordion
•Ancyra
•Iconium
Maeander
•Ephesus
•Miletus *Halys*
CARIA
•Xanthus
PERSIAN

GREECE
•Athens
•Marathon
•Sparta

Cyprus

Crete

Rhodes

•Cyrene

Upper
Sea

LIBYA

•Cyprus

•Pelusium
•Memphis
•Heliopolis
•Sais
•Temple of Amon
(Siwa)

EGYPT

Nile

•Thebes
•Syene
(Elephantine)

ETHIOPIA
(CUSH)

Libyan

Desert

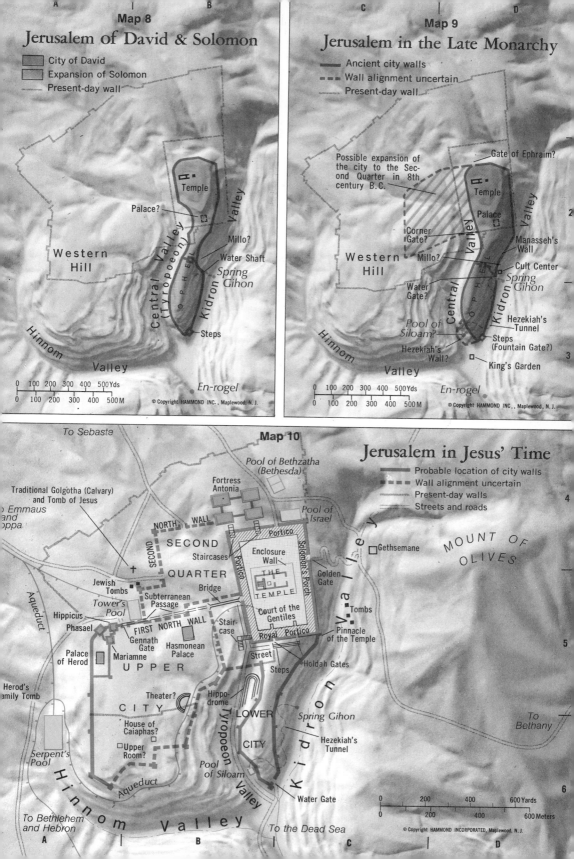

Map 8
Jerusalem of David & Solomon

- City of David
- Expansion of Solomon
- Present-day wall

Temple
Palace?
Millo?
Water Shaft
Western Hill
Central Valley (Tyropoeon)
OPHEL
Kidron Valley
Spring Gihon
Steps
Hinnom Valley
En-rogel

0 100 200 300 400 500Yds
0 100 200 300 400 500M
© Copyright HAMMOND INC., Maplewood, N.J.

Map 9
Jerusalem in the Late Monarchy

- Ancient city walls
- Wall alignment uncertain
- Present-day wall

Gate of Ephraim?
Possible expansion of the city to the Second Quarter in 8th century B.C.
Temple
Palace
Corner Gate?
Manasseh's Wall
Millo?
Cult Center
Western Hill
Water Gate?
Central Valley
OPHEL
Spring Gihon
Pool of Siloam?
Hezekiah's Tunnel
Hezekiah's Wall?
Steps (Fountain Gate?)
Kidron Valley
Hinnom Valley
King's Garden
En-rogel

0 100 200 300 400 500Yds
0 100 200 300 400 500M
© Copyright HAMMOND INC., Maplewood, N.J.

Map 10
Jerusalem in Jesus' Time

- Probable location of city walls
- Wall alignment uncertain
- Present-day walls
- Streets and roads

To Sebaste
Pool of Bethzatha (Bethesda)
Fortress Antonia
Traditional Golgotha (Calvary) and Tomb of Jesus
To Emmaus and Joppa
Pool of Israel
NORTH WALL
SECOND
Portico
SECOND QUARTER
Staircases
Portico
Enclosure Wall
Solomon's Porch
MOUNT OF OLIVES
Gethsemane
Bridge
Jewish Tombs
Tower's Pool
Subterranean Passage
THE TEMPLE
Golden Gate
Hippicus
FIRST NORTH WALL
Staircase
Court of the Gentiles
Tombs
Phasael
Gennath Gate
Hasmonean Palace
Royal Portico
Pinnacle of the Temple
Palace of Herod
Mariamne
UPPER
Street
Steps
Holdah Gates
Aqueduct
Herod's Family Tomb
Theater?
Hippodrome
CITY
House of Caiaphas?
Upper Room?
LOWER CITY
Spring Gihon
Hezekiah's Tunnel
To Bethany
Serpent's Pool
Tyropoeon Valley
Kidron Valley
Aqueduct
Pool of Siloam
Water Gate
To Bethlehem and Hebron
Hinnom Valley
To the Dead Sea

0 200 400 600 Yards
0 200 400 600 Meters
© Copyright HAMMOND INCORPORATED, Maplewood, N.J.

Map 11

Palestine in
New Testament Times

Political boundaries A.D. 6-44
☐ Cities of the Decapolis
⊠ Fortresses

0   10   20   30   40 Mls
0   20   40   60 Kms

© Copyright HAMMOND INCORPORATED, Maplewood, N.J.

Mediterranean

Sea

P h o e n i c i a

S Y R I A

MT. LEBANON

MT. HERMON

ABILENE

Iturea

•Abila

•Sidon

•Dama

•Sarepta

Paneas

•Caesarea Philippi

•Tyre

Leontes

Ulatha

Ladder
of Tyre

•Cadasa

Gaulanitis

Batane

•Ecdippa

•Gischala

•Ptolemais

•Chorazin

•Bethsaida-Julias

•Raphana

GALILEE

•Capernaum

•Cana •Magadan

Sea

☐Hippos

☐Dion?

•Asochis

•Tiberias

of

•Sepphoris

Galilee

•Abila

Mt. Carmel

•Nazareth

Yarmuk

☐Gadara

Plain

▲Mt.
Tabor

•Nain

•Capitolias

•Dora

of

•Agrippina

•Arbela

Esdraelon

•Caesarea

Scythopolis☐

DECAPOLIS

•Narbata

☐Pella

•Ginae

Salim

SAMARIA

•Aenon

•Sebaste
(Samaria)

•Amathus

☐Gerasa

•Neapolis ▲Mt. Ebal

Mt. Gerizim▲ •Sychar

Jordan

Jabbok

•Apollonia

Plain of Sharon

•Antipatris

•Alexandrium⊠

•Gadara

PEREA

☐Philadelphia

•Joppa

•Arimathea?

•Phasaelis

•Lydda

•Gophna

•Ephraim

•Archelais

•Jamnia

•Jericho

Betharamphtha
•(Livias, Julias)

•Emmaus
(Nicopolis)

•Emmaus?

•Cyprus

•Esbus

•Azotus

•Jerusalem •Bethany

•Qumran

•Medeba

•Bethlehem

⊠Hyrcania

JUDEA

⊠Herodium

•Callirrhoe

•Ascalon

•Marisa

•Bethsura

⊠Machaerus

•Agrippias

•Hebron

Lake
Asphaltitis
(Dead Sea)

Arnon

N A B A T E A

•Gaza

•Engaddi

•Masada⊠

IDUMEA

•Areopolis

•Bersabe

•Malatha⊠

•Charachmoba

The Roman World

━━━ Limits of direct Roman rule or political influence at the birth of Christ

- - - Provincial or state boundaries

SYRIA   Roman provinces

<u>LYCIA</u>   Client kingdoms or states

© Copyright HAMMOND INCORPORATED, Maplewood, N.J.

Map 12

Scale: 0 100 200 300 400 500 Mls
0 200 400 600 800 Kms

Atlantic Ocean

Britannia

Albis (Elbe)

Lost to Rome in A.D. 9

Rhine

Augusta Treverorum

Germania

Sarmatia

Rha (Volga)

Caspian Sea

CAUCASUS

Albania

Iberia

Colchis

Artaxata

ARMENIA

PARTHIAN EMPIRE

Ctesiphon

Arabia

BOSPORUS KDM.

Black Sea

Trapezus

Sinope

CAPPADOCIA

COMMAGENE

Antioch

SYRIA

Tarsus

CILICIA

KDM. OF HEROD

Jerusalem

NABATEA

Red Sea

BITHYNIA & PONTUS

Ancyra

GALATIA

Pergamum

ASIA

Ephesus

LYCIA

PAMPHYLIA

CYPRUS

Nile

Thebes

Memphis

EGYPT

Alexandria

Byzantium

THRACE

MACEDONIA

Thessalonica

Aegean Sea

Athens

ACHAIA

Corinth

CRETA

Cyrene

CYRENAICA

Carpathians

Dacia

Ister (Danube)

MOESIA

ILLYRICUM

Salonae

PANNONIA

NORICUM

Aquileia

Danube

Gaul

BELGICA

Lutetia

LUGDUNENSIS

Lugdunum

AQUITANIA

Burdigala

NARBONENSIS

Narbo

ALPES

RAETIA

Rubicon

ITALY

Rome

Tarentum

Sea of Adria

SICILIA

Syracuse

Leptis Magna

AFRICA

Carthage

Citta

MAURETANIA

Caesarea

CORSICA

AND

SARDINIA

Caralis

Mare Internum

(Mediterranean Sea)

TARRACONENSIS

Caesarea Augusta

Tarraco

Hispania

LUSITANIA

Emerita Augusta

BAETICA

Corduba

Tingis

Map 13

Journeys of the Apostles

- – – – Philip's journeys
- ——→ Saul's (Paul's) journeys
- ——→ Peter's journey
- ——→ Barnabas' journey
- ——→ Barnabas' and Paul's journey
- ······· Barnabas' and Mark's journey

```
0    10   25        50        75 MIs
0   20   40   60   80   100   120 Kms
```

© Copyright HAMMOND INCORPORATED, Maplewood, N.J.

CILICIA

Tarsus

Alexandria

AMANUS MTS.

Seleucia Tracheotis

Antioch

Seleucia Pieria

Laodicea
ad Mare

Apamea

Orontes

Epiphania

SYRIA

Salamis

CYPRUS

Ardus
(Arvad)

Emesa

Tripolis

Byblos

Heliopolis

LEBANON

Berytus

Chalcis

Abilene

Damascus

Sidon

Caesarea
Philippi

Tyre

Ptolemais

Galilee

Sea of
Galilee

Tiberias

Mediterranean Sea

Phoenicia

Leontes MT.

Caesarea

Scythopolis

Decapolis

Pella

Jordan

Gerasa

Samaria

Sebaste

Joppa

Lydda

Jerusalem

Jericho

Philadelphia

Azotus

Gaza

Judea

Dead
Sea

NABATEANS?

Map 14

GALATIA

CAPPADOCIA

Antioch

Lycaonia
Iconium

Pisidia

Lystra

Derbe

CILICIA

Tarsus

Perga
PAMPHYLIA

Attalia

Antioch

Sel

CYPRUS

SYR

Salamis

Paphos

Damasc

Caesa

Paul's First Journey

```
0          100        200 MIs
0    100   200   300 Kms
```

Jerusale

Judea

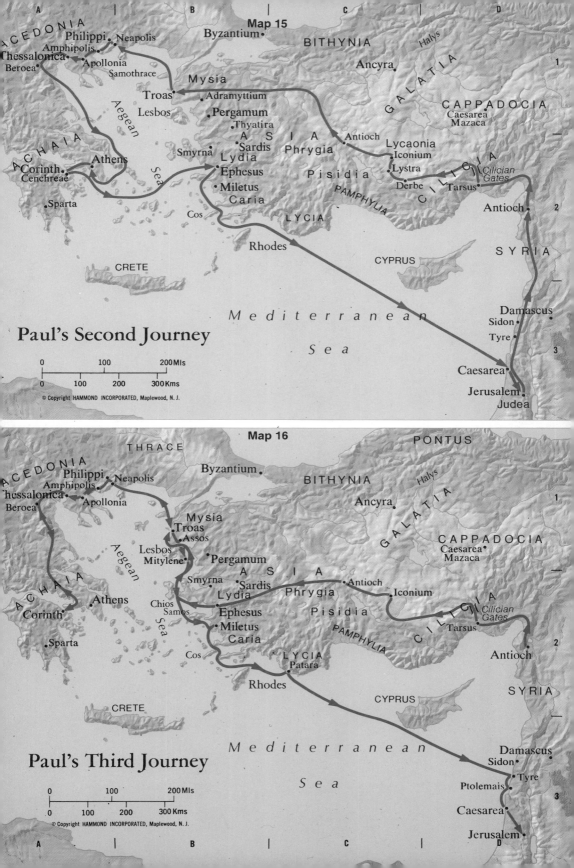

Map 15

A · · B · · C · · D

ACEDONIA
Philippi · Neapolis
Amphipolis
Thessalonica
Beroea · Apollonia
Samothrace
Byzantium
BITHYNIA
Ancyra
Halys
GALATIA
CAPPADOCIA
Caesarea
Mazaca · 1

Mysia
Troas · Adramyttium
Lesbos
Pergamum
Thyatira
A S I A
Smyrna
Sardis
Phrygia
Antioch
Lycaonia
Iconium
Lystra
CILICIA
Cilician
Gates

Aegean
Athens
Achaia
Corinth
Cenchreae
Lydia
Ephesus
Miletus
Caria
Pisidia
Derbe
Tarsus
Sea
Sparta
Cos
PAMPHYLIA
Antioch · 2
SYRIA

LYCIA
Rhodes
CYPRUS

M e d i t e r r a n e a n
S e a
Damascus
Sidon
Tyre
Caesarea
Jerusalem · 3
Judea

Paul's Second Journey

0 · 100 · 200 Mls
0 · 100 · 200 · 300 Kms
© Copyright HAMMOND INCORPORATED, Maplewood, N. J.

Map 16

THRACE
PONTUS

ACEDONIA
Philippi · Neapolis
Amphipolis
Thessalonica
Beroea · Apollonia
Byzantium
BITHYNIA
Ancyra
Halys
GALATIA
CAPPADOCIA
Caesarea
Mazaca · 1

Mysia
Troas · Assos
Lesbos
Mitylene
Pergamum
A S I A
Smyrna
Sardis
Phrygia
Antioch
Iconium
CILICIA
Cilician
Gates

Aegean
A C H A I A
Athens
Corinth
Chios
Samos
Lydia
Ephesus
Miletus
Caria
Pisidia
Tarsus
Sea
Sparta
Cos
PAMPHYLIA
Antioch · 2
SYRIA

LYCIA
Patara
Rhodes
CYPRUS

CRETE

M e d i t e r r a n e a n
S e a
Damascus
Sidon
Tyre
Ptolemais
Caesarea
Jerusalem · 3

Paul's Third Journey

0 · 100 · 200 Mls
0 · 100 · 200 · 300 Kms
© Copyright HAMMOND INCORPORATED, Maplewood, N. J.

A · · B · · C · · D

Map 17

Paul's Journey to Rome

© Copyright HAMMOND INCORPORATED, Maplewood, N.J.

Map 18

The Spread of Christianity

Extent of Christian communities by 1st century A.D.

Extent of Christian communities by A.D. 185 (the time of Irenaeus)

Early centers of Christianity

Boundary of the Roman Empire for most of the 1st and 2nd centuries A.D.

Boundary of the Roman Empire A.D. 114-117

© Copyright HAMMOND INCORPORATED, Maplewood, N.J.

100   200   300   400   500 Mls
200   400   600   800 Kms

GERMANIA

GAUL

Rhine

Colgne

Trier

Danube

Lyons

Vienne

SPAIN

Saragossa

Astorga

Merida

Corduba

Hispalis

CORSICA

SARDINIA

ITALY

Rome

Puteoli

SICILY

Syracuse

Salona

ILLYRICUM

Sea of Adria

Mediterranean Sea

Carthage

Cirta

NUMIDIA

AFRICA

MAURETANIA

DACIA

MOESIA

THRACE

Byzantium

Philippi

Thessalonica

Beroea

Larissa

Nicopolis

MACEDONIA

ACHAIA

Corinth

Athens

Black Sea

Amastris

Sinope

PONTUS

BITHYNIA

Nicomedia

Ancyra

GALATIA

CAPPADOCIA

Caesarea

Pergamum

Sardis

Smyrna

Ephesus

Miletus

Mysia

Troas

Phrygia

Laodicea

Iconium

Lystra

Tarsus

CILICIA

Patmos

Cnossus

CRETE

Myra

CYPRUS

Salamis

Paphos

Sidon

Damascus

Caesarea

Jerusalem

Antioch

SYRIA

ARMENIA

Edessa

Nisibis

Zabd

Beit

MESO-POTAMIA

Dura Europos

ARABIA

Red Sea

Nile

EGYPT

Memphis

Alexandria

Cyrene

CYRENAICA

Archaeological Sites
in Israel and Jordan

- Prehistoric cave sites
- Major excavated sites
- Other important excavations

0 5 10 15 20 25 Mls
0   10   20   30   40 Kms

© Copyright HAMMOND INCORPORATED, Maplewood, N.J.

Map 19

A | B | C | D

1

LEB.

Tyre

Dan

Kafr Bir'im

S Y R I A

Nahariyah

Meiron

HAZOR

Acco—
Ptolemais

Tabgha

Capernaum

Irbid
Tiberias

*Sea of
Galilee*

Sepphoris

2

Wadi el-Mughara

Beth Shearim

Beth-yerah

Dor

Beth Shearim

MEGIDDO

Beth-Alfa

Caesarea

Taanach

BETH-SHAN—SCYTHOPOLIS

Mediterranean

Dothan

TIRZAH

Tell es-Saidiyeh
(Zarethan?)

Jerash

Sea

SAMARIA—SEBASTE

SHECHEM

Tell Deir 'allā
(Succoth)

3

Qasile

Aphek—Antipatris

J O R D A N

Joppa

Shiloh

Yavne Yam

BETHEL

Ai

Kh. el-Mefjir
(Gilgal?)

Amman

'Araq el-Emir

Tell en-Nasbeh
(Mizpah?)

JERICHO

GEZER

Gibeon

Gibeah

Heshbon

I S R A E L

'Ain Karim

JERUSALEM

Ashdod

BETH-SHEMESH

Ramat
Rahel

Qumran

Teleilat el-Ghassul

4

Tell es-Safi

Bethlehem

'Ain Feshkha

Madaba

Ascalon

Azekah

Herodium

Hyrcania

Tell el-Judeideh

Beth-zur

Murabba'at Caves

LACHISH

Mareshah

Dead

Gaza

Tell el-Hesi
(Eglon?)

Hebron

Dibon

TELL AJJUL

TELL BEIT MIRSIM
(Debir?)

'Ain Gedi

Khirbet 'Ar'ir

Sea

Tell Jemmeh

Tell el-Far'a

Tell 'Arad

Masada

Bab edh 'Drah

5

Tell Abu Matar

Tell es-Seba

Khirbet el-Kerak

Khalasa

Karnub

Khirbet et-Tannur

Auja el-Hafir

Isbeita

6

E G Y P T

Avdat

Kadesh-barnea

A | B | C | D

CHAPTER XII

The Kingdom of Saul

THE KINGDOM OF SAUL
c. 1020-1000 B.C.

Copyright by C. S. HAMMOND & CO., N.Y.

Scale of Miles

0 5 10   20   30   40

Perennial Rivers
Seasonal Rivers & Streams
Capitals
Israelite Forces
Enemies of the Israelites
Kingdom of Saul at its greatest extent

The Philistines invaded Israel through the Plain of Jezreel. The Israelites were defeated and Saul slain at Mt. Gilboa.

The Great Sea
(Mediterranean Sea)

Saul defeated the Ammonites besieging Jabesh-gilead. For his triumph Saul was proclaimed king of all Israel.

Ramathaim-zophim Home of Samuel. Saul anointed here.

Jonathan's exploits at Michmash routed the Philistines.

Encounter of David and Goliath.

David, driven into exile by Saul, finally took refuge among the Philistines and settled in Ziklag.

Saul secured the southern border of Judah by defeating the Amalekites.

SYRIAN STATES
ZOBAH
Aramaeans
Basha

MOUNT LEBANON
MT. HERMON
MAACHAH
GESHUR
TOB
GILEAD
AMMON
Havoth-jair
Phoenicians
Canaanites
Plain of Sharon
Plain of Jezreel
MT. CARMEL
MT. GILBOA
PHILISTIA
Cherethites
JUDAH
Wilderness of Judah
Kenites
MOAB
EDOM
Amalekites
Salt Sea (Dead Sea)
River Jordan

Sidon
Zarephath
Tyre
Kanah
Achzib
Accho
Aphek
Cabul
Dor
Abana
Dam
Ijon
Abel-beth-maachah
Dan
Kedesh
Hazor
Chinnereth
Sea of Chinnereth
Karnaim
Ashtaroth
Edrei
Ramoth-gilead
Camon
Rimmon
Shimron
Hammath
Mt. Tabor
En-dor
Shunem
Jezreel
Beth-shan
Jabesh-gilead
Mahanaim
Megiddo
Taanach
Ibleam
Dothan
Bezek
Thebez
Mt. Ebal
Shechem
Mt. Gerizim
Succoth
Penuel
Jabbok R.
Adamah
Shiloh
Joppa
Aphek
Lod
Ophrah
Bethel
Michmash
Mizpah?
Geba
Gibeon
Ramah
Gibeah
Nob
Jebus (Jerusalem)
Gilgal
Rabbath-ammon
Heshbon
Mt. Nebo
Medeba
Jabneel
Gezer
Ekron
Kirjath-jearim
Timnah
Ashdod
Elah
Beth-shemesh
Azekah
Socoh
Bethlehem
Adullam
Keilah
Tekoa
Gath
Lachish
Eglon
Ashkelon
Gaza
Hebron
Ziph
Carmel
Maon
En-gedi
Dibon
Aroer
Gerar
Ziklag
Jattir
Raphia
Besor
Beer-sheba
Hormah
Aroer
Ar?
Kir-moab (Kir-haresheth)
Arnon R.
Yarmuk R.
Leontes R.
Kishon R.
Brook Zered

The Kingdom of Saul

The period of the Judges had been a theocracy in theory, but often anarchy in practice. Theoretically God was king; actually "every man did that which was right in his own eyes." During the wise judgeship of Samuel, Israel had no cause for complaint. With his advancing years, however, fear of the future became a paramount concern. Samuel's sons were not following the godly paths of their father, and Philistines continued to threaten the tribes of Israel. Under such circumstances the Israelites clamored for a king comparable to the rulers of neighboring lands.

Samuel was disheartened when his people requested a king. It seemed to be a rejection of the theocracy, and of Samuel himself. Assured, however, that it was God's will that he anoint a king over Israel, Samuel sought the one whom God would designate as the first king.

SAUL ANOINTED AS KING

Benjamin, Saul's tribe, was very small. The choice of a Benjamite for Israel's first king may be regarded as a conciliatory gesture toward the rival tribes of Ephraim, to the north, and Judah, to the south. Tribal rivalries were thus held in abeyance while Israel passed from a loose federation of tribes to a centralized monarchy.

Saul's life centers around four places.

Ramathaim. At Ramathaim, or Ramathaim-zophim ("double height of the watchers"), sometimes shortened to Ramah, Saul was privately anointed in Samuel's home. The New Testament form of this name, Arimathaea, is used to designate the home of Joseph who provided his sepulchre for the burial of Jesus. Although identified by some scholars with Ramah (*er-Râm*) north of Jerusalem, an ancient tradition placing it at Rentis on the western edge of Mount Ephraim appears to be correct.

Mizpeh. At Mizpeh ("watchtower"), northwest of Jerusalem, Saul was presented to the people as king. This Mizpeh, in the tribe of Benjamin, was a religious center with a sanctuary in the time of the Judges (Judg. 20; I Sam. 7; 10:17-27). It has been identified with *Tell en-Nasbeh*, seven miles north of Jerusalem on the main highway to Samaria and Galilee. The Palestine Institute, of the Pacific School of Religion, directed by William F. Bade, excavated the mound of *Tell en-Nasbeh* (1926-35). W. F. Albright and others, however, locate Mizpeh four miles southwest of *Tell en-Nasbeh* at *Nebî Samwîl* ("the prophet Samuel"), a 2,900 foot elevation overlooking Jerusalem.

Gibeah ("hill") of Benjamin, or Gibeah of Saul, was the home and capital of Israel's first king. It has been identified with *Tell el-Fûl* ("hill of beans"), four miles north of Jerusalem by the side of the main road leading to Samaria, on a summit with an elevation of about 2,750 feet above sea level.

Gilgal ("circle of stones") is probably

Nob, the City of Priests. Within
sight of Jerusalem is the site of Nob.
This photograph gives an unusually
good view of the landscape.
Copyright, Matson Photo Service

identical with the place of Joshua's first
military encampment west of the Jordan.
Some scholars, however, suggest a Gilgal
seven miles north of Bethel, now known
as *Jiljiliyeh*. At Gilgal, Saul was formally
received as king by the united tribes of
Israel.

It was while seeking the lost asses of
his father that Saul first met Samuel. His
journey took him through the land
of Shalisha ("the three"), a district
adjoining Mount Ephraim, north of
Lod (Lydda). Baal-shalisha (II Kings
4:42) was an important city in this district. It is now known as *Kefr Thilth*.
He also passed through the land of Sha-
lim, or Shaalim ("foxes"), which may
be identical with Shual ("fox") (I
Sam. 13:17), near Michmash. The exact
location is unknown. Saul continued

through the land of the Benjamites and
the land of Zuph, the section of the
hill country of Ephraim in which Ramathaim-zophim was located.

THE WARS OF SAUL (I Sam. 11—18)

Saul was anointed as king by Samuel,
but it was his prowess on the battlefield
which brought him the enthusiastic support of the people. Israel had requested
a king who would lead his people in
battle, and Saul was not a disappoint-
ment in that respect.

Ammonite War (I Sam. 11). The
Ammonites, who lived east of Moab,
and Gilead, were a roving, predatory
people. Under their king Nahash they

invaded the Israelite territory east of the Jordan and besieged Jabesh-gilead. Nelson Glueck identified Jabesh-gilead with the twin mounds: *Tell el-Meqbereh* ("burial place"), and *Tell Abu Kharaz*, its overshadowing fortress. Most recent scholarship, however, prefers a site in the sector of the valley which bears the name *Wadi Yâbis*. This site, *Tell el Maqlûb*, seems to be the Iabis mentioned by Eusebius as six Roman miles distant from Pella (*Khirbet Fahil*) on the road to Gerasa (Jarash). J. Simons states that this identification "can no longer be reasonably doubted."

When Saul learned of the threat to the men of Jabesh-gilead, he summoned the Israelite warriors to Bezek, known today as *Khirbet Ibzîq,* south of Mount Gilboa. Under Saul's leadership the Ammonites were put to flight. This decisive victory gave Saul prestige as a king who had proved himself successful on the field of battle.

First Philistine War (I Sam. 13—14). Since the time of the Judges, the Philistines had occupied strategic Israelite cities. Geba of Benjamin, modern *Jeba',* six miles north of Jerusalem, and Bethel, twelve miles north of Jerusalem on the Shechem road, were among the important cities in Philistine hands. Saul sought to deliver Israel from Philistine control. Jonathan, his son, struck the first blow by attacking the Philistines at Geba, and soon followed it with a victory at Michmash, across the valley from Geba. The Israelites then pursued the Philistines to their own borders. Philistines, however, continued to hold fortresses in Israel throughout the reign of Saul, and there was constant warfare between the two peoples.

Moabite War (I Sam. 14:47). The Moabites, who lived east of the Dead Sea, may have been associated with the neighboring Ammonites in attacking Israel. No battles are mentioned and, although the Moabites were defeated, Moab was not brought into subjection to Israel.

Edomite War (I Sam. 14:47). Edom, south of Moab, evidently joined her neighbors in seeking the defeat of Israel. Following Saul's victory at Jabesh-gilead he may have pursued the Ammonites. After defeating them he would have turned against the lands of their allies, Moab and Edom.

Syrian War (I Sam. 14:47). The Aramaean state of Zobah, north of Damascus, had frontiers extending as far as the Euphrates. Located in the Anti-Lebanon Range, Zobah was rich in silver. Its chariotry proved a serious obstacle to Israelite military power (I Chron. 19:6). Saul's campaign against Zobah was very likely a defensive one, designed to protect his borders against Aramaean invasions.

Amalekite War (I Sam. 14:48; 15:1-35). The marauding nomads to the south who attacked the Israelites during their migration from Egypt (Deut. 25:17-19) and were defeated by Joshua at Rephidim (Exod. 17:8-16) proved to be Israel's inveterate foes. Saul secured his southern border by defeating them in battle but he incurred the wrath of Samuel when he spared Agag, the Amalekite ruler, and refrained from killing the cattle. Although Saul excused his conduct on the ground that he wished to sacrifice the best of the cattle to the Lord, Samuel insisted that obedience is better than sacrifice. The beginning of the rift between Samuel and Saul may be traced to the Amalekite war.

Second Philistine War (I Sam. 17—18). There were doubtless many conflicts between Israelites and Philistines during the reign of Saul. The second war was notable in that David, who had been anointed privately by Samuel, appeared on the field of battle for the first time. In the Valley of Elah at Ephes-dammim (Pas-dammim in I Chron. 11:13), between Socoh and Azekah, David met and slew the Philistine champion, Goliath of Gath. The Israelite victory which followed made David a national hero. This, however, only enraged Saul who determined to rid himself of the youth who seemed to challenge his own popularity.

SAUL'S PURSUIT OF DAVID (I Sam. 19—28)

The tragic closing years of Saul's life were spent in the vain attempt to track down and slay one whom he supposed to be an enemy. David's flight from Saul brought him into contact with many communities in southern Palestine.

Gibeah. David was forced to flee for his life from Gibeah of Benjamin, the home of Saul and the Israelite capital during his reign.

Ramah (I Sam. 19:18-24). At Naioth, in or near Ramah, north of Jerusalem, David took refuge after he had escaped from Saul. The king's messengers pursued David, but at Ramah the Spirit of God came upon them. When Saul came to Sechu near Ramah, he, too, was so overcome by the Spirit that he began to prophesy. While this was going on, David was able to escape to Gibeah.

Nob, "the city of the priests," was David's first stopping place as he fled into exile from Gibeah (I Sam. 21:1-9). Nob was located near Jerusalem, probably on the east slope of Mount Scopus,

northeast of Jerusalem. Ahimelech, a descendant of Eli, leader of the priests of Nob, gave David food for his men and the sword with which Goliath had been slain. When a spy reported this to Saul, he ordered the murder of Ahimelech and the inhabitants of Nob.

Gath (I Sam. 21:10-15). David escaped from Nob and made his way down the mountains to the Philistine city of Gath ("wine press"). The location of Gath is still in dispute. Eusebius places it five miles north of Eleutheropolis (*Beit Jibrîn*), while Jerome places it south, on the road to Gaza. A mound known as *Tell Arâq-Menshîyeh* would fit Jerome's description. *Tell es-Sâfî,* ten miles east of Ashdod, is also suggested as a possible site. Whatever its location, Gath was the nearest of the large Philistine cities to Hebrew territory. David, although known as an enemy of Saul, was suspected by the Philistines at Gath of being their enemy also. He feigned insanity in order to escape.

Adullam. In Adullam, *Tell esh-Sheikh Madhkûr,* a town southwest of Jerusalem, about midway between Jerusalem and Lachish, David took refuge in a cave. Here he was joined by sympathizers, including his parents and brothers. Saul's murder of the priests of Nob doubtless served as a warning to others friendly to David that their lives were in danger.

Mizpeh of Moab. At this unidentified place David put his parents in the custody of the king of Moab. David and his men took up their abode in a place called "the stronghold" (I Sam. 22:3, 4), apparently a fortified point nearby.

Forest of Hareth (Hereth). At the advice of the prophet Gad, David and

his company traveled back to Judah, making their headquarters at the forest of Hareth, probably in the mountain country southwest of Adullam.

Keilah ("the spur"). The Philistines attacked Keilah, modern *Khirbet Qilâ,* in the Shephelah southeast of Adullam, and David rallied his men to defend the city. When he learned that the men of Keilah were preparing to betray him to Saul, David made a hasty departure for the wilderness between Hebron and the Dead Sea known as the Jeshimon ("devastation").

Ziph. At Ziph (*Khirbet ez-Zif*), in the wilderness four miles southeast of Hebron, David found a refuge. There he met Jonathan for the last time. David's followers had scattered, and he was in difficult straits. When the Ziphites prepared to betray him to Saul, David fled (I Sam. 23:14-24).

Maon. David was again threatened by Saul at Maon (*Tell Ma'în*), south of Hebron. Deliverance came, however, when a Philistine attack forced Saul

and his troops to leave (I Sam. 23:24-28). At Maon, David sought provisions from wealthy Nabal, who contemptuously refused to pay any tribute to David. David and his men were prepared to force the issue when Abigail, Nabal's wife, appeared with a generous gift. After the death of Nabal, David married Abigail (I Sam. 25).

En-gedi. Near the center of the western shore of the Dead Sea, about thirty miles southeast of Jerusalem, is the town of En-gedi ("well of the wild goat"), also called Hazezon-tamar ("sandy surface of the palm tree"). It is on the new road extending from Qumran south, past En-gedi and Masada to Sodom and the Arabah. In one of the caves near En-gedi David found a place of refuge (I Sam. 23:29). When Saul inadvertently entered the cave, David cut off a piece of the king's robe. David, however, did not take advantage of the opportunity to slay his persecutor. Reverence for the king as "the Lord's anointed" marked David's attitude throughout the lifetime of Saul.

Ziklag. Despairing of safety in Israel, David fled again to the Philistine country. The king of Gath assigned to David the city of Ziklag (possibly *Tell el-Khuweilifeh*) in the Negeb about twenty-five miles southeast of Gaza. There David remained until after Saul's death. He accompanied the Philistines in their campaign against Israel at Aphek, in Mount Ephraim. He was sent back, however, for the Philistines feared he might desert to Israel. Finding his home plundered by roving Amalekites, David pursued them, rescued his family and possessions, and took a great quantity of booty.

Hebron. Soon after the death of Saul, David left Ziklag and went up to the mountain region of Hebron. Here he was anointed king of the tribe of Judah (II Sam. 2:1-4). It was not until the death of Saul's son, Ish-bosheth, that all Israel recognized David as king.

SAUL'S DEATH

A number of locations take on additional significance as a result of events associated with the closing years of Saul's reign.

The last years of Saul's life were filled with tragedy. Literally insane with jealousy over David, Saul was in no position to lead his people into battle. The Philistines were a growing threat, as they prepared for an all-out victory over Israel. Meeting at Aphek in Ephraim, they marched northward toward the Israelite encampment on the Plain of Jezreel at the foot of Mount Gilboa. Saul, fearing for his life, left the Israelite camp by night and sought out a "woman having a familiar spirit" at En-dor, south of Mount Tabor. During this clandestine interview, the deceased Samuel warned Saul that he would die on the morrow. The next day a battle was fought between Israel and the Philistines at Mount Gilboa. Saul and three of his sons, including Jonathan, were killed. Saul's body was fastened to the wall of the Canaanite fortress city of Beth-shan, overlooking the Jezreel Valley. It was retrieved, however, by the warriors of Jabesh-gilead who remembered Saul's deliverance of their city when it had been attacked by the Ammonites. The Philistine victory at Gilboa thoroughly humbled Israel before a powerful foe. It also made possible the rise to power of David, an event which ushered in the golden age of Israelite power.

CHAPTER XIII

The Empire of David and Solomon

Gibeah of Benjamin. It was the site of a desperate attempt of the Turks to recapture Jerusalem on December 26, 1917.

Copyright, Matson Photo Service

The Empire of David and Solomon

When David became king of Israel he was responsible for territory measuring only six thousand square miles. He left to Solomon, his son and successor, an empire embracing about sixty thousand square miles.

DAVID'S REIGN OVER JUDAH
(II Sam. 1—4)

After the death of Saul, David left his place of refuge, the Philistine city of Ziklag, and went to Hebron where he was proclaimed king over Judah. In the meantime Saul's son Ish-bosheth ruled over the northern tribes, although Abner, who had been Saul's general, exercised the real power. The forces of Joab, David's general, and Abner, commander of Ish-bosheth's army, met at Gibeon (el-Jib). The ensuing battle resulted in victory for the partisans of David. In the retreat, however, Joab's brother, Asahel, was slain by Abner. After a stormy career, during which Abner changed allegiance to David, Ish-bosheth was murdered by two of his own courtiers who took his head to David at Hebron, expecting a reward. David hanged the criminals and gave the head of Ish-bosheth an honorable burial. Fearing the loss of his position, David's general, Joab, slew his potential rival, Abner, ostensibly to avenge the death of Asahel. King David mourned Abner, describing him as "a prince and a great man" (II Sam. 3:38).

With the death of Ish-bosheth, opposition to the kingship of David over the northern tribes was removed. He was subsequently anointed king over all Israel.

THE UNION OF PALESTINE
(II Sam. 5—7)

When David became heir to the kingdom of Saul he ruled the hill country of Ephraim and Judah; Philistines and Canaanites still occupied strategic cities on the coastal plain, the Shephelah, and the Jezreel Valley. The Jebusites, a Canaanite tribe (Gen. 10:16, cf. I Chron. 1:14), occupied the ancient city of Jerusalem which they called Jebus. In the Amarna Tablets, dated about 1400 B.C., the city was called *Urusalim*, meaning "city of peace" or "city of Salim," one of the gods worshiped in ancient Canaan. Abraham paid tithes to an Amorite priest-king, Melchizedek, at Salem (Gen. 14:18-20), which is usually identified with the *Urusalim* of the Amarna tablets and the Jerusalem of later history.

Although the Jebusites felt their fortress city high in the Judaean mountains to be impregnable, Joab, David's general, risked his life to conquer it for his king. Jebus bordered Judah and Benjamin, but had not been incorporated into the territory of either tribe during the period of Jebusite occupation. After capture by Joab, Jerusalem became "the city of David." It served as the political and spiritual center of Israel, a position Jerusalem continues to occupy in the hearts of Jews throughout the world.

Pool at Gibeon. Abner and the partisans of Ish-bosheth fought a strange battle with Joab and those loyal to David at the Pool of Gibeon (II Sam. 2:12-17). Twelve men were chosen to represent each contender for the throne. They killed one another, and in the battle which followed the forces of David prevailed. *Courtesy, James B. Pritchard*

The Philistines became apprehensive at the growing power of David and entered the Judaean mountain region with their armies. In the Valley of Rephaim, running about three miles southwest from Jerusalem toward Bethlehem, David utterly routed his Philistine foes, exclaiming, "The Lord has broken through my enemies before me like a bursting flood" (II Sam. 5:20).

Following up his victory in the Judaean highlands, David pursued the Philistines to the Shephelah and the Coastal Plain. To the southeast he took the stronghold of Gath (I Chron. 18:1), and so completely subjugated the Philistine confederacy that they could not trouble Israel again until after the division of the kingdom.

Although not permitted to build the Temple, David made the initial plans for it. He centralized worship in Jerusalem by bringing the ark from Kirjath-jearim on the western border of Benjamin to the new capital. At the threshing floor called Perez-uzzah, a man named

Uzzah irreverently touched the ark and died. Thereupon David turned aside from the main road to Jerusalem and left the ark in the house of Obed-edom (cf. I Chron. 13:3-14). The mission was subsequently completed and the ark brought to Jerusalem where it remained until the Exile (587 B.C.).

DAVID'S FOREIGN CONQUESTS
(II Sam. 8—11)

The reign of David marks, politically speaking, Israel's golden age. Periods of political weakness in both Egypt and Mesopotamia made it possible for the tribes which had entered Canaan under Joshua a few centuries earlier to become a mighty nation. The following lands were conquered by David.

Moab (II Sam. 8:2). Israel had not been able to pass through Moab at the time of the wilderness sojourn (Judg. 11:17-18). David now incorporated this land east of the Dead Sea into his empire.

Zobah (II Sam. 8:3-5). The Aramaean state of Zobah, or Aram-zobah, reached from Damascus northward to Riblah. During the time of David it was the most powerful Aramaean state, with considerable wealth in copper. David defeated Hadadezer of Zobah, even though a large contingent from other Aramaean states sought to aid the resistance to Israelite power.

Damascus (II Sam. 8:5, 6). Damascus, an ally of Zobah, was the largest city in Syria. It is located on a plain, approximately thirty by ten miles in extent, watered by the Abana River (modern *Nahr Baradâ*). The Abana divides into seven branches which further subdivide, making the entire Damascus plain a garden spot. The defeat of the coalition of the Aramaean state of Damascus and Zobah brought Damascus under Israelite control.

Edom (II Sam. 8:13-14). The battle with the Edomites was fought at the Valley of Salt, identified by some scholars with the *Wadi el-Milh,* a ravine running southeastward from Beer-sheba toward Petra (Sela) in Edom. It is probable, however, that the Valley of Salt is another name for the *Wadi 'Araba,* the southern continuation of the Dead Sea, or Salt Sea, as it was known to the Hebrews. In I Chronicles 18:12 and in the title of Psalm 60, Edom is described as the enemy which was defeated in the Valley of Salt. As this valley was in the territory of Edom and far from the scene of the defeat of the Aramaeans, the reading Edom is by most scholars preferred to Aram (Syria) in II Samuel 8:13.

Ammon (II Sam. 10—11). The Ammonite war was the longest in David's career. The Ammonites were aided by fighting men from these Aramaean states: Zobah; Maachah (Aram-maachah), a region south of Mount Hermon; Beth-rehob, a principality in the upper part of the Hula marshes near Dan; and Tob, possibly in the east-Jordan area to which Jephthah fled. The Ammonites were therefore able to put up stiff resistance to David.

The first battle was fought near Medeba, an old Moabite town about sixteen miles southeast of the place where the Jordan enters the Dead Sea. The Aramaeans were routed and the Ammonites took refuge within a fortress. Joab met the army of Hadadezer of Zobah, led by his chief, Shobach, at an unidentified place named Helam (II Sam. 10:16), in the east-Jordan country (possibly modern *'Alma*). After peace was concluded with the Aramaeans, David turned his attention to the siege of Rabbah, or Rabbath-ammon, (modern *'Amman*), northeast of the Dead Sea. It was during this, extended siege that David, at home in Jerusalem, ordered the death of Uriah, the Hittite, in order to cover his sin with Bath-sheba, Uriah's wife, and marry her. With the capture of "the city of the waters," evidently a term for the acropolis which controlled a brook in the vicinity of Rabbah, victory was assured for Israel. Joab sent for David so that he might supervise the final operations and so receive credit for being conqueror of Rabbah (cf. I Chron. 20:1-3). David put the crown of Milcom, the god of Ammon, on his head, thus taking to himself the title "King of the Ammonites," along with his sovereignty over Judah and Israel.

With the successful conclusion of the Ammonite war, David was king of an area extending from the River of Egypt to northern Syria. He was at the pinnacle of success; but already the seeds of future trouble were evident. From the death of Saul to the siege of Rabbah, David was successful in all his major undertakings. This was not true during the latter part of his life.

CALAMITIES OF DAVID'S REIGN (II Sam. 12—20; 24)

David experienced three great trials during his declining years.

Absalom's Rebellion. As David had once been the popular hero to the discomfiture of Saul, so now David's son Absalom took advantage of youth and prowess to lead a revolt against his father.

Absalom killed his half-brother, David's oldest son, Amnon, who had defiled and mistreated Tamar, Absalom's full sister. Fearing the anger of David, Absalom fled to the small Aramaean state of Geshur, east of the Sea of Galilee, the home of his maternal grandparents. Through a stratagem of "the wise woman of Tekoa" (*Khirbet Tequ'a*), south of Bethlehem, David was reconciled to Absalom and the youth returned home.

Difficulties continued, however, until Absalom took advantage of a sacrificial ceremony at Hebron to have himself declared king of Israel. David with his foreign mercenaries, Cherethites (probably Cretans) and Pelethites (from southern Philistia), fled from Jerusalem and made his way to the east-Jordan territory (II Sam. 8:18).

Before Absalom and his army crossed the stream (II Sam. 17:24), David and his retinue reached Mahanaim, probably *Khirbet Mahneh* north of the Jabbok. In the "Forest of Ephraim" nearby, a battle took place in which Absalom was killed. David's return to power was accompanied by grief over the death of his son.

Sheba's Rebellion. Soon after Absalom's rebellion, a Benjamite, Sheba, led a second revolt against David. Since Saul had been a Benjamite, Sheba's revolt may be interpreted as an effort to bring the throne back to the tribe of Benjamin. Joab pursued Sheba and his followers to Abel-beth-maachah, (modern *Tell Abil*), in northern Palestine west of Dan. There Sheba was decapitated by a "wise woman" in order to save her city from destruction by Joab's army.

Pestilence. Following the census which David took, a severe pestilence fell upon the people (II Sam. 24). David purchased a stone threshingfloor from Araunah, or Ornan, which was subsequently used as the base for an altar dedicated by David to the Lord (II Sam. 24:16-25). This became the site of Solomon's Temple, and is thought to be the rugged natural scarp preserved under the mosque known as the Dome of the Rock in the old city of Jerusalem.

CLOSE OF DAVID'S REIGN (I Kings 1—2; I Chron. 22—29).

Davids last days were comparatively uneventful. When his son Adonijah attempted to secure his own succession to the throne, David heeded the warning of Bath-sheba and Nathan and had Solomon anointed at the Spring Gihon, outside the east wall of Jerusalem.

SOLOMON'S REIGN

Solomon fell heir to an empire formed largely through the leadership of David. Early in his reign, Solomon went to Gibeon, five miles northwest of Jerusalem, where God promised him wisdom for his rule over Israel (I Kings 3:4-15).

Solomon soon reorganized the government of his kingdom, dividing it into twelve provinces or administrative districts (I Kings 4:7-19). Judah is not mentioned among the provinces. It may have been ruled directly from Jerusalem.

Solomon is said to have ruled from the Euphrates to the border of Egypt (I Kings 4:21). The Aramaean states as well as the people of Edom and Moab regularly presented their tribute to Solomon at Jerusalem. As a commercial outpost he built "Tadmor in the wilderness" (II Chron. 8:3, 4), about 140 miles northeast of Damascus. In Roman times Tadmor was known as Palmyra. Its famous queen, Zenobia, defied the entire Roman Empire until she was taken prisoner by Aurelian (A.D. 273), after which Palmyra quickly declined in importance.

Centers of Commerce. By a trade alliance with Hiram, king of the Phoenician seaport city of Tyre, Solomon was able to promote Israel's commercial interests. He personally developed Ezion-

Mediggo, Model of "Solomon's Stables." Solomon not only built the Temple in Jerusalem but also fortified strategic cities in his empire. The stables attributed to Solomon may actually be from the time of Ahab, who, according to the annals of Shalmaneser III, sent two thousand chariots against Assyria at Karkar. The Israeli archaeologist Yigael Yadin has suggested the later date.
Courtesy, Oriental Institute

geber, on the Gulf of Aqaba, as a port through which Israelite trade with Arabia and Africa could pass (I Kings 9: 26-28).

Hiram of Tyre was also of help to Solomon in providing building materials and skilled labor for the palace and Temple which he built in Jerusalem. Solomon was able to supply farm products to the Tyrians as a partial payment for their assistance. Ten thousand men are said to have been employed to cut down the cedars and transport them to the sea, where they were floated down to the Israelite port of Joppa (II Chron. 2:16). Stone for Solomon's building operations was quarried in the mountain country adjacent to Jerusalem.

The financial difficulties of Solomon are evident in the account of his ceding a tract of land in Galilee containing twenty towns as partial payment for his debt (I Kings 9:11-14). One of these towns was Cabul, a border city in the tribe of Asher. The territory was evidently not desirable, for Hiram expressed dissatisfaction over the payment.

The use of the camel greatly facilitated land transportation through desert areas. Solomon's control of Zobah, Damascus, Ammon, Moab, and Edom gave him a monopoly of the caravan routes between Arabia and the North. Horses from Cilicia (I Kings 10:28-29) and chariots from Egypt were handled at a fixed price by Solomon's merchants.

Chariotry Installations. Solomon's program of defense called for the building of chariotry installations at strategic sites. The great Canaanite strongholds of Hazor in Upper Galilee, and Megiddo overlooking the Plain of Jezreel, had extensive facilities for horses to be used in chariot warfare. Other chariotry cities included Accho (Acre), north of Mount Carmel; Achshaph, five miles southeast of Accho; and *Tell el-Hesi*

(perhaps Eglon), west of Lachish. There were also Solomonic chariotry installations at the towns on the border of Cilicia. The city of Gezer (*Tell Jezer*), west of Jerusalem, was given by the Egyptian Pharaoh to his daughter on the occasion of her marriage to Solomon (I Kings 9:16). Important chariotry installations were subsequently placed there.

Copper Mining Centers. Copper mining and smelting in the Arabah near Ezion-geber was a thriving and important business. The industry was also developed in the Jordan valley in the region between Succoth (*Tell Deir 'Allā*), near the Jabbok, and Zarethan (possibly *Tell es-Sa'īdīyeh*) twelve miles northeast of Adamah. The whole region between Succoth and Zarethan provided suitable clay for the molds in which the copper was cast. Metal objects produced here later adorned and equipped the Temple in Jerusalem.

Relations with Other Lands. International alliances were made not only with Egypt (through Solomon's marriage to an Egyptian princess) and Tyre but also with other states. Solomon's harem of a thousand wives and concubines represented many alliances sealed by marriage (I Kings 11:1-3). The visit of the Queen of Sheba, from Saba in southwestern Arabia, doubtless was concerned in part with commercial matters. Important caravan roads led from Saba northward along the western borders of Arabia (Job 6:19; Isa. 60:6; Jer. 6:20; Ezek. 27:22-23).

Solomon carried on trade with Ophir from which he imported "almug wood" and precious stone. Ophir was probably located in southwestern Arabia in the area now called Yemen. From distant lands Solomon's vessels brought gold, silver, ivory, apes, and peacocks (or "ba-

Copper Mining in the Negeb. The Promised Land was described as a land "out of whose hills thou mayest dig copper" (Deut. 8:9). Archaeology has not only given us the evidence of extensive copper mining in Solomonic Israel, but has provided the impetus for modern mining in the Negeb.

Courtesy, Israel Office of Information

Ezion-geber. At the head of the Gulf of Aqaba, Solomon developed Ezion-geber, near modern Elath, as a port through which trade with Arabia and Africa could pass.

boons") to Solomonic Israel (I Kings 10:22). Egypt (or, perhaps a northern Musri in Asia Minor) and Kue, a part of Cilicia, provided horses for Solomon's extensive chariotry installations (I Kings 10:28).

Solomon's Declining Years. The latter years of Solomon marked the beginning of Israel's economic and political decline. A change in dynasties in Egypt brought to the throne a Pharaoh unfriendly to Solomon. Hadad, an Edomite who had been in Egypt, returned to his native country to spark a rebellion against Solomon (I Kings 11:14-22).

Rezon, an Aramaean chief, seized Damascus and severed its ties with Israel. The loss of these territories resulted in a serious decline of revenue to the government of Solomon.

Further trouble came, from within Israel. Jeroboam, a high official of Solomon, who had the responsibility for the labor conscriptions in the "tribe of Joseph" (i.e. Ephraim and Manasseh), became the center of a revolt against the king. Although forced to flee to Egypt, Jeroboam remained in readiness to return when called upon by his countrymen.

The City of Jerusalem

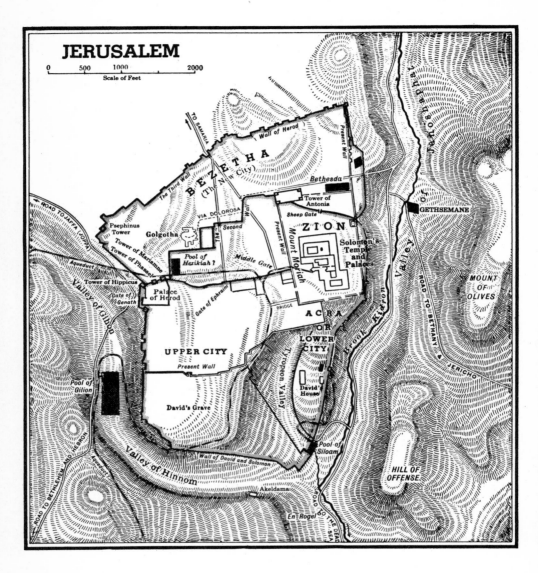

Outline Map of Ancient Jerusalem. This map shows very clearly the surface features of Jerusalem and its environs. It indicates the location of the various walls as well as the traditional sites significant in Bible history. This map can be used to good advantage throughout this chapter.   *Courtesy, C. S. Hammond and Company*

Use Maps 8, 9, and 10

The City of Jerusalem

NAMES. Egyptian records from the nineteenth century before Christ refer to a city of *Urusalimu*. Four centuries later the name appears in the Tell el-Amarna tablets as *Urusalim*. Subsequent Assyrian records speak of the city *Ursalimmu*. Within the Bible itself the first reference to Jerusalem appears in the account of Melchizedek's priestly kingdom of Salem, properly pronounced Shalem (Gen. 14:18; Ps. 76:2). The Jebusites, who occupied the city prior to the time of David, called it Jebus (Judg. 19:10). When the city was taken by the Israelites during the tenth century B.C. it became known as "the city of David" (I Kings 14:31) or Jerusalem.

The etymology of Jerusalem (Hebrew *Yerushalaim*) is uncertain. That it is a compound of the word *shalem* ("peace") is clear. Some scholars have suggested *yerush-shalaim* ("possession of peace"); others *yeru-shalaim* ("foundation of peace") as the meaning of the compound name. *Urusalim* has also been interpreted as "city of peace," or "city of Salim," an ancient Canaanite deity.

Secondary names have been applied to the city. Isaiah calls it Ariel, "the lion of God" (Isa. 29:1). It is also known as "the holy city" (Matt. 4:5; 27:53).

After the destruction of Jerusalem by Titus (A.D. 70), it was rebuilt by the emperor Aelius Hadrianus (A.D. 135) and named Aelia, or Aelia Capitolina. The ancient name, Jerusalem, was restored by Constantine, whose mother, Helena, made a pilgrimage to the city in A.D. 326. The Arabs call it *El Kuds,* "the holy."

LOCATION. Jerusalem is situated thirty-three miles east of the Mediterranean in a southeast direction from Joppa. It is fourteen miles west of the Dead Sea, one hundred and thirty-three miles southwest of Damascus, and five miles northeast of Bethlehem. The city of Jerusalem is higher than almost any other great capital of history. It reaches an elevation of about 2,550 feet above the level of the Mediterranean and 3,800 feet above the level of the Dead Sea.

MOUNTAINS

Jerusalem stood in ancient times on four distinct hills, with other hills or mountains on all sides. Our knowledge of its topography has increased greatly in recent years, and some of the traditional terminology has had to be corrected.

Mount Zion. The original Zion was the scarp of rock on the southern tip of the ridge between the Kidron and the Tyropoeon valleys. This area is south of the Temple hill and outside the present walls of Jerusalem. Zion had an ample water supply from the Spring Gihon, now called the *'Ain Sitti Mariam* ("Fountain of the Virgin") and En-rogel, now called *Bir Ayyûb* ("Job's Well"—probably originally named for Joab, David's commander, as there are no traditions which link Job with Jeru-

141

salem). Christian tradition from the fourth century A.D. to the present has erroneously located Zion on the southern portion of the west ridge of Jerusalem, between the Tyropoeon and Hinnom valleys. A traditional "tomb of David" (probably dating to Roman times) is shown here. Scriptural evidence and archaeological findings, however, locate Zion at the southeast rather than the southwest corner of Jerusalem.

The Temple Mount. The Temple Mount, the location of Araunah's Threshing-floor purchased by David and later used by Solomon as the site of the Temple, appears to have been north of the original Zion. It is traditionally associated with the place where Abraham offered Isaac—Mount Moriah (Gen. 22: 2; II Chron. 3:1), although the land of Moriah in the patriarchal record appears to have been a remote spot, removed from human activity. The Moriah of David's day is the central portion of the eastern hill, and the term Zion, initially used of the Jebusite fortress to the south, came to be applied to the Temple Mount as well (cf. Ps. 65:1; Jer. 31:6). Once the site of Solomon's Temple and the Temple built by the Jews who returned from Babylon, the Temple Mount is now the location of the Dome of the Rock, a beautiful octagonal structure built late in the seventh century to serve as a mosque. The sacred rock under the dome is probably the site of the ancient Jewish altar of burnt offering.

Ophel is the name given to the southern extremity of the Temple Mount. South of Ophel was the original Jebusite city of Mount Zion. The original Zion was known in later times as the Acra, or Mount Acra.

Bezetha. Northeast of the Temple Mount is a "suburb" known as Bezetha. Herod Agrippa enclosed Bezetha with walls. The Pool of Bethesda is located in this area.

Surrounding Jerusalem are mountains which have an important role in the Biblical narrative.

Mount of Olives. Paralleling the eastern elevation of Jerusalem, separated from it by the Kidron Valley, is the mile-long ridge of limestone hills known as the Mount of Olives, or Olivet (elevation about 2,680 feet).

North of the Mount of Olives, and sometimes regarded as a part of it, is Mount Scopus. When approaching Jerusalem from the north, the traveler gets a panoramic view of the city from Mount Scopus. Here the Roman general Titus is reputed to have had his first glimpse of Jerusalem, the city which he had come to destroy. Buildings of the Hebrew University and the Hadassah Hospital, built on Mount Scopus before the establishment of the State of Israel, form the nucleus for renewed building operations since the Israelis occupied the area in 1967.

South of Scopus is a hill known as *Viri Galiloei* ("men of Galilee") because of a tradition that the Ascension of Jesus took place there (cf. Acts 1:11). As this hill was covered with buildings in New Testament times, it is a most unlikely site for the ascension.

The next hill to the south, the central summit of Olivet, is often called the Mount of Ascension. It is directly opposite the site of the Temple and is marked today by a Russian Orthodox church with its tall Tower of Ascension visible from all the approaches to Jerusalem. The village of Bethphage (Matt. 21:1) has been identified with the Moslem *Kefr et-Tūr* on the southeastern

Aerial View of Jerusalem. You will find it interesting to compare this photograph of modern Jerusalem with the outline map of Ancient Jerusalem on page 140.

Copyright, Matson Photo Service

Jerusalem. This view of the southeast corner of the Old City is from the Jewish cemetery on the Mount of Olives. To the right in the photograph is the Dome of the Rock, which was built on the site of Solomon's Temple.

Copyright, Levant Photo Service

slope of the Mount of Ascension, near Bethany.

Moving southward we come to the peak called "the prophets" from the tradition that prophets were buried there facing the Kidron.

The southernmost part of the Mount of Olives is known as the Mount of Offense. It is so named because of the idolatries which Solomon practiced there (I Kings 11:7). The village of *Silwân,* or Siloam, is located above the juncture of the Kidron and Hinnom valleys. This is not the Biblical Siloam which was a district of Jerusalem.

Hill of Evil Counsel. South of the Valley of Hinnom, at the place where it joins the Kidron Valley, is an eminence known as the Hill of Evil Counsel (i.e. the counsel cf Judas to the High Priest). Here Judas is said to have bargained for the betrayal of his Lord. Upon the slope of this hill is the traditional Aceldama, "the field of blood" (Matt. 27:7-8).

VALLEYS

Jerusalem is built around three valleys which unite near the southeastern corner of the city.

The Kidron (Kedron, or Cedron of A.V.). The Kidron, or "the Valley of Jehoshaphat," is a valley three miles long. It bounds the eastern slope of Jerusalem and separates it from the Mount of Olives. During the summer the Kidron Valley is dry, but in the rainy season it is the bed of a brook. South of En-rogel Spring the Kidron continues as the *Wadi en-Nar* ("Valley of Fire").

The Tyropoeon. Inside Jerusalem the Tyropoeon, or "Valley of Cheesemakers," runs in a southeastward direction separating the western from the eastern

hills. It enters the Kidron at a point near its junction with the Valley of Hinnom. The Tyropoeon Valley was much deeper in ancient times than it is now. The debris of the centuries has tended to raise its level.

Valley of Hinnom. Bounding Jerusalem on the west and south was the Hinnom Valley, also called "the Valley of the Sons of Hinnom" or Gehenna (*Ge Hinnom*). It was once the seat of idolatrous Molech worship, and afterward served as the place where the offal of the city was burned. Southwest from the Valley of Hinnom in the direction of Bethlehem is the Valley of Rephaim.

WALLS

Jerusalem's present walls with their two and one-half miles of masonry, thirty-four towers, and eight gates are largely the work of the sixteenth century sultan Suleiman I ("the Magnificent"). Massive stones in the south and southeast sectors of the wall, however, go back to pre-Christian times.

There was doubtless a long history of walled cities on the site of Jerusalem before it became "the city of David." The Jebusite rampart, captured by David, is the "first wall" according to modern terminology. David repaired these Jebusite walls, which were subsequently enlarged by Solomon.

The wall of David's city was about two hundred yards south of the present south wall. Under Solomon the city was extended northward to include the Temple, built on Araunah's threshing-floor at Mount Moriah, and the royal palace built south of and adjacent to the Temple. The Palestine Exploration Fund was able to study a section of the Jebusite and Solomonic walls overlooking the Kidron. The results indicate that the Jerusalem of David's day was shaped like a gigantic human footprint about

Hill of Ophel, Jerusalem. This view, looking south, is a portion of Nehemiah's wall, which was excavated by the archaeologist Kathleen Kenyon.

1,250 feet long and 400 feet wide. The area of the city could not have been more than eight acres. By way of comparison, ancient Megiddo had an area of thirty acres.

There were doubtless many additions to the walls of Jerusalem during the years of the kings subsequent to Solomon, including that ascribed to Manasseh (II Chron. 33:14). Our fullest description of Jerusalem's walls, however, comes in the period after the return from Babylon. Nehemiah took a night ride to inspect the walls of the city. He went out the Valley Gate, probably in the Hinnom Valley shortly below the "Tower of Furnaces." Passing the Dung Gate and the Fountain Gate he was forced to dismount at the King's Pool (the upper Siloam Pool) because of the rubble left from the Babylonian destruction. Then he proceeded on foot a short way up "the brook" (Kidron) (Neh. 2:12-15). The archaeologist F. J. Bliss unearthed gates which he identified as the ones Nehemiah passed on his journey from the Valley Gate to the King's Pool (Neh. 2:13-15).

Herod the Great surrounded the Temple area which he developed in Jerusalem with beautifully fashioned walls. The "wailing wall" used by Jews for centuries as a place of prayer is a part of the Herodian structure. Two towers "Hippicus" and "Phasael"—named after a friend and a brother of Herod— are thought to be represented in the masonry of the present "David's Tower," near the Jaffa Gate. The Herodian walls were described by Josephus.

The location of the north wall of Herod's Jerusalem is one of the archaeological puzzles which vex New Testament scholars. The Church of the Holy Sepulchre is, of course, inside the present walls of Jerusalem. Jesus was, we know, crucified outside the city (Heb. 13:12). We cannot be sure, however, whether or not the Church of the Holy Sepulchre was inside or outside the walled city of Jesus' day.

Adequate archaeological work in Jerusalem is difficult because Jerusalem is an inhabited city. The type of systematic excavation which takes place at the mounds of the Near East is impossible under such circumstances.

The Divided Kingdom

THE KINGDOMS OF ISRAEL AND JUDAH

c. 925-842 B.C.

Copyright by C. S. HAMMOND & Co., N. Y.

Scale of Miles

0   10   20   30   40

Capitals - - - - - - - - - -

Sidon

Damascus

Zarephath

MOUNT LEBANON

Leontes R.

MT. HERMON

Tyre

PHOENICIA

Ijon

A R A M

Dan

S y r i a n s

Kedesh

Hazor

Accho

Chinnereth

GESHUR

Cabul

Sea of Chinnereth

Bashan

Hammath

Aphek

MT. CARMEL

Kishon R.

Mt. Tabor

Edrei

Dor

Shunem

Yarmuk R.

Megiddo

Jezreel

Ramoth-gilead

Taanach

Beth-shan

I S R A E L

Plain of Sharon

Jordan

G I L E A D

The Great Sea
(Mediterranean Sea)

Samaria

Mt. Ebal

Mt. Gerizim

Shechem

Penuel

A M M O N

Jabbok R.

Shiloh

Joppa

Beth-horon

Bethel

Jericho

Rabbath-ammon

Jabneel

Gilgal

Gezer

Heshbon

Ashdod

Ekron

Jerusalem

Mt. Nebo

Ashkelon

Bethlehem

Medeba

PHILISTIA

Salt Sea (Dead Sea)

Gaza

Lachish

Hebron

Aroer

J U D A H

Gerar

Arnon R.

M O A B

Raphia

Wilderness of Judah

Beer-sheba

Kir-moab

River of Egypt

Valley of Salt

Zered R.

E D O M

The Divided Kingdom

Solomon had received from David a powerful empire. During his latter years, however, it began to fall apart. Expensive building projects sapped the strength and loyalty of the native Israelites. As the tributary nations saw the opportunity to assert their independence they did so, and Solomon was unable to prevent the disintegration of the empire. Before Solomon's death the Aramaeans severed themselves from his kingdom, and shortly after he was succeeded by Rehoboam, a further split took place. With the breakdown of the monarchy, subject states declared their independence so that the territory once ruled by David was divided into autonomous units.

INDEPENDENT UNITS

Syria, or *Aram.* The portion of Solomon's empire north of Mount Hermon, extending as far as the Euphrates, revolted and formed the Kingdom of Syria or Aram, with Damascus as its capital. The area of Syria varied at different times. Generally speaking it was bounded on the west by the Mediterranean, on the south by Galilee and Bashan, and on the east by the Arabian desert. It is a fertile territory, watered by the Orontes, the Pharpar and Abana, the upper Euphrates, and numerous other streams.

Although Solomon was unable to maintain control over Syria, the kingdoms of Israel and Judah frequently made alliances with the Damascus government—sometimes in opposition to one another. Asa of Judah (*ca.* 913-878 B.C.) used gold and silver treasures from the Jerusalem palace and Temple to purchase the help of Ben-hadad of Syria against Baasha of Israel. Ahab of Israel (*ca.* 869-850 B.C.) put Ben-hadad of Syria to flight (I Kings 20:20), securing rights for Israelite merchants to open bazaars in Damascus (I Kings 20:34; cf. Ezek. 27:16). During the reign of Ahaz of Judah (*ca.* 735 B.C.), the Syrian king, Rezin, allied himself with Pekah of Israel against Judah. In this instance the kings of Syria and Israel attempted to force Judah into an alliance to resist the inroads of the Assyrian Empire in western Asia. The alliance was unsuccessful, and Assyrian power grew. In the first half of the eighth century Tiglath-pileser III conquered Damascus. The region around Hamath was taken by Sargon II in 720 B.C., two years after the fall of Samaria.

Israel. South of Syria was the kingdom of the ten tribes, known as Israel, or the Northern Kingdom. Shortly after the death of Solomon, Rehoboam, his son, refused to come to grips with the economic chaos of the nation. Jeroboam, a former officer of Solomon, returned from exile in Egypt to lead a revolt, the result of which was the establishment of an independent Northern Kingdom, with its capital at Shechem. The Northern Kingdom included the larger portion of Palestine proper, an area of about 9,400 square miles as over against 3,400 for the rival kingdom of Judah. The boundary line between Israel and Judah ran south of Jericho, Bethel, and Joppa. The line was variable, however, being moved northward or southward depending on the relative strength of the two nations. In addition to Shechem, Jeroboam established a capital at Peniel (Penuel) east of the Jordan, where Jacob had once wrestled with an angel. The capital was moved from Shechem to neighboring Tirzah by Baasha. Omri, the founder of the third dynasty, chose Samaria as the site of his permanent capital. It remained there until the kingdom was destroyed by the Assyrians. Religious sanctuaries were established by Jeroboam at Dan in northern Israel, and Bethel near the southern border.

Judah. The kingdom of Judah included the tribe of that name, a portion of Benjamin, and Simeon which had been incorporated earlier into Judah. The Shephelah and the Coastal Plain were nominally a part of Judah, but actually they seem to have been controlled by the Philistines who were never fully absorbed into the state of Judah. Kings of the Davidic line reigned over Judah until the fall of Jerusalem to Nebuchadnezzar, king of Babylon (587 B.C.) .

Moab. Solomon retained control over Moab (I Kings 11:1, 7); but his successors found the Moabites hard to keep in subjection. On the Moabite Stone, discovered at Dibon in Jordan in 1868, Mesha, king of Moab, records that his land had been subdued by Omri of Israel, and held by Omri's son Ahab until Mesha freed his country, during the latter part of Ahab's reign. According to Assyrian records, Moab paid tribute to Tiglath-pileser III after his invasion of the West (733-732 B.C.) , and subsequently to Sennacherib (701 B.C.) .

Moab disappeared as a political power when Nebuchadnezzar (605-562 B.C.) subjugated the country. Nabataean Arabs held the territory of Moab during the first two centuries B.C. and the first century A.D.

Edom. South of the Dead Sea was the kingdom of Edom which had been conquered by David and remained tributary during the reign of Solomon. Its

Moabite Stone. The Moabite Stone is an inscribed stele of black basalt consisting of thirty-four lines written in an alphabet similar to that used among the ancient Israelites. The inscription tells how Moab had been subdued by Omri and Ahab and how Mesha, in the name of his god Chemosh, had delivered his people from Israelite domination.
Courtesy, Oriental Institute

relationship to Judah was similar to that of Moab to Israel. When Judah was strong, Edom was forced to pay tribute. During the reign of Jehoram, son of Jehoshaphat (*ca.* 849-842 B.C.), the Edomites gained their independence (II Kings 8:20-22). Subsequently, Edom, along with the rest of western Asia, fell to Nebuchadnezzar. In the post-Exilic period the Edomites were pushed northward by the Nabataean Arabs into the southern part of Judaea (*see* Map 11), where they became known as Idumeans. They were conquered by John Hyrcanus, the Hasmonaean ruler of the Jews (134-104 B.C.) and forcibly incorporated into the Jewish state. An Idumaean, Antipater, was appointed procurator of Judaea, Samaria and Galilee by Julius Caesar (47 B.C.). Subsequently, Herod, his son, was crowned king of the Jews (37 B.C.). After the destruction of Jerusalem (A.D. 70), the Idumaeans as a people lost their identity.

THREE KINGDOMS

Striving for Supremacy. The three kingdoms which developed from Solomon's kingdom in western Palestine—Syria, Israel, and Judah—strove for supremacy during the period from Jeroboam to Jehu in the northern kingdom and from Rehoboam to Joash in Judah.

During the early part of this period wars were constant between Israel and Judah. With the threat to both Israel and Judah from the powerful Syrian state of Damascus, there developed a tendency for the two states to reconcile their differences.

Shortly after the division of the kingdom, Jeroboam of Israel encouraged Sheshonk of Egypt (Biblical Shishak) to invade Judah. This was an excellent military tactic, for Judah now had a war on two fronts—Israel to the north and Egypt to the south. Sheshonk despoiled the Temple and palace of treasures accumulated by David and Solomon (II Chron. 12:2-12), but he did not limit his Palestinian campaign to Judaean cities. Egyptian inscriptions at Karnak depict captives from the Northern Kingdom as well as from Judah.

During the reign of Asa, Judah was invaded by a large force of chariotry under Zerah, an Ethiopian or Cushite. This Zerah, who may be one of the Osorkons of the Twenty-second Dynasty of Egyptian history, was defeated at the Judaean city of Mareshah on the highway from Gaza to Hebron (II Chron. 14:8-15).

Under Ahab and his Phoenician wife, Jezebel, the worship of the Tyrian Baal became a serious challenge to the faith of Israel (I Kings 16:28—19:21). The ministry of the prophet Elijah helped stem the tide of Baalism. Meanwhile, Ahab was faced with serious trouble from Syria. After an initial defeat by Israel, Ben-hadad's Syrian forces concluded that Israel's God was "a God of the hills" (I Kings 20:23), and that victory for Syria would be achieved if Israel could be brought down from her mountain strongholds. This proved to be wishful thinking, however. At Aphek, a town about four miles east of the Sea of Galilee on the road between Damascus and Jezreel, Ben-hadad was decisively defeated. Cities earlier taken from Israel by the Syrians were restored and the Northern Kingdom was given commercial privileges in Damascus (I Kings 20:26-34).

Subsequently Ahab was numbered among the allies of Ben-hadad who fought against the Assyrian ruler, Shalmaneser III, at Karkar on the Orontes River (853 B.C.). The major threat from Assyria made it necessary for the smaller states of Syria-Palestine to reconcile their differences. Assyrian records tell us that Ahab placed in the field of battle two thousand chariots and ten thousand foot soldiers. Although Shalmaneser III claimed a great victory, it was not a decisive one. When the Assyrian armies returned home, things returned to "normal" in Syria and Palestine. War again broke out between Benhadad and Ahab. In a battle to regain Ramoth-gilead, east of the Jordan, Ahab was struck with an arrow. He bled to death and was buried in the Israelite capital, Samaria.

Contemporary with the reigns of Omri, Ahab, and Jehoram in Israel, Jehoshaphat reigned as Judah's fourth king. Early in his reign, Jehoshaphat sought to cement relations with Israel by marrying his son, the crown prince Jehoram, to Athaliah, a daughter of Ahab and Jezebel. This act, while politically expedient, gave Baal worship a

foothold in the Southern Kingdom comparable to its earlier hold upon the North.

Jehoshaphat was allied with Ahab against the Syrians at the battle of Ramoth-gilead, near the Syrian border (II Chron. 18:19). During his reign a strong confederacy of Edomites, Moabites, and Ammonites invaded Judah. Due to a misunderstanding, however, the invading peoples began fighting among themselves and Jehoshaphat won the day without drawing his sword. Having gained access to Ezion-geber on the Gulf of Aqaba, Jehoshaphat built a fleet of ocean-going ships. A storm wrecked the fleet before it sailed, however.

The Moabite Stone tells us that Moab had been subdued by Omri of Israel. Late in the reign of Omri's son, Ahab, the Moabites successfully rebelled against Israel. Mesha, the Moabite king, cele-

Shrine at Megiddo. Ruins of a shrine with its stone altar is reminiscent of the fact that many religions flourished in the land of Canaan. During the time of Elijah, Baalism was so popular that it threatened to eliminate the historic faith in the God who brought Israel out of Egypt.   *Courtesy, Oriental Institute*

brated his victory by erecting the monument which we know as the Moabite Stone at Dibon.

During the reign of Jehoram (Joram) of Judah, Edom revolted. Jehoram encamped at Zair, possibly *Sa'ir*, five miles northeast of Hebron, before successfully attacking the Edomites. Judah was unable to retain supremacy over Edom, however.

Aramaean (Syrian) Dominance. The dynasty of Omri in Israel was brought to a violent end by Jehu, who was as zealous for the worship of Israel's God as Ahab and Jezebel, had been for Baal. A counter movement took place in the South, when Athaliah, the daughter of Ahab and Jezebel seized the throne of Judah and attempted to force Baalism on her people. While both Israel and Judah were going through these periods of trial, Hazael succeeded Ben-hadad II as king of Syria (II Kings 8:7-15). Hazael was so powerful that, during a period of Assyrian weakness, he was able to dominate both Israel and Judah. He seized Israel's land east of the Jordan, the territories known as Gilead and Manasseh (II Kings 10:32, 33; cf. Amos 1:3), and spared Jerusalem only after plundering the city and Temple (II Kings 12:17, 18).

During this period the usurpation of Athaliah was ended through the activity of the High Priest Jehoiada who had rescued Joash "of the seed royal" from the murderous plans of Athaliah. Joash was instrumental, in co-operation with Jehoiada, in a program of renovation and repair of the Temple (II Kings 12:1-16). During the latter part of his reign, however, he lapsed into idolatry. It was during Joash's reign that Hazael conquered the Judaean city of Gath and plundered Jerusalem itself.

Political Strength. With the death of Hazael, Syrian power waned. Jero-

Black Obelisk of Shalmaneser. The Assyrian king, Shalmaneser III, gave a brief account of his conquests on this stone, which shows Jehu of Israel or his emissary kissing the ground at the king's feet. The inscription reads, "Tribute of Jehu the son of Omri."

Courtesy, Oriental Institute

boam (II), son of Joash (Jehoash) was a powerful and able king of Israel. Lost territory was regained, nearly all of Syria was reconquered, and Samaria was the capital of a nation which approached in size the empire over which Solomon had ruled. The period of Joash of Israel and his son, Jeroboam II, has been called the "Indian summer of Israel"—a brief time of prosperity before its fall.

The period of Israel's "Indian summer" was paralleled in Judah by the reigns of Amaziah and Uzziah (or Azariah). After a victorious campaign against Edom in which he took Sela (Petra) (see Map 4) the capital of Edom, Amaziah of Judah fought Jehoash of Israel at Beth-shemesh. Amaziah's Judaean army was defeated and Israel proceeded to attack Jerusalem itself. For the only time in Judah's history, an army from the Northern Kingdom entered Jerusalem as victor, plundered its treasures, and reduced Judah to virtual subjection to Israel.

The reign of Uzziah of Judah was more successful. He raised a large, well-equipped army (II Chron. 26:11-14) and provided for the defense of Jerusalem (II Chron. 26:9, 15). Successful military campaigns were carried on against the Philistines (II Chron. 26:6, 7), and Ammon was made tributary to Judah (II Chron. 26:8). Ezion-geber, or Elath, was recovered for the Southern Kingdom (II Kings 14:22).

The material prosperity during the reigns of Jeroboam II of Israel and Uzziah of Judah was not matched with spiritual progress. The prophets of the day, particularly Hosea and Amos in the North and Isaiah in the South, underscored the externalism and hypocrisy which characterized much of religious life. Sacrifices were brought to the altars and sacred seasons of the year were punctiliously observed. Oppression, bloodshed, and greed were characteristic of the people, however. The rich tended to grow richer and the poor grew progressively poorer. The prophets declared the imminent judgment of God upon a nation which had forgotten its Maker and Protector.

The Northern Kingdom Falls. Israel's prosperity under Jeroboam II was short-lived. Assyrian power was on the increase, and the entire Syria-Palestine area was considered suitable prey. In the reign of Menahem, Israel became tributary to Assyria. Northern Israel, including Naphtali, was carried into captivity by Tiglath-pileser III (733 B.C.). His son, Shalmaneser V, besieged the capital city, Samaria, which fell to Shalmaneser's successor, Sargon II (722 B.C.). Israel had placed confidence in Egypt for assistance against Assyria, but the days of Egyptian might were past.

The Assyrian policy of transportation had an important effect upon subsequent history. Captive peoples were transported to various new areas in an attempt to break up any possible national resistance. Israelites were taken to Halah and Gozan on the banks of the River Habor (*Khabur*) in northern Mesopotamia. Similarly, colonists from Babylonia, Syria, Elam, and elsewhere were settled in Samaria (II Kings 17:24). The intermarriage of these peoples with the Israelites who were left in the land produced the people known in subsequent history as Samaritans (II Kings 17:29). It was precisely this policy of transportation which made impossible the return of the people of the Northern Kingdom in a way comparable to the return of the Judaeans after the decree of Cyrus.

CHAPTER XVI

Judah Alone

A Judaean Landscape. This modern photo, looking southeastward from the Plain of Sharon, presents a clear picture of Judah of old.

Copyright, Matson Photo Service

CHAPTER XVI

Judah Alone

For almost a century and a half after the fall of Samaria, the southern kingdom of Judah maintained itself as a sovereign state with a king of the dynasty of David ruling in Jerusalem. This rule was at times very ineffective, and Judah was tributary to the Egyptians, Aramaeans, Assyrians, or Babylonians during much of the time before she finally was conquered by Nebuchadnezzar (587 B.C.).

During the reigns of Jotham and Ahaz, Judah had refused to join the coalition of Syria and Israel against Assyria. Tiglath-pileser, however, looked upon Judah as a subject state rather than an ally. Judah was, in fact, forced to pay heavy tribute to Assyria.

Religiously, Judah was at a low ebb. Pagan religious practices became the norm in the life of the Southern Kingdom. Children were actually burned as sacrifices in the Valley of Hinnom, near Jerusalem (Jer. 7:31).

Territory gained during the prosperous days of Uzziah had been in large measure lost. Edom, with the strategic port city of Ezion-geber at the Gulf of Aqaba, was no longer subject to Judah. Ahaz was forced to empty his royal treasury and strip the Temple in order to meet the demands of his Assyrian overlords.

Judah under Hezekiah. When Hezekiah succeeded his father Ahaz to the throne of Judah, important changes took place both within Judah and among the other nations of the Fertile Crescent. The ministries of Isaiah and Micah provided the spiritual impetus for the rejection of idolatrous practices and the revival of the worship of the God of Israel. Hezekiah sought to correct abuses and call the people back to the observance of the Law of God.

Important changes were taking place on the international scene which made it possible for Hezekiah to defy his Assyrian overlords. Sargon, who had transplanted the population of the Northern Kingdom after the fall of Samaria (722 B.C.), encountered rebellion in Babylon where Merodach-baladan (II Kings 20: 12) successfully defied the Assyrians for a dozen years. Egypt, too, had arisen from her slumber and attempted to make a name for herself on the political horizon. While Assyria was busy with troubles in the East, her vassals in Palestine were assured of help from Egypt if they should meet trouble when defying their overlord. Egyptian promises were vain in the long run, but her policy encouraged the states of western Asia to refuse tribute to Assyria, and, later, to Babylonia, on more than one occasion.

When Sargon was succeeded by his son Sennacherib (705 B.C.), Hezekiah decided to declare his political independence by refusing the payment of tribute (II Kings 18:7). This was, of course, an act of rebellion, but Sennacherib was unable to intervene at once. Aided by the Elamites, Merodach-baladan had established himself as king in Babylon, and Sennacherib was forced to intervene to save his empire in the east. Egypt, of course, took advantage of the situation to encourage rebellion among the western provinces.

We are aided in our understanding of the conflict between Hezekiah and Sennacherib by the annals which describe the various campaigns of the Assyrian ruler. There we learn that Hezekiah was a ringleader of the opposition. When Padi, king of Ekron, sought to maintain his loyalty to the Assyrians, his enraged subjects handed him over to Hezekiah for punishment.

In 701 B.C. Sennacherib was able to turn westward to defend his holdings and punish the insurgents. His annals tell how he crushed resistance at Tyre and placed his own puppet ruler at the head of its government. The rebellious king fled to Cyprus. The defeat of Tyre sparked a series of surrenders before the might of Assyria. Byblos, Arvad, Ashdod, Moab, Edom, and Ammon quickly made peace with Sennacherib. Judah, however, supported by Ashkelon and Ekron, held out. An Egyptian army came to help the rebels and encountered Sennacherib's forces at Eltekeh, near Ekron, but the Assyrians gained a quick victory. Ekron fell to Sennacherib, and the Assyrian ruler marched into Judah.

In his annals, Sennacherib boasts that he captured forty-six of Hezekiah's fortified cities and besieged Jerusalem. Hezekiah was shut up in his capital city "like a bird in a cage." Jerusalem, however, did not fall. As Isaiah had prophesied, the Assyrian was forced to leave Jerusalem untouched. Hezekiah did pay heavy tribute to Sennacherib, taking gold and silver from the palace and the Temple, but he maintained his independence.

Judah under Manasseh and Amon. The death of Hezekiah brought about a change in the affairs of Judah. Manas-seh, doubtless under strong political pressure, declared himself a loyal vassal of Assyria and abandoned Hezekiah's policy of resistance. The spiritual revival which Hezekiah had fostered was largely negated and idolatry again became common in Judah.

Sennacherib, himself, was murdered by certain of his sons (II Kings 19:37). His successor, Esarhaddon, proved to be a vigorous ruler who determined to crush the power of Assyria's perennial enemy, Egypt. Although partially successful in his first campaign, Esarhaddon was killed during a second attempt to conquer Egypt. Ashurbanipal, his son, continued the campaign, and actually destroyed Thebes, the ancient Egyptian capital, known as No or No-Amon (Nah. 3:8). The Egyptian Pharaoh fled south to Nubia.

During his long reign of forty-four years, Manasseh maintained his loyalty to Assyria. He paid his tribute regularly and was not molested. His reign is remembered for its idolatry, rather than its peace, however. Tradition says that the prophet Isaiah met a martyr's death, being "sawn asunder" (cf. Heb. 11:37) at this time.

Unrest was growing, however, and vassal states of Assyria were awaiting the moment when they could assert their independence. Babylon, Egypt, and the Lydians of Asia Minor were among the peoples whose hatred of Assyria knew no bounds. Then, too, new problems arose. From beyond the Caucasus Mountains barbaric peoples known as Cimmerians and Scythians invaded the Fertile Crescent. Arab tribes overran Edom, Moab, and much of eastern Palestine.

Ashurbanipal did enjoy a period of respite, however, although he was to be the last strong king of Assyria. Unable really to subdue Egypt, he had to be content with the submission of the rest

Mound of Megiddo. Excavations of this thirteen acre mound reveal a history of occupation from 3500 B.C. to 450 B.C. The mound covers thirteen acres and the accumulation of debris amounted to from thirty to forty feet. King Josiah was fatally wounded on the battlefield of Megiddo as he attempted to stop Pharaoh Necho from using the Esdraelon Valley to join the Assyrians at Carchemish.

Courtesy, Oriental Institute

of his empire. Yet Ashurbanipal's chief claim to fame does not come from the field of battle. He collected a great library containing the classics of the ancient world of cuneiform literature. Much of our knowledge of the history and mythology of the Sumerians, Babylonians, and Assyrians comes from the clay tablets which were assembled by Ashurbanipal and discovered during the nineteenth century by the excavators of Nineveh.

Two sons of Ashurbanipal succeeded their father in rapid succession. The tide of revolt continued, however, and they were unable to hold together the empire. A Chaldean prince, Nabopolassar, was able to defeat an Assyrian army at Babylon, thus gaining independence and becoming first ruler of the Neo-Babylonian, or Chaldean Empire. He subsequently joined forces with the Medes, under Cyaxeres, who were planning to attack the mighty Nineveh, the Assyrian capital to which the riches of

the East had been brought in tribute during the days of the powerful Assyrian kings. After a three-month siege, Nineveh fell, never to rise again. The Assyrians retreated northward and settled for a time at Haran, the city once visited by Abraham, but they could stage no comeback. Babylon was soon to become the great power of the East.

Judah's Last Revival. About eight years before the death of Ashurbanipal, Josiah came to the throne of Judah. The disorders which plagued the Assyrian monarch made it possible for Josiah to chart an independent course. Josiah rejected the idolatries of his predecessors, Manasseh and Amon, and determined to revive the worship of the God of Israel. The Bible knows Josiah as one of the greatest and most godly kings. Under his auspices the Temple was renovated and the ancient book of the Law of the Lord was found in the rubble of a building which had been neglected during the decades of idolatry. King and people recognized that they had sinned against the Lord and sought to bring the national life into conformity with His Law.

When Pharaoh Necho marched northward to join the Assyrian armies in a desperate attempt to turn back the forces of Babylon, Josiah led an army to Megiddo to intercept the Egyptian. Egypt and Assyria, former rivals, were preparing to unite to meet a new enemy, Babylon. Josiah, an ally of Babylon, died fighting the Egyptians on the battlefield of Megiddo (609 B.C.) .

Necho and the Assyrians were not successful, however. At Carchemish, on the Euphrates River, a decisive battle was fought (605 B.C.) which made the Babylonians undisputed rulers of the Tigris-Euphrates basin. As the conqueror of Assyria, Babylon laid claim to the entire empire once ruled from Nineveh. Egypt, however, had occupied much of Palestine, and sought to consolidate her position there. Judah was again a buffer state between two dominant powers—Egypt and Babylon this time.

Judah's Last Years. Suspecting that Jehoahaz, son of Josiah, was pro-Babylonian, Pharaoh Necho removed him from the throne of Judah and installed his brother Jehoiakim as an Egyptian puppet. In the meantime much of the effect of Josiah's spiritual impact had been neutralized and idolatry became rampant in Judah. Jeremiah stated that she worshiped as many gods as she had cities!

When Nebuchadnezzar returned to western Palestine after having succeeded his father Nabopolassar to the throne of Babylon, Jehoiakim found it advisable to shift his allegiance and pay tribute to the Babylonians. Following a temporary Babylonian set-back at the hands of Pharaoh Necho, Jehoiakim again shifted allegiance with sad results to Judah. Daniel and other youths were deported to Babylon. Jehoiakim died shortly after these events, and it is possible that he was murdered.

Within three months after eighteen year old Jehoiachin took the throne, the city of Jerusalem was surrendered to the Babylonians. Jehoichin had defied the Babylonians, trusting in Egyptian help which did not come. The young king and ten thousand Judaeans were taken to Babylon and Nebuchadnezzar appointed Zedekiah, twenty-one year old uncle of Jehoiachin, as ruler of Judah.

Things did not improve under Zedekiah, however. In spite of Jeremiah's warning, Zedekiah accepted the counsel of the pro-Egyptian party and refused tribute to Nebuchadnezzar. This time the Babylonian king determined to put down Judaean resistance violently. The city and its Temple were destroyed (587 B.C.) . Zedekiah's sons were slain before his eyes, and he was blinded and taken in chains to Babylon. Except for the poorest of the people, the population of Judah was deported.

Nebuchadnezzar attempted to rule the remnants of Judah by a puppet governor, Gedaliah. Even this failed. A small but active group of Jews, under the leadership of a man named Ishmael who claimed royal descent, murdered Gedaliah in his capital at Mizpeh in a vain attempt to set up a government independent of Babylonia. Fearing further reprisals from Nebuchadnezzar, a Jewish remnant made its way to Egypt (*ca.* 581 B.C.) taking along the prophet Jeremiah who had consistently warned against rebellion.

Exile and Restoration

Air View of Susa (Biblical Shushan). Susa was the royal winter residence of Darius the Great, and served as one of three capitals of the Persian Empire. The excavated ruins show levels of occupation from about 4000 B.C. to A.D. 1200.   Courtesy, Oriental Institute

Use Maps 6 and 7

Exile and Restoration

Nebuchadnezzar was one of history's most able administrators, but he is known to readers of Scripture as the Babylonian king who destroyed Jerusalem (587 B.C.) and carried the Judaeans into exile. Secular history also knows him as an efficient builder and organizer who made Babylon the center of the most successful empire of his age. His famous "Hanging Gardens," actually gardens built on stone terraces for his Median wife, were among the wonders of the ancient world.

Although the Babylonian captivity was interpreted as a just punishment for the idolatry of Judah, the Biblical writers note that God was with His people in the land of their exile. Daniel, a pious Jew, was advanced to positions of responsibility in the courts of Babylon and Persia in spite of opposition from jealous courtiers. Ezekiel ministered to a community of his countrymen who had been settled in a community known as Tel-abib ("mound of ears of grain"). Although the exact location of Tel-abib is not known, Ezekiel tells us that it was located on the River Chebar, thought to have been one of the canals southeast of the city of Babylon. A system of such canals made possible the cultivation of a large area in southern Mesopotamia.

Nebuchadnezzar did not impose any permanent religious restrictions on the Jews, but their very absence from the Jerusalem Temple brought about significant changes. While in Palestine, the Jew looked to the Temple as the one place where God might be worshiped with an acceptable sacrifice. Away from Jerusalem, the Jew in exile found a substitute for Temple worship in the institution of the synagogue. Pious Jews longed for the end of the Exile when they might return to rebuild the Temple. In the meantime, however, they gathered in small groups for prayer and Bible study. Instead of making them more amenable to idolatry, the Exile provided the environment in which devotion to the Law was nurtured. Prophets, such as Jeremiah, who had been largely discredited during the time of their oral ministry, took on new significance as their warnings and their promises were read and pondered by their countrymen in exile.

THE NEO-BABYLONIAN EMPIRE

Nabopolassar, the father of Nebuchadnezzar, had rebelled successfully against his Assyrian overlords and established the Neo-Babylonian Empire, the name given to the Babylon of his time to distinguish it from the earlier empire with its famous lawgiver, Hammurabi. The Neo-Babylonians are sometimes designated by their tribal name as Chaldeans.

As a general leading his father's armies, Nebuchadnezzar defeated Pharaoh Necho of Egypt at the Battle of Carchemish in upper Mesopotamia (605 B.C.). Carchemish marked the end of Egyptian power in Syria, and Nebuchadnezzar might have moved against Egypt itself but for word of the death of his father. Sensing the need to return home to establish his right to the throne, Nebuchadnezzar abandoned his campaign against Egypt.

Because Palestine was a kind of buffer state between Egyptian and Babylonian interests, the leaders of Judah were subjected to pressure from both directions. Egypt encouraged Judah to refuse the payment of tribute to Nebuchadnezzar with the assurance of military help in the event of invasion. Nebuchadnezzar demanded tribute, and Egypt was unable to offer effective help. After two such episodes, each of which ended with a partial deportation of Jews to Babylon, Nebuchadnezzar brought to an end the last rebellion with the destruction of Jerusalem and its Temple (587 B.C.).

In secular history Nebuchadnezzar is known as the king who was responsible for the rebuilding and ornamentation of Babylon. Nebuchadnezzar reigned for more than forty years, but he did not prepare successors who could effectively carry out his policies. In the first year of the reign of his son, Awil-Marduk (the Evil Merodach of Scripture), Jehoiachin, king of Judah, was released from prison in Babylon and given a position of honor among the vassal kings. Jehoiachin had been deported to Babylon after a reign of about three months. Although Zedekiah had been appointed by Nebuchadnezzar to take his place in Jerusalem, Jehoiachin was looked upon by many Jews as their true king. We know nothing of his history after the restoration, however. After a reign of but two years, Evil Merodach was assassinated by his brother-in-law, Neriglissar, who usurped the throne for himself.

Neriglissar's son, Labashi-Marduk, was in turn assassinated after a nine-month reign by Nabonidus who had no ability as a king. Nabonidus was more interested in religion and the study of antiq-uities than in the details of government. Consequently, he was unpopular with the priests, who wished to restrict his interest to the established religion, and with the populace who cared little for his unorthodox ways. Belshazzar, the son of Nabonidus, served as prince regent in the place of his father and is best known as the "king" under whom Babylon fell to the Persians.

THE PERSIAN EMPIRE

The founder of the Persian Empire came to the throne of the tiny Elamite state of Anshan (ca. 559 B.C.). Taking advantage of rebellion in the Median army, Cyrus defeated Astyages, king of the Medes, and entered his capital city, Ecbatana.

In an amazingly short time, Cyrus extended his borders westward and northward. He threatened the fabulously wealthy kingdom of Lydia, in Asia Minor, whose king Croesus sought an alliance with Nabonidus of Babylon and Amasis II of Egypt. Before help could come, Cyrus struck and added Lydia to his empire. This brought Cyrus into contact with the Greek cities of Asia Minor, and presaged the ultimate conflict with Greece. However, turning eastward toward the Tigris-Euphrates Valley, Cyrus moved his armies in the direction of Babylon. After a series of victories in the communities north of the capital, Babylon itself fell to the Persian armies in 538 B.C. There was no fighting, and Cyrus appeared as a liberator to the populace which had shown discontent with the policies of Nabonidus and Belshazzar.

Cyrus made it a point to reverse certain of the basic policies of his predecessors. Captive peoples were permitted to return to their homelands, and idols which had been taken to Babylon were restored to their local shrines. Although there was no "idol" for the God of Israel, Temple furnishings had been taken to Babylon by Nebuchadnezzar's armies. Cyrus granted permission to the Jews to return to Jerusalem with these furnishings and rebuild their Temple (Ezra 1:2-4).

Under Sheshbazzar, identified by some scholars with Zerubbabel, a company of Jewish exiles returned to Jerusalem and the work of rebuilding the Temple was begun. The native population of Judaea—Samaritans and others who had profited by the absence of the Jews in Babylon—exerted strong opposition to the Jews in their work of rebuilding the Temple and, subsequently, the walls of Jerusalem. After the building of an altar, little more was accomplished by the Jews during the lifetime of Cyrus. He is remembered, however, as the

Lord's anointed who made possible the return from Exile.

Under Cambyses (530-522 B.C.), son and heir of Cyrus, Persian power reached into Egypt. The Egyptian Pharaoh Psamtik was defeated at Pelusium (525 B.C.) after which Cambyses sacked the capital at Memphis. The defeat of the Egyptians by Cambyses brought an end to the independence of Egypt which had once been the greatest power in the Near East.

While following up his victories in Egypt, Cambyses learned of revolts at home and hastened to return to Persia in order to secure his throne. Before reaching home, Cambyses died. Some suggest that he committed suicide.

The period of confusion which marked the last days of Cambyses was ended when Darius "the Great" (522-486 B.C.) put down all opposition and ruled as

Stairway from Darius' Palace, Persepolis. Using gray marble from nearby quarries, Darius built a palace expressive of the might of Persia. The stairways depict, in relief, twenty-three nations bearing their tribute to the Persian ruler.

Courtesy, Oriental Institute

Gate of Xerxes, Persepolis. In these ruins of the palace of Darius we see huge figures of man-bulls guarding the eastern doorway to a hall of columns.

one of the strongest of Persian monarchs. Cyrus had tried to rule with a policy of clemency, but Darius thought it necessary to exert absolute control. His efficient organization made Persia a centralized state in which total power and control was vested in the king. Before the end of the sixth century B.C., the empire of Darius extended from the Indus Valley to the Aegean, from the Jaxartes (modern Syr Darya) in central Asia to Libya in North Africa.

Since the days of Cyrus, the Persian rulers dreamed of conquering Greece. Darius campaigned in Europe, and annexed Thrace and Macedonia with little difficulty. Greece, however, resisted successfully. The defeat of Darius at Marathon (490 B.C.) proved a major setback and kept from Darius the prize he sought most.

Darius was an efficient organizer, and his rule left nothing to be desired from the administrative standpoint. Legal and fiscal reforms promoted commerce and industry. A postal system facilitated communication throughout his vast empire. Roads were built everywhere. Engineers of Darius designed a canal to be dug in Egypt linking the Nile River with the Red Sea and serving the same purpose as the modern Suez Canal. The great palace which Darius built at Persepolis was a veritable beehive of activity which rivaled in efficiency a modern capital.

Judaea was a small dependency in the two million square mile kingdom of Darius, who made no change in official policy toward the Jews. When Tattenai, the Persian governor of Samaria, joined others in making complaint against the Jews, Darius searched the archives and found the decree of Cyrus which authorized the construction of the Temple. Thereupon Darius issued a new edict forbidding hindrance to the project and ordering a generous contribution from the royal treasury. During the sixth year of the reign of Darius the Temple was finished and dedicated (Ezra 6:15).

Xerxes I (486-465 B.C.) was the son of Darius and Atossa, a daughter of

Cyrus, a relationship which insured him the strongest claim to the throne. Early in his reign he found it necessary to put down rebellion in Egypt, and shortly thereafter (482 B.C.) he turned against insurgents in Babylon, demolished the walls of the city and destroyed its famous temple to Marduk. Having accomplished this, he prepared for the invasion of Greece, Persia's sole remaining rival. Xerxes crossed the Hellespont (480 B.C.) and moved through Macedonia with a large army. In a short time the brave Spartans were defeated at Thermopylae (480 B.C.) and Athens was occupied and pillaged. At Salamis, however, the Persians lost a third of their fleet to the Greeks, and the tide of battle turned. Xerxes gave the command of the Persian armies to his general, Mardonius, and returned to Asia. Mardonius, however, could not restore Persian prestige. At Plataea (479 B.C.) the Persian army was decisively defeated, and the remnant of the Persian fleet was destroyed the same year near Samos. Back in Persia, Xerxes the king was assassinated by one of his guards.

Xerxes was the Ahasuerus of the Book of Esther. When peeved at the virtuous conduct of his wife, Vashti, he divorced her and sought a substitute. Esther, a beautiful Jewess, was brought to the king at Susa (Biblical Shushan) and, as his wife, saved her people from the evil designs of their enemies, notably a courtier named Haman. The Jewish feast of Purim commemorates the victory of the Jews over their enemies in the days of Esther.

Artaxerxes I, Longimanus (465-424 B.C.), a son of Xerxes, succeeded to the throne after the assassination of his father. The empire was again restive, and Artaxerxes had to put down Greek attacks on Cyprus and rebellion in Egypt. At the peace of Callias (449 B.C.) the Greek cities of Asia Minor which were

in league with Athens were conceded their freedom. Persian troops were permitted in the portion of Asia Minor east of the Halys River, but the Persian fleet agreed not to enter the Aegean.

It was during the reign of Artaxerxes that Ezra "the scribe" led a group of exiles back to Jerusalem, and Nehemiah, the king's cupbearer, secured a leave of absence to encourage the Jews to activity in rebuilding the walls of the city. The Persian kings exhibited a concern for the welfare of their subjects, and the Jews seem to have been loyal and trusted subjects.

About ninety years passed between the death of Artaxerxes I and the death of Darius III (331 B.C.), the last of the Achaemenid Persian rulers. Six Persian rulers reigned with varying success, but none was able to restore Persia to its former greatness. The most celebrated dynastic quarrel of this period was the rebellion of Cyrus the Younger, a Persian prince who hired an army of Greek mercenaries (the "Ten Thousand") to support his cause in opposition to Artaxerxes II. Cyrus was killed in the battle of Cunaxa (401 B.C.) and his mercenaries had to fight their way back to Greece in the dead of winter. Xenophon, one of the "Ten Thousand," wrote the history of this famed retreat in the *Anabasis*. Harassed by the Persians, they went up the Tigris valley into Armenia, going northward through the mountains and then down to the Black Sea at Trapezus (Trebizond), thence back to Greece.

Although there were temporary periods of splendor, the latter kings of Persia lived during times of intrigue, rebellion, and bloodshed. In 334 B.C. Alexander of Macedon invaded Asia Minor and, the next year, he defeated a Persian army at Issus in northern Syria. The end came for the Persian empire when Alexander defeated Darius III at Gaugamela in northern Mesopotamia (331 B.C.). The last of the Persian kings fled to the re- mote province of Bactria where he was assassinated by his own cousin.

Persepolis.   Two guards, a Median (left) and a Persian (right), each holding a spear, are pictured on this closeup of the stairway of Darius' palace.   *Courtesy, Oriental Institute*

The Hellenistic Age

Ancient Greek Theatre, Epidaurus, Greece. The most beautiful of ancient Greek theatres was located at Epidaurus, on an inlet of the Saronic Gulf in the northeastern Peloponnesus.

Copyright Ewing Galloway

The Hellenistic Age

Alexander the Great was an apostle of Hellenism. His teacher, Aristotle, helped Alexander appreciate the literature and cultural institutions of Greece. A conqueror and empire-builder often has little time for the "nicer" things. Not so, Alexander. Convinced of the superiority of Greek institutions, Alexander spread Hellenism so effectively that it continued to be the dominant pattern of life long after his death and the disintegration of his kingdom.

ALEXANDER'S EMPIRE

Succeeding to the throne of Macedon at the death of his father Philip, Alexander proved his military prowess by bringing order into the restive political life of Greece. He succeeded in putting down rebellion in Thrace and Illyria as a prelude to his greater conquests. By 334 B.C. he was ready to cross the Hellespont and undertake the war on Persia which his father had planned. Soon after entering Asia Minor, Alexander met and defeated a Persian army at the Granicus River, near the Hellespont. The strategic cities of Sardis, Miletus, and Halicarnassus were quickly occupied. From Asia Minor he moved on to northern Syria where an army of the Persian king Darius III was routed at Issus (333 B.C.). Alexander proceeded southward along the Mediterranean coast, and spent another year in subduing Tyre and Gaza, and then entered Egypt. The Egyptians, who resented Persian rule, welcomed Alexander as a liberator, acknowledging

him to be the son of Amon-Re, the Egyptian sun god. He founded the city of Alexandria in Egypt to serve as a model Hellenistic city. Jews were encouraged to settle there. Alexandria became the cultural center of Hellenistic Judaism and, later, of the Christian church.

From Egypt, Alexander retraced his steps northward through Syria and met the armies of Darius at Gaugamela in northern Mesopotamia. After a bitter battle there, Alexander was able to move southward and take Babylon. He then pressed on and successively conquered the Persian capitals at Susa, Persepolis, and Ecbatana. Farther east, Alexander's forces occupied Bactria and penetrated into the Punjab region of India.

This, however, was the extent of Alexander's conquests. His desire to be treated as a god, his arbitrary treatment of trusted associates, and his attempt to force his officers to intermingle with and marry Persians brought much resentment. The apostle of Hellenism had changed, and his popularity began to slip.

Alexander died a natural death, however. While in the city of Babylon on the return trip to Greece, he died of a fever at the age of thirty-three (323 B.C.). It had been just eleven years since Alexander left Macedonia on an expedition destined to change the course of history.

THE KINGDOM OF ALEXANDER'S SUCCESSORS

When Alexander died he left no heir. A son was born posthumously to Roxanna, his Bactrian wife, but both mother and child were killed during the wars among Alexander's generals who were desirous of seizing the throne for themselves.

In 301 B.C. at Ipsus in Phrygia, Antigonus "the One-Eyed" who laid claim to the entire empire of Alexander was defeated and slain by his rivals, Seleucus and Lysimachus. In the meantime Ptolemy I (Soter), the son of a Macedonian named Lagus, managed to gain control of Egypt. Ptolemy had been one of Alexander's greatest generals, but he was not present at Ipsus and did not share in the division of the empire. As part of the spoils of war Seleucus was assigned the whole of Syria and, in theory at least, the Egyptian territory ruled by Ptolemy. Palestine was ruled by the Ptolemies, but the Seleucids considered it part of their rightful territory.

PALESTINE IN THE HELLENISTIC AGE

Palestine under the Ptolemies (321-198 B.C.)

The century and a quarter during which Palestine was subject to the Ptolemies was a time of prosperity for the Jews. High Priests were responsible for the internal affairs of the Palestinian Jews. At Alexandria, about 285 B.C., the Jewish Law was translated into the Greek language for the benefit of the Jewish community there which had come to use the Greek tongue instead of Hebrew. Subsequently the remaining books of the Old Testament were translated into Greek. This translation, known as the Septuagint, acquainted non-Jews for the first time with the Hebrew Scriptures and thus helped prepare the Hellenistic world for the Christian gospel.

Palestine under the Seleucids (198-166 B.C.)

Most of Asia Minor, Mesopotamia, Syria, Babylonia, and Persia were incorporated into the kingdom of Seleucus. At this time the terms "Seleucid" and "Syrian" were synonymous, and the Syrian Seleucid rulers were regarded by the Jews as cruel oppressors.

At Panium (Panias) near the headwaters of the Jordan Antiochus III of Syria defeated an Egyptian army (198 B.C.) and Palestine passed into Syrian control. It was not long before the Jews went through times of great suffering. Antiochus IV ("Epiphanes"), faced with financial problems and the need to unify his empire, backed the pro-Hellenistic party in Palestine and outlawed the practice of the Jewish religion. Copies of the Law were burned, Sabbath observance was not permitted and the rite of circumcision declared illicit.

The Maccabean Reaction (166-40 B.C.)

The challenge of Hellenism had produced a mixed reaction among the Jews. To some of them the life which centered in a Greek city was a great advance over the traditional Jewish folkways. Greek thinking which found expression in the schools of philosophy, and Greek action exemplified by the gymnasium constituted a real challenge. Other Jews, however, looked upon Hellenism as a threat to the religious attitudes and institutions which had been hallowed since time immemorial. Hellenism was not all good, or all bad, but it must be admitted that Palestine did not see it at its best.

When Antiochus Epiphanes appointed a High Priest who would be favorable to his Hellenizing program he doubtless thought he was acting within his rights as the rightful ruler of Palestine. To the pious in Israel, however, he was guilty of trifling with holy things. His sacrifice of swine on the altar of the

Temple in Jerusalem was an act of desecration which could not soon be forgotten. Zeus was worshiped instead of the God of Israel.

Revolt was not long delayed. When the aged priest of Modin, seventeen miles northwest of Jerusalem, refused to take part in a heathen sacrifice, a frightened Jew prepared to do so. Mattathias, the priest, killed both the cowardly Jew and the emissary of Antiochus and, with his sons, fled to the mountains where they waged guerrilla warfare. Mattathias did not live long after the beginning of the revolt, but his son Judas "the Maccabee" led a band of pious Jews who determined to resist the policy of Antiochus even at the cost of their lives.

Antiochus did not take this band of faithful Jews seriously. His major forces were busy elsewhere, so small detachments were sent against the Maccabees. The impossible took place, however. Judas led his ill-equipped army to victory after victory. When Lysias, the Syrian general, decided personally to command the Syrian troops in an effort to stamp out the Jewish revolt, the Syrians were defeated with heavy losses.

In 165 B.C. Judas entered Jerusalem as victor. He purified the Temple and re-established the rites which had been suspended by the edict of Antiochus. The Jewish community still celebrates the feast of Hanukkah (the feast of Lights) each December in commemoration of the cleansing of the Temple.

The death of Antiochus precipitated a contest for the Syrian throne. Lysias seized the reins of government and prepared to attack the Jews. While besieging Jerusalem, however, he found it necessary to hasten home to defend his throne against a rival claimant. In this extremity he offered full religious liberty to the Jews on condition that they recognize his political sovereignty.

Although this seemed to resolve the problems of the Jews, the crisis was soon renewed. The throne of Syria changed hands again and the ·Jews found that they were forced to recognize Alcimus, a hated High Priest with Hellenistic sympathies, as their spiritual leader. Antagonism was so great that Alcimus had to flee. The Syrians, who backed Alcimus, prepared to attack the Jews. At Elasa, north of Jerusalem, Judas himself died in battle in 160 B.C.

Jonathan, the youngest brother of Judas, inherited his brother's command of the Maccabean forces. The political situation again favored him. Rome and Sparta made treaties of alliance, and Demetrius II, the new king of Syria, named Jonathan civil and military governor of Judaea. Jonathan was murdered, however, by Trypho, a pretender to the Syrian throne, in 142 B.C.

A third son of Mattathias, Simon, took up the work of his murdered brother Jonathan. Demetrius II, in return for Jewish assistance in resisting Trypho, renounced all claim to tribute and gave the Jews full independence. Simon was made hereditary High Priest and Ethnarch. His rule was marked by tragedy, however. A new Syrian ruler, Antiochus VII, wished to impose tribute on Judaea, but met effective resistance from John and Judas, sons of Simon. A son-in-law, Ptolemy, murdered the aged Simon in a plot to gain power for himself. The dynasty of Simon (known as the Hasmonaean dynasty) continued, however, for his son John Hyrcanus became ruler of Judaea in 134 B.C.

The early years of Hyrcanus were difficult. Syria again besieged Jerusalem demanding heavy tribute and the leveling of the city's fortifications. Hyrcanus refused to acknowledge defeat. He built up a personal army and began a program designed to make Judaea a powerful sovereign state. When Syrian power declined and the Syrian armies were

The Erechtheum, Athens. One of the finest examples of Greek architecture, the Erechtheum was built of marble on the Acropolis (420-409 B.C.). It contained shrines to four of the deities of the ancient Greece. During the reign of Justinian it was made into a Christian church.   *Courtesy, Trans World Airlines*

removed from Palestine, Hyrcanus determined to fill the vacuum. He conquered Samaria and destroyed the temple which the Samaritans had built on Mount Gerizim. Idumaea, the portion of southern Palestine occupied by the descendants of the Edomites, was conquered and its people forced to embrace Judaism.

The policies of John Hyrcanus could hardly be popular among the pious in Israel. Hyrcanus actually broke with the party of the Pharisees—the spiritual descendants of the pious who had stood out against Syrian tyranny in the days of Antiochus Epiphanes. He joined the Sadducees, the party with Hellenistic leanings.

Under Alexander Jannaeus, brother of Hyrcanus, things went from bad to worse. The borders were further extended but the nation was plunged into civil war. In their bitter opposition to the Sadducees, the Pharisees actually requested help of Demetrius III, the Syrian ruler. Jannaeus, however, emerged victorious and organized a celebration during which eight hundred of his captives were crucified while their wives and children were slaughtered before their eyes.

Things were somewhat improved under Salome Alexandra, wife of Jannaeus, who took control of the government after his death. Her son Hyrcanus II served as High Priest. Alexandra favored the Pharisees, but civil strife continued as the Pharisees sought vengeance on their enemies, the Sadducees.

At the death of Salome Alexandra, a fresh contest broke out among rival claimants for the throne, backed by the rival parties. Salome's second son, Aristobulus II, with the help of the Sadducees, gained the throne, but his brother, Hyrcanus II, plotted a return to power. A man named Antipater, an Idumaean by birth, supported Hyrcanus. It is significant that Antipater arranged things so efficiently that his son Herod subsequently became king of Judaea.

During the civil war between Hyrcanus II and Aristobulus II, the Roman general Pompey appeared in the East. After conquering Syria he turned his attention to the problems in Judaea. He heard the rival claims of the two brothers. Suspicious of the motives of Aristobulus, Pompey ordered the siege of Jerusalem, and in 63 B.C. it fell to the Romans. Although the Hasmonaean dynasty continued in nominal control until 37 B.C., Roman power continued to be exerted in Palestine until the end of Biblical history.

The Roman Empire

Caspian Sea
(Mare Hyrcanium)

Caspian Sea
(Mare Hyrcanium)

Crassus killed by Parthians at Carrhae in 53 B.C.

Under Caesar the Jews enjoyed semi-independent rule with religious freedom and deferral from military service.

Red Sea (Sinus Arabicus)

Pompey was murdered at Alexandria in 48 B.C. Caesar defeated the Egyptians and placed Cleopatra on the throne in 47 B.C.

Caesar "came, saw and conquered" Pharnaces II at Zela in 47 B.C.

In 49 B.C. Caesar crossed the Rubicon, the boundary of his province of Cisalpine Gaul, precipitating civil war.

Caesar raided Britain in 55 and 54 B.C.

Caesar conquered Gaul in 58-51 B.C.

Caesar defeated Pompey at Pharsalus in 48 B.C.

THE ROMAN WORLD
IN THE TIME OF CAESAR
60 TO 44 B.C.

Copyright by C. S. HAMMOND & CO., N.Y.

Scale of Miles

0 100 200 400 600

Limits of Roman control at the death of Caesar-44 B.C. ———
Major battles fought by Caesar ..... ✕
Capitals ..... ⊹

The Roman Empire

Like the other great empires of antiquity, Rome was the extension of the rule of a city-state. Unlike its predecessors, however, the Roman Empire was not the creation of a single gifted leader—a Cyrus or an Alexander—but of a self-governing people whose periods of conquest span many centuries.

THE ROMAN EMPIRE IS FOUNDED

During the eighth century before Christ a people known as the Etruscans took the fortified elevation of the Palatine Hill near the midpoint of the west coast of the Italian peninsula. They soon amalgamated the tiny hamlets about the Palatine into the city of Rome—the city of seven hills. Tradition states that Rome was founded by Romulus and Remus in 753 B.C.

In subsequent years the Romans slowly gained control of the Italian peninsula. A powerful Greek state at the southeastern sector of the peninsula (the "heel" of the Italian "boot") temporarily defeated the Romans (280 B.C.) but the Tarentines fell before the Romans five years later. From southern Italy it was a short step to Sicily where Roman interests clashed with those of Carthage, the north African city-state founded by Phoenicians from Tyre. The First Punic (i.e. Phoenician) War began at Messana, opposite the "toe" of the Italian "boot" in 264 B.C. The war brought disaster to Carthage but brought Roman power beyond the Italian peninsula for the first time. Sardinia and Corsica as well as Sicily became subject to Rome.

THE ROMAN EMPIRE EXPANDS

By 220 B.C. both the Romans and the Carthaginians were seeking additional territory. Rome had expanded north of the Po Valley and the Carthaginians were making inroads into Spain. When the Carthaginian general Hannibal attacked Saguntum on the east coast of Spain, Rome intervened and the Second Punic War began. For a time it looked as though the forces of Hannibal were going to reach Rome itself. With his famed battle elephants, Hannibal crossed the Alps (218 B.C.) and marched down the Po Valley. The tide of battle turned, however. The brilliant young Roman general, Scipio, took the initiative and Hannibal was forced to retreat. At Zama, southwest of Carthage, the Carthaginians suffered a defeat which ended their threat to the growth of Rome (202 B.C.).

With the close of the Second Punic War, Rome was the uncontested ruler of the western Mediterranean. Next she turned eastward and gradually absorbed most of the territory which had been a part of Alexander's empire. Roman power was established in Macedonia with the defeat of its king at Cynoscephalae (197 B.C.). In 192 B.C. the Romans repelled an invasion of Greece by Antiochus III, Seleucid ruler of Syria. Following a series of revolts against Roman power (149-146 B.C.), Macedonia was organized as a Roman province and the territory around Carthage became the Roman province of Africa. A large province in Asia Minor became Roman as a result of the bequest of Attalus I, king of Pergamum. In 129 B.C. it was organized as the province of Asia. The king of Bythinia also willed his kingdom to the Romans (75 B.C.) but in order to claim it they had to fight a war with a rival claimant, Mithradates, king of Pontus. The Roman general, Pompey, defeated Mithradates and Bithynia became a Roman province. The other states of Asia Minor were made vassals to Rome. The remains of the once powerful Seleucid empire were annexed to Rome as the province of Syria.

Roman power was first felt in Judaea when Pompey intervened at the time of the dispute between rival heirs to the Hasmonaean throne, Aristobulus II and Hyrcanus II. In 63 B.C. Pompey captured Jerusalem, breaking down part of its wall. Aristobulus was thrown into chains and Hyrcanus restored to the office of High Priest. Antigonus, a son of Aristobulus, secured help from the Parthians, eastern rivals of Rome, and for a time (40-37 B.C.) occupied Jerusalem. With the recapture of the Holy City (37 B.C.) Roman power was established in Judaea with Herod the Great (37-4 B.C.) reigning as "King of the Jews."

While Pompey was exerting power in the east and adding to the power of Rome there, his bitter rival Julius Caesar was busy in the west. During the years 58-51 B.C. he conquered Gaul and immortalized his campaigns there in his annals which are still read—particularly by Latin students!

The Roman senate, under pressure from Pompey, removed Caesar from his army command. Caesar, however, marched his armies across the Rubicon,

the river which served as the boundary between his province and Italy, and within sixty days was in command of the whole of Italy.

A show-down battle was fought between the forces of Caesar and Pompey at Pharsalus in east central Greece. Pompey was defeated (48 B.C.) and fled to Egypt where he was promptly murdered. Caesar himself sailed for Egypt in pursuit of Pompey. After a narrow escape there, Caesar received assistance from an army from Syria in which Antipater, the father of Herod the Great, played a conspicuous part. Antipater had acted as the power behind Hyrcanus II, whom Pompey had appointed High Priest over Judaea. With the rise of Caesar to political power in the east, Antipater developed new loyalties for which he was amply rewarded.

The famous Cleopatra was Caesar's choice for the throne of Egypt. As heiress to the dynasty of the Ptolemies she had a legitimate claim to office. It was expected, of course, that she would be subservient to Rome. After the death of Caesar, Cleopatra became involved in the struggle for power between Octavian and Antony. At the Battle of Actium (31 B.C.) the forces of Antony and Cleopatra were crushed. Egypt became a Roman province and Octavian emerged as the first Roman emperor, Augustus Caesar.

ROME RULES THE WORLD

Before the death of Augustus (A.D. 14) the empire was vastly increased. Spain was wholly occupied and the Alpine provinces of Raetia, Noricum, Pannonia, Illyricum, and Moesia were incorporated into the Roman territories. In Asia Minor, Augustus took Galatia, Lycaonia, and Pisidia. The basins of the Rhine and the Danube formed the northern border of Roman influence in Europe. Augustus held the upper Euphrates and the edge of the Arabian desert as his natural frontiers with Parthia, which was never conquered.

The successors of Augustus continued his policy of expansion. Tiberius (A.D. 14-37) annexed Cappadocia in Asia Minor. Caligula (A.D. 37-41) added to his empire Mauretania (modern Morocco) in northern Africa opposite Spain. Under Claudius (A.D. 41-54), Thrace and Lycia were occupied by Rome and the empire was extended northward to include Britain. During the reigns of the Flavian emperors (A.D. 69-96) Roman civilization reached into southern Germany. Rome also claimed the territory southeast of the Black Sea known as Lesser Armenia and extended the Syrian frontier.

The empire reached its maximum extent under Trajan (A.D. 98-117). Dacia, north of Thrace, was incorporated into the empire, as was the portion of northern Arabia known as Arabia Petraea. Armenia and Mesopotamia were temporarily occupied, but Rome was unable to maintain these eastern territories.

Pisidia. Warlike tribes maintained their independence in the mountains of Pisidia, part of the Taurus range, until the country became a Roman province. Ruins of an ancient aqueduct appear in the background.
Courtesy, Kelsey Museum of Archaeology
The University of Michigan

THE ROMAN EMPIRE
DISINTEGRATES

Disintegration became apparent in Rome's far-flung empire after the second century. Gaul and Britain were separated from the imperial power during a portion of the third century, and Egypt and Syria were ruled from the rich caravan city-state of Palmyra, northeast of Damascus, before Aurelian (A.D. 270-275) restored Rome's shrinking prestige. The empire lasted in the west until A.D. 476 when it fell before invaders from the north. The eastern, or Byzantine Empire, continued, however, until the fall of Constantinople (A.D. 1453), considered by some historians to be the event which marks the end of the Middle Ages.

The Latin language, continuing in modified form in the so-called Romance languages, including Italian, French and Spanish; and Roman law, which is basic to all modern western systems of jurisprudence, are continuing Roman contributions to civilization. On the material side, the remains of Roman roads can still be seen throughout southern Europe and Britain. The unity of the empire, although for a time unfriendly to the Christian gospel, made possible the rapid spread of Christianity during the earliest period of church history.

Gerasa. Thirty-five miles southeast of the Sea of Galilee, this ancient Decapolis city (modern Jerash) demonstrates through its extensive Roman ruins, such as in this scene of the Street of the Columns, that it was a flourishing Roman city in the second and third centuries A.D. *Copyright, Levant Photo Service*

CHAPTER XX

New Testament Palestine

PALESTINE IN THE TIME OF CHRIST

Copyright by C. S. HAMMOND & CO., N. Y.

Scale of Miles

0   5   10   20   30   40

Perennial Rivers
Seasonal Rivers & Streams
Capitals
Roads & Trade Routes
Cities of the Decapolis

The Decapolis and Ascalon retained their independence under the Roman governor of the province of Syria.

The Great Sea

(Mediterranean Sea)

Archelaus, upon Herod's death, became ruler of Judaea, Samaria and Idumaea. His reign lasted until 6 A.D. when he was removed and exiled. His territory then was placed under a Roman procurator.

Salome, Herod's sister, was given Jamnia, Azotus and Phasaelis. They, in turn, passed to Livia, wife of Augustus and then to Emperor Tiberius.

ABILENE
Abila
Damascus

PHOENICIA
MOUNT LEBANON
Sidon
Sarepta (Zarephath)
Leontes R.
River Jordan
MT. HERMON
PANIAS
ITURAEA
Tyre
Dan · Caesarea Philippi
ULATHA
Lake Semechonitis
TRACHONITIS
Cadasa (Kedesh)
Ladder of Tyre
Gischala
Seleucia
GAULANITIS
BATANAEA
BASHAN
Raphana
Horns of Hattin (Kurûn Hattin) is a possible site of the Sermon on the Mount.
Chorazin · Bethsaida (Julias)
Ptolemais (Accho)
Jotapata
Cana
Magdala (Dalmanutha)
Capernaum
Tabigha
Gergesa
Gamala
Sepphoris
Horns of Hattin +
Sea of Galilee
Hippos
Dion
AURANITIS
GALILEE
Tiberias
Nazareth
Philoteria
Yarmuk R.
Abila
Edrei
Mt. Tabor
Plain of Esdraelon
Gadara
Capitolias
Dora
Nain
Bethabara
En-gannim (Ginaea)
Scythopolis (Beth-shan)
Pella
DECAPOLIS
Caesarea Residence of Roman procurators.
SAMARIA
Gerasa
Apollonia
Samaria (Sebaste)
Mt. Ebal
Shechem + Sychar
Mt. Gerizim + Jacob's Well
River Jordan
Jabbok R.
Antipatris
Amathus
PERAEA
Joppa
Arimathaea (Ramathaim)
Phasaelis
Philadelphia (Rabbath-ammon)
Lydda (Diospolis)
Gophna
Archelais
Beth-nimrah
Gezer (Gazara)
Bethel
Ephraim
Jamnia
Ramah
Jericho
Ekron
Emmaus
Mt. of Olives
Julias (Livias, Beth-haram)
Heshbon
Nicopolis (Emmaus)
Jerusalem
Bethany
Khirbet Qumran
The Dead Sea Scrolls were found in a cave here; also the ruins of an Essene monastery.
Azotus (Ashdod)
Bethlehem
Herodium
Ascalon
Callirhoe
Here John the Baptist was imprisoned and beheaded by order of Herod Antipas.
JUDAEA
Machaerus
Dibon
Mareshah (Marisa)
Hebron
Ziph
Gaza
Juttah
Carmel
En-gedi
Arnon R.
Gerar
Wilderness of Judah
IDUMAEA
Salt or Dead Sea (L. Asphaltitis)
Masada
Rabbath Moab (Areopolis, Rabba)
AMMON
Raphia
Beersheba
Kir-moab (Kir-haresheth)
MOAB
Zered R.
ARABIA
NABATAEANS

New Testament Palestine

The Romans were never successful in ruling Palestine. Their various attempts at finding a solution to the "Palestine problem" resulted not only in changes of personnel, but also in the titles they bore and the division of the land itself.

THE PROVINCES

The Jordan River has always formed a natural line for the divisions of Palestine.

West of the Jordan, from south to north, were three provinces:

Judaea. The territories once belonging to the tribes of Judah, Dan, Benjamin, and Simeon comprised Judaea—the largest of the Palestinian provinces. The area south of Hebron was known as Idumaea, a term reminiscent of the fact that the Edomites, hereditary enemies of the Jews, settled in that section between the sixth and fourth centuries B.C. The Philistine Plain and the Negeb, or "Southland," were known as Daroma, an Aramaic word meaning "the South."

Samaria. Between Judaea and the Carmel range was Samaria, a district politically annexed to Judaea in New Testament times. The section of Samaria bordering the Mediterranean was known as Saron (i.e. Sharon) and was occupied largely by gentiles. The mountain districts in the interior of the country were inhabited by a people of mixed race descended from the remnants of the ten northern tribes and from the non-

Israelites brought into the territory after the fall of Samaria (cf. II Kings 17). Following the return of the Jews from Babylonian exile, Samaritan and Jew clashed, and the two peoples became bitter rivals. A Samaritan temple was built on Mount Gerizim during the fourth century B.C. Although destroyed by the Maccabean prince, John Hyrcanus (*ca.* 128 B.C.), the site of the temple continued to be a Samaritan "holy place." The Samaritan woman (John 4) attempted to argue the proper place for acceptable worship with Jesus, but He focused attention on the nature of true worship. Prejudice was so great that many Jews chose to detour across the Jordan and travel through Peraea, rather than go through the land of the despised Samaritan, when making trips from Galilee to Judah. Jesus, however, insisted that the Samaritan was a potential neighbor and made a conspicuous place for the Samaritans in His ministry. A small number of them still live in and around the village of Nablus.

Galilee. At the time of Christ, Galilee extended southward from the highlands west of Lake Semechonitis (or Hula) to the ridges of Mount Carmel and Gilboa and westward from the Jordan Valley to Phoenicia. Its proximity to the non-Jewish world caused the orthodox to stigmatize it as "Galilee of the Gentiles." Once the territory of the tribe of Naphtali, it included a mixture of races during the Hellenistic Age. The province was naturally divided into two sectors. It included Lower Galilee, the territory south of Tiberias and Accho (or Ptolemaïs as it was called in New Testament times), with the Plain of Esdraelon and its offshoots reaching southward toward Samaria. Upper Galilee, on the other hand, is a mountainous region. The fertile plains of Lower Galilee produce an abundance of grain, but the mountains of Upper Galilee are noted for their olive groves. We know that Jews lived in Galilee during Maccabean times, for we read that Simon brought Jews from Galilee to Jerusalem (I Macc. 5:14-23). Under John Hyrcanus, Samaria was subjugated and the borders of the Jewish kingdom extended northward to Galilee. Jerusalem Jews tended to frown on the Galileans because of their peculiar dialect and their distance from the center of Jewish life. Galileans, however, were intensely loyal to the Jewish faith and nation. Eleven of the twelve disciples of Jesus were Galileans, and the greater part of our Lord's ministry was performed there. After the destruction of Jerusalem, Galilee became the center of Judaism in Palestine.

East of Jordan were two districts:

Peraea. The area east of the Jordan and the Dead Sea, extending northward from the Arnon to the town of Pella, was known as Peraea (the Greek equivalent of Transjordan, "the land beyond"). Peraea was about the size of the territory earlier occupied by the tribes of Reuben and Gad. During New Testament times it was largely occupied by Jews, although gentiles lived in a number of its villages.

Decapolis. The Decapolis was a region southeast of the Sea of Galilee, comprising ten Greek cities, nine east of the Jordan and one (Beth-shan) west. These cities were founded by followers of Alex-

ander the Great, and were re-established by Pompey (63 B.C.) who hoped to use them to establish Roman rule in Palestine. Pliny, the first writer to mention the Decapolis, lists the original ten cities as: Beth-shan (Scythopolis), Pella, Dion, Kanatha, Raphana, Hippos, Gadara, Philadelphia (Rabbath-ammon), Damascus, and Gerasa (Jarash). At times this Hellenistic league included as many as eighteen cities. Each city controlled the region immediately around it, but the exact extent of the control is not known. The ruins of Gerasa, a city which flourished during the second and third centuries A.D., indicate the high culture of the Decapolis league.

POLITICAL HISTORY
(40 B.C.-A.D. 70).

Kingdom of Herod the Great. The Herodian family was descended from an Idumaean governor named Antipater, or Antipas who is thought to have come from Ascalon in the country once controlled by Phoenicians. During the reign of John Hyrcanus, the Hasmonaean ruler of Judaea, Antipater and his family were forced to adopt the Jewish religion and accept the rite of circumcision. While Julius Caesar was gaining control of the Roman Empire, a son of Antipater, bearing the same name as his father, became virtual ruler of Palestine.

When, following Caesar's assassination, Cassius appeared as proconsul of Syria, Antipater was given the task of raising a large sum of money—about a million and a half dollars at present values—for Rome. Resentment against Antipater reached its climax when he was poisoned by Malichus, a man who posed as a friend of Antipater while planning to seize the government for himself.

About the time Antony and Octavian

Tiberias on the Sea of Galilee. Built by Herod Antipas (Antipater) on the southwestern shore of the Sea of Galilee, Tiberias was largely a gentile city until the fall of Jerusalem (A.D. 70). In subsequent years, however, it became a center of Talmudic study and a Jewish holy place. *Courtesy, Israel Government Tourist Office*

defeated Cassius on the plains of Philippi in Macedonia, a son of the Hasmonaean ruler Aristobulus II determined to wrest Judaea from the control of his uncle Hyrcanus II. The youth, named Antigonus, enlisted the aid of the Parthians, a warlike people who had never been conquered by Rome. Jerusalem was occupied by the Parthians. Of the sons of Antipater, Phasael was captured and, at length, committed suicide, and Herod escaped to Egypt, and then to Rome (40 B.C.).

In Rome, Herod, a son of Antipater, was able to impress Antony and Octavian so that they named him king of the Jews. Herod, however, had to fight for his kingdom. Although he found many sympathizers when he returned to Judaea, it was only with the aid of Roman arms that he was able to occupy Jerusalem, which had been beseiged for five months before it fell.

Herod attempted to win the favor of the Jews by publicly observing the Law. He made every effort to build and adorn his realm. Strato's Tower, on the Mediterranean, was rebuilt as a port city and named Caesarea in honor of Octavian (Augustus) to whom Herod gave his support after the Battle of Actium. Samaria was rebuilt as Sebaste, named after the wife of Augustus.

The Temple which was in Jerusalem during the time of Christ was begun about 20 B.C. by Herod who doubtless wished to give his subjects a Temple comparable with those being erected to the gods of other peoples all over Palestine. Out of deference to the Mosaic Law, Herod placed no statues in the Jerusalem Temple.

Herod attempted to win the favor of the Jews by publicly observing the Jewish law, and by the rebuilding on a grand scale of the Temple begun by the Jews who returned from Babylon under Zerubbabel. The Jews were not appreciative of his labors, however. His personal cruelties outweighed his religious acts, and his Idumaean blood rendered him suspect in any case.

In his latter years Herod appears to have been insane. Domestic troubles plagued him. He murdered Mariamne, the favorite of his ten wives, her grandfather Hyrcanus, her brother Aristobulus, and several of his own children. This accords with the Biblical description of Herod who, when he heard the report of the birth of one who was to be a "King of the Jews," ordered the massacre of the infants in Bethlehem and its environs (Matt. 2:16).

Although history calls Herod "the Great," he knew that his death would bring rejoicing among the Jews. He actually ordered that the leaders of the Jews

be executed at the time of his death that there might be mourning throughout the land. Happily this murderous project was not carried out, and we suspect that there were few to weep at the death of the tyrant.

The Tetrarchy (4 B.C.-A.D. 41). After Herod's death, his kingdom was divided among rulers known as Tetrarchs (a term which originally signified "ruler of a fourth part"). Archelaus became Tetrarch of Judaea and Samaria, ruling Palestine south of the Valley of Esdraelon. Herod Antipas, or "Herod the Tetrarch" who ordered the death of John the Baptist, was ruler of Galilee and Peraea. When Herod Antipas rejected his wife, a daughter of a Nabataean king, Aretas, to marry Herodias, wife of his brother, Philip, many pious Jews were infuriated. Although his reign spanned the time of Jesus' ministry, he was finally banished by Caligula (A.D. 39). Philip was assigned a district east of the Sea of Galilee including Batanaea, Trachonitis, Auranitis, Gaulanitis, and parts of Panias. This was non-Jewish territory which Philip succeeded in Romanizing. He erected a marble temple in honor of Augustus on the majestic rocks above the older city of Panias, which he rebuilt as Caesarea—or, to distinguish it from the coastal city of the same name, Caesarea Philippi. Bethsaida-Julias at the head of the Sea of Galilee was also rebuilt by Philip and named in honor of the daughter of Augustus. Philip had a peaceful rule of thirty-seven years and is reputed to have been the best of the sons of Herod the Great. Lysanius ruled the small district of Abilene (Luke 3:1), between Baalbek, on the north side of Mount Hermon, and Damascus. This area had not been in Herod's kingdom.

When Archelaus was deposed (A.D. 6), Judaea and Samaria were annexed to the Empire and governed by a series

The Treasury at Petra. This imposing structure, with its front carved in the red sandstone side of the valley, is over ninety feet high. It is dated in the second century A.D. or earlier, and is popularly called the "Treasury of Pharaoh." It actually served as a royal tomb, and is the best preserved monument of the Nabataean Arabs.   *Courtesy, Jordan Tourist Department*

of procurators. At the time of the crucifixion of Christ, the fifth procurator, Pontius Pilate, was in office. The procurators were never able to reconcile their Jewish constituents to Roman rule, and the Jews were restive until the time of the revolt which brought on the destruction of Jerusalem (A.D. 70).

Kingdom of Herod Agrippa I (A.D. 41-44). The Roman Emperor Caligula befriended Herod Agrippa and made him king over the territory east of Galilee which had earlier been the domain of his uncle, Philip, and of the territory west of Damascus known as Abilene. At the accession of Claudius, Agrippa was also given rule over southern Syria and Palestine—a territory including practically all of the kingdom of his grandfather, Herod the Great. Agrippa espoused the cause of the Pharisees, and Josephus speaks of his zeal for Jewish religion. To win favor with the Jews he persecuted the church, causing James the apostle to be slain and Peter to be imprisoned. Josephus tells us that Herod Agrippa was seized by severe pains during a celebration at Caesarea, when he was being acclaimed a god. Five days later he died (cf. Acts 12:20-23).

The Provinces Divided (A.D. 44-70). When Herod Agrippa died, his son, Herod Agrippa II, was a youth of seventeen. The Emperor Claudius divided the kingdom. The southern section, Judaea, Samaria, Galilee, and Peraea, became the province of Judaea, which was subsequently ruled by Roman procurators with headquarters at Caesarea. The northern section east of the Jordan, territory earlier ruled by Philip and Lysanius, was later assigned to Herod Agrippa II (A.D. 49). To this Herod, "expert in all customs and questions which are among the Jews," Paul was brought by Festus (Acts 25:13—26:32).

Failing in his attempt to dissuade his subjects from revolt (A.D. 60), Herod Agrippa II sided with the Romans and fought alongside Vespasian. After the fall of Jerusalem (A.D. 70) he went to Rome where he died (ca. A.D. 100), holding the rank of praetor.

The Nabataean Kingdom. During New Testament times an energetic people of Arab background known as the Nabataeans ruled a kingdom including southern Palestine (the Negeb), most of Transjordan, and northern Arabia. Under their greatest king, Aretas IV (9 B.C.-A.D. 40), Nabataean power reached as far as Damascus (cf. II Cor. 11:32).

The Nabataean city of Petra (Sela), south of the Dead Sea (*see* Map 3), with buildings cut out of red sandstone high in the mountainous district of Edom, was located on one of the important trade routes of antiquity. Here could be seen caravans bound, ultimately, for Greece and Rome.

Irrigation projects enabled the Nabataeans to maintain settlements in the barren Negeb. Huge cisterns were built, along with dams, aqueducts, and water channels. The hills were terraced to keep the earth from being swept away. Thus every drop of water was conserved and otherwise barren territory was rendered prosperous. The Israeli people are currently attempting to use similar principles in reclaiming the southern part of their country. In some cases old Nabataean constructions are being repaired and used.

The Nabataean era came to an end in A.D. 105 when the Roman emperor, Trajan, occupied their land and made it a Roman province—Arabia Petraea.

Petra. The *ed-Deir* (the Monastery) is another example of buildings carved out of sandstone rock at Petra. The strength of this fortress city in ancient times was secured by access restricted to one narrow gorge, known as the "Siq."   *Copyright, Levant Photo Service*

CHAPTER XXI

The Life of Christ

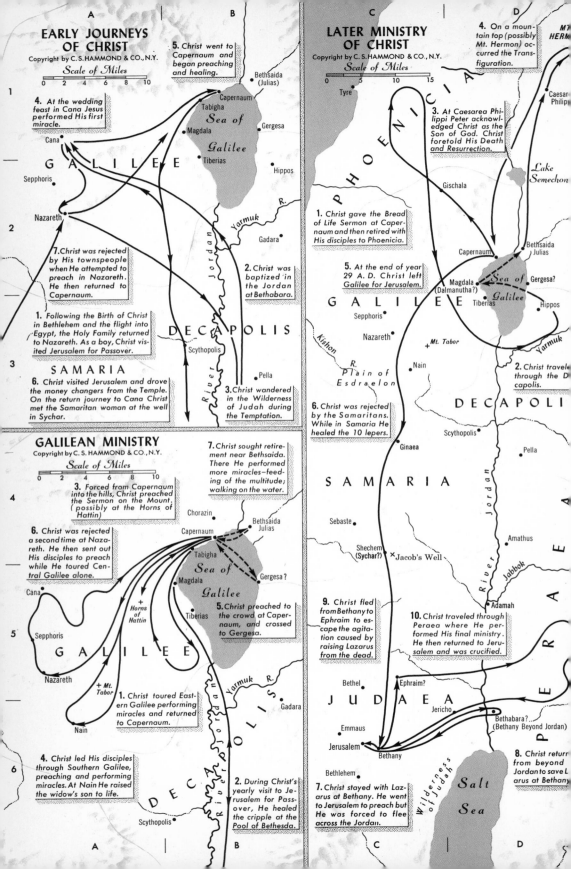

EARLY JOURNEYS OF CHRIST

Copyright by C. S. HAMMOND & CO., N.Y.

Scale of Miles
0 2 4 6 8 10

4. At the wedding feast in Cana Jesus performed His first miracle.

5. Christ went to Capernaum and began preaching and healing.

7. Christ was rejected by His townspeople when He attempted to preach in Nazareth. He then returned to Capernaum.

1. Following the Birth of Christ in Bethlehem and the flight into Egypt, the Holy Family returned to Nazareth. As a boy, Christ visited Jerusalem for Passover.

6. Christ visited Jerusalem and drove the money changers from the Temple. On the return journey to Cana Christ met the Samaritan woman at the well in Sychar.

2. Christ was baptized in the Jordan at Bethabara.

3. Christ wandered in the Wilderness of Judah during the Temptation.

GALILEE
SAMARIA
DECAPOLIS

Sephoris • Cana • Nazareth
Capernaum • Tabigha • Magdala • Tiberias
Bethsaida (Julias) • Gergesa • Hippos
Sea of Galilee
Gadara
Scythopolis • Pella
Jordan River • Yarmuk R.

LATER MINISTRY OF CHRIST

Copyright by C. S. HAMMOND & CO., N.Y.

Scale of Miles
0 5 10 15

4. On a mountain top (possibly Mt. Hermon) occurred the Transfiguration.

3. At Caesarea Philippi Peter acknowledged Christ as the Son of God. Christ foretold His Death and Resurrection.

1. Christ gave the Bread of Life Sermon at Capernaum and then retired with His disciples to Phoenicia.

5. At the end of year 29 A.D. Christ left Galilee for Jerusalem.

6. Christ was rejected by the Samaritans. While in Samaria He healed the 10 lepers.

2. Christ traveled through the Decapolis.

9. Christ fled from Bethany to Ephraim to escape the agitation caused by raising Lazarus from the dead.

10. Christ traveled through Peraea where He performed His final ministry. He then returned to Jerusalem and was crucified.

7. Christ stayed with Lazarus at Bethany. He went to Jerusalem to preach but He was forced to flee across the Jordan.

8. Christ returned from beyond Jordan to save Lazarus at Bethany.

PHOENICIA
GALILEE
DECAPOLIS
SAMARIA
JUDAEA
PERAEA

Tyre • Caesarea Philippi
Lake Semechon
Gischala
Capernaum • Bethsaida Julias • Gergesa?
Magdala (Dalmanutha?) • Sea of Galilee • Hippos
Tiberias • Yarmuk
Sephoris • Nazareth • Mt. Tabor • Nain
Kishon R. • Plain of Esdraelon
Ginaea
Sebaste
Shechem (Sychar?) × Jacob's Well • Amathus
Scythopolis • Pella • Adamah
River Jordan • Jabbok R.
Bethel • Ephraim?
Emmaus • Jerusalem • Bethany • Jericho • Bethabara? (Bethany Beyond Jordan)
Bethlehem • Wilderness of Judah • Salt Sea

GALILEAN MINISTRY

Copyright by C. S. HAMMOND & CO., N.Y.

Scale of Miles
0 2 4 6 8 10

3. Forced from Capernaum into the hills, Christ preached the Sermon on the Mount. (possibly at the Horns of Hattin)

7. Christ sought retirement near Bethsaida. There He performed more miracles—feeding of the multitude; walking on the water.

6. Christ was rejected a second time at Nazareth. He then sent out His disciples to preach while He toured Central Galilee alone.

5. Christ preached to the crowd at Capernaum, and crossed to Gergesa.

1. Christ toured Eastern Galilee performing miracles and returned to Capernaum.

4. Christ led His disciples through Southern Galilee, preaching and performing miracles. At Nain He raised the widow's son to life.

2. During Christ's yearly visit to Jerusalem for Passover, He healed the cripple at the Pool of Bethesda.

GALILEE
DECAPOLIS

Cana • Sephoris • Nazareth • Nain
Horns of Hattin • Mt. Tabor
Chorazin • Capernaum • Tabigha • Bethsaida Julias
Magdala • Tiberias • Sea of Galilee • Gergesa?
Gadara • Scythopolis
River Jordan • Yarmuk R.

Use Map 11

The Life of Christ

The four Gospels comprise our primary source material for the study of the life of Christ. Other collections of sayings of Jesus, including the Gnostic "gospels" discovered in Egypt, while suggestive of early ideas about Jesus, give us no help in the attempt to outline the ministry of our Lord. The Gospels themselves were not written as books of history, but as extracts from the ministry of Jesus designed to impart faith (cf. John 20:30-31). As such they frequently perplex the modern historical student who is concerned with details of chronology and geography. We shall attempt to follow the broad outlines suggested by the Gospel narratives, recognizing that there are many gaps in our knowledge.

BIRTH TO BAPTISM

The canonical Gospels give few details concerning the infancy and boyhood of Jesus. With the exception of the journey to Jerusalem at the age of twelve, we possess no records of the life of Jesus from his infancy until the beginning of his public ministry. The infancy narrative, however, is quite detailed.

Bethlehem. Five miles south of Jerusalem, on a limestone ridge along the main highway to Hebron and Egypt, is Bethlehem. Centuries before the birth of Jesus, Ruth the Moabitess came with her mother-in-law to Bethlehem. Here David, the son of Jesse, tended his fa-

ther's flocks and was anointed by Samuel to reign over Israel. The second chapter of Matthew records the birth of Jesus at Bethlehem and the subsequent arrival there of Wise Men from the East. It tells of the departure of the Holy Family from Bethlehem when they learned of Herod's threat to the infant's life. Luke relates the account of the birth of Jesus in a manger at Bethlehem. On the nearby hillside angels proclaimed the tidings of the birth of the "King of the Jews" to shepherds who were tending their flocks.

Jerusalem. When but forty days old, the infant Jesus was taken to Jerusalem to be solemnly presented to the Lord in the Temple. There the aged Simeon and Anna recognized Him as the promised Messiah (Luke 2:22-38). Although most of Jesus' life was centered in Galilee, it was outside the wall of Jerusalem that He was crucified, and His ascension took place from the Mount of Olives, east of the city.

Egypt. Because of the insane jealousy of Herod the Great (37-4 B.C.) the infant Jesus was taken by Mary and Joseph to Egypt for protection. Since Herod's jurisdiction did not extend beyond the borders of Judaea, he could not harm the child there. When Mary and Joseph received word that Herod had died, they took Jesus to Nazareth in Galilee.

Nazareth. Nazareth had been the early home of Mary and Joseph. It was an

Road from Nazareth. The valley in which Nazareth is located is in one of the southernmost slopes of the Lebanon Mountains. South of Nazareth the ridge drops to the Plain of Esdraelon. The road winding down the mountain may be seen at the right of the picture.   *Courtesy, Israel Office of Information*

obscure town, not being so much as mentioned in the Old Testament, the writings of Josephus, or the Talmud. "Can any good thing come out of Nazareth?" (John 1:46) expressed the popular contempt for this small Galilean village. Yet, within walking distance of Nazareth many of the great events of Old Testament history took place. From the nearby mountains, a keen eye can observe the countryside for a distance of thirty miles. To the east the mountains of Gilead can be seen across the Jordan Valley. Southward lies the Plain of Esdraelon with Mount Tabor and Mount Gilboa and the mounds of Bethshan and Megiddo in the distance. To the west the Carmel Ridge may be seen as it approaches the Mediterranean.

Although nestled on a mountain slope, Nazareth was not isolated from the military and commercial life of the day. Nearby highways ran east to the fords of the Jordan and the region known as Decapolis; south to Samaria, Jerusalem, and Egypt; west to Ptolemaïs (O.T. Accho) and the Mediterranean; and north to Damascus.

From Nazareth Jesus was taken to Jerusalem, a journey of eighty miles by the most direct route, at the age of twelve. During the remainder of the "silent years" in Nazareth we presume he attended the local synagogue, learned the carpenters' trade and did those things which accord with the evangelist's statement: "Jesus increased in wisdom and stature, and in favor with God and man" (Luke 2:52).

Jesus declared that a prophet was not without honor save in his own country. On the occasion of his baptism, He left Nazareth (Mark 1:9), but returned again a short time after the Temptation. Subsequently, however, the opposition and murderous intent of its citizens caused Jesus to leave the town and settle in Capernaum (Matt. 4:12-13). There is no evidence that He ever returned to Nazareth.

Bethabara ("house of crossing") was the place on the east bank of the Jordan where John was baptizing. Some ancient versions call it "Bethany beyond the Jordan." The exact location is not known. Here Jesus was baptized by John and received from heaven the testimony to His Sonship.

The Wilderness of Judah. For a period of forty days, Jesus was tempted by Satan in the Judaean Wilderness. This is the region of rugged gorges and bad lands in the eastern part of Judah where the land slopes off toward the Jordan Valley. In ancient times this area was infested with wild animals. Except for a brief time during the spring rains the wilderness is arid.

GALILEAN MINISTRY

All of the disciples of Jesus except Judas Iscariot were Galileans and much of the teaching and ministry of Jesus took place there. Important places of ministry in Galilee include:

Cana. The first two miracles were performed in the village of Cana. Here Jesus changed the water into wine at a wedding feast (John 2:1-11) and healed, at a distance, the son of a nobleman from Capernaum (John 4:46-54). Bartholomew, otherwise called Nathaniel, a disciple of Jesus, was from Cana (John 21:2).

Two sites vie for the distinction of being the Biblical Cana. *Kefr Kennā*, the Cana of ecclesiastical tradition, is

Synagogue at Capernaum. The synagogue is thought to have been built during the third century A.D. but it may stand on the site of the Capernaum synagogue in which Jesus ministered. The steps lead to entrances on the south. The colonnade of pillars supported a balcony for women which went around the west, north, and east sides. The balcony was entered by an outside stairway from the north.

Courtesy, Israel Office of Information

near Nazareth on the road to Tiberias and the Sea of Galilee. Farther to the north is the site of *Khirbet Qâna*, near Jotapata, a fortress of the Jews where, a generation later, Josephus was taken prisoner by the Romans. *Khirbet Qâna* awaits excavation. It is, however, the probable site of New Testament Cana.

Capernaum. On the northwest shore of the Sea of Galilee was *Kefr-Nahum*, "the town of Nahum" or Capernaum. Its site has been identified with *Tell Hûm*, an excavated mound located between Bethsaida and Tabigha, about two and one-half miles southwest of the point where the Jordan enters the Sea of Galilee.

Capernaum was evidently a Roman military post along the highway which went through Galilee en route from Damascus to Jerusalem. It was from a tax-collector's booth along this road that Matthew was called to discipleship (Matt. 9:9). Peter's house (Mark 9:35) probably served as headquarters for Jesus at Capernaum. Although He was "brought up" in Nazareth, Capernaum was emphatically "his own city" (Matt. 9:1). Here Jesus performed many miracles and preached to the multitudes. In the synagogue He proclaimed Himself the bread of life (John 6:48). Periodically Jesus found it necessary to leave Capernaum and find a place of retirement on the other side of the lake (Matt. 8:18).

Excavated ruins of Capernaum include a white limestone synagogue dating from the third century A.D. This

Jacob's Well. The well near which Jesus met the Samaritan woman (John 4:6) is located near Sychar, on the eastern slope of Mount Ebal.
Copyright, Matson Photo Service

The Village of Sychar. Mount Gerizim appears in the background.
Copyright, Levant Photo Service

structure, while assuredly later than the ministry of Christ, may have been built on the site of the structure in which Jesus ministered. It is located near the northern shore of the Sea of Galilee in a picturesque setting surrounded by palm trees.

Sychar. From Capernaum Jesus went to Jerusalem, probably by way of the Jordan Valley, to attend the Passover (John 2:13). On the return journey He paused at Sychar in Samaria "near the parcel of ground that Jacob gave to his son Joseph" (John 4:5). Sychar may be the modern *'Askar,* a short distance southeast of Shechem. Mount Ebal rises behind the village. About one-half mile south of *'Askar* on a slope of Mount Gerizim along the road from Beth-shan to Jerusalem is the traditional well of Jacob. The ancient stone well curb is seven and one-half feet in diameter with a shaft which is eighty-five feet deep today, although it is believed to have been deeper in antiquity. The "well" is actually a cistern from which accumulated rainfall is dispensed. This gives point to the words of Jesus, "the water that I shall give him will become in him a spring of living water, welling up to eternal life" (John 4:14).

"Horns of Hattin." During His ministry in Galilee, Jesus delivered the familiar Sermon on the Mount. Tradition places the scene of Jesus' ministry at the Horns of Hattin, a twin-peaked elevation overlooking the Sea of Galilee and the plain of Genesareth. From Hattin a magnificent panorama extends northward as far as Mount Hermon. Tiberias and the Sea of Galilee can be seen toward the east. Erich Kiel has suggested the area near Tabigha and Capernaum as a probable site for the Sermon on the Mount. The exact location, of

course, must remain a matter of conjecture.

Nain. After a time of preaching in Lower Galilee, Jesus came to Nain, where He raised a widow's only son to life (Luke 7:11-16). Nain, modern *Nein,* is a small village on the northern slope of "the hill of Moreh," or "Little Hermon," a hillock about 1,690 feet high overlooking the Valley of Esdraelon, six miles southeast of Nazareth.

Gergesa, Gadara, Gerasa. After preaching at Capernaum, Jesus crossed the Sea of Galilee to a place named Gergesa (see Matt. 8:28, A.V.) or Gadara (Mark 5:1-17; Luke 8:26-37 A.V.). Gergesa may be modern *Kursī,* on the eastern shore of the Sea of Galilee. Gadara was a city of the Decapolis southeast of the Sea of Galilee, now known as *Muqeis,* or *Umm Qeis.* Some scholars, on the basis of the study of ancient Greek texts, read "Gerasenes" as the name of the people among whom Jesus healed the demoniac. It is agreed, however, that this does not refer to Gerasa, Semitic *Jarash,* the impressive Decapolis city thirty-seven miles southeast of the Sea of Galilee. The reading "Gerasenes" occurs, however, in the best ancient manuscripts of Mark and Luke. Matthew 8 reads "Gadarenes" in the best texts. Scholars have spent much time discussing the textual and geographical phenomena but no certain conclusions have been reached. There is a steep cliff at *Kursī* such as is presupposed in the Gospel narrative; however, no tombs are there.

Bethsaida. After further ministry in central Galilee we read of Jesus' retirement to Bethsaida ("House of Fishers"). On the northern shore of the Sea of Galilee. Philip the Tetrarch rebuilt an older Bethsaida and named it Julias in honor of the daughter of his emperor, Augustus. The full name of the city appears as Bethsaida-Julias. The mound *et Tell*, thought to contain the remains of Bethsaida-Julias, is nearly a mile north of the shore. Kraeling suggests that the fishing village known as Bethsaida remained distinct from Julias, and was on the shore of the lake. Others, however, believe that a second Bethsaida, located at Tabigha on the western shore of the Sea of Galilee, was the Bethsaida of the gospel records. It is argued that several communities may have borne the name "House of Fishing" in view of the importance of the fishing industry on the Sea of Galilee. Peter, Andrew, and Philip made their home at Bethsaida (John 1:44; 12:21). Here Jesus healed a blind man brought to Him by sympathetic friends (Mark 8:22-26). In a barren region outside the town, Jesus miraculously fed the Five Thousand who had listened to His preaching (Matt. 14:13-21).

LATER MINISTRY

Jesus spent some time instructing His disciples, after which He engaged in a wider ministry.

Phoenicia. On a journey which took Him to the borders of the ancient Phoenician cities of Tyre and Sidon, Jesus restored to health the demoniac daughter of a "Syro-Phoenician" woman. Matthew (15:22) calls her "a woman of Canaan," an appropriate description because the Phoenicians were descendants of the ancient Canaanites. Although Jesus' ministry was directed primarily to "the lost sheep of the house of Israel," the faith of this gentile woman was honored and contrasted with the faithlessness of Israel.

Decapolis. During our Lord's first ministry in Galilee He was attended by crowds from all over Palestine. Some had come from the Decapolis region (Matt.

4:25) to hear Him. The maniac who was cured by Jesus subsequently spread the good news throughout the region of Decapolis. We read that, as part of His later ministry, Jesus journeyed "through the midst of the coasts of Decapolis" (Mark 7:31). There were many Jews in this region. The Scriptures, however, do not hint that Jesus ever went to the great Hellenistic cities of the Decapolis district.

Caesarea Philippi. The site of Caesarea Philippi, at the base of Mount Hermon, northeast of the Sea of Galilee, had long been associated with the Canaanite fertility cult. From a nearby cave there flowed a spring which became one of the principal sources of the Jordan River. The place had been named Panias, for it served as the favorite seat of Pan, a Greek fertility god. Philip, a son of Herod the Great, rebuilt Panias and named it Caesaraea Philippi in honor of his Caesar, Tiberius. Here Peter by divine revelation acknowledged Christ as the Son of God. Many New Testament scholars identify Caesaraea Philippi as the site of the transfiguration of Jesus.

Bethany ("House of Figs"). Jesus traveled southward through Samaria to Bethany, a suburb of Jerusalem. This town has been identified as *el-'Azarîyeh*, "Lazarus Village." It is located one and three-quarter miles from Jerusalem on the eastern slope of the Mount of Olives. In ancient times a footpath led over the Mount from Jerusalem to Bethany. There Jesus often visited the home of Mary and Martha. In a time of sorrow in the Bethany home, He exhibited His power by raising their brother Lazarus from the dead. While a guest of Simon, at Bethany, Jesus was anointed in anticipation of His burial, and from Bethany Jesus sent two of His disciples to find the ass on which He made His triumphal entry into Jerusalem. The traditional place of the ascension is within sight of Bethany.

Ephraim. To escape the agitation caused by the raising of Lazarus from the dead, Jesus withdrew with His disciples to Ephraim, a town on a steep hill about five miles northeast of Bethel. Its modern name is *et-Taiyibeh.* Jesus' sojourn in Ephraim probably lasted about two weeks, after which He made the fifteen mile journey back to Jerusalem.

Peraea. In returning to Jerusalem, Jesus traveled by way of Peraea, the province east of the Jordan, south and west of the Decapolis region. Here He performed His last acts before the final entrance into the Holy City.

Jerusalem. More details are given concerning Passion Week than any comparable period. Jesus made the Bethany home of Mary, Martha, and Lazarus His headquarters during the early part of the week. He journeyed to Jerusalem on Palm Sunday and on the two following days, each evening returning to Bethany. The traditional place of the last supper was the *Coenaculum,* or supper room, in the southwest sector of Jerusalem.

Gethsemane was the name of a garden across the Kidron Valley, east of the Temple area, at the foot of the Mount of Olives. There Jesus went with His disciples to agonize in prayer. The quiet of the hour was interrupted with the appearance of Judas and the arrest of Jesus.

Tradition has attempted to locate the place of the betrayal, trial, and crucifixion of Christ. In view of the fact that Jerusalem has been destroyed several times since our Lord walked its streets, no identification can be considered final.

Calvary was near a highway (Matt. 27:39) and "without the gate" (Heb. 13:12). The line of Jerusalem's north wall as it existed in New Testament times is not known, so an appraisal of existing evidence must at best be tentative. The site known as Gordon's Calvary, outside the present north wall, has appealed to many Protestants because of its quiet contrast to the seeming commercialism of the older "holy places." There is no evidence for its authenticity, however, beyond its apparent appropriateness. The identification was first suggested during the nineteenth century.

The present Church of the Holy Sepulchre represents a tradition of the site of the crucifixion which is traced to Helena, the mother of Constantine, who made a pilgrimage to the Holy Land, A.D. 326. However much Christians of later centuries wished to locate the scenes of the Passion narrative, the earliest believers had no such desire. For them it was enough to know that Christ was alive, and that He would return.

Even such a term as "Place of the Skull" defies definition. Three suggestions have been given. Some writers consider the site as one where actual skulls could be seen. Others mention ancient legends of the skulls of famous men located at Golgotha. According to one such legend, the skull of Adam was buried there. In some artistic representations of the crucifixion a skull can be seen at the foot of the cross. Those who consider Gordon's Calvary as the site of the crucifixion point to the rock formation which appears in the shape of a skull, as both the interpretation of the word Golgotha and the justification for their identification of it.

Although neither Calvary nor the empty tomb can be positively located, the Mount of Olives has been, of course, identified beyond dispute. From one of the summits of this mount the "men of Galilee" gazed heavenward, only to be reminded that their Lord would so come in like manner as they had seen Him go into heaven.

Early Apostolic History

Antioch-on-the-Orontes. Ancient Syrian Antioch is now known as Antakya, Turkey. The Orontes River (in the foreground) passes through the city.

Early Apostolic History

In its earliest history Christianity was closely related to Judaism. Christians were Jews who believed that Jesus of Nazareth 'was the promised Messiah. This belief was not, of course, merely a mental assent to academic propositions. It involved a personal commitment to One who had died and was raised from the dead. Early Christians were convinced that God, in the person of Jesus the Christ, had become man to redeem His people from sin. They looked for the consummation of history at the return of Christ, in the not distant future. As they awaited this return of their Lord, the primitive church remembered, in a lesser or greater degree, His command, "Occupy till I Come."

The outreach beyond the confines of Judaism was relatively slow. It took the martyrdom of Stephen and the subsequent dispersion of Christians to spur the church on to serious effort in its evangelistic witness. Only after a miraculous vision did Peter preach Christ to the Roman centurion, Cornelius.

SEVEN CITIES

The events of the apostolic period gather around seven cities:

Jerusalem. The crucifixion, resurrection, and ascension of Jesus took place in and near the Holy City. There Peter preached his Pentecost sermon and the early church developed a rudimentary organization.

Samaria (Acts 8:5-25). Samaria, thirty miles north of Jerusalem, was the field of Philip's early ministry. Once the capital of Israel, the city of Samaria had been rebuilt by Herod the Great and renamed Sebaste, in honor of Augustus Caesar. The present-day village of *Sebastiyeh* still bears its ancient name.

Caesarea (Acts 10). The conversion of Cornelius, a gentile centurion at Caesarea, was an important moment in the missionary outreach of the Church. Caesarea was the Roman capital of Palestine and the residence of the procurators. Located along the Mediterranean, twenty-three miles south of Mount Carmel and sixty-four miles northwest of Jerusalem, Caesarea was built on the site of Strato's Tower by Herod the Great and named in honor of Caesar Augustus. It was sometimes called Caesarea Stratonis to distinguish it from Caesarea Philippi near Mount Hermon.

In antiquity Caesarea had a wonderful artificial harbor which is now in ruins. A modern Jewish colony on the Plain of Sharon is located nearby and bears the name of its ancient counterpart, *Keisâriyeh.*

Joppa. Thirty miles south of Caesarea and thirty-four miles northwest of Jerusalem is the city of Joppa, or Jaffa, as it is now called. Here Dorcas was raised to life (Acts 9:36-43) and Peter received his vision (Acts 10:11). In Old Testament times Joppa had the only harbor between Mount Carmel and Egypt. Today it is contiguous with Tel Aviv, the largest city in the state of Israel.

Damascus. The conversion of Saul of Tarsus took place while he was on the road to Damascus, reputed to be the oldest continually occupied city in the world. Located east of snow-capped Mount Hermon, Damascus is a garden spot of beauty and fertility. Caravans from East and West stopped at Damascus, the city which reminded Mohammed of paradise. Once the center of an Aramaean kingdom, modern Damascus is the chief city of Syria, and one of the capitals of the United Arab Republic.

Antioch. Syrian Antioch was about twenty miles from the Mediterranean at the point where the Orontes River turns abruptly to the west. It is located in the fertile plain which separates the Lebanons from the Taurus Mountains. Seleucus I founded the city about 300 B.C. as one of sixteen Antiochs built in honor of his father. The quarter known as the New City was built by Antiochus III (223-187 B.C.). Under the Romans it was beautified and made the capital of the province of Syria. Antioch was the third largest city in the Roman Empire and served as a melting pot between East and West. Its lighted streets and beautiful buildings made it the "Queen of the East." At Antioch, culture and degradation went hand in hand. It was a mission field as well as a center from which the Christian gospel could be carried to more remote regions.

Tarsus. The city of Tarsus was the capital of Cilicia in southern Asia Minor. It was situated on the Cydnus River, ten miles from the Mediterranean and thirty miles south of the Taurus Mountains. Ancient trade routes from the Euphrates Valley to Asia Minor passed through Tarsus before going through the "Cilician Gates"—one of the most important mountain passes of the ancient world. East and West met at Tarsus and both influences had important bearing on the life of its most illustrious son, Paul.

The Tarsians had, according to the historian Strabo, an enthusiasm for education and philosophy which surpassed that of the Athenians and the Alexandrians. The University of Tarsus was largely attended by Cilician students and was supported by the state. This cosmopolitan atmosphere, coupled with orthodox Jewish piety, formed the background for the life of the famous "apostle to the gentiles."

FIVE JOURNEYS

During the early history of the church we read of five journeys:

Philip's Journey (Acts 8:5-40). One of the seven "deacons" (Acts 6:3-5), Philip left Jerusalem for Samaria a short time after the martyrdom of Stephen. The preaching of the gospel in Samaria was the first step in the outreach of the gospel to the ends of the earth. Traditionally the Jews had no dealings with the Samaritans, yet Jesus had ministered there and included Samaria in the missionary program of His church. From Samaria, Philip went southward "unto the way that goeth down from Jerusalem to Gaza, which is desert" (Acts 8:26). There he met a nobleman from Ethiopia whom he instructed in the gospel and baptized as a believer. Philip next appeared in Azotus (Old Testament Ashdod) in the Philistine Plain. The diversified ministry of Philip at Samaria, to an Ethiopian, and among the essentially gentile Philistine cities, gave evidence of a concern for men beyond the confines of Judaism, which was rare in the church of his day.

Harbor of Caesarea. Built by Herod the Great and named in honor of Caesar Augustus, Caesarea was the seat of government for the Roman procurator during New Testament times. Here Peter preached to a gentile centurion and Paul spent two years in jail. From the harbor of Caesarea, Paul sailed for Rome. *Courtesy, Israel Office of Information*

Paul's Journey (Acts 9:1-30). Saul of Tarsus was an orthodox Pharisee who looked upon Christians as enemies of his ancestral faith. Desirous of stamping out Christianity, he went to Damascus in order to bring back followers of Jesus for trial before the Jewish authorities. On the road to Damascus, however, Saul had an experience which changed the entire direction of his life. He met the risen Christ and entered the city convinced that Israel's Messiah had come.

After a brief stay in Damascus, Saul, whose name later became Paul, spent some time in Arabia. The term "Arabia" can be used of any part of the vast peninsula which bears that name, and it is probable that Paul's sojourn was in the desert bordering Syria, not far from Damascus (Gal. 1:17).

Back in Damascus, Paul met persecution for the first time. He escaped capture by being lowered over the city wall in a basket. Returning to Jerusalem, where he had earlier studied under Rabbi Gamaliel, Paul was welcomed by Barnabas who knew of his conversion, and introduced him to the apostles Peter and James.

When Paul's preaching at Jerusalem evoked further opposition, he was taken to the seaport city of Caesarea from which he sailed northward to Tarsus. There, in his home town, he spent several quiet years before beginning his missionary career.

Peter's Journey (Acts 9:32—11:18). Following the conversion of Paul, persecution of Christians temporarily subsided. Peter took the opportunity to visit and encourage the churches. At Lydda, a town in the Plain of Sharon on a direct route from Joppa to Jerusalem, he healed a palsied man, Aeneas. This act brought many to faith in Christ (Acts 9:32-35).

Peter was next summoned to Joppa, about eleven miles northwest of Lydda. Joppa was an old city with a history dating to the Egyptian conqueror Thutmose III (fifteenth century B.C.). It served as the port of Jerusalem in Old Testament times. During Peter's ministry there he healed Dorcas, a woman of "good works and almsdeeds" (Acts 9:36-42) and received a summons to bring the gospel to Cornelius at Caesarea.

A journey of thirty miles north from Joppa brought Peter to Caesarea, where he preached to Cornelius, a Roman centurion, who gave evidence of true Christian faith without having first undergone the rite of circumcision (Acts 10). When the leaders of the church at Jerusalem were suspicious of the conversion of gentiles, Peter returned to the city and argued from the experience of Cornelius that this was a work of God (Acts 11:1-18).

Barnabas' Journey (Acts 11:22-26). After the death of Stephen and the ensuing persecution, a number of disciples were driven from Jerusalem. They traveled northward past Tyre and Sidon to the cosmopolitan city of Antioch-on-the-Orontes. Faithful to their Christian convictions, they became the nucleus around which a new church was formed. Here, at Antioch, the disciples were first called Christians, and from this city the first missionaries were sent out as heralds of the gospel. The Jerusalem church, still suspicious of work not directly related to Jewish Christianity, appointed Barnabas to investigate the new converts. Barnabas, sensing the work of the Holy Spirit, gave his hearty endorsement to the Antioch church. He remained there for a time to help in the ministry, but soon realized the need for additional assistance. Remembering Paul, whose Hellenistic background at Tarsus would be of help in this Syrian city, Barnabas traveled northward to Cilicia and persuaded Paul to leave home and return with him to Antioch.

The Journey of Barnabas and Paul (Acts 11:26-30; 12:25). From Tarsus, Barnabas and Paul journeyed by sea southward to Seleucia, the port of Antioch, near the mouth of the Orontes River. A short trip up the Orontes brought them to Antioch, one of the great cities of the ancient world. There they worked for a year, helping to found a church which became a leading Christian center. In a time of famine in Judaea the church at Antioch sent Barnabas and Paul with a contribution for the impoverished disciples in Jerusalem. This mission was typical of the attitude of Christian love which characterized the early church and proved such a testimony to the heathen world. Returning to Antioch, the two evangelists labored there until they went on their first missionary journey, the first self-conscious effort to bring the gospel to those who had never heard the Christian message.

Journeys of the Apostle Paul

The Appian Way. The oldest of the famous Roman roads was begun in 312 B.C. and was extended southward to join Rome with Brundisium. Paul made use of the Appian Way on his historic journey to Rome.

Courtesy, Trans-World Airlines

Use Maps 14, 15, 16, and 17

Journeys of the Apostle Paul

Little is known concerning the later years of most of the apostles of Christ. Peter, to be sure, occupied an important place in the early chapters of Acts, and John was associated with him on at least one occasion (Acts 3:1). James was slain early in the apostolic age at the command of Herod (Acts 12:2). The central figure in most of the Book of the Acts was the great missionary, Paul, the "apostle to the gentiles." During his lifetime, Christianity assumed its true international complexion. When Paul began his ministry a gentile was an oddity in the church. Before his death the eastern part of the Roman Empire had in large measure heard the gospel message.

ASIA MINOR

Asia Minor was an important area at the time of Paul.

Paul's first missionary journey was largely confined to Asia Minor, a peninsula of about 156,000 square miles, about two-thirds the size of Texas. The Black, Aegean, and Mediterranean seas bound Asia Minor on the north, west, and south respectively. Armenia, Mesopotamia, and Syria shared its eastern (land) border.

The term "Asia" as used in the New Testament does not refer to the continent of that name or even to the whole of Asia Minor. Four districts of western Asia Minor—Caria, Lydia, Mysia, and Phrygia—were united as the Province of Asia. The provinces of Bithynia and Pontus were located on the southern shore of the Black Sea. Between them was the area known as Paphlagonia, watered by the Halys River. Politically the territory south of the Black Sea was united under the name Bithynia and Pontus. Similarly Lycaonia and Pisidia were considered a part of Galatia.

DISTRICTS ON THE BLACK SEA

Pontus (Acts 2:9; 18:2; I Peter 1:1). The province of Pontus takes its name from the *Pontus Euxinus*, or Black Sea. It was the northeastern province of Asia Minor located between Paphlagonia and Armenia, and bounded by Cappadocia on the south. A dynasty of kings named Mithridates ruled this rugged area from 337 B.C. to 63 B.C. Jews from Pontus were in Jerusalem on the Day of Pentecost. Aquila, a helper of Paul, had come from Pontus, and Peter addressed the Christians of this region, among others, in his first epistle.

Paphlagonia. Between Pontus and Bithynia, in the area north of Galatia, was the district of Paphlagonia. It is not mentioned in the New Testament, and was not a political unit during the apostolic age.

Bithynia (Acts 16:7; I Peter 1:1). Bounded by the Propontis (now known as the Sea of Marmara) on the west, and Paphlagonia on the east, the province of Bithynia occupied the northwestern sector of Asia Minor. Mysia and Phrygia form the southern border of this moun-

207

The Ruins at Ephesus. The apostle Paul ministered in Ephesus, the city of Asia Minor dedicated to the goddess Diana. Some of the ancient glory of Ephesus can be seen in its significant ruins.   *Courtesy H. Gokberg*

tainous, thickly wooded area. Bithynia is only incidentally named in the New Testament, although it played an important part in early church history. The letters of the Roman consul, Pliny, to his emperor, Trajan, express concern over the large number of Christians in his province (Pontus-Bithynia). Nicomedia in Bithynia served as the eastern imperial capital under Diocletian, and Nicaea was the site of the first ecumenical council (A.D. 323) convened by Constantine the Great.

DISTRICTS ON THE AEGEAN SEA

The Province of Asia included the following districts on the Aegean coast:

Mysia (Acts 16:7, 8). Separated from Europe by the Hellespont (now called the Dardanelles) and the Propontis, and from the Black Sea by Bithynia, was the district of Mysia. It included the city of Troas, ten miles south of Homer's Ilium, the Troy of the Trojan wars. From Troas, Paul could see the hills of Europe. There he received his vision of the "man of Macedonia" whose call for help led Paul to carry the gospel into Europe.

Lydia. In the days of Croesus, Lydia was an important and wealthy empire. In 546 B.C. the country was conquered by Cyrus and absorbed into the Persian Empire. Subsequently it fell to Alexander and later to the Romans. In apostolic times Lydia extended from Mysia to Caria along the Aegean, and eastward as far as Phrygia. Ephesus, the leading city of the province of Asia, was in Lydia. The temple of Artemis (Diana) in Ephesus is regarded as one of the "Seven Wonders of the Ancient World." Ephesus was one of Paul's most important fields of labor. Along with Sardis, Thyatira, and Philadelphia, all in Lydia, Ephesus was addressed by John in the Revelation.

Caria. The southwestern part of the Province of Asia, Caria, is not named in the New Testament. Its cities of Cnidus and Miletus are mentioned, however. Paul's touching farewell to the Ephesian elders took place in Miletus (Acts 20:15-17). Caria had been ruled by native princes from their capital at Halicarnassus until their land was taken by Lydia, which subsequently fell to Cyrus.

DISTRICTS ON THE MEDITERRANEAN

Bounded on the south by the Mediterranean, and on the north by the Taurus mountains were three provinces.

Lycia (Acts 27:5). South of the Taurus Mountains and northeast of the island of Rhodes was the small province of Lycia. The fertile Xanthus valley and wooded mountains of Lycia made it a wealthy province. Two of its cities, Patara and Myra (Acts 21:1; 27:5), were visited by Paul.

Pamphylia (Acts 13:13). East of Lycia was Pamphylia, whose capital, Perga, was the first city in Asia Minor visited during Paul's first missionary journey. He later preached at the seaport city of Attalia (Acts 13:13; 14:25). Pamphylia was notorious for its pirates, some of whom were suppressed by Pompey (67 B.C.).

Cilicia (Acts 21:39). Between Pamphylia and Syria, south of Cappadocia, was Cilicia, famed for its cloth made of goat's hair known as *cilicium*. The capital of Cilicia, Tarsus, was the birthplace of Paul. An ancient highway from Cappadocia to Cilicia passes through the Ciliciae Pylae, or Cilician Gates, a pass in the Taurus Mountains north of Tarsus. Travelers from Syria used this route on journeys to the interior of Asia Minor.

DISTRICTS OF THE INTERIOR

Galatia. Galatia received its name from the Gauls who became masters of the Halys River valley in central Asia Minor during the third century before Christ. When Rome under Pompey (64 B.C.) conquered this territory, a Roman province was given the name of Galatia. This included Pisidia and Lycaonia, districts to the south of the earlier Galatian territory. Iconium, Derbe, Lystra, and Pisidian Antioch are Galatian cities in which Paul preached and suffered persecution.

Cappadocia. South of Pontus and southeast of Galatia was the large province of Cappadocia, mentioned as a place from which people came to Jerusalem on Pentecost (Acts 2:9) and referred to by Peter in his First Epistle (1:1). Silver was mined in Cappadocia and sent to Assyria as early as 1900 B.C. Iron from the Taurus Mountains was also smelted at an early date. Horses from Cappadocia were prized in antiquity.

Lycaonia (Acts 14:1-23). Actually a part of Galatia during Roman times, Lycaonia was the name given to the district including Iconium, Derbe, and Lystra. It comprised the high tableland north of the Taurus Mountains and had a population regarded as uncivilized.

Pisidia. In Paul's time Pisidia was a part of Galatia. Pisidian Antioch was visited at least twice by the apostle (Acts 13:14; 14:21).

Phrygia. A fertile inland region of Asia Minor, varying in size from time to time, was known as Phrygia. Phrygians were related to the Trojans. They are said to have aided King Priam of Troy in return for his help to them against a powerful people, possibly the Hittites. Gordius and Midas were Phrygian kings familiar in Greek folk lore. In New Testament times, Phrygia was not a political entity, but served as the name of the high plateau between Lycaonia, Pisidia, Lydia, Mysia, Bithynia, and Galatia. On his missionary journeys, Paul is said to have traveled through "the region of Phrygia and Galatia" (Acts 16:6; 18:23). Phrygia included the cities of Laodicea, Hierapolis, and Colossae, all mentioned in New Testament epistles.

FIRST MISSIONARY JOURNEY

Antioch in Syria was the point of departure for the first missionary journey. Paul and Barnabas, accompanied by John Mark, left Antioch, the metropolis of Syria, descending the mountains toward Seleucia, the port which served Antioch, sixteen miles away. Built on level ground at the foot of Mount Pieria, five miles north of the mouth of the Orontes, Seleucia was one of the most important harbors of the eastern Mediterranean during New Testament times.

Cyprus. The first stop was the Island of Cyprus, sixty miles west of Syria and forty miles south of Asia Minor. Cyprus is one hundred and forty miles long and is shaped like a fist with the forefinger pointing to Syrian Antioch. In ancient times Cyprus was valued for its copper mines (whence the name "Cyprus") and its timber. It had been ruled by Rome since 58 B.C. and numbered among its governors the great orator Cicero. Paul and his companions stopped first at Salamis (Acts 13:5) on the eastern shore of Cyprus where they preached in a Jewish synagogue. Salamis is said to have been founded by Phoenician colonists from Tyre centuries before the Roman occupation of the city.

Crossing the island from east to west, Paul and his companions continued their preaching mission. At the southwest tip of the island they came to Paphos (Acts 13:6), the capital city and seat of the Roman administration. Here Paul and Barnabas met the proconsul Sergius Paulus who, in spite of opposition from Elymas the sorcerer, sent for the apostle to inquire concerning "the Word of God" (Acts 13:7). Paul's first presentation of Christianity to a Roman official resulted in conversion. This was a great victory for the cause of Christ, for Paphos was a stronghold of the worship of Aphrodite who was believed to have sprung from the sea there. She had a famous temple at Paphos, similar to that of Artemis at Ephesus, and was worshiped with sensuous rites. Sergius Paulus, like many another, was to turn in disgust from the heathenism of his day to the purity of the gospel of Christ. Cyprus early became a Christian stronghold. Its influence was such that it was able to send three bishops to the Council of Nicaea (A.D. 325).

Asia Minor. Sailing in a northwesterly direction a distance of one hundred and seventy miles, the missionary party reached the province of Pamphylia in Asia Minor. Passing by Attalia they went up the river Kestros and landed at Perga (Acts 13:13), twelve miles inland. On a hill outside the town stood a temple of Artemis (Diana), the Asiatic nature-goddess who was regarded as "queen of Perga." When Paul determined to press on from Perga to the hinterland of Asia Minor, John Mark left the party and returned to Jerusalem. From Perga, Paul and Barnabas traveled northward to Antioch in Pisidia, a center of Hellenistic influence in the mountainous terrain near the Phrygian border. In Pisidian Antioch and the adjacent Galatian region were many Jews who had come to Asia Minor on business ventures with the encouragement of the Seleucid kings. When Paul preached in the synagogues some Jews enthusiastically received his message and passed it on to their gentile neighbors (Acts 13:14-48). Others, however, bitterly opposed the preaching of the gospel and drove Paul and Barnabas out of town (Acts 13:50-51).

Driven out of Pisidian Antioch, Paul and Barnabas journeyed eighty miles southeast to the Phrygian town of Iconium, still a populous Turkish city named *Konya*. Here the threat of being stoned caused the missionaries to leave hastily. Paul's harsh treatment at Iconium remained a painful memory to the end of his life (Acts 14:1-6; II Tim. 3:11).

About eighteen miles southwest of Iconium was Lystra, founded by Augus-

tus Caesar as a Roman colony in 6 B.C. Impressed by the cure of a man crippled from birth, the men of Lystra offered worship to Paul as Mercury, the god of eloquence, and to Barnabas, evidently the more imposing of the two, as Jupiter. The crowd proved fickle, however. When Jews from Pisidian Antioch and Iconium brought charges against Paul and Barnabas, the men of Lystra stoned the missionaries and Paul was carried almost lifeless from the city.

Paul and Barnabas next traveled thirty miles southeast to Derbe, where they preached with power after the difficult time at Lystra. Derbe was the farthest point reached on the first missionary journey, a city to which Paul would later return. From Derbe it was a comparatively short trip through the Cilician Gates to Tarsus, and then by sea or land to Syria. This, however, was not the route chosen by Paul and Barnabas.

Instead, the missionaries chose to retrace their steps, revisiting Lystra, Iconium, and Pisidian Antioch and confirm-

Ancient Aqueduct, Pisidia. In the foreground are the ruins of an aqueduct which brought water to Pisidian Antioch. The Taurus mountains are in the background.
Courtesy, Kelsey Museum of Archaeology
University of Michigan

ing the churches which they had established earlier. They also preached in some places which had been missed during the first part of the journey. From Attalia (modern *Adalia*), a seaport on the coast of Pamphylia, sixteen miles from Perga, Paul and Barnabas sailed directly to Antioch in Syria where they were warmly received by the church which had sent them forth.

SECOND MISSIONARY JOURNEY

Between the first and second missionary journeys Paul went to Jerusalem to attend a council called to establish the principle upon which gentiles were to be received into the church (Acts 15:1-30). This was in itself a testimony to the fact that Christianity had, in a significant way, exceeded the bounds of Judaism and that gentiles did not have to pass through the corridor of the Law to enter the church of Jesus Christ.

The second missionary journey began with a disagreement between Paul and Barnabas over John Mark. Mark had left the missionaries during their first journey, and Paul refused to take him a second time. Barnabas espoused the cause of Mark, separated from Paul, and went with Mark to Cyprus. Paul with Silas journeyed to Asia Minor and then on to Europe. Timothy and Luke later joined Paul's missionary party.

Asia Minor. As in the first journey, Syrian Antioch was the point of departure for the new evangelistic mission. This time, however, Paul traveled by land northward toward Asia Minor which he probably entered through the Syrian Gates, a famous pass in the Amanus Mountains. The important cities of Issus and (Syrian) Alexandria, modern Alexandrette, were along this route but there is no record of Paul's ministry in either of these places.

Entering Cilicia (Acts 15:41), Paul may have traveled through Mopsuestia and Anana on his way to Tarsus, his birthplace. From Tarsus he traveled northwestward through the Cilician Gates to the plain of Lycaonia. There he revisited Derbe and Lystra where he had planted churches on his first journey. Timothy, Paul's "son" in the faith and lifelong companion, joined the evangelistic party at Lystra (Acts 16:1-4).

Next we read that Paul and Silas went "throughout Phrygia." As no mention is made of the establishing of new churches in this area, New Testament scholars usually suggest that this refers to a tour among the churches at Iconium and Pisidian Antioch, the fruits of the first journey.

Reference is also made to Paul's travels in Galatia (Acts 16:6). Older geographies presumed that this meant a northern trip through Pessinus, Ancyra, and Tavium. Since the time of William M. Ramsay, however, it has been recognized that Lycaonia was a part of the province of Galatia, and that the Galatian journey was probably in the district of Derbe, Lystra, and Iconium rather than the North Galatian cities.

Paul desired to continue his evangelistic ministry in the Roman proconsular province of Asia, comprising Phrygia and the Aegean districts of Mysia, Lydia, and Caria. Here, as in Bithynia, Paul did not sense the divine leading in the matter of gospel witness. He kept traveling westward, however, finally reaching Troas (Acts 16:6-8).

Troas had important historical associations, being near the Troy of Homer's epics. It is probable that a church was established in this city by Paul, for there he was joined by Luke "the beloved physician" and historian of the early church. On a later journey he met his companions at Troas (Acts 20:6, 7). Here Paul saw the vision of the "man of Macedonia" asking for help. This vision,

Neapolis. At the harbor of Neapolis, modern Kavalla, Paul first landed in Europe (Acts 16:11). Neapolis is the seaport of Philippi, and the eastern terminus of the Egnatian Road.   *Courtesy, Royal Greek Embassy*

and Paul's response to it, marked the beginning of Christian ministry in Europe.

Europe. From Troas, Paul journeyed by boat to Macedonia, the province north of Greece. Macedonia had been the home of Alexander the Great who had earlier undertaken another type of missionary enterprise, spreading Greek culture in the East. Under the Romans, Macedonia was divided into four districts with capitals at Amphipolis, Thessalonica (the residence of the provincial proconsul), Pella (the birthplace of Alexander the Great), and Pelagonia. Amphipolis, however, had become less important than the rival city of Philippi, in the same district.

After spending a night on the island of Samothrace, "Thracian Samos," a rocky island near the coast of Thrace, Paul and his companions anchored in the harbor of Neapolis (modern *Kavalla*), the port of Philippi in Macedonia. The missionary party did not remain in the port city, but proceeded on foot to Philippi itself.

Philippi, built on a spur of the Pangaean mountain range, was named for Philip of Macedon, its conqueror, during the fourth century B.C. On the plains below Philippi, the great battle of Augustus and Antony against Brutus and Cassius was fought in 42 B.C. In commemoration of the victory of Augustus, the city was designated a colony and regarded as a branch of Rome itself. Its inhabitants were always proud of their Roman prerogatives (Acts 16:21).

The Jewish colony of Philippi met on the banks of the River Gangites

(Modern Angista) at a spot which offered both privacy and facilities for ceremonial purifications. In ministering to the Jewish congregation at Philippi, Paul was able to lead to Christ his first European convert—Lydia, a business woman of Philippi, who had become a proselyte to Judaism (Acts 16:14).

Paul and Silas were thrown into jail at Philippi after having relieved a young woman of a "spirit of divination," thus bringing down the wrath of those who had profited by her unfortunate plight. In the sequel the Philippian jailor and his household believed on Christ (Acts 16:25-34) and, when morning came, the officials of the city were made to tremble on learning that they had inflicted violence on a citizen of Rome.

Paul had many warm friends in Philippi. At a later date he revisited Macedonia and observed the Passover with the brethren there (Acts 20:6). The Philippian church sent gifts to Paul, and his Epistle to the Philippians was a "thank you" letter for their fellowship with him in the gospel.

In leaving Philippi, Paul and his missionary associates traveled along the Egnatian Way, the great military and commercial highway that linked the Aegean with the Adriatic. Thirty-three miles southwest of Philippi, they stopped for a day in Amphipolis, on the River Strymon. Amphipolis was founded by the Athenians in 437 B.C., and subsequently was the scene of a famous battle in the Peloponnesian War. Under Rome it became a free city and the capital of the first of the four districts into which Macedonia was divided. Continuing along the Egnatian Way, Paul's party next came to Apollonia, twenty-eight miles southwest of Amphipolis (Acts 17:1). There they probably spent the night en route to Thessalonica.

A journey of forty miles along the Egnatian Way brought the missionaries to Thessalonica, the most important seaport of Macedonia, situated on the northern part of the Thermaic Gulf. Thessalonica was named by Cassander for his wife, the sister of Alexander the Great (ca. 315 B.C.). It had earlier been known as Therma ("Hot Springs"). This seaport had the advantages of a strategic location, a good harbor, and nearby fertile lands. Because of its allegiance to Augustus and Antony in their struggle with Brutus and Cassius it was made a free city and served as the capital of one of the four districts of Macedonia during Roman times. Thessalonica was given autonomy in internal affairs (Acts 17:6, 8), its rulers being known as "politarchs." This town which in modern times has been called *Saloniki* is now officially known as *Thessaloniki* and continues to occupy a place of importance.

Paul found an influential group of Jews at Thessalonica. They not only had a synagogue of their own but had attracted a significant number of Greeks who attended as "God-fearers." Paul's ministry was not devoid of results. In three weeks time he had "some" converts from among the Jews, "a great multitude" of adherents from among the "devout Greeks" and of the "chief women not a few" (Acts 17:4). Under pressure from the unbelieving Jews, the politarchs prevailed on Paul to leave the city. He later revisited Thessalonica (I Cor. 16:5) and addressed the earliest of his epistles to the church there.

Fifty miles southwest of Thessalonica, Paul stopped at Berea, modern *Verria* (Acts 17:10-13), at the foot of Mount Bermius, near Pella. Berea had a Jewish synagogue whose members eagerly listened to Paul's message and "searched the Scriptures" to check his claims. Many Bereans accepted the gospel and, when Jews from Thessalonica came to stir up trouble, they helped Paul to reach Athens safely.

Areopagus. Mars Hills, another name for the Areopagus, was a rocky place, 377 feet high, northwest of the acropolis. It was the meeting place of a court, also known as the Areopagus. Paul's address (Acts 17: 19, 22) was probably delivered here, as it was the usual meeting place of the court. This photograph was taken in 1951, on the 1900th anniversary of the arrival of St. Paul in Athens.

Courtesy,
Royal Greek Embassy

On leaving Berea, Paul and his companions left Macedonia going south to Achaia, the Roman name for Greece. During the apostolic age, Corinth was the capital and chief city of Achaia, although Athens retained its fame as a cultural center.

Athens is located five miles northeast of the Saronic Gulf between two little streams, the Gephissus and the Ilissus. It was connected with its seaport, the Piraeus, by two long parallel walls, built two hundred yards apart. As Paul journeyed along the two-mile road from the Piraeus to Athens he noted the altars dedicated "to the unknown god" which served as a basis for his sermon on Mars Hill. These altars along the highway and elsewhere in Athens are mentioned by the second century Greek writers, Pausanias and Philostratus.

The "Golden Age" of Athens dates back to the fifth century before Christ when it produced its great philosophy, art, and literature. It was a religious center with shrines to many deities, including the patron goddess Athena. After the Peloponnesian War between Athens and Sparta (431-404 B.C.), internal dissensions among the Greek states led to political weakness and opened the way for Macedonian conquest of Greece by Philip (338 B.C.) and Alexander the Great (335 B.C.). Following 146 B.C., Athens became for all practical purposes a free city-state under Roman protection.

The city of Athens circled the base of the Acropolis, a hill five hundred feet high on which numerous temples were built. Here the visitor may still see the ruins of the Temple of the Wingless Victory, the Erechtheum with its graceful Ionic columns, and the Parthenon with its simpler Doric pillars.

North of the Acropolis was the agora, or market place where the Athenians met to transact business and argue philosophy (Acts 17:17). The agora has been excavated by the American School of Classical Studies and the buildings and street of the area have been charted.

At the western approach to the Acropolis was Mars Hill, or the Areopagus. The latter name is that of the city court of Athens which met at Mars Hill on stated occasions to pass judgment on such matters as pertained to the welfare of the city.

Paul, as a teacher of a new "philosophy" was brought before the Areopagus for a hearing (Acts 17:15-34). The popular Greek philosophies of the day were those which we designate as Platonic, Epicurean, and Stoic. Paul presented a polemic against polytheism, arguing for the spiritual nature of God and His claims on all men. We do not read of the organization of a church at Athens, but there were significant converts including

Steps to the Areopagus. Did Paul climb these stone steps?   Courtesy, Royal Greek Embassy

Dionysius, an "Areopagite," or member of the council of the Areopagus.

Paul next crossed the isthmus between the gulfs of Lepanto and Aegina, connecting the mainland of Greece with the Peloponnesus. Here, forty miles west of Athens, he entered Corinth, the capital of the Roman province of Achaia, which had been made a Roman colony by Julius Caesar (46 B.C.). The ancient city was about three miles southwest of the present site. It was connected by a double wall with its western seaport Lechaeum, which faced toward Italy, and by fortifications with its eastern seaport, Cenchrea, which faced toward Asia.

As Athens had a reputation for culture, so Corinth was known for its corruption. Greeks, Romans, Jews, and adventurers from the entire Mediterranean world came to Corinth for trade and vice in all its forms. "To live like a Corinthian," became synonymous with a life of luxury and licentiousness. Paul found Corinth a promising mission field. Plying his trade of tentmaking in order to meet expenses, he spent a year and a half in Corinth making his home with Aquila and Priscilla, who had been driven from Rome by the anti-Jewish legislation of Claudius (Acts 18:2). At Corinth, Paul reached individuals from all levels of society. Although cast out of the synagogue himself, he was able to lead Crispus, the chief ruler of the synagogue, to Christ. Another convert, a Roman named Justus who had attended Jewish synagogue worship, opened his house for the meetings of the first church at Corinth. Erastus, the city treasurer, was another well-known convert.

Corinthian Jews accused Paul of persuading men to "worship God contrary to law" and brought him before the Roman Proconsul, Gallio. This Gallio is known from history as a brother of the Roman philosopher, Seneca. Pliny

Antioch-on-the-Orontes. This was Paul's point of departure on his first missionary journey, and in a way served as his "headquarters." Here the believers were first called Christians. Antioch-on-the-Orontes should not be confused with Antioch in Pisidia, where Paul was persecuted.

Courtesy, Religious News Service

mentions that Gallio went to Egypt after finishing his term in Corinth, a victim of lung hemorrhage.

Gallio refused to take the charge of the Jews against Paul seriously. He found no "wrong or wicked lewdness" (Acts 18:14) in the apostle and dismissed the case. Paul thereupon sailed from the port of Cenchrea for Ephesus, in Asia Minor, but he subsequently revisited Corinth and wrote epistles to the church there.

We do not read of any public ministry at Cenchrea, although it is reasonable to assume that the ministry in Corinth touched some lives in its port on the Saronic Gulf. Paul's letter to the Romans speaks of a deaconess from Cenchrea (Rom. 16:1-2).

The Return Trip. The return journey from Corinth to Antioch was more than a thousand miles in length. Stops were made at Ephesus, Caesarea and Jerusalem (Acts 18:18-22).

Directly eastward, across the Aegean Sea, Paul traveled two hundred fifty miles to reach the city of Ephesus, which, with Syrian Antioch and Egyptian Alexandria, ranked as one of the three greatest cities of the eastern Mediterranean. Ephesus was a transportation junction where highways and seaways converged. People and merchandise from East and West constantly passed through Ephesus. A Lydian fertility goddess similar to the Phoenician Astarte (Greek Artemis, Roman Diana) dominated the life of the city. The Temple of Diana at Ephesus was regarded as one of the wonders of the ancient world. The Greek geographer Pausanias called it the largest building in existence in his day. Religious prostitution and the superstitious veneration of images presented the more sordid side of the worship of Diana.

Paul's first visit to Ephesus was short. The Jews to whom he ministered desired

him to stay longer, but eager to continue his journey, he moved on assuring them of his intention to return. Paul left behind him warm friends, including Aquila and Priscilla. He visited Ephesus again during the Third Missionary Journey.

From Ephesus, Paul took a boat and sailed for Caesarea, the seat of government and seaport of Roman Palestine. Continuing by land he traveled sixty-four miles southeast to the city of Jerusalem, high in the Judaean mountains. Gifts from the gentile Christians were probably sent with Paul for the poor saints in the Holy City. From Jerusalem, Paul returned to his "headquarters" at Antioch. The church at Antioch had sent him out on his missionary journeys, and Paul seems to have made his home there.

THIRD MISSIONARY JOURNEY

Paul's third journey took him from Antioch, through Asia Minor, to Corinth, and back again to Jerusalem. Three years were spent in Ephesus on the westward part of the journey. Much of the third missionary journey was spent in visiting churches which had been established earlier.

The Outward Journey (Acts 18:23— 20:3). From Syrian Antioch, Paul took the land route northward through Cilicia and the Cilician Gates into Galatia where he visited the churches at Derbe, Lystra, and Iconium. Continuing westward he passed through Phrygia, and then moved on to Ephesus where he remained longer than at any other place during his active ministry.

Working at his trade through the week, and preaching in the synagogues on the sabbath days, Paul was able to bring many to Christ. Jewish opposition ultimately forced Paul out of the synagogues, but he was able to gather the believers into churches.

Although Paul did not make a frontal attack on idolatry (Acts 19:37), he won converts from Diana worship, the popular form of religion at Ephesus. This stirred up Demetrius, a silversmith, whose trade in idols had been jeopardized. He organized a mass meeting at the Great Theatre of Ephesus, overlooking the city from the western shore of Mount Pion. Demetrius gathered a large crowd in the theatre which could seat twenty-five thousand people. He insisted that Ephesus was "temple keeper" or "warden" of Diana, hence responsible to maintain her worship. Paul was rescued from possible mob violence by the tactful town clerk who assured the Ephesians that he was neither a blasphemer of Diana nor "a robber of churches" (Acts 19:35-40).

From Ephesus, Paul went north to Troas (II Cor. 2:12, 13), where he hoped to meet Titus with news from the church at Corinth. While waiting he found opportunity for missionary activity. When the expected tidings did not come, Paul sailed again from Troas to Europe.

The cities of Macedonia which were next visited (Acts 20:1-2) probably included Philippi, Thessalonica, and Berea. It may be that at this time Paul "fully preached the gospel of Christ" (Rom. 15:19) in the region of Illyricum, the name given to the coastal region east of the Adriatic. This was later known as Dalmatia, and is now called Yugoslavia.

Greece or Achaia (Acts 20:2, 3) was the farthest extent of the third journey. After three months the missionary party headed home.

The Return Journey (Acts 20:3—21:17). Paul traveled back toward Palestine with the desire to reach Jerusalem in time for the Pentecost observance. He did not return directly, but took the land route around the Aegean by way of Philippi and Troas. The report of a plot to murder him may have caused Paul to take this route, accompanied by friends.

From Corinth, Paul and his companions journeyed overland through Greece and Macedonia to Philippi (Acts 20:3-6). There Luke the "beloved physician" joined Paul and accompanied him during the remainder of his recorded journeys.

Most of Paul's company sailed ahead to Troas, where they waited until Paul and Luke rejoined them (Acts 20:4-6). During the stay of a week in Troas, a young man named Eutychus was restored to life by the apostle.

From Troas most of the missionary company set sail for Palestine, but Paul went on foot to Assos, a Mysian seaport twenty miles southeast of Troas. There he was taken on board ship.

After a voyage of thirty miles, the ship anchored for the night at Mitylene, the most important city on the island of Lesbos and home of the Greek poetess, Sappho. Another night was spent at Chios, an island of the Greek archipelago between Samos and Lesbos, reputedly the birthplace of Homer. The difficulty of following the island-studded channel at night may have been responsible for these stops.

After a very brief stop at Samos, an important Greek commercial center a mile from the mainland of Asia Minor, Paul's boat went on to Trogyllium, a promontory extending into the Aegean south of Ephesus. Here another night was passed.

At Miletus, thirty-six miles south of Ephesus at the mouth of the Meander River, the ship was delayed for two days. Miletus was founded by Ionians in the eleventh century B.C. and, although destroyed by Alexander the Great (334 B.C.), it was soon rebuilt.

The island is known as the birthplace of Thales, one of the sages of ancient Greece, and of Anaximander, the philosopher. One of the largest amphitheaters of Asia Minor has been excavated there. Paul took the opportunity of the delay at Miletus to send for the elders of Ephesus and give them a farewell address which is considered one of the most touching passages of the New Testament.

The ship next anchored at Cos (Coos, A.V.), a small island off the southwest tip of Asia Minor. During the fourth century B.C., Cos became famous for its shrine of Aesculapius, the god of healing. It had a well-known medical school and was the home of Hippocrates, the "father of medicine." The production of silk, ointments, wine, and wheat made Cos a prosperous island.

Rhodes, the "island of roses" (Acts 21:1), also had had a significant history before Paul stopped there. Located twelve miles south of Cape Krio on the southwestern tip of Asia Minor it was at the crossroads for ships traveling between the Aegean and the eastern Mediterranean. The island, forty-five miles long and twenty-two miles wide, was famous for its Colossus, an 105 foot statue of the sun god built in 280 B.C. to commemorate successful resistance to a siege and regarded as one of the wonders of the ancient world. It fell into the harbor waters during an earthquake in 224 B.C. Cicero and Julius Caesar are said to have studied at Rhodes, and Strabo boasted of its harbors, streets, and walls. Thousands of jars of wine were exported from Rhodes in ancient times, a fact verified by the jar handles bearing the name of their maker found in many parts of Palestine.

Paul's vessel ended its voyage at Patara, a seaport in the province of Lycia directly east of Rhodes. Patara was famous for its oracle of Apollo. The missionary party found there another ship bound for Phoenicia.

The ship from Patara sailed directly to Tyre, formerly the great Phoenician seaport. The city had been besieged by Nebuchadnezzar and destroyed by Alexander the Great. Rebuilt under the Seleucids, Tyre enjoyed a measure of prosperity for some centuries although it never was free from the great world empires.

At Tyre, Paul boarded ship again, sailing twenty-five miles southward along the Palestinian coast to Ptolemaïs (Old Testament Accho), eight miles north of Mount Carmel at the head of the Bay of Acre. It was a "Key to Palestine" in ancient times because of its strategic location in respect to the approaches to the Plain of Esdraelon. Solomon had used Accho as a chariot city where he kept the horses which he imported from Cilicia.

Caesarea, the Roman capital of Palestine, was the next city visited by Paul as he traveled by land from Ptolemaïs. At Caesarea, Paul received warning from the aged prophet Agabus that he should not go to Jerusalem. He did not heed the warning, however, but traveled on to Jerusalem. When Paul left the holy city he was a "prisoner of the Lord," bound for Rome.

The Voyage to Rome (Acts 21:26—28:31). The last recorded journey of Paul is that which took him to Rome as a prisoner. Seized by a Jewish mob in the Temple, he would have been slain but for the timely arrival of a company of Roman soldiers from the adjacent Tower of Antonia. Paul addressed the throng from the stairs, leading out of the Temple Court of the Gentiles into the Tower, after which he was imprisoned in the Tower.

When the Roman officer in charge of the Tower learned that a band of Jews had plotted to slay Paul, he hastened to provide protection for his prisoner. Under a strong escort, Paul was brought safely from the city.

By night the apostle was taken to Antipatris (Old Testament Aphek), thirty-nine miles from Jerusalem on the Roman military road. The next morning the foot soldiers were sent back to Jerusalem, and the apostle continued with a cavalry escort (Acts 23:31, 32).

The prison in Caesarea was "home" to Paul for two years. Here he was tried by Felix and made his defense before Herod Agrippa (Acts 24—26). Having appealed as a Roman citizen to the supreme court at Rome, Paul was put on a boat with a company of prisoners and a guard commanded by the centurion Julius. Luke and Aristarchus accompanied Paul (Acts 27:1, 2).

The second day out from Caesarea the boat stopped at Sidon, and Paul was permitted to go ashore (Acts 27:3). Sidon was an ancient Phoenician city twenty miles north of Tyre. Following a revolt against the Persian King Artaxerxes III (351 B.C.), Sidon was burned to the ground but it was re-established during the third century B.C. by the Seleucid rulers.

From Sidon the vessel traveled north of Cyprus along the southern shores of Asia Minor to Myra in the Province of Lycia. Myra was one of the great ports of call for the grain ships between Egypt and Rome. An early bishop of Myra, St. Nicholas, became the patron saint of sailors in the eastern Mediterranean. At Myra the centurion placed his prisoner on an Alexandrian grain ship bound for Italy (Acts 27:6).

The grain ship sailed toward Cnidus, a harbor on Cape Krio, the southwestern tip of Asia Minor adjacent to Rhodes and Cos. Unable to enter the harbor of Cnidus because of contrary winds, the boat turned southward toward the island of Crete, the large island (140 miles long by 35 miles wide) at the entrance to the Aegean Sea.

Crete is about equidistant from Europe, Asia and Africa. In the Old Testament, it was called Caphtor, and is considered the home of the Philistines who invaded Canaan (Jer. 47:4; Amos 9:7). The great Minoan Cretan culture suffered a catastrophe about 1200 B.C., the very time when large numbers of Philistines poured into southern Palestine after having made an unsuccessful attempt to enter Egypt.

The Mycenaean culture which sprang from Minoan Crete has provided us with many artifacts. In later times various ethnic groups, including Jews, settled there. Jews from Crete were in Jerusalem on the day of Pentecost.

The boat on which Paul was a prisoner rounded Cape Salmone at the eastern point of the island and anchored at a bay known as Fair Havens on the southern shore. The ship remained there for a considerable time. The reference to the "fast" (Acts 27:9), referring to the Day of Atonement, indicates that the journey took place during the fall of the year. Mediterranean navigation was very dangerous at this season and it was often suspended entirely from early November to early February.

Paul urged the centurion to stay at Fair Havens for the winter to insure the safety of cargo, passengers, and crew. The owner of the ship, however, argued that the harbor of Phenice (or Phoenix, modern Lutro), fifty miles west, would be a safer and more adequate harbor. The name of Phenice is reminiscent of the Phoenician traders who early colonized the Mediterranean islands.

A gentle south wind enabled the vessel to leave Fair Havens and round Cape Matapan (Acts 27:13), but it never reached Phenice. A storm, called Euroclydon (A.V.) or Euraquilo, which is a violent "northeaster," drove the ship off its course. At the small island of Clauda (Cauda), which lay off the southwest shore of Crete, the sailors were able to strengthen the vessel by winding the ropes around the hull.

After this the boat was driven before the wind for fourteen days and nights. The cargo and the ship's furnishings had to be cast into the sea as the situation grew hopeless. Paul, who had urged a delay at Fair Havens, now expressed confidence that God would preserve the lives of all on board. The boat was wrecked in a bay on the northeastern shore of Malta (now called St. Paul's Bay), an island sixty-two miles south of Sicily, but no lives were lost.

Malta, or Melita ("honey"), had been colonized by the Phoenicians, and subsequently ruled by Greeks, Carthaginians, and Romans. Paul and his companions were hospitably received and entertained during a three-month stay on the island. Christian influences have been traced in the art of second century Malta, but the first clear references to a church on the island date in the fifth century.

Following the winter at Malta the shipwrecked party boarded an Alexandrian vessel bound for Rome. The first stopping place during this part of the voyage was the city of Syracuse at the southeastern corner of Sicily, the largest island in the Mediterranean. Syracuse was a Greek city, founded by Archias of Corinth about 735 B.C. It boasted a temple of Athena, built during the fifth century before Christ, and a rock-cut semicircular theater. Paul and his associates spent three days at Syracuse before crossing the Straits of Messina to Rhegium at the "toe" of the Italian "boot," opposite Sicily.

Rhegium, modern Reggio di Calabria in Italy, was also a Greek city. Here, according to legend, was the home of Scylla, the dreaded monster feared by

mariners. After a day at Rhegium the vessel traveled northward along the western coast of Italy to Puteoli, eight miles west of Naples. Puteoli (modern Pozzuoli) was probably founded by settlers from Cumae (*ca.* 520 B.C.). Although 141 miles from Rome, excellent roads connecting it with the capital made the port a favorite for ships from the East. Paul left the Alexandrian grain ship at Puteoli where he was entertained for seven days by local Christians.

Christians met Paul at two places along the Appian Way, over which he passed en route to Rome: at Appii Forum ("Market of Appius"), forty miles from the capital, and at a place known as "Three Taverns," ten miles closer. The end of Paul's journey was Rome itself, the capital of the Empire. For two years he lived in "his own hired house" chained to a Roman soldier. Here the history of the Book of the Acts comes to an end. Other details of Paul's life are matters of tradition and of inference from his letters.

In the period of its greatness Rome occupied ten hills with the valleys between them, and a plain near the River Tiber.

The site of Paul's "hired house" is not known. While in Rome, Paul doubtless saw the palaces of the Caesars on the Palatine Hill. In walking through the Forum he passed the Temple of Saturn which had been converted into the treasury storehouse of the Roman people. The Temple of Castor and Pollux served as a kind of "bureau of weights and measures" where metals were assayed for coins.

At the time of Paul's imprisonment, Rome had a population of approximately 1,200,000 inhabitants. About half of these people were slaves and the majority of the rest were paupers supported in idleness by the free distribution of food.

The Geography of the Book of Revelation

The Taurus Mountains. Along the southern coast of Asia Minor, the Taurus (or Silver) Mountains reach as high as 12,250 feet above sea level.

Courtesy,
The Turkish Information Service

Use Maps 14 and 15

The Geography of the Book of Revelation

The last book of the Bible was written on the small island of Patmos in the Sporades group, southwest of Asia Minor and west of Rhodes.

Patmos is located about seventy miles southwest of Ephesus. It is approximately twenty miles in circumference and covers a territory of about fifty square miles. In rocky, barren seclusion, it was a suitable place for the banishment of criminals. Today the Monastery of St. John owns most of the southern half of the island.

THE SEVEN CHURCHES OF ASIA. The Book of the Revelation, chapters two and three, contains letters to seven churches of proconsular Asia, the name given to the lands of Mysia, Lydia, Caria, and a part of Phrygia. This territory had belonged to Pergamum, a city-state which attained the peak of its culture under Eumenes II (197-159 B.C.). The independence of Pergamum ended dramatically when Attalus III (d. 133 B.C.) bequeathed his kingdom to the Roman people. It subsequently became the Province of Asia, with Pergamum its capital and Ephesus and Smyrna its principal cities.

The letters were addressed to:

Ephesus (Rev. 2:1). Ephesus was the most important city of the district in which the seven churches were located and served as capital of Roman Asia. It had been visited by Paul during his Second Missionary Journey, and an extended ministry of over two years in Ephesus took place during the apostle's third journey.

Smyrna (Rev. 2:8). About forty miles directly north of Ephesus is Smyrna, modern *Izmir,* an important Aegean port of western Turkey. Smyrna was founded in the twelfth century B.C. by Aeolic Greeks, and became rich through trade between Asia and the West. It was rebuilt by Alexander the Great. Although its only Biblical mention is in the Book of the Revelation, it subsequently became an important Christian center. Polycarp was bishop of Smyrna before his martyrdom about A.D. 155. The letter in the Revelation suggests that the Smyrna church was poor and had suffered persecution as a result of refusal to participate in the Roman cult of emperor worship.

Pergamum (Pergamos) (Rev. 2:12). Sixty miles northeast of Smyrna, in the district of Mysia, was the city of Pergamum. It had served as the capital of one of the small kingdoms which arose after the breakup of Alexander's kingdom.

Pergamene sculpture became famous throughout the ancient world. The *Dying Gaul* is an example of the realism in art which served to depict the victory of Attalus I of Pergamum over the Galatians (*ca.* 230 B.C.). The defeat of Antiochus III by the Roman fleet aided by squadrons from Rhodes and Pergamum at Magnesia in Lydia (190 B.C.) is commemorated in a frieze for the great altar of Zeus in Pergamum.

The great library at Pergamum is said to have contained 200,000 manuscripts. Legend suggests that Ptolemy Philadelphus of Egypt, fearful lest his library at Alexandria be overshadowed, forbade the export of papyrus to Pergamum. Thereupon, we are told, the people of Pergamum developed parchment, termed in Greek, *pergamenos*.

The author of the Revelation speaks of "Satan's throne" at Pergamum (Rev. 2:13). This may have been the great altar of Zeus which stood nearly fifty feet high in a colonnaded enclosure on the lower terrace of the city. Its base was more than one hundred feet square.

Thyatira (Rev. 2:18). Thyatira was a city of ancient Lydia on the road from Pergamum to Sardis. It was established by Seleucus I during the third century B.C. on a key commercial highway. The town gained prestige from its Macedonian colonists who formed guilds of weavers, dyers, leather-workers, and metal craftsmen. Lydia, Paul's first convert in Europe, was a cloth merchant from Thyatira who did business in Philippi (Acts 16:14). The church was commended for its good works, charity, faith, and patience but chastised because some of its members had been guilty of immorality and had eaten things sacrificed to idols (Rev. 2:20 ff.). The modern town of *Ackisar* stands on the site of Thyatira.

Sardis (Rev. 3:1). Thirty miles south of Thyatira, between the River Hermus and Mount Tmolus, was the city of Sardis, founded about 1200 B.C. It later served as the capital of the powerful Kingdom of Lydia. Under the fabulously rich Croesus (*ca.* 560—*ca.* 540 B.C.) the Lydians minted the first coins in history. Greeks later adopted the practice which soon became commonplace among all civilized peoples.

Ephesus Today. Ephesus was the most important city of the district in which the seven churches were located. It is abandoned today.   *Courtesy, H. Gokberg*

Pergamum. This once great city has also been
reduced to a field of ruins.   Courtesy, H. Gokberg

The wealth of Sardis came in part from commerce, in part from its location on the productive plains of the Tmolus River, and in part from the textiles and jewelry produced by its artisans. It was located on the east-west crossroads of the Lydian Empire.

In Roman times the mystery cults of the ancient East had wealthy devotees at Sardis. Adherents to the cult of Cybele claimed power to restore the dead. Praise was given in Revelation to the "few" in Sardis who "have not defiled their garments" and who thus were worthy to walk in white with Christ (Rev. 3:4).

Sardis early became a center of Christianity in Asia Minor. Beside the remains of an impressive temple of Artemis, dating to the fourth century B.C., archaeologists discovered the remains of a Christian church built before the fourth century A.D. The city was destroyed in the early fifteenth century by the Mongol, Tamerlane.

Philadelphia (Rev. 3:7). About twenty-eight miles southeast of Sardis, on the Cogamus River, a branch of the Hermus, was the city of Philadelphia, named for its founder Attalus Philadelphus of Pergamum (d. 138 B.C.). Philadelphia was destroyed by earthquakes several times, but its history continues under the modern name, *Alashehir*. The Philadelphia church was commended for keeping God's Word and assured that God would keep His faithful people "from the hour of temptation, which shall come upon all the world."

Laodicea (Rev. 3:14). Laodicea, the capital of Phrygia, was about fifty miles from Philadelphia. It was situated in the fertile Lycus River valley at the crossroads of the trade route from the East to Pergamum and Ephesus. Its ancient name was Diospolis, but it was renamed by the Syrian king, Seleucus II, in honor of his wife, Laodice. After an

earthquake in A.D. 60 the city was rebuilt by its citizens without aid from
Rome (cf. Rev. 3:17). Laodicea produced a fine black wool from the local
sheep. It boasted a medical school which
produced a well-known eye medicine
known as Phrygian powder. Laodicean
bankers negotiated with the entire
empire.

The Laodicean church received the
sharpest rebuke. It had become infected
by the worldly prosperity of the city.

Today, Laodicea is in ruins. A theater,
an aqueduct, a gymnasium, and sar-
cophagi speak of a glory long since departed.

The order of the churches described
in Revelation is in the form of a circuit, starting from Ephesus, traveling
north to Smyrna and Pergamum, then
southeast to Thyatira, Sardis, and Philadelphia, until the southern and eastern
limit is reached at Laodicea.

Patmos.   This small island was the site of John's banishment and the setting for writing the last book of the Bible. Patmos is located about seventy miles southwest of Ephesus.
Religious News Service Photo

CHAPTER XXV

The Centuries Between

THE SPREAD OF CHRISTIANITY

Copyright by C. S. HAMMOND & CO., N.Y.

Scale of Miles

0   100   200   400   600

Northern limit of area permanently lost to Mohammedanism..........

During the 7th cent. the Church introduced Nestorian Christianity into Central Asia.

The Christian Coptic Church was introduced on the Upper Nile and in Ethiopia in the 4th cent.

Christianity in Roman Britain was wiped out by the Anglo-Saxon invasion. The faith was reëstablished in the 7th cent. by Irish missionaries.

Caspian Sea

Black Sea

Sea of Azov

North Sea

Baltic Sea

Atlantic Ocean

Mediterranean Sea

Red Sea

Volga R.

Don R.

Dnieper R.

Dniester R.

Danube R.

Rhine R.

Tagus R.

Duero R.

Nile R.

Tigris R.

Euphrates R.

Russians (989-1015)

Prussians (13th Cent.)

Lithuanians (13th Cent.)

Poles (962-1025)

Czechs (c. 1000)

Magyars (950-1050)

Saxons (785-805)

Thuringians (8th Cent.)

Alamanni (4th Cent.)

Pomeranians (1122-1130)

IRELAND

BRITAIN

GAUL

SPAIN

ITALY

ARMENIA

EGYPT

SICILY

SARDINIA

CORSICA

CRETE

CYPRUS

RHODES

BALEARIC IS.

Clonard
York
Lincoln
London
Canterbury
Caerleon
Riga
Marienburg
Gnesen
Magdeburg
Bremen
Utrecht
Cologne
Fulda
Mainz
Luxeuil
Trier
Regensburg
Augsburg
Esztergom
Sirmium
Siscia
Singidunum
Salona
Durazzo
Kiew
Preslav
Sardica
Philippi
Beroea
Nicopolis
Thessalonica
Larissa
Athens
Corinth
Sparta
Durana
Benevenrum
Naples
Puteoli
Rome
Ravenna
Ancona
Florence
Pisa
Genoa
Verona
Milan
Aquileia
Vienne
Lyons
Arles
Marseille
Narbonne
Toulouse
Bordeaux
Tours
Nantes
Rouen
Paris
Reims
Bourges
Leon
Astorga
Merida
Evora
Faro
Cadiz
Seville
Cordova
Malaga
Tingis
Toledo
Valencia
Cartagena
Tarragona
Saragossa
Beneventum
Messina
Syracuse
Caesarea
Hippo Regius
Cirta
Madaura
Lambaesis
Carthage
Hadrumetum
Leptis Magna
Berenice
Cyrene
Alexandria
Memphis
Oxyrhynchus
Hermopolis
Ptolemais
Thebes
Jerusalem
Tyre
Caesarea
Damascus
Palmyra
Antioch
Edessa
Meliene
Nisibis
Arbela
Seleucia
Ctesiphon
Vagarshapat
Ancyra
Nicomedia
Nicaea
Chalcedon
Constantinople
Troas
Pergamum
Thyatira
Sardis
Smyrna
Ephesus
Laodicea
Perga
Iconium
Tarsus
Myra
Paphos
Salamis
Cnossus
Gortyna
Sinope
Piyus
Chersonesus
Tomi
Anchialus
Develtum
Amastris

The Centuries Between

The destruction of Jerusalem by the Romans under Titus (A.D. 70) and the subsequent suppression of the Bar Cochba revolt (A.D. 132-135) marked the end of the Jewish commonwealth. These events serve as important landmarks in the development of both Judaism and Christianity. In the years before A.D. 70, Judaism had developed distinctive traits in the many lands in which Jews had settled. Each community with a sizable Jewish population had its own synagogue and, although separated from the Jerusalem Temple, the Jews of the dispersion maintained a loyalty to the homeland through rigid observance of the sabbath and other legal requirements and by sending gifts to the Temple. The destruction of Jerusalem (A.D. 70) brought the Temple services to an end. Sacrifice and priesthood became matters of concern in the academies, but they were not part of Jewish worship. The synagogue, instead of the Temple, became the primary institution of religious life.

The Jew, however, continued to look to Jerusalem as his Holy City. Some Jews were taken by the Romans as slaves and dispersed throughout the empire. A remnant continued to live in Palestine, cultivating the soil and maintaining their religious schools. Galilee took on a distinctly Jewish character and Tiberias, once a gentile city, became a center of Jewish life.

Following the tragic Second Jewish Revolt (A.D. 132-135), the new city of Aelia Capitolina was built on the site of Jerusalem and Jews were excluded. The Jew, however, whether in the villages of Palestine or in the "dispersion" still looked to former Jerusalem as the city which was central to his life and faith.

During the years when Christianity was developing its distinctive traits and ceasing to be thought of as a Jewish sect, its geographical ties with Jerusalem and the Holy Land were also broken. Although Christians might have an attachment to Jerusalem because of its association with the passion and resurrection of Jesus, no one spot was accorded sacred status in the Christian faith. Jesus had told the Samaritan woman that it was neither in Mount Gerizim, nor in Jerusalem, that worship was to be offered, but wherever men would worship "in spirit and in truth" (John 4:20-24).

Christian communities sprang up along the coastal plain and in the mountainous districts of Judaea, Samaria, and Galilee before the end of the first century. We know of important groups at Joppa, Caesarea, Lydda, and Samaria. Before the destruction of Jerusalem, Christians left the Holy City and fled to Pella, in Transjordan, where other Christians had earlier settled.

SPREAD OF CHRISTIANITY

The first three centuries of the Christian era were times of unprecedented missionary outreach. In spite of the opposition of Imperial Rome, Christianity

Air View of Dura-Europus. Excavations at Dura, east of Palmyra, have supplied information on life, history, and art in Mesopotamia from Hellenistic and Roman times.
Courtesy, Yale University

spread to the most remote reaches of the Empire. It gained a firm foothold in Lower Egypt, particularly in Alexandria, from which it spread southward to Upper Egypt, and westward to the Roman provinces of northern Africa. In Europe it spread to Gaul, up the Danube River, and toward the Roman provinces in Germany. Tertullian (A.D. 160-220) states that Christianity was brought to Britain by the end of the second century.

Equally significant with the advance of Christianity westward was its conquest of the East. Edessa, not far from Syrian Antioch, on the great trade route between Armenia and the Syrian desert, early became the center of the Syriac church. King Abgar of Edessa is said to have written to Jesus asking Him to come and work a miraculous cure. After the resurrection, legend states, one of the Seventy arrived at Edessa, healed the king, and won the city to the Faith. The Syrian Christians spoke a language

known as Syriac, closely akin to Aramaic. They produced a Bible translation (the Peshitta), commentaries and other works expounding and defending the Christian faith.

Archaeological work at Dura-Europus, on the Euphrates along the road between Ctesiphon and Antioch, has unearthed the remains of a small building used as a church (A.D. 232). We know that Christianity reached northward into Armenia by the third century, and that it had a foothold in Georgia, north of Armenia, by the time of Constantine.

The eastern branches of Christianity also moved southward and eastward into Mesopotamia, Persia, Parthia, and Bactria. The traditions that Bartholomew brought Matthew's Gospel to India and that Thomas ministered both in Parthia and in India cannot always be taken seriously, but they do bear witness to the spread of the gospel to those lands at an early date.

Western Christianity was to experience

significant changes following the conversion of Constantine (A.D. 288-337). Although the church had made rapid strides, Christianity was for the most part a minority religion. Asia Minor was something of an exception, for the Christian church seems to have achieved majority status there, and it was making inroads into the older native population of Egypt. On the whole, however, Christianity was limited to the larger cities of the Empire, and even there it was one among many competing religions and philosophies.

Christianity, however, had survived a series of persecutions, and had attracted many of the finest minds of the Empire. When the Emperor Constantine professed the Christian faith the church entered a new era. Instead of being persecuted, Christianity became the favored religion and, ultimately, under Theodosius, the religion of the state itself. In fact Christianity soon was equated with Graeco-Roman civilization, and the state took it upon itself to define and enforce theological orthodoxy.

Although this process served to strengthen the church in the West, it had the opposite effect upon eastern Christianity. Zoroastrian Persia was an hereditary enemy of Rome. The equation of Christianity with Roman culture and political life put the Christians there in a most unfavorable light. The differences between the eastern and western forms of Christianity were, in part at least, due to these political pressures.

The establishment of an eastern capital at Byzantium, to serve as a "new Rome" in the East (A.D. 330) had important consequences for both the state and the church. Byzantium, or Constantinople as it was to be called, became the center of the Eastern Roman Empire, and of the eastern church.

The western empire was destroyed (A.D. 476) when Teutonic tribes from the north sacked the city of Rome and put an end to the imperial government. The church, however, although closely associated with Rome, survived its fall. The tribes which conquered Rome had accepted the Christian faith, and it was the bishops, priests, monks, and missionaries who kept Christian culture from disintegrating after the empire fell. The year of the fall of Rome is sometimes regarded as the dividing line between ancient history and the Middle Ages.

Although Constantinople was to maintain its imperial status for another millennium, Christians in the East were less successful than those in Europe in meeting their next crisis. During the seventh century the forces of Islam, the religion of Mohammed, swept out of Arabia and soon engulfed the East, and posed a serious threat to Christian Europe.

SPREAD OF ISLAM

In the seventh century the religion of Mohammed became a decisive voice in the East. During Mohammed's lifetime the Byzantine Empire, the successor to Rome, was being challenged by the Persian Empire, the successor to the old empire of Cyrus. There were religious overtones, for Byzantium was Christian; Persia, Zoroastrian. The two had fought bitterly in Palestine and Jerusalem frequently changed hands. Mohammed himself called on both Byzantine and Persian emperors to accept Islam.

Shortly after the death of Mohammed, one of his lieutenants led an army into Palestine and within two years conquered the entire country. A decisive battle was fought on the bank of the Yarmuk (A.D. 636). The conqueror, Omar, took both Damascus, the capital of Syria, and the city of Jerusalem. Under Moslem rule a small number of Jews made their way back to Palestine where they, as well as the Christians, were granted liberty to worship without fear of molestation.

Another lieutenant of Mohammed turned toward the East. He conquered Mesopotamia (modern Iraq; ancient Babylon and Assyria), and Persia. Within a few years a third Moslem prince captured Alexandria (A.D. 642) and proceeded to set up headquarters in Fustat (now Cairo) at the head of the Delta. From Egypt, the Arabs went on to take the island of Cyprus in the Mediterranean and then advanced westward along the coast of North Africa as far as Morocco and the Atlantic Ocean. In the year 710, the Arab, Tarq, invaded Spain with seven thousand men. The place where he landed was named Gebel (mountain) Tariq, and is now known as Gibraltar. Moslem arms threatened western Europe, but they were decisively defeated at Tours, in central France, by the armies of Charles Martel (A.D. 732).

The Arabs advanced in the East with lightning speed also. Their empire and religion was carried through central Asia to Samarkand and Bokhara, and on to western India and Afghanistan. Arabic became the common tongue of the Islamic Empire as Latin had been used in all parts of the Roman Empire.

The Arab nation was ruled by the Caliph ("successor," i.e. to Mohammed). A brother-in-law of Mohammed, Moawiya, founded the Omayad dynasty. From their capital at Damascus they ruled an empire from the Indus River to the Atlantic Ocean. Dynastic struggles ended the Omayad rule after about a century, and a **Persian** named Abbas became the first of the Abbassid Caliphs. In A.D. 762 the Abbassids built a new capital at Baghdad on the Tigris.

By the ninth century the supremacy of the families which claimed descent from Mohammed began to be challenged. Egypt became an independent Arab power and extended control over Syria and Palestine. The tenth century brought the rise of a new Fatimid dynasty in Egypt, which claimed descent from Fatima, a daughter of Mohammed. These rulers were less tolerant than the older dynasties and Christians from Europe began to experience trouble in their pilgrimages to the holy places. This trouble was increased early in the eleventh century when the Seljuks from Turkistan conquered Palestine. The oppression of the Christian pilgrims which followed, brought on the crusades—the attempts of Christians from western Europe to recover the Holy Land for Christianity.

THE CRUSADES

For more than two centuries the crusaders (i.e. followers of the *crux* or cross) fought the Moslems in the Near East. At the end of the eleventh century an army estimated at one million marched to the Holy Land from western Europe. Syria and Palestine were captured and Jerusalem became the capital of a Latin-Christian Kingdom (1099) with a Norman baron, Baldwin, as its first king. For eighty-five years the Latin Kingdom maintained its power. The land was divided into fiefs belonging to feudal barons who built impressive castles at strategic positions. The ruins of some of these still can be seen in the Holy Land.

The Moslems, however, did not acquiesce to Christian rule. They staged a comeback under the leadership of the vizier of the Sultan of Damascus and Egypt, Salah-ed-Din, better known as Saladin. The Christian knights lost an important battle at the Horns of Hattin in Galilee, and in 1189 Moslem power was restored to Jerusalem. The English king, Richard the Lionhearted, led a crusade against Saladin in the hope of

Crusader Castle at Sidon. For more than two centuries the crusaders fought the Moslems in the Near East. Ruins of their castles can still be seen today.
Courtesy,
Zion Research Library

reconquering the Holy City. This crusade was a failure. The Christian knights, however, maintained possession of the coastal plain of Palestine and Syria for about a century longer because they held strongly fortified cities such as Acre and Athlit. It was after fresh invasions of nomadic Mongols and Tartars that the Christians had to withdraw completely.

DECLINE OF ARAB CULTURE

During the Middle Ages the culture of the Moslem East was far ahead of the Christian West. Although the Crusaders fought to rescue the holy places from the hand of the "infidel," they found much in the Moslem world which was worth bringing back to Europe. The philosophy, the mathematics, the arts, and the material goods of the East provided one of the sparks which produced the European Renaissance. When the philosophers of ancient Greece had been forgotten in their homeland they were being studied by the Arabs of Baghdad in Arabic translations.

Soon after the Crusades, however, the East suffered a series of invasions from eastern Asia which resulted in the cultural stagnation from which it is now

arising. The Mongols and Tartars threatened both Christian and Moslem in the Near East before the dissolution of the Latin Kingdom. The nomads were finally defeated in a decisive battle near Beisan (Beth-shan) in Palestine. By that time, however, they had destroyed the chief centers of Arab civilization in Mesopotamia and had laid waste a large part of Palestine.

During the thirteenth and fourteenth centuries still other nomads from central Asia invaded the Middle East. These nomads, known to us as the Ottoman Turks, adopted Islam after they came in touch with the Arab kingdoms. By the end of the fifteenth century they controlled the entire Arab Empire. In 1453 they captured Constantinople (Byzantium) and brought to an end the Byzantine Empire which had lasted a thousand years. They conquered the Balkan countries and several times reached the very gates of Vienna.

The Turkish conquests marked the end of Arab political power for four centuries. The Turks, being Moslems, did not oppress their Arab co-religionists, but the Arabs remained socially, culturally, and economically stagnant. Following the Renaissance, the western nations became the bearers of culture and, in

At the Mount of Olives.   This ground-level view of the Chapel of the Ascension clearly shows the Crusader architecture of the lower level, which supports the Islamic dome above it. This is one example of the various cultural influences on the face of Palestine.

time, western ideas began to penetrate the East. The Portuguese, the Dutch, and finally the British established trading stations and gained legal concessions from the Turkish sultans. During the eighteenth and nineteenth centuries Britain was the dominant power in the East. In general the British were sympathetic to the Arabs. This found expression during World War I when Colonel Lawrence negotiated with Arab leaders a "Revolt in the Desert" against the Turks. The defeat of the Central Powers, including Turkey, during World War I, made possible the realization of a revived Arab nationalism. At the same time, however, the promise contained in the Balfour Declaration that Palestine would become a national homeland for the Jews complicated the picture.

CHAPTER XXVI

Bible Lands Today

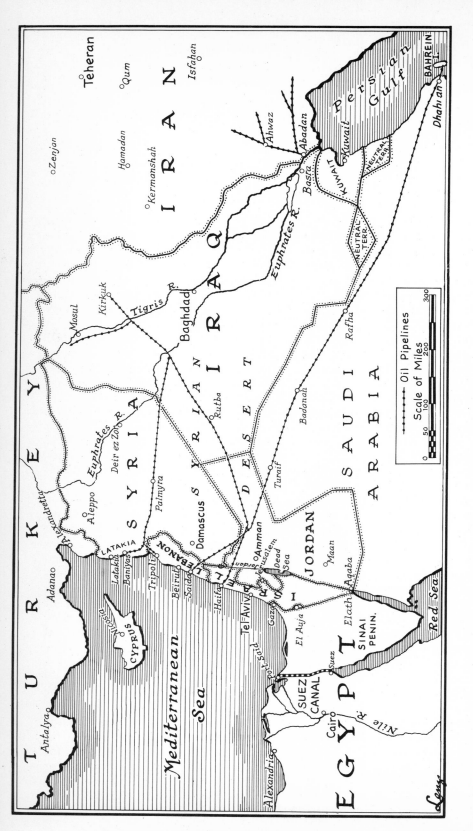

The Modern Near East. The state of Israel is predominantly Jewish in religion; Lebanon, about 50 per cent Christian and 50 per cent Moslem; the United Arab Republic (Egypt and Syria), Jordan, Saudi Arabia, Iraq, and Iran are predominantly Moslem. The map indicates oil pipelines which are a major factor in the economy of the Near East. Since the establishment of the state of Israel the section of the line terminating at Haifa has not been used.

Courtesy, The Christian Science Monitor

Bible Lands Today

EUROPEAN INTEREST

Napoleon's campaign in the Holy Land (1798-99) marked the beginning of European political interest in the Near East. Although his aim was utilitarian, there were cultural results of Napoleon's expedition. He succeeded in gaining control of the Near East and thus cutting off the British route through Egypt to India. The savants who accompanied Napoleon discovered the Rosetta Stone, a tri-lingual inscription in Greek and two forms of ancient Egyptian writing, which provided the clue to the decipherment of the hieroglyphs, thus opening a new chapter in the study of the literature and history of ancient Egypt.

After occupying Cairo and extending French control over the whole of Egypt, Napoleon marched into southern Palestine through the coastal plain which once had been occupied by the Philistines. The cities of Gaza and Joppa fell to the French, but the tide of battle then turned. Admiral Nelson with the British navy defeated the French fleet at the Battle of the Nile. The French land forces were decisively defeated at Acre (O.T. Accho; N.T. Ptolemaïs), north of Haifa. Acre is located north of the Bay of Acre, and it served as the chief harbor of the crusaders during the Middle Ages. Napoleon never recovered from his defeat at Acre. It marked the end of his dream for empire in the East. Even the Rosetta Stone was taken by the British and it can be seen today in the British Museum.

At the time of Napoleon's invasion, Palestine was a neglected, disease-ridden land with a population of between 100,000 and 200,000 people, most of whom were Arabs. There were, however, some Jews, Greeks, Negroes, and other minority peoples. Palestine, and the entire Near East, belonged to the Turkish (Ottoman) Empire.

Religious interest in Palestine had continued, however. Christian pilgrims visited Jerusalem, Bethlehem, Nazareth, and other holy places. They were zealous in building monasteries, convents, and churches. European Jews settled in Jerusalem and Hebron. Tiberias, on the Sea of Galilee, and Safad, farther north, were revered as holy places associated with rabbinical leaders of the post-Biblical period.

Following Napoleon's unsuccessful campaign, other European powers gave attention to Middle Eastern affairs. Britain wished to avoid any further threat to her route to India. Since part of it was overland, from Alexandria on the Mediterranean to Suez on the Red Sea, it was important that Egypt be kept out of enemy hands. The building of the Suez Canal (1859-69) eliminated the land part of the trip, but did not lessen the desirability of having Egypt ruled by a people friendly to Britain.

In the mid-nineteenth century the European nations actively took an interest in Palestine. Under Lord Palmerston, the British appointed a consul in Jerusalem who had the responsibility for the protection of all Jews, whether or not they were British subjects. The

French appointed a consul who protected the rights of the Latin (Roman Catholic) Church, and the Russians undertook similar responsibility for the Orthodox (Greek Orthodox) community. Italians, Germans, and Austrians also supported the Latin Church. Claims to rights at the holy places frequently resulted in friction. In 1853 a dispute between France and Russia touched off the Crimean War, which resulted in a lessening of Russian influence in the Middle East.

In 1870 several groups of German Christians settled in Jerusalem, Nazareth, Jaffa, and Haifa. They became pioneers in land-reclamation, and brought European methods of agriculture and trade to Palestine. They were followed by groups of Jewish idealists from eastern Europe who established a number of agricultural communities. The ravages of disease (particularly malaria) and Arab marauders took a heavy toll, but encouragement came through the munificence of the French financier, Baron Edmund Rothschild, whose financial help made possible the establishment of fifty villages.

Although not active in the politics of the Near East, nineteenth century America was interested in the lands of the Bible because of their religious significance. Edward Robinson, a teacher of Hebrew at Andover (Massachusetts) Theological Seminary, traveled to the Bible lands in 1838 in order to gain knowledge sufficient to write a Bible Geography. A second visit was made in 1852. Although subsequent research has made many changes in Robinson's work, he must be recognized as the pioneer in the study of the topography of Palestine. The excavation of Palestinian mounds had not yet begun in the days of Robinson. He and his followers did, however, explore the country, noting names and

geographical features which conformed to the description of sites mentioned in Scripture. Robinson did not blindly follow tradition, however. His Puritan background is often conspicuous, especially in the discussion of the so-called holy places.

Scholarly interest in the Holy Land led to the formation, in Britain, of the Palestine Exploration Fund. This society, founded in 1865, sponsored a survey of Palestine which resulted in the publication of a map of the country, to the scale of one inch to one mile, accompanied by volumes on Topography, Place-names, Fauna and Flora of the land. Underground explorations of Jerusalem formed one of the early projects of the Palestine Exploration Fund.

The work of Sir Flinders Petrie at Tell el-Hesi, near Gaza, formed one of the great contributions of the Palestine Exploration Fund to the science of archaeology. Petrie pointed to the fact that broken pieces of pottery, found in every ancient community, can be used to establish chronology. Each generation develops its own style and shape of pottery, so that an experienced archaeologist can date his find on the basis of the pottery discovered at a given site.

Other nations made their contributions to Palestinian archaeological research. The *Deutsche Palastina-Verein* ("German Palestine Society") published a journal dealing with Palestinian studies beginning in 1878. The French Dominican fathers had earlier established the *Ècole Biblique* ("Biblical School") in Jerusalem. They edited a scholarly journal known as *La Revue Biblique*. Scholars representing differing religious backgrounds, major educational institutions, and a variety of national organizations for the promotion of scholarly research, worked harmoniously during the years before World War I to provide a proper background for Biblical study.

While scholars were working together, national rivalries were building up tensions which were to result in a World War. German interest in the Near East was not all academic and religious. Kaiser Wilhelm II personally visited Turkey and Palestine in 1898, and proclaimed himself a friend of the Moslems. Germany pushed hard for a "Berlin to Baghdad" railroad which would have important political and economic overtones. Turkey was won over to the Ger-man side. Her alliance with the Central Powers during World War I resulted in the dismemberment of her empire following the victory of the allies.

ISRAEL

Following World War I, Palestine, the territory west of the Jordan, and Trans-Jordan, the land east of the Jordan, were assigned to the British as mandates by the League of Nations. According to the Balfour declaration (1917), Palestine was to become a na-

Tiberias on the Sea of Galilee. In Roman times Tiberias was famed for its mineral baths. It later became a center of Jewish life and is now a popular winter resort.

Courtesy, Consulate General of Israel

tional homeland for the Jews, with due regard to the rights of non-Jewish residents.

This provision, accepted in the best of faith, contained elements which history has shown to be irreconcilable. The Jew, represented by the Jewish Agency, and the Arab, represented by the Moslem Supreme Council, were soon pitted against one another. Rioting and bloodshed resulted. The Arabs, although the majority group, were alarmed at the population increase among the Jews, particularly in the years following Hitler's rise to power in Germany (1933). Britain suggested that the country be divided into Arab and Jewish sectors (1936), but the Arabs rejected any plan to partition the country. When Britain announced a plan to restrict further Jewish immigration (1939) the Jews, already suffering under Nazi Germany, refused to co-operate.

The Palestine problem was held in abeyance during World War II, but Arab and Jewish interests again clashed at the termination of the war. Desiring to provide a homeland for the surviving remnant of Jews who had escaped the massacres of Europe during World War II, the Jews sought to quicken the pace of immigration. The Arabs, on the other hand, wanted immigration to stop. In 1946 an Anglo-American commission appointed to study the problem recommended that 100,000 displaced European Jews be admitted into Palestine. No permanent solution to the problem was presented, however. When the British decided to admit but 2,000 Jews a month, secret Jewish terrorist groups began to attack British military installations. The situation deteriorated rapidly. Jews were smuggled into Palestine, and the British sought to intercept the ships. Britain found herself unable to cope with the mounting tensions.

In 1947 the United Nations established the United Nations Special Committee on Palestine to provide an answer to the impasse. The committee recommended that the land be partitioned into a Jewish state, an Arab state, and an international zone including Jerusalem. Against strong Arab protest the plan was accepted by the necessary two-thirds vote of the United Nations on November 29, 1947. When the British began to withdraw from Palestine early in 1948, Arab and Jew prepared for war. The British High Commissioner left Palestine on May 14, 1948, and Israel was immediately proclaimed as a sovereign state at Tel Aviv. The combined Arab armies of Lebanon, Syria, Jordan, Egypt, and Iraq immediately attacked the new Jewish state. Fighting continued, in spite of attempts at truce arrangements under United Nations auspices, until January 1949 when armistice arrangements were made.

At the time of the armistice Israel had increased the territory assigned to her in the United Nations partition plan by about one-half. Israeli territory included Galilee, the Coastal Plain, and the Negeb, with her southern boundary at Eilat (Elath) on the Gulf of Aqaba. Israel also occupied the New City of Jerusalem, i.e. the western suburbs of the walled city, which was in Jordan. Jerusalem is the seat of Israel's government. It was connected to the coastal plain by a corridor of land which was also part of Israel's territory. Israel after 1949 was comparable in size to the American state of New Jersey. It covered approximately 8,000 square miles of land area. At its greatest extent Israel's length was 280 miles and its maximum width was 41 miles. Following the Arab-Israeli war of 1967 Israel annexed the former Arab sector of Jesusalem and occupied the east bank of the Jordan, the Sinai Peninsula, and the Golan Heights east of the Sea of Galilee.

Bay of Haifa. Haifa, at the foot of Mount Carmel, is the port city of modern Israel. Oil refineries and diversified industry give it a significant place in the economy of the Near East.

Courtesy, Israel Office of Information

JORDAN

From the sixteenth century to the close of World War I the area which comprises the state of Jordan was a part of the Ottoman (Turkish) Empire. From 1922-1946 the land east of the Jordan, corresponding roughly with the Old Testament lands of Gilead, Moab, and Edom, comprised the British mandated territory of Trans-Jordan, or Transjordania—an area about 34,750 square miles in extent.

In 1923 Britain agreed to recognize the independence of Trans-Jordan under a prince of the Hashemite (Arab) family named Abdullah. An administrative agreement was subsequently reached whereby Britain was granted authority to maintain garrisons in the land. Following World War II, however, the official ties with Britain were severed and an Arab kingdom proclaimed (1946). Britain was permitted garrisons at the principal airports of the land and, in return, paid the Jordanians a subsidy of two million pounds each year for the maintenance of the Jordan Legion.

When the State of Israel was established (1948), Jordan joined the other Arab states in an attempt to thwart the Zionist aims. Although unsuccessful in preventing the functioning of the Jewish state, Jordan was able to occupy most of central Palestine west of the Jordan and south of Galilee.

The annexation of the territory west of the Jordan increased the territory of the former Trans-Jordan, now officially named the Hashemite Kingdom of Jordan, to 37,500 square miles. As a result of a desire to be fully freed from British influence, British troops have been completely removed, and Britain no longer subsidizes the Jordanian government.

All Jordanian territory west of the Jordan River fell to Israel in June 1967. It is now regarded as occupied territory.

The capital of Jordan is the city of Amman, situated on the famous King's Highway which was in use as early as the time of Abraham. Amman was known as Rabbah, or Rabbath-ammon in Old Testament times. It was during

David's siege of Rabbah that Uriah the Hittite died at the decree of the king who had taken the wife of his faithful soldier.

SYRIA

With the dismemberment of the Turkish Empire following World War I, the state of Syria was given its independence (1920) and, with neighboring Lebanon, was ruled as a French mandated territory (1920-41). In September 1941, during World War II, the occupying French authorities proclaimed Syria a republic. Since 1946 the land has been free of French troops.

Syria touches the Mediterranean north of Lebanon, and includes territory extending eastward to the Tigris River, north of ancient Nineveh. It covers 72,234 square miles of territory, much of which is desert. The Euphrates irrigates a narrow strip in the northeastern part of the country, and there are fertile areas around Homs and Hama (ancient Hamath) in the northwest, and Damascus and the *Jebel ed-Druz* sections of the southwest.

Damascus, the capital of modern Syria, is one of the oldest of occupied sites, its history going back to a period earlier than that of the Biblical patriarchs. One hundred forty miles north of Damascus is Hama, the Hamath of the Old Testament, located on the Orontes River. The city was once a center of Hittite culture, and it is still strategic because of its commercial position in the upper Orontes valley.

Aleppo, in northwestern Syria, was also the center of a Hittite state in ancient times. Located on important trade routes it was an important trading and commercial city. Silk and cotton textile

Hebron. The mosque *Al-Haram al-Ibrahimi* in the foreground was built over the traditional site of Machpelah, the field which Abraham purchased from Ephron the Hittite as a burial place.
Courtesy, Jordan Tourist Department

industries flourish there today. An ancient Roman road between Aleppo and Antioch (*Antakya, Turkey*) is reminiscent of the great part these cities played in ancient history.

LEBANON

About four thousand square miles of territory along the Mediterranean coast between Israel and Syria comprise the state of Lebanon. Formerly part of the Turkish Empire, Lebanon became independent under a French mandate from the League of Nations in 1920. The population of one and one-half million is about equally divided between Christian and Moslem.

Lebanon, once famed for its cedar trees, is a mountainous country with a fertile valley between the Lebanon Mountains which flank its west coast and the Anti-Lebanons which form the border between Lebanon and Syria on the east.

The ancient Phoenician cities of Tyre and Sidon are along the Mediterranean coast of Lebanon, as is Byblos (Gebal) once a center for the manufacture of papyrus ("paper"). The modern capital is at Beirut (ancient Berytus), a seaport at the foot of the Lebanons which was an important center of trade with Egypt as early as 1500 B.C. The American University at Beirut has made an important contribution to education in the Near East since it was founded by Americans in the 1860's.

IRAQ

The land between the Tigris and Euphrates rivers in the northern and eastern sections of the Fertile Crescent, including ancient Mesopotamia, is now called by its Arabic name, Iraq. During World War I, Iraq was taken from Tur-

key and it was subsequently assigned to Britain as a League of Nations mandate. In 1932 the mandate was ended and Iraq was recognized as a sovereign state.

Iraq is rich in historical lore, for it contains the ruins of the great Sumerian, Babylonian, and Assyrian cities of antiquity. From Ur of the Chaldees, in southern Iraq, Abraham and Terah began their pilgrimage. The ancient capitals at Babylon and Nineveh were once the greatest cities of the world. Babylonian and Assyrian kings ruled the Fertile Crescent area and beautified their cities with the fruits of their conquests.

The capital of modern Iraq is Baghdad, the city of the medieval caliphs, known to the West through the *Arabian Nights*. Baghdad, on the Tigris River, was the cultural center of medieval Islam.

Opposite the site of ancient Nineveh, along the Tigris River in the Zagros Mountain area, is the important city of Mosul. The valuable oil deposits of northern Iraq are piped from Mosul to Tripoli, on the Mediterranean coast.

A third important city of modern Iraq is Basra, located in the southeastern part of the country at the junction of the Tigris and Euphrates rivers. Basra is an important commercial city, serving as the port for Baghdad.

IRAN

The greater part of the plateau between the Indus and the Tigris rivers is occupied by the kingdom of Iran, the official name of the nation once known as Persia. Except for narrow strips of fertile territory along the Caspian Sea and the Persian Gulf, most of the 628,060 miles of Iranian territory is too dry to sustain a large population.

Not a part of the Arab world, the Iranians, although Moslem in religion, are adherents of the Shiite form of that faith. During World War I, Iran was neutral, although British and Russian troops occupied the country. A treaty with the British following the war (1919) affirmed Iranian independence but virtually established a British protectorate over the country. This treaty was subsequently abolished (1925) and the country is ruled as a constitutional monarchy under a shah.

The Iranian oil fields give the land strategic importance in the modern world. It also has valuable deposits of coal, iron, copper, lead, and manganese. Iranians are largely an agricultural people, raising wheat, barley and other grains.

The capital and intellectual center of Iran is the city of Teheran, in the northern part of the country. The second city of the country is Tabriz, a summer resort and center of trade between the north (Russia) and the west (Turkey).

Scene in Modern Jordan. This is a view of Mount Nebo with the "Spring of Moses" in the foreground.
Copyright,
Matson Photo Service

EGYPT

On the eve of World War I, Great Britain declared Egypt a British protectorate to counteract the influence of Turkey which had just joined the Central Powers. After the war, vigorous demands were made for the freedom of Egypt and a treaty was concluded in 1922. Egypt was proclaimed a kingdom under Fuad I, who was to rule by means of a parliament. Britain, however, reserved the right to maintain troops in Egypt, and the status of the Anglo-Egyptian Sudan was left indefinite.

Another treaty (1936) proclaimed Britain and Egypt as allies, but promised the eventual withdrawal of British troops. During World War II, Britain undertook the defense of Egypt which served as a key to the defense of the Empire. Alexandria became an important allied base, and the Suez Canal became the focus of attention.

A German advance which threatened Alexandria and the canal was stopped at El Alamein, a short distance west of Alexandria. This proved to be the turning point in the African phase of the war.

Since the close of World War II both Egyptian and Arab nationalism have brought about a withdrawal of British interests from Egypt. In June 1953 Egypt was proclaimed a republic. Since that time she has taken over control of the Suez Canal (1956) and combined with Syria to form the United Arab Republic (1958). The union was short-lived, but a new union, including Libya, has been formed. Egypt itself contains about 386,198 square miles of territory. Except for the Nile Valley, most of this is desert. The building of the Aswan High Dam made possible the irrigation of thousands of acres of previously useless land. The population growth of Egypt, however, has offset the benefit which the dam was expected to bring to the Egyptian standard of living.

The capital and business center of modern Egypt is Cairo, a city of over two million people at the head of the Nile Delta, directly across the river from the ancient capital, Memphis. It is but a short distance from the pyramids, impressive monuments to the Pharaohs who were buried within those gigantic stone structures 4500 years ago. The medieval mosques of Cairo and its Museum of Antiquities add to its interest as a tourist attraction.

Alexandria, at the western extremity of the Nile Delta, boasts a modern harbor and handles much of Egypt's foreign trade. The city has a population of nearly one million, and is connected by rail with Cairo and much of the Nile Valley.

Ancient Alexandria, the greatest seaport of the Hellenistic age, boasted one of the so-called wonders of the ancient world. The Pharos, or lighthouse, designed to point ships to the harbor and warn them of the shoals nearby, was built by Ptolemy Philadelphus, son and successor of Alexander's general, Ptolemy, who became ruler of Egypt following the break-up of the kingdom after Alexander's death. Ruins of the famed Pharos can still be seen in the harbor.

The loss of Sinai and the Gaza Strip to Israel in 1967 was a blow to Egypt. Although Russia provided planes and tanks to replace those lost in war, Egypt desires to be a leader of the Arab world free from domination by Russia or the West.

TURKEY

Most of the 287,500 square mile territory of modern Turkey is located in Asia Minor, once the center of ancient Hittite empires and later the birthplace and major field of labor of the apostle Paul. Turkey's association with the Central Powers during World War I brought

about important changes after the victory of the Allies. The empire was dismembered, the sultanate abolished, and the new Republic of Turkey set up (1923).

The chief city and seaport of modern Turkey is Istanbul, known before 1930 as Constantinople. With a colorful history going back to the days when it was the capital of the Byzantine Empire and the largest European city of the Middle Ages, Istanbul maintains its polyglot character which is reflected in its varied churches and numerous mosques.

The centrally located capital of modern Turkey is Ankara, anciently known as Ancyra. For centuries Ankara was a small town of no importance. It was rebuilt, however (1920-23), and made the seat of government, after which it grew quickly.

The lands of the Near East present a study in contrasts. In many of its cities the camel and the automobile can be seen simultaneously. Ancient methods of agriculture, however, are rapidly giving way to modern farming techniques. Oil has brought sudden riches to parts of the world which were regarded as remote and primitive a few decades ago. As in the days of Alexander the Great, East and West are meeting. Slowly the changeless Orient is experiencing change. Cultures long forgotten are being studied. Sons of the Pharaohs dream of the grandeur of a civilization only recently re-discovered. The mounds of Iraq speak of the days when Assyrians and Babylonians ruled the Fertile Crescent. The Bible lands have arisen from their slumbers and the Near East continues to occupy a central point in the affairs of nations.

Biblical Archaeology in the Twentieth Century

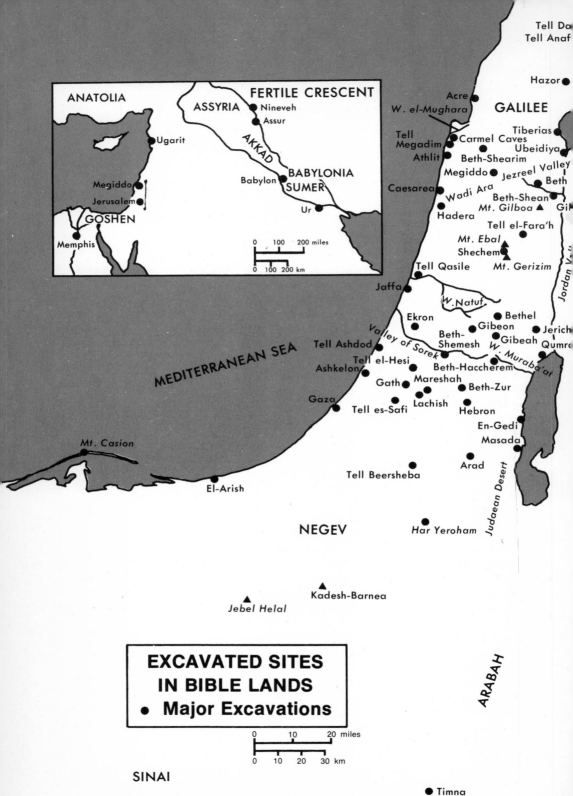

Tell Da
Tell Anaf

Hazor

ANATOLIA   FERTILE CRESCENT
ASSYRIA   Nineveh
                 Assur
                                        Acre   GALILEE
AKKAD   W. el-Mughara
                 Ugarit   Tiberias
                          BABYLONIA   Tell   Carmel Caves   Ubeidiya
Megiddo   Babylon   SUMER   Megadim   Carmel Caves
Jerusalem   Athlit   Beth-Shearim
           Ur   Megiddo   Jezreel Valley   Beth
GOSHEN   Caesarea   Wadi Ara
                                                    Beth-Shean
Memphis   Hadera   Mt. Gilboa ▲   Gi

0   100   200 miles   Tell el-Fara'h
0   100   200 km   Mt. Ebal ▲
                                                   Shechem
                                          Tell Qasile   Mt. Gerizim

MEDITERRANEAN SEA   Jaffa
                                                   W. Natuf
                                          Ekron   Bethel
                                                    Gibeon   Jericho
                                          Beth-   Gibeah
                                          Shemesh   Qumran
                                          Tell Ashdod   Valley of Sorek   W. Muraba'at
                                          Tell el-Hesi
                                          Ashkelon   Beth-Haccherem
                                          Gath   Mareshah   Beth-Zur
                                          Gaza   Lachish
Mt. Casion   Tell es-Safi   Hebron
                                                    En-Gedi
                                                    Masada
El-Arish   Tell Beersheba   Arad

                                          Judaean Desert
NEGEV   Har Yeroham

                     Kadesh-Barnea ▲
          Jebel Helal ▲

EXCAVATED SITES
IN BIBLE LANDS
• Major Excavations
                                                    ARABAH

0   10   20 miles
0   10   20   30 km

SINAI
                                          ● Timna

                                          ● Ezion-Geber

Biblical Archaeology in the Twentieth Century

In its broadest terms archaeology is concerned with the study of ancient things, and Biblical archaeology deals with Biblical antiquities. Pilgrims and travelers in the Bible lands are in a sense, amateur archaeologists, i.e. they are interested in seeing and discovering items which are related in some way to the Biblical record. Occasionally valuable materials are found by people with no specific archaeological training.

Modern archaeology, however, has developed scientific techniques which remove it from the realm of the "treasure hunt" of former years. When a mound is excavated great care is taken to place each item in its proper context. Mounds which contain the ruins of ancient cities frequently have many layers, or "strata," the top stratum representing the most recent settlement at the site. In stratigraphic excavations a stratum is removed to its foundations. Walls and rooms are carefully traced and each object is photographed at the spot where it was discovered. When this process is completed the next stratum is cleared away and the process repeated.

The careful archaeologist makes it a point to keep an accurate record of all objects found in every stratum. He does this by means of maps, plans, drawings, and photography, which are subsequently published so that other archaeologists may have the benefit of his work.

After records are carefully made, the archaeologist usually offers an interpretation of his discoveries. He is often able to date his finds by observing the forms of pottery found in each stratum. Archaeologists have made careful research in the development of shapes and designs in pottery and, as a result, are able to date these objects with a remarkable degree of accuracy. Inscribed material frequently gives a clue to the date of a given stratum, but pottery alone is often enough to provide an accurate chronological record. The comparison of objects from a given stratum with similar discoveries in other places frequently provides information concerning the cultural movements and relationships of ancient civilizations.

PALESTINE

It was not until the latter part of the nineteenth century that serious archaeological work began in Palestine. In 1890 the Palestine Exploration Fund sent Flinders Petrie, already a veteran Egyptian archaeologist, to locate Lachish in southern Palestine. He selected *Tell el-Hesī* for a trial excavation of six weeks, after which F. J. Bliss continued the work.

Tell el-Hesī is a mound which rose 120 feet beside an intermittent stream. Excavations indicated that eight cities had successively been built there. The first settlement was, according to Bliss, to be dated about 1700 B.C. The third city from the bottom contained a cunei-

Step-Trench, *Tell Jedeidah*, Syria. The excavator of a tell is apt to find a series of civilizations superimposed on one another. At *Tell Jedeidah* evidences of fourteen distinct occupations from about 5500 B.C. to A.D. 600 can be traced, showing the way in which a tell is built up from century to century. Typical objects are shown from each level.

Courtesy, Oriental Institute

I. A.D. 600-300. The level of an early Christian church. On a near-by site are even later Byzantine ruins and bronze crosses of the priests.

II. A.D. 300-64 B.C. A village partly contemporary with Paul and early Christian missionary activity in Antioch. Coins of the Caesars and Roman lamps.

III. ca. 64-500 B.C. An occupation of the period of the Persian Empire and of the Greek empires which followed the conquests of Alexander the Great.

IV. ca. 500-1000 B.C. Layers of the Syrian Hittite kingdom, contemporary with the later Assyrian Empire and the Babylonian Nebuchadnezzar. Hittite Hieroglyphs.

V. ca. 1000-1200 B.C. Ceramic traces of the "Peoples of the Sea," some of whom are known as the Philistines, others as the Achaeans who sacked Troy.

VI. ca. 1200-1600 B.C. A period rich in imported pottery of Cypriote and Aegean type, contemporary with the culture at Ugarit.

VII. ca. 1600-1900 B.C. The beginning of marked technological advances in the second millennium B.C. Grotesque "mother-goddess" figurines are characteristic of this period.

VIII. ca. 1900-2000 B.C. A period of transition (probably of a relatively short time) during which certain distinct types of pottery were manufactured.

IX. ca. 2000-2300 B.C. A time of brilliant work in metal and pottery, climaxing the technological achievements of the third millennium B.C.

X. ca. 2300-2600 B.C. The beginnings of a range of goblets and small drinking vessels; a period rich in connections with the south and east.

XI. ca. 2600-3000 B.C. A range marked by a fine red-and-black pottery series, by excellent metalwork, and by cylinder seals of Mesopotamian type.

XII. ca. 3000-3500 B.C. A period of technological advancement, at the end of which appear the earliest known castings of human figures in metal. Links to both Egypt and Mesopotamia.

XIII. ca. 3500-3900 B.C. Levels yielding rather drab pottery but the earliest types of tectonically conceived metal tools. The technological traditions have links to the east.

GAP

XIV. ca. 5000-5500 B.C.(?) Traces of materials in the range of the earliest known villages of Syro-Cilicia. Hand-made, polished pottery; simple tools in bone and flint.

VIRGIN SOIL   Six feet under the present water level.

form tablet with the name of one of the men mentioned in the Egyptian Tell el Amarna tablets (1400-1350 B.C.). Pottery of Greek origin was found in the stratum which should be dated from 550 to 350 B.C.

Subsequent archaeological work has identified Lachish with *Tell ed-Duweir*, with the result that Petrie's identification of *Tell el-Hesī* must be corrected. Although we cannot be certain, some scholars identify *Tell el-Hesī* with Eglon (Josh. 10:3; 12:12).

After spending some years in the city of Jerusalem (1894-97), during which he attempted to recover the line of the ancient south wall of the city, Bliss turned again to the excavation of other sites. He was attracted to the Shephelah, the onetime borderland between Judah and the Philistines. Work began at *Tell Zakariyeh,* Biblical Azekah, where he discovered a fortress with foundations dating to early Israelite times. These may be the fortifications built by Rehoboam (II Chron. 11:5-10).

The expedition moved on to *Tell es-Sâfi,* possibly Biblical Libnah. This city had been occupied from about 1700 B.C. to Seleucid times (250 B.C.). Further excavations were carried on at *Tell el-Judeideh,* Biblical Moresheth-gath.

The Palestine Exploration Fund sent R. A. Stewart Macalister, formerly assistant to Dr. Bliss, to *Tell Jezer,* about six miles southeast of Ramle, which had been identified as the site of Biblical Gezer. A series of expeditions (1902-09) produced many artifacts, but the permanent results were meager. Scientific techniques of archaeological research were just being developed, and the work of Bliss was primitive by modern standards.

Advances were made in the excavations at Jericho by Sellin and Watzinger (1907-09) and at Megiddo by Reisner and Fisher (1908-10). In both instances

excellent work was done which prepared the way for more definitive excavating at a later time.

During part of three seasons from 1908 to 1910, Harvard University conducted a campaign at *Sebastiyeh,* the site of ancient Samaria. Remains of a large palace erected on native rock are thought to go back to the Israelite king Omri who transferred the seat of his government to Samaria (I Kings 16:24). Above this were ruins of a larger palace faced with white marble which may be the "ivory house" built by Ahab (I Kings 22:39). On a level with this latter house was a building containing a large number of inscribed potsherds which proved to be receipts for wine and oil stored there. Above the "Ahab" palace was still a third palace, thought to date from the time of Jeroboam II. Higher up in the mound were remains from the period of Assyrian control and from the time of Herod the Great, who rebuilt the city.

Following World War I, Palestinian archaeology was pursued with renewed vigor. The limitations imposed by the Turkish government were now lifted and Palestine was assigned to Britain under a League of Nations mandate. In 1920 this government organized a Department of Antiquities headed by John Garstang. During the years 1921-22, Garstang and W. J. Phythian-Adams carried on excavations at the old Philistine cities of Ashkelon and Gaza. These were not extensive campaigns although they produced some interesting results. Gaza was found to have been largely abandoned from about 300 B.C. until Roman times, a fact which coincides with the statement of the historian Strabo that it was destroyed by Alexander the Great and remained deserted. Garstang and Phythian-Adams also worked for a short time (October, 1922) at *Tell Jemmeh,* eight miles southeast of Gaza, which was tentatively identified with Biblical Gerar (Gen. 10:19; 20:1, 2). The city was on the main caravan route to Egypt and it seems to have been maintained by exacting toll from passing traffic.

Excavations at Beth-shan, located at the point where the Valley of Esdraelon descends into the Jordan Valley, were undertaken by the University of Pennsylvania Museum during the years 1921-33 in a series of expeditions directed by Clarence S. Fisher, A. Rowe, and G. M. Fitzgerald. The site, it was discovered, was occupied from 3000 B.C. and contained inscribed pillars from the time of the Egyptian Pharaohs Seti I and Rameses II (1290 B.C.). The fortress was later in the hands of the Philistines and subsequently burned, probably by David. Successive strata of temples at Beth-shan illustrate the religious practices of the non-Israelites in ancient Canaan.

The mound of *Tell Beit Mirsim* was excavated during a series of campaigns from 1926 to 1933 by Melvin Grove Kyle of the Pittsburgh-Xenia Theological Seminary and William Foxwell Albright representing the American Schools of Oriental Research. The mound, twelve miles southwest of Hebron, had been occupied by ten successive settlements, the earliest of which was founded about 2200 B.C.

The excavators identified *Tell Beit Mirsim* with Kirjath-sepher, or Debir (Josh. 15:15, 16; Judg. 1:11, 12). Archaeological remains indicate that the city was destroyed ten times, one of which, according to the Biblical text, was by Pharaoh Shishak (Egyptian, Sheshonk), about 930 B.C. (I Kings 14:25). The last settlement was destroyed by the armies of Nebuchadnezzar who burned Jerusalem in 587 B.C.

In the upper level of the mound a seal was found bearing the inscription, "Eliakim, servant of Jehoiachin." This may well have belonged to a servant of the Judaean king, Jehoiachin, who reigned but three months before being taken to Babylon by Nebuchadnezzar and replaced by his uncle Zedekiah.

During the years 1926-35, Professor F. W. Badè of the Pacific School of Religion, assisted by members of the staff of the American Schools of Oriental Research, excavated *Tell en-Nasbeh,* a large mound about seven miles north of Jerusalem. Jar handles stamped with the word "Mizpeh" in old Hebrew letters seem to identify the site with Mizpeh of Benjamin (Judg. 20:1; I Sam. 7:5).

The city of Beth-shemesh, which had been partially explored by Duncan Mackenzie in 1911-12, was excavated by Professor Elihu Grant of Haverford College between the years 1928 and 1933. Four strata have been distinguished from Hyksos times to the Babylonian Exile. Discoveries include a potsherd inscribed in ink with old Hebrew characters and a tablet written in the Ugaritic alphabet of northern Phoenicia.

William F. Albright conducted important excavations at *Tell el-Fûl,* the Biblical Gibeah of Saul. At the bottom of the mound he found ruins of a fortress built of massive stone blocks which was destroyed by fire, as evidenced by the layer of ashes covering the stones. Albright connects this destruction with that mentioned in the Biblical account of the war between Benjamin and Israel (Judg. 20:40).

Between 1925 and 1936 systematic excavations were carried on by the Oriental Institute of the University of Chicago at *Tell el-Mutesellim,* the mound of ancient Megiddo. Work was done by Clarence S. Fisher, P. L. O. Guy and G. Loud. Among the discoveries at Megiddo are the famous "Solomon's Stables" equipped with mangers for the horses, space for housing chariots and quarters for the grooms. Recent Israeli studies suggest that the stables may actually be from the time of Ahab.

Protohistoric finds of the Chalcolithic period (4500-3000 B.C.) in Palestine resulted from work at *Teleilât el-Ghassûl* on the east bank of the Jordan near Jericho, conducted by the Pontifical Biblical Institute and directed by Père A. Mallon and Robert Koppel (1929-38). Houses at *Teleilât el-Ghassûl* were made of mud brick and many of the plastered interiors were adorned with paintings.

The American Schools of Oriental Research in Jerusalem and the Presbyterian Theological Seminary (now McCormick), Chicago, jointly sponsored an expedition at *Khirbet et-Tubeiqeh,* Biblical Beth-zur, north of Hebron, in 1931. W. F. Albright directed the work, assisted by O. R. Sellers. Although further work was not possible in the intervening years, Sellers was able to return in 1957 for a second campaign. Archaeological evidence indicates that the city was founded about 1600 B.C. and destroyed about a century later, perhaps by the Egyptian Pharaoh Thutmose III. During the thirteenth century B.C. Beth-zur was rebuilt.

The modern village of *Beitin,* about twelve miles north of Jerusalem, is on the site of ancient Bethel. In 1934 W. F. Albright, who had earlier determined that at least half of the ancient city was outside the modern village, returned with James L. Kelso, of Pittsburgh-Xenia Seminary to excavate as much of the city as possible. Kelso went again in 1954 and 1957 for further work. The objects discovered indicate that the first settlement was made about 2000 B.C. After a checkered history, Bethel, in the thirteenth century B.C., was destroyed by fire. This destruction is thought to have been the work of Israelites at the time of the conquest of Canaan. The city was rebuilt, but inferior workmanship marks the Bethel of the time of the Judges.

During the ninth or tenth century B.C. the city was again built with houses and walls, but the workmanship was much better. This was the period of Jeroboam I who established Bethel as an important religious center for the Northern Kingdom. A later destruction is probably to be attributed to Nebuchadnezzar in the sixth century. The site then remained unoccupied until about 400 B.C.

In 1926 Professor Ernst Sellin resumed excavations at *Tell Balâta,* near Shechem, which had been begun during the 1913-14 season. A large palace with massive walls was discovered along with a temple which the excavators identified with the El-berith shrine (Judg. 9:46). Two cuneiform tablets, similar in character and contents to those discovered at *Tell el-Amarna* were also found by Sellin. The temple seems to have been built about 1300 B.C. and burned about 1150 B.C. Although the German excavators were unable to complete the excavation of *Tell Balâta,* the work was resumed as a joint project of Drew University and McCormick Theological Seminary in 1957 under the direction of G. Ernest Wright.

In 1927 Sir W. M. Flinders Petrie, the veteran explorer of Egypt, returned to southern Palestine and excavated *Tell Jemmeh* which he, like his predecessor Garstang, identified with Gerar. Being unimpressed with the work at *Tell Jemmeh,* Petrie transferred his activities to *Tell el-Fâr'ah,* southeast of Gaza, which he identified with Beth-palet (Josh. 15:27). Albright, however suggests that *Tell el-Fâr'ah* may have been Sharuhen, a prominent city on the southern border of Palestine. Later Petrie excavated at *Tell el-'Ajjûl* in the southwestern Negev.

Work at Samaria, begun in 1908, was resumed by Harvard University in 1931 in co-operation with the Hebrew University, the British School of Archaeology,

The Gulf of Aqaba. Here we see Nelson Glueck reading the Bible to members of his expedition, on a hilltop overlooking the north end of the Gulf of Aqaba.
Courtesy, Nelson Glueck

and the Palestine Exploration Fund. J. M. Crowfoot, E. Sukenik, and others worked at Samaria from 1931 to 1935. The old Hebrew wall from the time of Omri and Ahab was discovered, as were numerous carved ivories.

Jericho, excavated by Ernst Sellin in 1908-09, became the scene of a series of campaigns by John Garstang (1930-36). Garstang found many strata at Jericho, evidence that the site had been occupied for many centuries. Through the study of pottery he dated a severe conflagration at about 1400 B.C., stating that Joshua captured the city at that time (Josh. 6:1-21).

From 1952 to 1956 Jericho was again the subject of serious archaeological work, this time directed by Kathleen Kenyon for the British School of Archaeology and a number of co-operating institutions. Miss Kenyon has shown that virtually nothing remains at the site of Jericho from the period between 1500 and 1200 B.C. The walls which Garstang believed to have been destroyed by earthquake and fire in 1400 are now dated much earlier.

In the spring of 1933, J. L. Starkey began the excavation of *Tell ed-Duweir* not far from *Tell Beit-Mirsim*. The expedition continued through 1938 although Starkey was murdered by Arabs and the work had to be carried on by G. Lankester Harding and Charles Inge. *Tell ed-Duweir* proved to be one of the frontier fortresses of the kingdom of Judah, and it is now identified with Biblical Lachish. Discoveries include a cemetery with objects dating to 3000 B.C. or earlier and a small temple which seems to have been built during the reign of the Egyptian Pharaoh Amenhotep III and repaired during the reign of Rameses II.

The most spectacular of the finds at *Tell ed-Duweir* was a group of eighteen potsherds inscribed with ancient Hebrew

characters. They were letters, written to a Judaean officer or governor shortly before the whole of Palestine was conquered by Nebuchadnezzar. One of the letters refers to the smoke signals by which the cities of Judah communicated with each other: "We are watching the signal-station of Lachish, according to all the signals you are giving, because we cannot see the signals of Azekah." Apparently Azekah had already fallen to the Babylonians.

Madame Judith Marquet-Krause carried on extensive excavations at *et-Tell* (Biblical Ai) two miles southeast of Bethel in 1934 and 1935. Three city levels were unearthed, the earliest of which dates from about 3000 B.C. The mound was not inhabited from 2000 to about 1050 B.C. when the foundations of a building designated as "the palace" appear. Professor Joseph Callaway of the Southern Baptist Seminary has resumed excavation of *et-Tell*. He is convinced that the identification of the mound with Ai is correct.

The Biblical word Ai means "the ruin." It may have been a military outpost of Bethel at the time of the Israelite conquest of Canaan.

Professor Nelson Glueck of Hebrew Union College, Cincinnati, conducted an archaeological survey of Trans-Jordan (1933-1943). Several hundred mounds were examined and information gathered concerning localities in ancient Moab, Edom, and the Nabataean Kingdom. A number of copper and iron mines were discovered in the area south of the Dead Sea, where raw ore actually protrudes above the surface of the ground.

Glueck excavated *Tell el Kheleifeh*, ancient Ezion-geber, during the years 1937-40. Here Solomon maintained his seaport on the Gulf of Aqaba. Remains of a large smelting refinery first built in the tenth century B.C. were discovered. Ore mined in the area south of the Dead

Caves overlooking Wadi Qumran. In these caves, about two miles west of the Dead Sea on the edge of the Judaean wilderness, the library of a monastic Jewish community was discovered. The manuscripts, popularly known as the Dead Sea Scrolls contain copies of most of our Old Testament books as well as other literature prized by the Qumran community.
Copyright, Matson Photo Service

Sea received a preliminary smelting near the mines, after which it was brought to Ezion-geber and placed in crucibles inside the smelters. There it was further refined and worked into ingots for shipment.

The expedition of Pére R. de Vaux and the French Dominican Fathers at *Tell el-Fâr'ah,* seven miles northeast of Shechem, begun in 1947, has unearthed remains of a city going back to the fourth millennium. The site tentatively identified with Tirzah (I Kings 15:21, 33) was destroyed during the ninth century B.C. about the time the Israelite capital was transferred to Samaria (I Kings 16:23-24).

In 1947 Maisler commenced the excavation of *Tell Qasileh* near Tel Aviv under the auspices of the Israel Exploration Society. Remains from the Philistine, Israelite, Persian, and Hellenistic periods have been discovered but the ancient name of the community is still unknown.

Since 1947 a series of discoveries in the vicinity of the *Wadi Qumrân* have given a clearer picture of Jewish life in the decades before the birth of Christ. The finding of a library of Biblical and other literature once belonging to a community of Essenes, a group of Jewish ascetics, has provided students of the Old Testament and of New Testament backgrounds with a wealth of material.

Following the discovery of the first of the scrolls the mound known as *Khirbet Qumrân* was excavated by Lankester Harding, then of the Jordan Department of Antiquities, and Père R. de Vaux of the Dominican École Biblique. The mound was found to contain the community center of the sect. In one of the rooms, known as the scriptorium, were found tables and benches for writing. An inkpot with dried ink was discovered in the scriptorium. This was probably the place where some of the scrolls found in the caves nearby were copied from originals brought by members of the community to their wilderness retreat. In subsequent years other scrolls were found in caves nearby, adding further light on the text of the Old Testament and of sectarian Judaism during New Testament times.

Shortly after the discovery of the Qumran scrolls, another group of ancient documents was discovered in the *Wadi Murabba'at*, about fifteen miles southeast of Jerusalem. Most of these documents date from the time of the Second Jewish Revolt (A.D. 132-135). A third group of writings, dating around the eighth century A.D., was discovered at *Khirbet el-Mird*, nine miles southeast of Jerusalem.

J. L. Kelso and J. B. Pritchard worked at the New Testament city of Jericho (*Tulul Abu el-'Alayiq*) during the years 1950-51. A large civic center attributed to Herod Archelaus was one of the more spectacular discoveries. It is known that Jericho served as the winter capital of Judah during the days of the Herods, and the ruins discovered there are architecturally similar to the civic buildings of Rome itself. Coins from the reign of Herod Archelaus assist in the dating of these important structures.

Joseph P. Free of Wheaton College conducted a series of summer excavations beginning in 1953 at Dothan, *Tell Dotan,* a mound which rises two hundred feet above the surrounding countryside eleven miles north of Samaria. Dr. Free has traced the history of Dothan from about 3000 B.C. to the Hellenistic age (*ca.* 100 B.C.). Dothan was the place where Joseph, Jacob's favorite son, was placed in a cistern by his jealous brothers and, subsequently, sold into slavery. Cistern pits, such as the one in which Joseph was placed, may still be seen near Dothan.

Tell el-Qedah, ancient Hazor in Galilee, west of Lake Hula, has been excavated by Professor Yigael Yadin of the Hebrew University. His first campaign there in 1955 produced evidence of seventeen strata of occupation, the earliest about 4000 B.C. The Canaanite city of Hazor appears to have been destroyed by the Israelites some time during the thirteenth century, and the Israelite city was evidently destroyed by Tiglath-pileser III (*ca.* 733 B.C.).

During the summer of 1956, James B. Pritchard began excavations at *el-Jib,*

six miles north of Jerusalem, which had been tentatively identified with the Biblical city of Gibeon.

Among the more interesting discoveries at *el-Jib* was a rock-cut pool which is now believed to be the site of the tournament between the twelve men of Abner and the twelve men of David (II Sam 2:12-17).

The Israel Exploration Society conducted major excavations at Beth Yerah (*Khirbet Kerak*), at the southwest corner of the Sea of Galilee beginning in 1944. Two Israeli scholars, M. Stekelis and B. Maisler, directed the expedition. In 1950 the Department of Antiquities of the state of Israel did further work there. Excavations show that in the middle of the third millennium B.C. the settlement at Khirbet Kerak enjoyed a remarkably high level of culture. The streets were straight and paved with basalt. In all there were sixteen strata, indicating levels of occupation from chalcolithic times until the eighth or ninth centuries A.D.

Each summer the Hebrew University and the University of Tel Aviv conduct major expeditions. Work continues at Tel Arad, Tel Beer Sheva, at the Western ("Wailing") Wall in Jerusalem and at many other sites. The Hebrew Union College is working at Gezer. The former Jerusalem school of the American School of Oriental Research, now the Albright Institute, is active in much of the archaeological work in the area. Another center in Amman, Jordan, sponsors work there. In addition to work in Amman itself, notable work has been done by Sigfried Horn at Heshbon. Never has there been more activity in Palestinian archaeology than at the present time.

ARABIA
Although closely related to the Biblical world, Arabia has been often neglected in archaeological research. Dur-

ing the nineteenth century the great Hebraists Wilhelm Gesenius and Emil Roediger deciphered Sabaean inscriptions and made available a fresh body of Semitic literature for the Old Testament scholars. Subsequently the area known as Yemen was explored by Arnaud, Halévy, and Glaser (1882-94) with the result that thousands of copies of Sabaean, Minaean, and Qatabanian inscriptions were collected.

The American Foundation for the Study of Man undertook in 1950 a campaign to study the culture of South Arabia under the direction of Wendell Phillips with W. F. Albright as chief archaeologist. Excavations were first conducted at Qataban, in and around the ancient capital city of Timna. Through a study of pottery, masonry, and forms of writing it is now possible to date events in the history of South Arabia with a high degree of accuracy.

In 1952 excavations were conducted at Marib, the ancient capital of Saba (Biblical Sheba). Here the ruins indicate the advanced state of South Arabian culture during Biblical times.

Meanwhile archaeologists in northern Arabia have endeavored to collect accessible inscriptions on walls and rock scarps. Thousands of such writings have been found there which date from 1000 B.C. to A.D. 600.

SYRIA AND LEBANON

A German expedition working at Sinjirli (ancient Samal), in Syria (1889-91) discovered many Hittite sculptures and a number of Aramaic inscriptions from the time of Tiglath-pileser III and Esarhaddon. Particularly impressive was the victory stele set up by Esarhaddon (680-669 B.C.) to commemorate the victory of his Assyrian forces over Egypt. John Garstang subsequently excavated another Hittite site nearby (1908-11). Much of the material found

during these excavations was clearly Hittite in origin and bore witness to the fact that a Hittite kingdom once had its center there.

Carchemish on the Euphrates was excavated by Sir Leonard Woolley and T. E. Lawrence for the British Museum (1911-14). Inscriptions in Hieroglyphic Hittite were discovered there along with many seals, pieces of jewelry, and other small objects. The ruins of an acropolis built by Sargon the Assyrian (ca. 717 B.C.) who wrested Carchemish from the Hittites, were also found.

Shortly after the close of World War I, the French archaeologist M. Montet began the excavation of Jebeil, ancient Gebal or Byblos, twenty-five miles north of Beirut. Tombs were discovered containing objects from early Egyptian dynasties which indicate Egyptian contacts with Phoenicia at a very early date. A sarcophagus discovered at Jebeil bears an inscription which is the oldest known example of Phoenician writing (ca. 1100 B.C.). The inscription contains the names Hiram and Ethbaal which occur in the Old Testament although, of course, in reference to different people.

The excavation at Dura, west of the Euphrates, began during the early days of the British occupation of Iraq following World War I. In the process of digging trenches the British military authorities discovered some remarkable paintings which they brought to the attention of Professor James Breasted (1920). Eight years later Yale University sponsored an expedition directed by M. I. Rostovtzeff, Franz Cumont, and René Dussaud to explore the site. In the course of the excavation they discovered a Jewish synagogue and a Christian church both of which had walls decorated with Biblical scenes. The city was identified with Dura, a flourishing town during the early centuries of the Christian era.

The accidental finding by a Syrian peasant of clay tablets in a previously unknown cuneiform alphabet proved to be one of the most important finds of the twentieth century. The discovery was made at a place known as Ras Shamra, on the Syrian coast, opposite Cyprus. It led to the excavation of the site over a period of years, beginning in 1929.

F. A. Schaeffer, a French archaeologist began the excavation of Ras Shamra, which proved to be the ancient city of Ugarit, known from other literature to have had commercial dealings with Babylonian and Hittite kings. The excavation at Ugarit brought to light buildings, a variety of utensils and works of art, and an archive of written documents.

In addition to such business documents as an important Near Eastern city might possess, Ugaritic texts also include a series of epics which describe the exploits of their gods (notably Baal) and the heroic kings of the legendary past. The language and idiom of Ugarit was similar to Biblical Hebrew, and the mythology exhibits the features of Canaanite religion which were condemned by the prophets of Israel.

Excavations at *Tell Hariri*, ancient Mari on the Middle Euphrates, were carried on from 1933 to 1938 by the Louvre under the direction of the French archaeologist André Parrot. Mari is now known to have been one of the greatest cities of ancient Mesopotamia. It contained an Ishtar temple and a ziggurat. More important, however, from the archaeological viewpoint, was the royal palace which contained the correspondence of Zimri-Lim, Mari's last king. Over twenty thousand cuneiform tablets comprising his diplomatic correspondence were recovered. Among those mentioned in these documents is Hammurabi of Babylon, the king who conquered Mari about 1697 B.C. and added it to his growing kingdom. The Mari tablets help us to understand the political and social backgrounds of the age of the Biblical patriarchs. Names such as Serug, Peleg, and Nahor appear in the letters (cf. Gen. 11:16, 22, 24, 27) and reference is made to a tribe of Bana-yamina, a name which is similar to Biblical Benjamin.

The ancient Hittite city of Alalakh, now the north Syrian mound known as *Tell 'Atshâneh*, was excavated by Sir Leonard Woolley during the 1938-39 season. Architectural discoveries included a palace (*ca.* 2000 B.C.) and a temple (*ca.* 1700-1583 B.C.) with statuary implying a high degree or artistic and technological competence. Some of the potsherds discovered at Alalakh are similar to those found at Knossus in Crete. Commerce and communication between Western and Eastern civilizations is thus illustrated from excavations dealing with Hittite times.

The German diplomat and explorer Baron Max von Oppenheim first discovered the site of *Tell Halâf* on the Habor River in northern Syria in 1899. He conducted extensive excavations there in 1911-13 and returned in 1927 and 1929. At *Tell Halâf* a number of Hittite statues were found, including a number of lions with gods standing on them. In lower levels of the mound Oppenheim found a large amount of prehistoric pottery now known as Halafian.

The Oriental Institute of the University of Chicago conducted excavations at Jarmo in Syria between 1948 and 1951. Robert Braidwood, a specialist in prehistory, was leader of the project. Braidwood also worked with Bruce Howe at nearby *Karim Shahir*, an excavation sponsored by the American Schools of Oriental Research. *Karim Shahir* presents evidence of man's earliest ventures into agriculture. The prehistorian notes the way in which man ceased being simply a "food gatherer" and began to become a "food producer." Progress is noted at Jarmo where food production was more refined and the community became more permanent.

BABYLONIA AND ASSYRIA

During the nineteenth century the cultures of Babylon and Assyria were rediscovered through the decipherment of cuneiform writing and the discovery of large numbers of cuneiform inscriptions. The work of Botta (1842) and Layard (1845) at Nineveh opened new chapters of ancient history.

The non-Semitic Sumerians also came to life during the nineteenth century. Sarzac's work at Lagash (1877) and the University of Pennsylvania excavations at Nippur (1889) brought to light evidences of the culture of a people who were settled at the head of the Persian Gulf at the dawn of history.

In 1899 the Germans organized a society for the purpose of scientific study of oriental cultures and sent Robert Koldewey to excavate Babylon, a work which continued until the outbreak of World War I. Koldewey recovered the walls of Nebuchadnezzar's Babylon and the palace and temples with which the city was once adorned. Minor excavations at other mounds of ancient Babylon were also conducted under Koldewey's direction. During the season 1903-04 other work was done in Babylon by an American expedition sponsored by the University of Chicago and directed by Professors Robert Harper and Edgar Banks. The mound of *Bismâya,* ancient Adab, was excavated but troubles with the Turkish government brought the expedition to an end.

The Germans also worked farther north in the Tigris-Euphrates valley at *Qala 'ah Sherqât,* ancient Ashur (Gen. 10:11) on the Tigris. The project was directed by Andrae and continued from 1902 to 1914. Temples and palaces were excavated and an abundance of inscribed material was found.

Although J. E. Taylor began excavation of Ur in 1859, and H. R. Hall conducted a campaign in 1918, the principal work at Ur (*el-Muqaiyar*) was begun in 1922 by Sir Leonard Woolley. Woolley subsequently conducted a joint expedition there for the British Museum and the University of Pennsylvania which lasted until 1934. The ancient Sumerian culture was well illustrated by the discoveries at Ur. The famous royal cemeteries (*ca.* 2500 B.C.) yielded beautiful jewelry and art treasures. Temples to the moon god (Nannar) and his consort (Nin-gal) were discovered. Nearby was a well-equipped kitchen with great ovens for roasting meat and cauldrons where meat could be boiled.

Excavations indicate that, at the time of Abraham, houses stood adjacent to the temple area. In one house there was discovered a private chapel with an altar, niche, and family burial vault.

Professor Edward Chiera, working with the American Schools of Oriental Research at Baghdad and with the Department of Antiquities of the Iraq government, began, in 1925, the excavation of *Yorghan Tepe,* near *Kirkuk,* southeast of ancient Nineveh. Among the ruins of the house of a prosperous citizen he found about one thousand clay tablets containing the business and legal records of its occupants. They indicated that the ancient city was named Nuzi or Nuzu and that it was occupied by a non-Semitic people known as Hurrians. The tablets were written in the Semitic language common to Assyria and Babylon and known to us as Akkadian. In successive years the work was continued by Robert H. Pfeiffer of Harvard (1928-29) and Richard F. S. Starr of the Fogg Museum, Harvard (1929-31). A large palace was discovered along with smaller buildings, works of art, and many more cuneiform tablets.

The site of *Yorghan Tepe* was occupied in the fourth millennium B.C. and there are fifteen levels of occupation in the mound. The most important level is dated about the fifteenth century B.C. The contracts and business documents from this time give parallels to many of the episodes in the Biblical patriarchal records.

The University of Chicago also contributed to the field of Mesopotamian exploration in sending Dr. Henri Frankfort to the mounds east of the Diala, a river which empties into the Tigris about fifteen miles below Baghdad. The Diala region is now desert, but it contains numerous mounds which give evidence of a significant past. In 1930 Dr. Frankfort began the excavation of *Tell 'Asmar* fifty miles northeast of Baghdad. Two large structures which appear to have served as combination temple and palace were discovered, one dated about 2300 B.C., the other 2600 B.C. Among the seals discovered at *Tell 'Asmar* were some identical in type with seals found at Mohenjo-daro in the Indus Valley. They bear witness to commerce between Mesopotamia and India at this early period. Other mounds near *Tell 'Asmar* were excavated at the same time.

EGYPT

During the first quarter of the nineteenth century the riddle of Egyptian hieroglyphs was solved by a French scholar, Champollion, although later Egyptologists were to refine and in a measure modify his work. Champollion used the tri-lingual Rosetta Stone as his key to the decipherment of the Egyptian hieroglyphic writing which had been

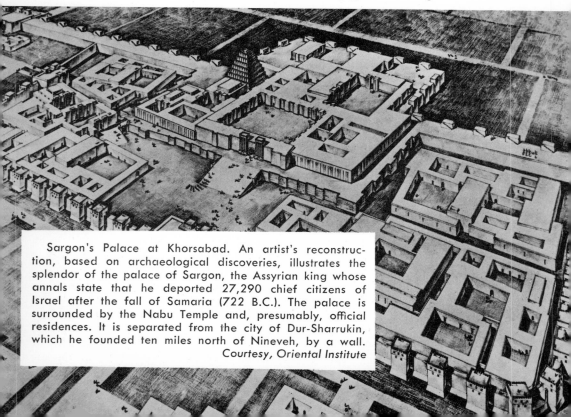

Sargon's Palace at Khorsabad. An artist's reconstruction, based on archaeological discoveries, illustrates the splendor of the palace of Sargon, the Assyrian king whose annals state that he deported 27,290 chief citizens of Israel after the fall of Samaria (722 B.C.). The palace is surrounded by the Nabu Temple and, presumably, official residences. It is separated from the city of Dur-Sharrukin, which he founded ten miles north of Nineveh, by a wall.
Courtesy, Oriental Institute

used for over three thousand years by the priests and scribes of ancient Egypt.

Unlike the buried remains of the civilizations of the Tigris-Euphrates valley, Egyptian monuments were usually above ground in the desert areas adjacent to the Nile. During the nineteenth century a series of archaeological pioneers began the study of the remains of Egypt's significant past.

Richard Lepsius, a brilliant young scholar from the University of Berlin, led an expedition to Egypt in 1843 during which he undertook the task of recording the writing on Egyptian monuments. Casts were made of reliefs and inscriptions preparatory to a systematic study of Egyptian antiquities.

For thirty years (1850-80) the French archaeologist Auguste Mariette had a virtual monopoly on Egyptian archaeology, but a new era began when in 1880 William M. Flinders Petrie arrived in Egypt. He first gave his attention to a scientific survey of the pyramids of Giza, but he became noted particularly for his careful attention to archaeological detail. It was Petrie who developed the system of digging known as stratigraphy whereby each layer, or stratum of a mound, is studied before the next layer is excavated. Through a careful study of the fragments of pottery discovered in a mound, Petrie found that he could date a stratum with considerable accuracy.

Although written in Akkadian cuneiform rather than Egyptian hieroglyphics, the *Tell el-Amarna* letters, discovered accidentally by an Egyptian peasant in 1887, have been a major source for our knowledge of Egypt during the reign of Akhenaten (Amenhotep IV). The letters comprise the diplomatic correspondence of Pharaohs Amenhotep III, and Amenhotep IV with kings of city-states in western Asia, including Palestine. Cities mentioned include Jerusalem, Byblos, Tyre, Sidon, Gezer, and Accho. Light is thrown on the political situation of western Asia during the period between 1400 B.C. and 1350 B.C. when Egyptian power was on the decline.

Early in the twentieth century James Henry Breasted, founder of the Oriental Institute at Chicago, spent a decade in Egypt during which time he copied, translated, and edited the inscriptions which he found there. These were published under the title *Ancient Records of Egypt* (5 volumes, 1906-07).

With the help of outside groups such as the Oriental Institute, Egypt has continued to encourage archaeological research. Artifacts are preserved in the excellent Archaeological Museum in Cairo.

The step pyramid of Dzoser at Sakkara has been completely excavated and in large measure restored. In the chamber under the pyramid, about twenty thousand alabaster vessels have been found, many of which contain inscriptions in the Hieratic form of Egyptian writing. The step pyramid is the first great stone structure of history.

In 1942, at the time of the excavation of Sakkara, an Egyptian archaeologist, Zaki Saad, discovered an Aramaic letter written on papyrus which had been placed in a pottery jar (cf. Jer. 32:14). The letter was from Adon, king of Ashkelon or some nearby Palestinian town and addressed to an Egyptian Pharaoh (probably Necho). The letter warned the Pharaoh of Babylonian troops which had reached Aphek and asked Egyptian aid in the defense of Palestine. The document is probably to be dated during the sixth century when Nebuchadnezzar was threatening Judah and its neighbors.

The neighborhood of the great pyramids of Giza has also been explored and many new monuments have been discovered including the tomb and possessions of Queen Hetep-heres, mother of Khufu, the Pharaoh who built the Great Pyramid. Many of the articles found in the queen's tomb were of gold and silver. In 1954 two gigantic solar barks were also discovered. These barks were thought to convey the spirit of the deceased to his eternal abode.

Excavations sponsored by the Metropolitan Museum of New York in Upper Egypt have uncovered a large quantity of tomb equipment which throws light on the daily life of the ancient Egyptians.

Howard Carter's spectacular discovery of the tomb of Tutankhamun in the Valley of the Kings (1922) produced an unprecedented interest in Egyptian antiquities. Although not directly related to the Bible, the discoveries show something of the fabulous wealth of Egypt even in its period of decline following the days of Akhenaten. Tutankhamun was a relatively unimportant Pharaoh.

At Tanis, in the eastern Delta, French excavations have brought to light a royal cemetery with rich burial furnishings from the family of Sheshonk I (Biblical Shishak, I Kings 14:25). The gold-masked body of Sheshonk was uncovered intact in his burial chamber.

About the year 1945 a discovery of particular interest to New Testament scholars was made near a village known as Nag Hammadi, far up the Nile River. An Egyptian peasant found there a large earthen jar which contained thirteen leather-bound volumes of papyrus manuscripts, written in Coptic during the fourth century A.D. The volumes included forty-nine treatises which reflected the ideas of Christian Gnostics of Egypt during the early centuries of the Christian era. One of these is called *The Gospel of Truth*, which proved to be a mystical treatment of ideas derived in part from our canonical Gospels, and in part from ancient speculation. It is com-

pletely different from the Gospels in our Bibles, for the central theme is not the Person of Christ but the meaning of the salvation which the Gnostics preached. Another, *The Gospel of Thomas*, presents Jesus and His gospel in terms of ancient Gnosticism. The result is a garbled picture of Christ, made to fit the theological framework of the Gnostic who was, in reality, a rival to the Christian, rather than a fellow-believer. The Nag Hammadi discoveries help us to understand the early church in its historical setting, and they exhibit attitudes toward Jesus which came in part from tradition and in part from Scripture.

IRAN (Persia)

In 1900 a French expedition directed by J. de Morgan began the excavation of Susa, Biblical Shushan. Of particular interest was the discovery of two inscribed pillars, one of which was the inscription of an ancient king of the Sumerian city of Kish, and the second was the black basalt pillar containing the law code of the Babylonian king Hammurabi. These pillars had been taken from lower Mesopotamia as trophies of war by Elamite conquerors.

Persepolis, the ancient capital of Persia, was excavated by the Oriental Institute and directed by Ernst Herzfeld of Berlin (1931-34) and Erick Schmidt of the Oriental Institute (1935-37). Among the more impressive discoveries was the great audience hall of Darius and Xerxes approached by a formal stairway containing reliefs depicting emissaries of subject nations with tribute for Persia. The foundation deposits of the audience hall contained solid gold tablets inscribed with records of Darius. Thousands of clay tablets were discovered at Persepolis written in Elamite, Old Persian, and Akkadian. These tablets pro-

Pergamum. This photo gives a clear view of the results of archaeological activity at Pergamum.

Courtesy, H. Gokberg

vide an insight into conditions in Persia during the sixth and fifth centuries B.C. —the time between the building of the Second Temple in Jerusalem and the ministry of Nehemiah.

Darius I of Persia left an impressive memorial of his victory over his enemies on the Rock of Behistun which rises above a spring-fed pool of water on the caravan road from Ecbatana to Babylon. Carved on the side of a mountain are figures of the victorious king lording it over his prostrate enemies. An inscription is written in three languages—Old Persian, Elamite, and Akkadian. The first serious effort to copy the inscriptions was made by Henry C. Rawlinson in 1835 and further studies have been made as recently as 1948 by George G. Cameron.

It was the trilingual Behistun Inscription that unlocked the cuneiform script just as the trilingual Rosetta Stone proved the key to the decipherment of Egyptian hieroglyphs.

ASIA MINOR

Professor Hugo Winckler of Berlin excavated the site of Bogaskoy, at the great bend of the Halys River in Turkey in 1906. Winckler worked with the authorities of the Turkish Museum in Constantinople (now Istanbul). Among his discoveries were numerous clay tablets written in cuneiform characters in the Hittite tongue. Others, however, were written in the Semitic Akkadian language. One of these was a copy of a peace treaty between the Hittite king Hattusil and Rameses II of Egypt. Of particular interest to the linguist were tablets which gave the Sumerian and Semitic equivalents of Hittite words.

Bogaskoy was known in Hittite times as Hattushash. It was the center of a great Hittite culture in Asia Minor which, during Old Testament times, penetrated Syria and Palestine.

New Testament archaeology found its great champion in Sir William M. Ramsay, who made careful studies of the cities visited by Paul and those mentioned in the Revelation. He travelled extensively in Asiatic Turkey (1880-91, 1898, 1901-05). Early in life, Ramsay followed the fashion of his generation in distrusting the Biblical records in their witness to the geography and political nomenclature of the Pauline era, but his careful studies caused him to reverse his earlier prejudices and see in the Scriptures a source of authentic geographical and historical information.

Excavators have been busy in Asia Minor, with the result that we now have a considerable body of knowledge concerning life in its flourishing cities during Greek and Roman times. The theater at Ephesus, and its marble street nearby, bear witness to the wealth and cosmopolitan atmosphere of the city once dedicated to Diana. In Sardis we find remains of a magnificent temple of Artemis (4th century B.C.) and a temple of Zeus which is thought to stand above the foundations of Croesus' palace. Excavations at Sardis are continuing. Smyrna (modern Izmir), contains ruins of a Roman agora (market place), with statues of Poseidon, the sea-god, and Demeter, personifying the earth. Pergamum, the most important city of Anatolia during Roman times, had a famous Aesculapium, or medical center, which was in use from the fourth century B.C. to the second century A.D. It had a library, temples, and baths, all of which are remarkably well preserved.

GREECE AND ROME

Biblical and classical archaeology converge when we move into Greece and Rome. The cultures there have never been completely forgotten, as were those of the Hittites of Asia Minor or the Sumerians of the southeastern Fertile Crescent. Archaeologists have kept busy in the classical lands, however. Since

Athens. The cultural center of pre-Christian Greece nestled around the 512-foot-high hill known as the Acropolis (left).

Courtesy, Royal Greek Embassy

Corinth Canal. Strategically situated on the Isthmus of Corinth, the city of Corinth was one of the oldest, most powerful, and wealthiest in Greece.

Copyright, Ewing Galloway

1930 the American School of Classical Studies has conducted systematic excavations at the agora (in the city) of Athens, where Paul reasoned with the philosophically-minded Athenians. Work began at Corinth in 1898, and the American School of Classical Studies purchased the modern village on the site of the ancient city in order to do a thorough job of excavation. On the hill which rises above the city, ruins of a temple to Aphrodite (Astarte, Semitic Ashtoreth) were discovered. The history of Corinth goes back to the fourth millennium before Christ. In Paul's day, it was a Roman colony enjoying a period of increasing prosperity.

Between 1914 and 1938, French archaeologists conducted excavations at an-cient Philippi. Among the discoveries was the old market place of the city and a large arched gateway at its northwest edge (cf. Acts 16:13). About a mile from the gate is a stream of water, on the banks of which the gospel was first preached in Europe.

Biblical archaeology is interested in Rome, the destination of Paul on his final voyage, and the traditional site of the martyrdoms of both Peter and Paul. The antiquities of Rome, including its catacombs, have been appreciated for centuries. The Italian government has done much, during the present century, to make them more easily accessible to visitors and to beautify the environment in which the principal ruins of Imperial Rome are located.

Time Line of Bible History

EARLY ISRAEL AND HER NEIGHBORS:

Egypt	Date	Mesopotamia	
	3000 B.C.		
Old Kingdom (29th-23rd centuries) Pyramid Age (26th-25th centuries)		Early Sumerians 2800-2360	
	2500		
		Sargon of Akkad dynasty *ca.* 2360-2180	
Middle Kingdom (21st-18th centuries)	2000	Ur III 2060-1950 Abraham leaves Ur	**Syria-Palestine**
	1750		
Hyksos *ca.* 1720-1550		**Asia Minor** Old Hittite Empire 1740-1460	
New Kingdom *ca.* 1570-1310 Amarna Letters *ca.* 1400-1350 Exodus of Hebrews *ca.* 1280 (?)	1500	New Hittite Empire 1460-1200	Ugaritic Texts (14th century)
Rameses II 1290-1224 End of Egyptian Empire, *ca.* 1100	1250	Assyria strong under Tiglath-pileser I 1118-1078	Hebrew Conquest 1250-1200 Judges 1200-1020 Saul 1020-1000
	1000	Assyria weak until	David 1000-961 Solomon 961-922
		Ashur-dan II 934-912	

THE DIVIDED KINGDOM:

Kings of Judah (Davidic Dynasty throughout)	Events and Prophets	Date	Contemporary Rulers	Kings of Israel (Italics indicate separate dynasties)
Rehoboam Abijam Asa	Pharaoh Shishak invaded Judah and Israel	925	(Assyrian) Adad-nirari II	Jeroboam I
	Asa allied with Ben-hadad of Syria against Baasha	900	Tukulti-ninurta II	*Nadab* Baasha
Jehoshaphat	Elijah prophesied during period of apostasy	875	Ashurnasirpal II	*Elah* *Zimri* Omri Ahab
Jehoram Ahaziah (Athaliah) Joash	Battle of Karkar Elisha	850	Shalmaneser III	Ahaziah Jehoram
	Jehu pays tribute to Shalmaneser	825	Shamshi-adad V	Jehu Jehoahaz

271

THE DIVIDED KINGDOM: (Con't)

Judah	Events / Prophets	Date	Assyria / Babylon / Persia	Israel
	Hazael of Damascus oppressed Judah			
Amaziah		800	Adad-nirari III	Joash (Jehoash)
				Jeroboam II
Uzziah			Shalmaneser IV	
	Hosea			
	Amos	775		
	Jonah		Ashur-dan III	
	Isaiah			
		750	Ashur-nirari I	*Zachariah*
				Shallum
Jotham	Micah		Tiglath-pileser III (Pul)	Menahem
				Pekahiah
Ahaz	Joel (?)			*Peka*
	Obadiah (?)	725	Shalmaneser V	Hoshea
Hezekiah			Sargon II	(Fall of Samaria, 722 B.C.)
	Sennacherib invades Judah	700	Sennacherib	
Manasseh			Esarhaddon	
	Assyria fought Egypt	675	Ashurbanipal	
	Manasseh carried to Babylon	650		
Amon			Ashur-etil-ilani	
Josiah			Sin-shar-ishkun	
	Nahum			
	Zephaniah	625	Nabopolassar established Neo-Babylonian Empire	
	Jeremiah			
	Fall of Nineveh (612)		(Babylonian)	
	Josiah killed at Megiddo (608)			
Jehoahaz	Battle of		Nebuchadnezzar	
Jehoiakim	Carchemish (605)			
Jehoiachin	Habakkuk	600		
Zedekiah				
(Fall of Jerusalem, 587 B.C.)				

THE EXILE AND RETURN:

Judah	Events / Prophets	Date	Babylon / Persia
		575	
	Nebuchadnezzar invades Egypt		Evil-Merodach
			Neriglissar
		550	Nabonidus (defeated by Cyrus the Persian)
	Fall of Babylon (539)		(Persian)
	Decree of Cyrus		
	Zerubbabel leads a party of Jews to Jerusalem		
	Haggai		Cambyses
	Zechariah	525	
	Malachi		
	Completion of second Temple (515)		Darius the Great
		500	Xerxes
	Esther saved her people in Persia		
		475	
			Artaxerxes
	Ezra led a party of Jews to Jerusalem.	450	

JUDAEA UNDER PERSIANS, GREEKS, AND ROMANS:

Greece	Date	Persia	Judaea
	500		
Battle of Marathon, 490		Xerxes	
Battle of Salamis, 480		486-465	
	475	Artaxerxes (Ahasuerus)	
Socrates, 470-399		465-424	
			Ezra's mission
			458 (?)
	450		
Xenophon, 431-354			
Plato, 428-348	425	Xerxes II, 323-	
	400	Darius II, 423-404	
		Artaxerxes II, 404-358	
Aristotle, 384-322		Artaxerxes III, 358-338	
		Arses, 338-336	
	350	Darius III, 336-331	
Alexander of Macedon		Persia defeated	
invades Asia, 334		by Alexander, 331	

Egypt		Syria	
Ptolemaic Empire in		Seleucid Empire in	
Egypt, 323-30	300	Syria, 312-64	
Egypt dominates			
Palestine	275		
Translation of			
Pentateuch into Greek	250		
	200	Antiochus III took	
		Palestine from Egypt, 198	
	175	Antiochus IV (Epiphanes),	
		175-163, persecutes Jews.	
			Maccabean
			Revolt, 166
			Judas the
Jewish temple built			Maccabee, 166-160
at Leontopolis, 161			Jonathan, 160-143
	150		
			Simon, 142-134
			John Hyrcanus,
			134-104
	125		
			Aristobolus I, 104
Rome	100		Alexander Jannaeus,
			103-76
			Alexandra, 76-67
		Pompey enters	
Caesar invades Britain, 55		Syria, 64	
			Pompey conquers
	50		Jerusalem, 63
			Antipater, procurator
Egypt becomes			of Judaea, 55-43
Roman province, 30			Herod, King of
Augustus, 31 B.C.-A.D. 14			Judaea 40-4
	A.D.		Birth of Jesus, 6 B.C.

273

JUDAEA UNDER PERSIANS, GREEKS, AND ROMANS: (Con't)

Tiberius, AD 14-37

Crucifixion, A.D. 32
Herod Agrippa I,
Caligula, 37-41   king of Judaea,
Claudius, 41-54   39-44

50   Felix, procurator of
Nero, 54-68   Judaea, 52-58
Vespasian, 69-79   Festus, procurator of
Titus, 79-81   Judaea, 58
Domitian, 81-96   Jerusalem taken,
Nerva, 96-98   Temple destroyed, 70
Trajan, 98-117.   100

GAZETTEER

This gazetteer is intended to describe the principal geographical features of Palestine and the ancient world and to indicate their locations on the maps included in this atlas. Most entries include a location reference consisting of a letter and number, followed by the number of the map on which the name appears. For example, the location reference for *Abila* is D1-11. Location references appear at the edges of each map, and the map number appears at the top of each map.

ca.—*circa* (Latin for "around, about, approximately")
J.—*jebel* (Arabic for "mount")
Kh.—*khirbet* (Arabic for "ruin, mound")
mod.—modern
mt(s).—mount, mountain(s)
N (S, E, W, NE, NW, etc.)—north(ern)
N.T.—New Testament
O.T.—Old Testament

poss.—possibly
prob.—probably
q.v.—*quod* or *quae vide* (Latin for "which see")
R.—river
W.—*wadi* (Arabic for "channel of a watercourse that is dry except in the rainy season")

A

Abana R. River of Damascus (II Kings 5:12). It has its source 19 miles NW of Damascus and flows through the city. Prob. mod. *Nahr Barada*. D1—1

Abdon. Town in the territory of Asher, 10 miles NE of Acre (Josh. 21:30; I Chron. 6:74). Mod. *Kh. 'Abde*.

Abel. Fortified town in the territory of Naphtali where Sheba, a rebel against David, was killed (II Sam. 20:15). Prob. mod. *Tell Abil*, 12 miles N of Lake Hula, opposite Dan. B3—4

Abela-Bethmaacha. *See* Abel

Abel-beth-maachah. C1—5. *See* Abel

Abel-maim. *See* Abel

Abel-meholah. City in the territory of Manasseh. It was W of the Jordan, about half way between the Sea of Galilee and the Dead Sea (Judg. 7:22; I Kings 4:12). C3—5

Abel-mehula. *See* Abel-meholah

Abel-sattim. *See* Abel-shittim

Abel-shittim. Settlement in Moab occupied by the Israelites before the capture of Jericho (Num. 33:49). It was also called Shittim (Num. 25:1; Josh. 2:1; 3:1). Poss. mod. *Tell Kefrein*, E of Jericho.

Abila (in Abilene). Capital of Abilene (Luke 3:1), on the Barada R. *ca*. 20 miles NW of Damascus. D1—11

Abila (in Batanea). City of the Decapolis (*q.v.*), S of the Yarmuk R., *ca*. 17 miles E of the S tip of the Sea of Galilee. Mod. *Tell Abil*. D3—11

Abilene. Tetrarchy in the region of the Anti-Lebanon Mts. (Luke 3:1). Its capital was Abila (*q.v.*). D1—11; B-C4—13

Abydos (in Asia Minor). Town in Phrygia, on the Asiatic side of the Hellespont, opposite Sestos.

Abydos (in Egypt). City dedicated to Osiris, Egyptian god of the underworld. *Ca*. 50 miles NW of Thebes. C6—2

Accad. *See* Akkad

Accaron. *See* Ekron

Acchad. *See* Akkad

Accho. *See* Acco

Acco (Ptolemais). City of Asher (Judg. 1:31) on a small promontory of the Palestinian coast about 25 miles S of Tyre, 8 miles N of Mt. Carmel (mod. *Haifa*) across the Bay of Acco. N.T. *Ptolemais*, medieval *Acre*. B2—1, 5; D2—3; B3—4; B1—19

Aceldama (Field of Blood). Parcel of ground known as the potter's field, traditionally located on the S side of the Hinnom Valley, Jerusalem.

Achad. *See* Akkad

Achaia. Originally a state of Greece located in the N Peloponnesus. Under the Romans, Achaia included the whole of the Peloponnesus with continental Greece S of Illyricum, Epirus, and Thessaly. Corinth was its capital (Acts 18:27; I Cor. 16:15; II Cor. 1:1). D3—12; A2—15, 16; C2—17; D3—18

Achazib. *See* Achzib

Achmetha. *See* Ecbatana

Achsaph. *See* Achshaph

Achshaph. Canaanite royal city (Josh. 11:1) captured by Joshua (Josh. 12:20), located in the territory of Asher *ca.* 8 miles SE of Acco. Poss. mod. *et-Tell*.

Achzib. Town on the seacoast of Asher (Josh. 19:29), 8.5 miles N of Acco, from which the Canaanites were not expelled (Judg. 1:31). It was known to the Greeks and Romans as *Ecdippa*. Poss. mod. *ez-Zib*.

Acrabathane. Region SW of the Dead Sea in the vicinity of the Ascent of Akrabim (*q.v.*). Acrabathane was the site of a victory of Judas the Maccabee over the Idumeans.

Acrabbim, Ascent of. *See* Akrabbim, Ascent of

Acre. *See* Acco

Acron. *See* Ekron

Actium. Promontory in NW Acarnania, Greece. It was the site of the victory of the forces of Octavian (Augustus) over Antony and Cleopatra (31 B.C.).

Adad. *See* Hadid

Adada(h). *See* Aroer (in Judah)

Adam. City on the E bank of the Jordan, mod. *Tell ed-Damieh*, less than a mile below the mouth of the Jabbok and 18 miles N of Jericho. Here the waters were held back for the miraculous crossing of the Israelites (Josh. 3:16).

Adamah. *See* Adam

Adana. City on the Sarus (mod. *Seyhan*) R. in S Turkey.

Adarsa. *See* Adasa

Adasa. Town near Beth-horon at the junction of 2 important roads, N of Jerusalem. Judas the Maccabee encamped there (I Macc. 7:40). Poss. mod. *Kh. 'Addaseh*.

Adida (Hadid). Town 3 miles NE of Lydda (I Macc. 12:38; 13:13). *See* Hadid

Adora. *See* Adoraim

Adoraim. City of Judah fortified by Rehoboam (II Chron. 11:9). It is mod. *Dura*, a village on a hillside *ca.* 5 miles SW of Hebron. B5—5

Adramyttium. Port in Mysia, NW Asia Minor. Paul embarked in a vessel of Adramyttium on his journey to Rome (Acts 27:2). B1—15; D2—17

Adria, Sea of. In the narrow sense, Sea of Adria was the portion of the Adriatic Sea near the commercial town of Adria, on the lower Po R. in Italy. The term was extended, however, to include the Tarentine Gulf, the Sicilian Sea, the Ionian Sea, the Corinthian Gulf, and the waters between Crete and Malta (Acts 27:27). C2—12; A1-B2—17

Adriatic Sea. Arm of the Mediterranean between Italy and the Balkan Peninsula. It extends from the Gulf of Venice SE to the Strait of Otranto, which leads into the Ionian Sea.

Adrumythium. *See* Adramyttium

Adullam. Town in Judah between Jarmuth and Socoh (Josh. 15:35). Nearby was the Cave of Adullam, which David used as a refuge and a headquarters for his activities (I Sam. 22:1; II Sam. 23:13). Prob. mod. *Tell esh-Sheikh-Madhkur*, near *'Id el-Ma*. B5—5

Aegean Sea. Arm of the Mediterranean between Greece and Asia Minor. The strait of the Dardanelles connects the Aegean with the Sea of Marmara. A1—6; D3—12; B1—15, 16; C-D2—17

Aenon. Place where John the Baptist exercised his ministry (John 3:23). It was near Salim (*q.v.*), the location of which is disputed. C4—11

Aestii. A Germanic people settled in N-central Europe along the E coast of the Baltic.

Africa. Continent situated S. of the Mediterranean, E of the Atlantic and W of the Red Sea and Indian Ocean. The Roman province named Africa embraced the territory NW of Syrtus Minor (*q.v.*). Its cities included Utica, Carthage, Hadrumetum, and Thapsus. C3—12; B-C3—18

Africa Nova. *See* Numidia

Agade (Akkad). One of the principal cities founded by Nimrod in the land of Shinar (Gen. 10:10—Accad). Its exact location is unknown. Poss. *Tell ed-Der* or *Tell Sheshubar*. F3—2

Agrigentum. City in S Sicily founded (*ca.* 580 B.C.) as Acragas (or Akragas) by Greek colonists.

Agrippias. City on the Mediterranean coast of Palestine N of Gaza. It was destroyed by Alexander Jannaeus but rebuilt by Augustus and added to the dominion of Herod, who renamed it Agrippium. A6—11

Agrippina. Fortress from which, according to the Talmud, the signals given by the Sanhedrin in Jerusalem were repeated. Poss. mod. *Kaukab el-Hawa*. C3—11

Agrippium. *See* Agrippias

Ai (Hai). Town E of Bethel that fell to Joshua after Jericho (Josh. 7—8). Aiath and Avvim may be variants of the same name. Prob. mod. *et-Tell*, 10 miles N of Jerusalem. D3—3; C4—19

Aialon. *See* Aijalon

Aijalon. City near the Philistine frontier (I Sam. 14:31) that at one time belonged to the tribe of Dan (Josh. 19:42; Judg. 1:35). Mod. *Yalo*, 14 miles NW of Jerusalem. B4—5

Aijalon, Valley of. Valley extending from the mts. N of Jerusalem in a generally NW direction to the Plain of Sharon, N of Joppa. Here Joshua gained victory over a coalition of kings from S Canaan (Josh. 10:12).

Aijalon R. B4—1. *See* Aijalon, Valley of

Aila. *See* Elath

Ailath. *See* Elath

'Ain Feshkha. Spring NW of the Dead Sea, near Qumran (*q.v.*). C4—19

'Ain Gedi. C5—19. *See* En-gedi

'Ain Karem. *See* 'Ain Karim

'Ain Karim. Village 4.5 miles W of Jerusalem. Tradition makes this the birthplace of John the Baptist. *See* Beth-haccherem. B4—19

Aion. *See* Ijon

Ajalon. *See* Aijalon

Ajalon, Valley of. *See* Aijalon, Valley of

'Ajlun. Town in Transjordan, NW of Jerash, part of whose wealth may be traced to iron mines in the 'Ajlun hills.

Akeldama. *See* Aceldama

Akhetaton (Tell el-Amarna). Capital of Egypt under Akhenaten (Amenhotep IV). Mod. *Tell el-Amarna*. C5—2; A6—3

Akkad. District in N Babylonia. It was the region between the Tigris and the Euphrates where they are closest together and almost parallel. In addition to the city of Akkad (poss. mod. *Tell ed-Der*), the cities of Babylon and Cuthah were in the city-state that bore this name. S of Akkad was the district known as Sumer. *See* Agade. F-G3—2

Akkrabattine. *See* Acrabathane

Akrabbim, Ascent of. The "ascent of scorpions" between the Arabah and the hill country of Judah (Num. 34:4; Josh. 15:3). Prob. mod. *Naqb es-Safa*. B6—5

Alaca Huyuk. Hittite ruins, including the famous "royal tombs," located in N-central Anatolia (*ca*. 100 miles NE of Ankara). D1—2

Alalakh. City on the Orontes R., N Syria. Mod. *Tell 'Atshaneh*. D2—2

Alamanni. A Germanic tribe from central Germany that engaged in numerous conflicts with the Romans. In A.D. 357 they were defeated by Julian (afterward emperor) at Strassburg. Their kingdom lasted until A.D. 495, when they were conquered by Clovis.

Alans. A division of the Sarmatia, a pastoral people related to the Scythians. The Alans were settled N of the Caucasus in Roman times.

Alashiya. C3—2. *See* Cyprus

Albania. Ancient name of a region in the E Caucasus bordering the Caspian Sea. It is now part of *Azerbaijan*, U.S.S.R. F2—12

Albis (Elbe) **R.** Rises in the Giant Mts. of NE Bohemia and flows generally NW through Saxony and the N German plain to the North Sea. It marked the farthest advance northward of the Romans under Drusus (9 B.C.). C1—12

Aleppo. *See* Haleb

Alesia. Town of Celtic and Roman Gaul, near mod. Dijon. Besieged by Caesar (52 B.C.), the town was starved out and Gallic resistance to Rome ended.

Alexandria (in Egypt). City founded by Alexander the Great (332 B.C.) at the Canopic mouth of the Nile at the W extremity of the Delta. Mod. *Al-Iskandariya*. D3—12; E4—17, 18

Alexandria (in India). City founded by Alexander the Great where the Four Rivers emptied into the Indus.

Alexandria (in Syria). City founded by Alexander the Great after defeating Darius near there in 333 B.C. It was located *ca*. 25 miles N of Antioch on the coast. Mod. *Iskanderun*. B1—13

Alexandria Arachosiorum. City founded by Alexander the Great in Arachosia (*q.v.*).

Alexandria Arion. *See* Herat

Alexandria Eschate. City founded by Alexander the Great on the Jaxartes R. to mark the proposed N limit of his kingdom. Mod. *Chodjend*.

Alexandrium. Fortress of the Hasmoneans and of Herod. Mod. *Qarn Sartabeh*, 17 miles N of Jericho. C4—11

Alisar Huyuk. *See* Kushshar

Alpes. Roman province between Italy on the E and Narbonensis on the W. B2—12

Alps. Mt. system of S-central Europe that swings in a great arc N, E, and SE between France and Italy to the Adriatic coast of Yugoslavia. Its northernmost point is in S Bavaria. B-C2—12

Alus. *See* Alush

Alush. Encampment of the Israelites between Egypt and Mt. Sinai (Num. 33:13–14). Poss. mod. *W. el-'Eshsh*. C5—3

Amadoci. Ancient people of W Sarmatia who lived in the area W of the Borysthenes R.

Amalecites. *See* Amalekites

Amalek. A5—4. *See* Amalekites

Amalekites. A nomadic people who wandered between the Negeb and the Sinai Peninsula. They are mentioned as enemies of Israel as late as David's reign.

Amanus Mts. Range E of the plain of Cilicia. C1—13

Amardi. Ancient people who inhabited the Elburz Mt. region, S of the Caspian Sea.

Amardos R. River of W. Asia that rises on the W slopes of the Zagros Mts. and flows generally NE, entering the S end of the Caspian Sea. It flows through the land of the Amardi (*q.v.*).

Amarna, Tell el-. C5—2; A6—3. *See* Akhetaton

Amasia. Ancient city of Galatia, in NE Asia Minor.

Amastris. Ancient port on the Black Sea in W Paphlagonia. E2—18

Amathus. Ancient town on the S coast of Cyprus, near the copper mines. A famous temple of Aphrodite was located there. C4—11

Amisus. Black Sea port of ancient Pontus, E of Sinope.

Amman (Rabbah). City at the headwaters of the Jabbok, 23 miles E of the Jordan. The chief city of the Ammonites, it was besieged by Joab, David's general (II Sam. 11:1; 12:26–31). Later the Ammonites won it back. It was denounced by Jeremiah (Jer. 49:2–6). Embellished by Ptolemy Philadelphus (285–246 B.C.), it was renamed Philadelphia. Mod. *'Amman*, capital of Jordan. D4—1; D3—19

Ammaus. *See* Emmaus

Ammon. A people descended from Ben-ammi, Lot's second son (Gen. 19:38). Ammonite settlements were located E of the Dead Sea, N of Moab. D4—1, 5; D3—3; C4—4

Ammonium. *See* Temple of Amon

Amon, Temple of (Siwa). Ancient town in the Libyan Desert, N Africa. It had a famed shrine to Amon, identified by the Greeks as Jupiter. Alexander the Great journeyed there—a 12-day pilgrimage from Memphis in Lower Egypt—and was hailed as a son of Amon. A3—6, 7

Amorites. Nomadic inhabitants of Palestine before and during the Israelite occupation (Gen. 10:16; 15:21; Josh. 7:7; 9:1; 11:3).

Amorrhites. *See* Amorites

Amorrites. *See* Amorites

Amphipolis. City of Thrace, situated at the mouth of the Strymon on a bend of the river. It was located on the Egnatian Way, 33 miles SW of Philippi. Paul passed through it while traveling from Philippi to Thessalonica (Acts 17:1). Mod. *Neochori*. A1—15, 16; C1—17

Amygdalon, Pool of. Pool in the Bethesda sector of N.T. Jerusalem, N of the E gate of the Palace of Herod.

Anab. Town in the hill country of Judah (Josh. 11:21; 15:50). Mod. *Kh. 'Anab*, 10 miles SW of Hebron.

Ananla(h). *See* Bethany

Anas R. River in Spain, dividing Lusitania and Baetica, spanned at Emerita Augusta by a bridge of 64 arches built by Trajan.

Anat. Ancient city on the middle Euphrates. Some scholars identify it with Hena (II Kings 18:34), which was overthrown by Sennacherib before his invasion of Judah. Mod. *Tell 'Ana*. C2—6

Anatho. *See* Anat

Anathoth. Levitical city in the territory of Benjamin (Josh. 21:18; I Chron. 6:60). It was the birthplace of Jeremiah (Jer. 1:1). Mod. *Ras el-Kharrubeh*, near *'Anata*, 2.5 miles NE of Jerusalem.

Anchialus. Port on the W end of the Black Sea, in mod. Bulgaria. Symeon, a Bulgarian ruler, defeated the Greeks near Anchialus (A.D. 917). A Christian church is known to have been there during the 3rd century A.D. Mod. *Ancheylo*, Bulgaria. E2—18

Ancona. Port city on the Adriatic, in central Italy. It was settled in the 4th century B.C. by Greeks from Syracuse.

Ancyra. Commercial center of central Anatolia (Asia Minor), dating to the 2nd millennium B.C. Mod. *Ankara*, capital of Turkey since 1923. B2—7; E2—12, 17; C1—15, 16; E2—18

Ankara. *See* Ancyra

Ankuwa. Hittite city in Anatolia, on the Konak R. Mod. *Alisar*, Turkey. D2—2

Anthedon. *See* Agrippias

Anti-Lebanon Mts. Mt. chain separated from the Lebanon Mts. by the valley of the Leontes and Orontes (the Beqa'a Valley). The greatest elevation of the Anti-Lebanon range is at its S end, Mt. Hermon.

Antioch (in Pisidia). Town in Asia Minor that served as center of civil and military administration for the S part of the Roman province of Galatia. Barnabas and Paul visited it on their First Missionary Journey (Acts 13:14–52; 14:19–21). Mod. *Yalovatch*. C4—14; C2—15, 16; E2—17

Antioch (in Syria). Syrian metropolis founded *ca.* 300 B.C. by Seleucus Nicator, situated on the S side of the Orontes *ca.* 15 miles from its mouth. It became a center of the early church (Acts 11:19–26; 13:1–3). Mod. *Antakya*, Turkey. E3—12; B1—13; D5—14; D2—15, 16; F2—17; F3—18

Antipatris (Aphek). Aphek was a Canaanite royal city (Josh. 12:18), 39 miles NW of Jerusalem, identical with ancient Capharsaba (*q.v.*). Herod the Great founded Antipatris on the same site. It was the limit of Paul's journey the first night when being taken as a prisoner from Jerusalem to Caesarea (Acts 23:31). Prob. mod. *Ras el-'Ain*. B4—11; B3—19

Anti-Taurus Mts. N extension of the Taurus Mts. (*q.v.*), across the Seyhan R.

Antonia, Fortress. Herod the Great's fortress-residence on the NW corner of the temple area in Jerusalem. Herod named it in honor of Mark Antony. B4—10

Anxa. Town in S Italy on a rocky island in the Gulf of Taranto, joined to the mainland by a bridge. The city was of Greek origin and was known also as Callipolis. Mod. *Gallipoli*.

Apamea. Important Hellenistic city founded by the Seleucids, S of Hamath, on the Orontes. Mod. *Qala'at el-Mudiq*. C2—13

Aphek (in Asher). City within the territory of Asher (Josh. 19:30; Judg. 1:31). Prob. mod. *Tell Kurdaneh*, near the sources of the Na'aman R., which flows into the Mediterranean SE of Acco. C2—3; B4—5

Aphek (in Ephraim). B3—19. *See* Antipatris

Aphek (in Transjordan). Site of Ahab's defeat by Ben-hadad of Damascus (I Kings 20:26, 30; cf. II Kings 13:17). Poss. mod. *Fiq*, E of the Sea of Galilee. C2—5

Apherema. *See* Ephraim, city of

Aphik. *See* Aphek (in Asher)

Apollonia (in E Macedonia). Town on the Egnatian Way, 28 miles W of Amphipolis (Acts 17:1). Mod. *Pollina*. A1—15, 16

Apollonia (in W Macedonia). Town on the Adriatic. Used as a base by Julius Caesar.

Apollonia (in Palestine). Town on the Mediterranean coast, in the Plain of Sharon, 12 miles N of Joppa. A4—11

Apollonia (in Thrace). City built by Greeks on the W shore of the Black Sea. Mod. *Burgas*, Bulgaria. B1—7

Appii Forum. *See* Appius, Forum of

Appius, Forum of. Town in Italy, on the Appian Way *ca.* 40 miles SE of Rome. Christians from Rome met Paul there (Acts 28:15). Mod. *Foro Appio.* A1—17

'Aqaba. Mod. name of a small town at the head of the Gulf of Aqaba (*q.v.*). Ancient Ezion-geber was near 'Aqaba.

Aqaba, Gulf of. The NE arm of the Red Sea, lying between Egypt and Arabia. Mod. *Eilat*, Israel, and 'Aqaba, Jordan, are located at its head, as was ancient Ezion-geber. The Gulf of Aqaba provides access to the Red Sea, and thence to the Indian Ocean. C6-D5—3

Aquileia. Town in NE Italy near the Adriatic. It was a Roman stronghold against barbarians from the N. C2—12

Aquitania. Former duchy and kingdom in SW France. It was conquered by one of Julius Caesar's lieutenants in 56 B.C. A2—12

Ar (Ar Moab). Ar, sometimes used as a synonym for Moab (Deut. 2:9), means "city" and may be the designation of the Moabite capital (cf. Num. 21:28; Isa. 15:1). The city has not been positively identified. C5—5

'Araba. *See* Arabah

Arabah. Term frequently used in the O.T. for the Jordan Valley (Deut. 1:7; 3:17; Josh. 11:2) and variously translated as "plain," "plains," "desert," "valley," or "wilderness." The Dead Sea was known as the Sea of Arabah (Deut. 3:17; Josh. 12:3). The term *Arabah* (W. *'Araba*) is now used of the 100-mile-long depression extending from the S end of the Dead Sea to the Gulf of Aqaba. C6—1; D4—3; B6—4

Arabella. *See* Arbela

Arabia. Peninsula comprising a desert area bounded by the Red Sea (W), the Persian Gulf and the Gulf of Oman (E), the Gulf of Aden and the Arabian Sea (S). The Fertile Crescent forms an arc around the N of Arabia. E-F5—2; C3—7; E-F4—12; F3—18

Arabian Desert. Part of an enormous belt of desert, commencing near the Atlantic coast of Africa with the Sahara, and extending through Chinese Turkestan to the Pacific Ocean. Arabia is largely desert. In Scripture the term *Arabian* designates an inhabitant of the Arabian Desert (Jer. 3:2), whether near Babylonia (Isa. 13:20) or Ethiopia (II Chron. 21:16).

Arabian Gulf. *See* Red Sea

Arabian Sea. NW part of the Indian Ocean, between Arabia and India. The Gulf of Aden, an extension of the Red Sea, and the Gulf of Oman, an extension of the Persian Gulf, are its principal arms.

Arabs. Tribes from the desert portions of the Arabian Peninsula. *See* Arabian Desert. C3—6

Arach. *See* Erech

Arachosia. E province of the Median and (later) Persian empires, bordering India. Alexander the Great founded there the city Alexandria Arachosiorum. E-F2—7

Arad (Malatha). Town in Palestine, *ca.* 15 miles S of Hebron (Josh. 12:14; Judg. 1:16). Mod. *Tell 'Arad.* D3—3; B5—4, 5

Aradus. *See* Arvad

Aral Sea. Inland sea, 175 miles E of the Caspian, fed by the Oxus and Jaxartes rivers. E1—6, 7

Aram. D1—5. *See* Syria

Arama. *See* Hormah

Aram-Damascus. C3—4. *See* Damascus, kingdom of

Aramean Kingdom. *See* Hamath, district of

Arameans. *See* Syrians

Aram-Maacah. *See* Maacah

Aram-naharaim. *See* Paddan-aram

Aram-zobah. Aramean kingdom that flourished W of the Euphrates in the days of David and Solomon (I Sam. 14:47). At one time it controlled territory S from Hamath to Damascus. C2—4

'Araq el-Emir. City that was the home of the Tobiads of Ammon, a wealthy and influential family, especially in the Persian period. It was located on a straight line between Jericho and Amman, *ca.* 18 miles E of Jericho and 10 miles W of Amman. D4—19

Ararat, Mt. Traditionally located midway between the Black and Caspian seas. It is known by the Turks as *Aghri Dagh*. F1—2

Ararat, region of. *See* Armenia *and* Urartu

Araunah, threshing floor of. Located on Mt. Moriah, Jerusalem. It became the site of the temple of Solomon (II Chron. 3:1).

Araxes R. River that rises in Armenia, near Erzerum, flows 550 miles in a generally E direction, then empties into the Caspian Sea. Mod. *Aras R.* G1—2; C2—7

Arbela (in Assyria). City *ca.* 50 miles W of Nineveh. Mod. *Erbil.* F2—2; C2—7

Arbela (in Decapolis). Town *ca.* 45 miles N of Philadelphia. C3—11

Arbela (in Palestine). Town W of Sea of Galilee, 5 miles NW of Tiberias. The area around the Horns of Hattin (*q.v.*) is known as the Arbel Valley. Mod. *Kh. Irbid.*

Arbella. *See* Arbela

Archelais. Town in Palestine, *ca.* 7.5 miles N of Jericho on an important trade route of N.T. times. C5—11

Ardus. B3—13. *See* Arvad

Areopolis (Rabbath-Moab). Rabbath-Moab was a city of ancient Moab, E of the Lisan Peninsula and S of the Arnon R. It was located on the N-S trade route through Transjordan. It was known to the Romans as Areopolis. Mod. *Rabbah.* D6—11

Areuna, threshing floor of. *See* Araunah, threshing floor of

Argob. Section of Bashan E of Geshur (Deut. 3:4, 13, 14; Josh. 13:30). C3—4

Aria. Province of the ancient Median (later Persian) Empire, comprising the region about the Arius (mod. *Hari*) R. E2—7

Arib. *See* Arabs

Arimathea (Ramathaim). Ramathaim in the O.T., Arimathea in the N.T. Ramah (in Ephraim) bears the fuller form Ramathaim, or Ramathaim-zophim. Ramathaim was the home of Samuel (I Sam. 1:19; 28:3). Arimathea was the town of Joseph, a member of the Sanhedrin who, after the crucifixion, placed the body of Jesus in his new tomb (Matt. 27:57–60; Luke 23:50–53; John 19:38). Poss. mod. *Rentis*, 20 miles NW of Jerusalem on the W edge of the hill-country of Ephraim. B4—11

'Arish, W. el (R. of Egypt). The great wadi that formed the SW border of Canaan. Normally dry, it is only during the rainy season that the wadi is a river, depositing its waters in the Mediterranean *ca*. 50 miles S of Gaza.

Arles. City on the Rhone Delta in SE France. In Roman times it was a flourishing town named Arelas.

Ar Moab. *See* Ar

Armenia. Regions of Asia Minor forming a continuation of the Anatolian Plateau. The Armenian Kingdom originated in the region around Lake Van. Assyrian inscriptions mention it as Urartu. It is the O.T. Ararat. C2—7; F2—12, 18

Armorica. Region of NW France across the English Channel from Great Britain. Mod. *Brittany*.

Arnon R. (W. el-Mujib). Stream on the E bank of the Dead Sea crossed by the Israelites on their way to Canaan (Deut. 2:24). It was the N boundary of Moab (Judg. 11:18). C5—1, 5; D3—3; C-D6—11

Aroer (in Judah). Town 12 miles SE of Beer-sheba in the *W. 'Ar'ara* (I Sam. 30:28). Mod. *Ararah*.

Aroer (in Moab). Town on the N bank of the Arnon, southernmost point ruled by Sihon (Deut. 2:36; Josh. 12:2). Mod. *Kh. 'Ar'ir*, S of Dibon, 13 miles W of the Dead Sea. B5—4; D5—5

Arpad. City frequently associated with Hamath (II Kings 18:34; 19:13), near which it was located. Mod. *Tell Erfad*, 13 miles N of Aleppo.

Arphachsad. *See* Arphaxad

Arphad. *See* Arpad

Arphaxad. A people descended from Shem. They settled in Chaldea NW of the Persian Gulf.

Arrapakha. Assyrian city E of Ashur, the center of a small Hurrian kingdom (including Nuzi) *ca*. 1800–1500 B.C.

Arsinoe. *See* Crocodilopolis

Artaxata. City on the Araxes R. in Armenia. After its capture by Corbulo, Nero's general, in A.D. 58, it became a dependency of Rome. F2—12

Arvad (Ardus). The most northerly of important Philistine centers. It is an island off the Syrian coast, N of Tripoli. Mod. *Ruad*. D3—2; B2—4, 7; B3—13

Aryans. *See* Indo-Iranians

Arzawa. Ancient name of district in NW Asia Minor. B-C2—2

Asasonthamas. *See* En-gedi

Ascalon. A5—11; A4—19. *See* Ashkelon

Ascent of Akrabbim. *See* Akrabbim, Ascent of

Aschenez. *See* Ashkenaz

Aser, allotment of. *See* Asher, allotment of

Ashdod (Azotus), city of. One of 5 leading Philistine cities. It was located 9 miles NE of Ashkelon, 3 miles E of the Mediterranean, 18 miles N of Gaza. Mod. *Esdud*. C3—3; A4—4, 5; B4—19

Ashdod, district of. District of S Palestine that derived its name from the city of Ashdod (*q.v.*).

Asher, allotment of. Territory assigned to Asher on the Mediterranean coast in N Palestine (Josh. 19:24–31).

Ashkelon (Ascalon). One of 5 leading Philistine cities. It was located in a valley along the Mediterranean, 12 miles N of Gaza (Jer. 47:5, 7). Mod. *'Askalon*. C3—3; A4—4; A5—5

Ashkenaz. A people of the race of Gomer who dwelt in the region of Ararat, E Armenia (Jer. 51:27).

Ashtaroth. City in Bashan (Josh. 9:10; 12:4; 13:12, 31) ruled by Og before the Israelite conquest. It was later a Levitical city (I Chron. 6:71). Mod. *Tell 'Ashtara*, E of the Sea of Galilee. D2—3, 5; C3—4

Ashur. Ancient city on the Tigris R. (Gen. 2:14). It was the oldest capital of the Assyrians. Near mod. *Qala'ah Sherqat*.

Asia, Roman province of. The territory in Asia Minor S of Bithynia, N of Lycia, W of Galatia, and E of the Aegean (Acts 19:10, 22, 26, 27; 20:4, 16, 18; 21:27). The term *Asia* can also refer to the continent E of Europe and Africa, or to the kingdom of the Seleucids during the Maccabean times. D3—12; B-C2—15, 16; D2—17; E3—18

Asia Minor. Peninsula in W Asia, also known as Anatolia, bounded on the N by the Black Sea, on the S by the Mediterranean, and on the W by the Aegean arm of the Mediterranean.

Askelon. *See* Ashkelon

Asochis (Hannathon). Place on N boundary of Zebulun (Josh. 19:14). Poss. mod. *Tell el-Bedeiwiyeh*. C3—11

Asophon. Town on the E bank of the Jordan, about midway between the Sea of Galilee and the Dead Sea.

Asor. *See* Hazor

Aspadana. *See* Gabae

Asphaltitis, Lake. C6—11. *See* Dead Sea

Asshur. F3—2; C2—7. *See* Assyria

Assos. Ancient city in Mysia, in NW Asia Minor, on the Gulf of Adramyttium, E of Point Lectum, westernmost point of Asia. Paul passed through Assos (Acts 20:13–14). B1—16

Assur. *See* Assyria

Assuwa. Ancient district of NW Asia Minor. B1—2

Assyria. Country E of the middle Tigris, bounded on the N by the mts. of Armenia, on the E by the Median mt. ranges, and on the S by the environs of Nineveh, its later capital. In the period of the Assyrian Empire (*q.v.*) this territory was extended to reach the Persian Gulf on the S and the Mediterranean on the W. F3—2; C2—6

Assyrian Empire. Empire that developed from the city of Ashur, on the upper Tigris. The period of greatness dates from the 9th century B.C. when Nineveh was its capital. The Assyrians captured Samaria and took the Israelites into captivity (722 B.C.). Nineveh was destroyed by the Baby-

Ionians and the Medes (612 B.C.), and Assyrian power was forever broken.

Astacus. City of ancient Bithynia, in N Asia Minor, at the E end of an arm of the Sea of Marmara. It was later named Nicomedia (*q.v.*) and is near mod. *Izmit*, Turkey.

Astharoth. *See* Ashtaroth

Astorga. Town in the Asturias region, in NW Spain. A2—18

Astures. An Iberian people who lived in NW Spain before the Roman conquest (2nd century B.C.). They were later absorbed by the Visigoths.

Asturica. *See* Astorga

Ataroth (in Ephraim). Town in the Jordan Valley, in NE Ephraim. Poss. mod. *Tell Sheikh edh-Dhiab*.

Ataroth (in Moab). Town taken from Gad by the Moabites (cf. Moabite Stone). Mod. *Kh. Attarus*, NW of Dibon. C5—5

Athens. Capital of the Greek state of Attica. In the 6th and 5th centuries B.C., Athens became the cultural center of the world, making contributions in the areas of government, architecture, literature, art, and philosophy. In N.T. times Athens was subject to Rome, having been taken by Sulla in 86 B.C. Paul preached to the Athenians from Mars Hill, a short distance W of the Acropolis (Acts 17:15–18:1). A2—6, 7, 15, 16; D3—12, 18; C2—17

Atlantic Ocean. Body of water extending from the Arctic to the Antarctic regions between the Americas on the W and Europe and Africa on the E. A1—12

Atlas Mts. System of nonvolcanic mt. ranges in NW Africa, extending *ca.* 1,500 miles NE from Morocco through Algeria to Cape Bon in Tunisia. It was inhabited in antiquity by Berbers.

Attalia. Mediterranean seaport in SW Asia Minor, the port whence Paul and Barnabas sailed for Antioch (Acts 14:25). Mod. *Adalia*. C5—14; E2—17

Augsburg. City in W. Bavaria, on the Lech R. It was founded by Augustus (15 B.C.) as the Roman colony Augusta Vindelicorum.

Augusta Treverorum. B1—12. *See* Trier

Augusta Vindelicorum. *See* Augsburg

Auja el-Hafir. Ancient town of the Negeb that was situated on a trade route from Palestine to Egypt. Neolithic tools have been found in the neighborhood, and deep wells there date to Nabatean and Byzantine times. It is also known as El 'Auja, or Nitsanah. A6—19

Auran. *See* Hauran

Auranitis. Name used in Greco-Roman times for a small district lying between Gaulanitis and the mod. *J. Hauran*. Auranitis, Trachonitis, and Batanea were assigned to Herod the Great by Augustus (*ca.* 23 B.C.).

Avaricum. *See* Bourges

Avaris (Zoan). C4—2. *See* Ramses

Avdat. Nabatean city S of Beer-sheba in the section of the Negeb known in biblical times as the Wilderness of Zin (*q.v.*). B6—19

Azeca. *See* Azekah

Azecha. *See* Azekah

Azekah. City in the lowlands of Judah a short distance NE of Lachish (*q.v.*). It, with Lachish, was strengthened by Rehoboam (II Chron. 11:9), and the two were among the last cities to fall to Nebuchadnezzar (Jer. 34:7). Mod. *Tell Zakari-yeh*. B4—19

Azotus. A5—11; A6—13. *See* Ashdod

Azov, Sea of. N arm of the Black Sea, bounded on the SW by the Crimea, on the N by the Ukraine, on the E by the Kuban lowland, and on the SE by the Taman Peninsula. It is fed by the Don and the Kuban rivers.

Azzah. *See* Gaza

B

Baalbek. *See* Heliopolis

Baal-meon. Town of the Reubenites (Num. 32:38; I Chron. 5:8). It was later a Moabite city (Ezek. 25:9; "Beth-meon" in Jer. 48:23), mentioned on the Moabite Stone. Mod. *Ma'in*, SW of Medeba, 9 miles E of the Dead Sea.

Baal-moan. *See* Baal-meon

Baal-saphon. *See* Baal-zephon

Baal-zephon. Place in Egypt on the border of the Red Sea where Israel encamped during the Exodus (Exod. 14:2, 9; Num. 33:7). Poss. mod. *J. Murr*. A4—3

Bab edh 'Drah. Site E of the Dead Sea where the remains of a sanctuary (dated 2800–1800 B.C.) have been discovered. C5—19

Babel. *See* Babylon

Babylon. Capital of Babylonia. It was an important city in S Mesopotamia that reached its zenith under Nebuchadnezzar. F4—2; C3—6, 7

Babylonia. Empire in the E Fertile Crescent area, N of the Persian Gulf, that had Babylon for its capital. It was also known as Shinar (Gen. 10:10; 11:2; Isa. 11:11) and the "land of the Chaldeans" (Jer. 24:5; Ezek. 12:13). F3-G4—2; D3—6; C3—7

Babylonian Empire, New. Name by which the Babylonia (*q.v.*) of the 6th and 5th centuries B.C. is known. Under its best-known king, Nebuchadnezzar, Judah was taken into exile (587 B.C.). C2-3—6

Babylonian Empire, Old. Name by which the Babylonia (*q.v.*) of the late 2nd millennium B.C.—the age of the biblical patriarchs—is known. Hammurabi was its most illustrious king.

Bactra. Capital of ancient Bactria (*q.v.*). Mod. *Balkh* in N Afghanistan. F2—7

Bactria. Ancient country that comprised the N slope of the Hindu Kush as far as the Oxus R. It was an E province of the Persian Empire before the conquest of Alexander (328 B.C.). A Greco-Bactrian kingdom was established there *ca.* 250 B.C. E-F2—7

Baetica. Roman province in Spain. It was bounded by the Anas R. on the N and W and by the Mediterranean Sea on the S. A2—12

Bagae. Ancient city on the Oxus R. in Sogdiana. In his battles with the E satrapies of the Persian Empire, Alexander fought in the vicinity of Bagae.

Balearic Islands. Group of 4 large and 11 small islands in the Mediterranean, off the E coast of Spain. They were colonized by Phoenicians and Carthaginians, and conquered by the Romans (123 B.C.).

Balikh R. Tributary of the upper Euphrates. The city of Haran (*q.v.*) was located on the Balikh, 60 miles N of its junction with the Euphrates.

Ballah, Lake. Lake on the border between Egypt and Sinai, E of Goshen and N of Lake Timsah. The Suez Canal now flows through the ancient lake region.

Baltic Sea. The E arm of the Atlantic Ocean, indenting N Europe. Countries surrounding the Baltic are: Denmark, Germany, Poland, Russia, Finland, and Sweden.

Baniyas. *See* Caesarea Philippi

Barasa. *See* Bostra

Barca. City of ancient Cyrenaica. Mod. *Barce* in Libya.

Basan. *See* Bashan

Bashan. Transjordan territory extending N from Gilead to Mt. Hermon. Before the Israelite conquest it was ruled by Og (Num. 21:33; Deut. 3:1; Josh. 12:5; 13:11), subsequently occupied by the half-tribe of Manasseh (Josh. 13:30; 17:1, 5; 21:6; 22:7; I Chron. 5:23), and at times settled by the tribe of Gad (I Chron. 5:11, 16). It was described as a fertile area, famed for its pasture lands (Deut. 32:14; Ezek. 39:18; Mic. 7:14). D2—1, 3; C-D2—5

Bastarnae. Ancient people of SE Sarmatia who settled in the region N of the Carpathian Mts.

Batanea. District of Transjordan E of Gualanitis. It was part of the kingdom of Herod the Great (37–4 B.C.) and subsequently assigned to Philip the Tetrarch (4 B.C.–A.D. 34). D2—11

Batavi. A Germanic people, settled N of the lower Rhine, S of the Frisians.

Beas R. *See* Hyphasis R.

Beautiful Gate. The E gate of Herod's temple. The Talmud terms it Nicanor's Gate, or the Great Gate. It was made of Corinthian brass, richly ornamented with precious metals. It was the largest of the temple gates, being 50 cubits high and 40 cubits wide. It was later called the Golden Gate, which is now sealed up.

Beelmeon. *See* Baal-meon

Beelsephon. *See* Baal-zephon

Beer Ora. Settlement in the Israeli Negeb, 12 miles N of Elath.

Beeroth. City of the Gibeonite Confederation (Josh. 9:17), subsequently subdued by Joshua and assigned to Benjamin (Josh. 18:25). It was repopulated after the Babylonian Exile (Ezra 2:25; Neh. 7:29). Poss. mod. *el-Bire*, N of Jerusalem.

Beer-sheba. City in S Palestine, midway between the Mediterranean and S end of the Dead Sea. Settled in patriarchal times (Gen. 21:14), it subsequently marked the S boundary of Israelite territory ("from Dan to Beer-sheba," Judg. 20:1; I Sam. 3:20; II Sam. 17:11). Beer-sheba (or Beer-sheva) is an important center for mod. Israeli settlements in the Negeb. B5—1; D4—2; C3—3; A5—4; B6—5

Beeshterah. *See* Ashtaroth

Behistun. Town in W Iran (ancient Persia) on the road from Hamadan to Babylon. On a mt. nearby, Darius I had reliefs and inscriptions carved to celebrate his victories. The trilingual inscriptions (Old Persian, Elamite, and Akkadian) provided the key to the decipherment of Akkadian cuneiform writing. C2—7

Beit Shean. *See* Beth-shan

Beit Shemesh. Name of the mod. Israeli community built near the mound of the same name that was excavated by the British Palestine Exploration Fund (1911–1912) and Haverford (Pa.) College (1928–1933). *See* Beth-shemesh

Beit Zabde. City in Zabdizene that was already Christian by *ca.* A.D. 100. F2—18

Bela. *See* Zoar

Belgica. Roman province in N Gaul, bounded by the North Sea and the Marne, Seine, and Rhine rivers. B1—12

Bene-barac. *See* Bene-berak

Bene-berak. City in Dan (Josh. 19:45), located 4 miles E of Joppa. Mod. *Ibn Ibraq*.

Benenennom Valley. *See* Hinnom Valley

Beneventum. Important commercial center on the Appian Way on a small plain of the Apennines in the Campania region of S Italy. A1—17

Beni Hasan. Village on the Nile, in Upper Egypt, in the vicinity of which have been found Middle Empire tombs with well-preserved murals.

Benjamin, allotment of. Tribe bounded on the N by Ephraim, on the S by Judah, on the W by Dan, and on the E by the Jordan.

Berea. *See* Beroea

Berenice (in Cyrenaica). Port on the Mediterranean on the N coast of Africa. Mod. *Bengasi*, Libya.

Berenice (in Egypt). Port city on the Red Sea, founded by Ptolemy II, that commanded trade with Arabia.

Beroea. City at the foot of Mt. Bermius in Macedonia. Paul commended the Beroeans for their careful study of Scripture (Acts 17:10–13). Mod. *Verria*. A1—15, 16; D2—18

Beroth. *See* Beeroth

Berotha. *See* Berothai

Berothai. Aramean city from which David took much bronze after defeating Hadadezer, its ruler (II Sam. 8:8). Mod. *Bereitan* in the Beqa'a, 35 miles N of Damascus. C2—4

Bersabe(e). B6—11. *See* Beer-sheba

Berytus. Ancient city on the Phoenician coast of the Mediterranean at the foot of the Lebanon range. Mod. *Beirut* or *Beyrouth*, Lebanon. D1—3; B3—4; B4—13

Besor R. Stream that flows into the Mediterranean *ca.* 5 miles S of Gaza. A5—1; A6—5

Bethabara. Place on the E bank of the Jordan where John was baptizing (John 1:28). Poss. mod.

'Abarah N of Scythopolis (Beth-shan). Many Greek manuscripts read "'Bethany beyond Jordan'' instead of "Bethabara."

Beth-Alfa. Town 4 miles W of Beth-shan. The remains of a synagogue (6th century A.D.) have been discovered there. C2—19

Bethania. *See* Bethany

Bethany. Village on the E slope of the Mt. of Olives, *ca.* 2 miles from Jerusalem. The home of Mary, Martha, and Lazarus (John 11:1; 12:1). Mod. *el-'Azariyeh.* C5—11

Bethany beyond Jordan. *See* Bethabara

Beth-aram. *See* Betharamphtha

Betharamphtha (Livias, Julias). Town in the Jordan Valley assigned to the tribe of Gad, also known as Beth-haram (Josh. 13:27) and Beth-haran (Num. 32:36). On this site was built the city of Livias, or Julias, where Herod the Great built a palace. Poss. mod. *Tell Iqtanu,* E of *Tell er-Rameh.* C5—11

Beth-aran. *See* Betharamphtha

Beth-dagon. Village *ca.* 5 miles NW of Lydda near Philistia (Josh. 15:41). Mod. *Kh. Dajun.*

Bethel. Town *ca.* 12 miles N of Jerusalem. Here the patriarch Abraham encamped (Gen. 12:8; 13:3). In the days of Jeroboam I of Israel, Bethel was chosen as a shrine to offset the influence of the Jerusalem temple (I Kings 12:28–33). Mod. *Beitin.* B4—1, 4, 5; D3—3; C4—19

Beth-emec. *See* Beth-emek

Beth-emek. Town in Asher (Josh. 19:27). Poss. mod. *Tell Mimas.*

Bethesda, Pool of. B4—10. *See* Bethzatha, Pool of

Beth-haccherem. Judean town that served as a place for signaling during times of invasion (Jer. 6:1). Commonly identified with 'Ain Karim (*q.v.*), 4.5 miles W of Jerusalem. Mod. *Beit-hakerem.*

Beth-hagla. *See* Beth-hoglah

Beth-haram. *See* Betharamphtha

Beth-haran. *See* Betharamphtha

Beth-hoglah. Town on the border between the territories of Benjamin and Judah (Josh. 15:6; 18:19, 21), SE of Jericho. Mod. *'Ain Hajlah.*

Beth-horon. Town on the boundary between the territories of Ephraim and Benjamin (Josh. 18:13). It is divided into 2 communities: Lower Beth-horon, mod. *Beit 'Ur et-Tahta,* which has an altitude of 1,240 feet; and Upper Beth-horon, mod. *Beit 'Ur el-Foqa,* which has an altitude of 1,730 feet. B4—4

Bethiesimoth. *See* Beth-jeshimoth

Beth-jeshimoth. Settlement in Transjordan N of the Dead Sea. It was the stopping place of Israel during the final stage of the Exodus (Num. 33:49). Later it became part of Moabite territory (Ezek. 25:9). Prob. mod. *Tell el-'Azeimeh.*

Beth-jesimoth. *See* Beth-jeshimoth

Bethlehem. Town located 5 miles S of Jerusalem on the road to Hebron. It was the city of David and the birthplace of Jesus. Mod. *Beit Lahm.* B5—1, 5, 11; B4—19

Beth-maachah. *See* Abel

Beth-nemra. *See* Beth-nimrah

Beth-nimrah. Town in the territory of Gad (Josh. 13:27), identical with Nimrah (Num. 32:3). Poss. mod. *Tell Bileibil,* near *Tell Nimrin.*

Bethoron. *See* Beth-horon

Beth-palet. Town in S Judah (the Negeb), the exact location of which is uncertain (Josh. 15:27; Neh. 11:26).

Beth-phaleth. *See* Beth-palet

Beth-pelet. *See* Beth-palet

Beth-rehob. An Aramean territory generally W of Damascus (II Sam. 10:6). Its precise location is uncertain, but it may be identical with Beth-rehob near Dan (Judg. 18:28). B-C3—4

Bethsaida-Julias. Town located E of the point where the Jordan flows into the Sea of Galilee. It was the home of Andrew, Peter, and Philip (John 1:44; 12:21). Poss. mod. *et-Tell.* C2—11

Beth-sames. *See* Beth-shemesh

Beth-san. *See* Beth-shan

Beth-shan (Scythopolis). Ancient fortress strategically located at the junction of the Plain of Jezreel with the Jordan Valley. Occupied by Canaanites before the conquest (Josh. 17:16), it was subsequently located on the border between the territories of Issachar and Manasseh (Josh. 17:11; I Chron. 7:29). Following the Battle of Gilboa (*ca.* 1000 B.C.) the Philistines fastened the bodies of Saul and his sons to the wall of the city (I Sam. 31:10–13). During Hellenistic times Beth-shan was known as Scythopolis. It was the one city W of the Jordan in the federation of Greek cities known as Decapolis. Beth-shan has been identified with *Tell el-Hosn,* near the village of Beisan. C3—1, 5; D2—3; B4—4; C2—19

Beth-shean. *See* Beth-shan

Beth Shearim. Jewish necropolis between Nazareth and Haifa, including more than 25 rock-hewn catacombs dating from the 2nd to the 4th centuries A.D. C2—19

Beth-shemesh. Town in the Valley of Sorek about 23.5 miles W of Jerusalem, on the border between the territories of Judah and Dan (Josh. 15:10), also known as Irshemesh (Josh. 19:41). Mod. *Tell er-Rumeileh.* B4—4, 19; B5—5

Bethsimoth. *See* Beth-jeshimoth

Bethsur. *See* Beth-zur

Bethsura. B5—11. *See* Beth-zur

Beth-togarmah. *See* Togarmah

Beth-yerah (Philoteria). Canaanite city near the S end of the Sea of Galilee. It became the Hellenistic city of Philoteria. Antiochus III of Syria (218 B.C.) occupied it, then crossed the Jordan and conquered Transjordan. C2—19

Beth-zacharam. *See* Beth-zacharias

Beth-zacharias. Town *ca.* 10 miles SW of Jerusalem. Mod. *Kh. Beit Sakaria.*

Bethzatha (Bethesda), Pool of. Name used in some manuscripts for the pool near the Sheep Gate in Jerusalem (John 5:2). Other manuscripts read Bethesda. B4—10

Beth-zur. Town in the hill-country of Judah, 4 miles N of Hebron. It was fortified by Rehoboam (II Chron. 11:7). Mod. *Kh. et-Tubeiqeh,* near *Burjes-Sur.* B5—5; C4—19

Betonim. Town in Gad (Josh. 13:26). Mod. *Kh. Batneh.*

Beycesultan. Ancient town on the Maeander R., in W Asia Minor. Excavations indicate a Greek culture here during the patriarchal age (2000–1600 B.C.). C2—2

Bezec. *See* Bezek

Bezek. Town in the territory of Manasseh, S of Mt. Gilboa. Prob. mod. *Kh. Ibziq.*

Bibracte. Town in central France, ancient Gaul, where Caesar defeated the Helvetii (58 B.C.).

Bile-am. *See* Ibleam

Bira. Town in Jordan, NE of Ramallah. *See* Beeroth

Birs Nimrud. *See* Borsippa

Bithynia. Region in N Asia Minor (Acts 16:7). E2—12, 18; C1—15, 16; D-F1—17

Bitter Lakes. Lakes in Egypt N of the Gulf of Suez. B4—3

Black Sea. Inland sea located N of Asia Minor. Enclosed by Russia on the N and E, by Turkey on the S, and by Bulgaria and Romania on the W. It is connected with the Mediterranean by the Bosporus, the Sea of Marmara, and the Dardanelles. C-D1—2; B-C1—6; B1—7; E2—12, 18; E-F1—17

Bogaskoy. *See* Hattusas

Bordeaux. City of SW France with a port accessible to the Atlantic through the Gironde R.

Borsippa. Town a few miles S of Babylon, also known as Birs Nimrud. Ruins of a great temple (*ziggurat*) are reminiscent of the biblical Tower of Babel.

Borysthenes (Dnieper) **R.** River flowing generally S from the Valdai Hills (W of Moscow) into the Black Sea, a distance of *ca.* 1,420 miles.

Bosor. City *ca.* 40 miles E of the Sea of Galilee. Mod. *Busr el-Hariri.*

Bosora. *See* Bostra

Bosporus Kingdom. State occupying the territory surrounding the Palus Maeotis, N of the Black Sea. The region produced grain for Rome. It was a client kingdom and not a kingdom subject to Rome. E2—12

Bosra. *See* Bozrah

Bostra (Busra). Town in the Hauran highlands of Transjordan, S of Kanatha.

Bourges (Avaricum). Avaricum, a town in central Gaul, was the site of a major battle described by Julius Caesar in his *Gallic Wars*. Augustus made it the capital of Aquitania N of the Garonne. Its mod. name is Bourges.

Bozrah. Important city of Edom situated in an oasis of the Syrian Desert. Prob. mod. *Buseira,* 25 miles SE of the Dead Sea. D4—3; B5—4

Bremen. City of the Saxons on the Weser R. in what is now N Germany.

Brick Walls, City of. *See* Kir-hareseth

Brigantium. Town on the NW coast of Spain, prob. to be identified with mod. *La Coruña.*

Britain. *See* Britannia

Britannia. Term applied to Great Britain before the Germanic invasions of the 5th and 6th centuries.

The Romans arrived in Britain in 55 B.C. and reached their period of greatest power there during the first half of the 3rd century A.D. B1—12

Brook of Cherith. *See* Cherith, Brook

Brundisium. Adriatic Sea port in S Italy, since ancient times a center of trade with the East. Products could be brought by sea to Brundisium and carried overland to Rome by the Appian Way, which terminated there. Mod. *Brindisi.*

Bubastis. A4—3. *See* Pibeseth

Bubastus. *See* Bubastis

Bucephala. Ancient town on the Hydaspes R. in India.

Burdigala. A2—12. *See* Bordeaux

Busra. *See* Bostra

Buxentum (Capo della Foresta). Town in SW Italy on the Gulf of Policastro.

Byblos. D3—2; B4—13. *See* Gebal

Byzantium (Istanbul). City located on both sides of the Bosporus at its entrance into the Sea of Marmara. As Constantinople it was the capital of the Byzantine Empire. In 1930 the name was officially changed to Istanbul, which serves as the chief city and seaport of Turkey. B1—7, 15, 16; D2—12, 18; D1—17

C

Cabul. Village of Asher (Josh. 19:27), 9 miles SE of Acco. Mod. *Kabul.* B3—4; B2—5

Cadasa. C2—11. *See* Kedesh (in Naphtali)

Cades. *See* Kedesh (in Naphtali)

Cadesbarne. *See* Kadesh-barnea

Cadiz. *See* Gades

Cadusii. An ancient people settled in the mts. W of the Caspian Sea.

Caerleon. Town on the Usk R. NE of Newport in W Britain. It was the site of the Roman fortress Isca. It is known as Camelot in the Arthurian legend.

Caesarea (in Mauretania). Important city on the Mediterranean in Mauretania, the westernmost African province of Rome. It was sacked by the vandals in the 5th century. The site is now occupied by Cherchell, Algeria. B3—12

Caesarea (in Palestine). Seaport, formerly Strato's Tower, *ca.* 23 miles S of Mt. Carmel, on the Mediterranean. It was built by Herod the Great. Mod. *Keisariyeh,* Israel. B3—1, 11; A5—13; D6—14; D3—15, 16; F4—17; E3—18; B2—19

Caesarea Augusta (Saragossa). City founded by Augustus Caesar on the Ebro R. in NE Spain. A2—12

Caesarea Mazaca. Called also Caesarea of Cappadocia, this was an important trading center in E Asia Minor and, as Mazaca, served as the residence of Cappadocian kings. Mod. *Kayseri,* Turkey. D1—15, 16; F2—17; E2—18

Caesarea Philippi (Baniyas). City near the source of the Jordan in N Palestine. It was built by the tetrarch Philip near a sanctuary of the god Pan, hence Panias, or Paneion. Its mod. name is Baniyas. C2—11; B4—13

Caesar's Bridge. Bridge that Caesar built across the Rhine, the boundary between Gaul and Germania. Caesar used bridges to invade Germania but made no permanent conquests.

Cagliari. *See* Caralis

Caiaphas, House of. Located in the Upper City of Jerusalem NE of the House of the Last Supper. B6—10

Calah (Nimrud). Ancient Assyrian city *ca.* 25 miles SE of Nineveh. Ashurnasirpal III built a great palace there and made it the center of his government. F3—2

Caleb. The clan of Caleb lived in the territory around Hebron and was incorporated into the tribe of Judah (Josh. 15:13–19).

Callirhoe. *See* Callirrhoe

Callirrhoe. Community in Perea (Transjordan) NW of Machaerus. It was noted for its baths, in which Herod bathed shortly before his death. C5—11

Calvary. A4—10. *See* Golgotha

Camon. Place mentioned in Judges 10:5 as the burial place of Jair. Poss. mod. *Qamm*, SE of the Sea of Galilee.

Cana. Village in Galilee where Jesus performed His first miracle (John 2:1–11). Prob. mod. *Kh. Qana*, 9 miles N of Nazareth. It is traditionally identified with *Kafr Kenna*. C2—11

Canaan. Biblical Canaan was the land promised to Abraham and his descendants (Gen. 17:8). It refers to Palestine W of the Jordan (Gen. 13:12). In a more restricted sense it may refer to Phoenicia (Isa. 23:11), or the land of the Philistines (Zeph. 2:5). According to Genesis 10:15–20, Canaanite territory extended from Sidon to Gaza, W of the Jordan. Canaanite settlements reached as far N as Arvad. D1-3—3

Canaanites. Term used of the inhabitants of Canaan who were in the land during patriarchal times and who were defeated in battle during the Israelite conquest under Joshua. Canaan is called a son of Ham (Gen. 10:6, 15–20), reminiscent of the fact that Canaan had long been dominated by the Egyptians (*Mizraim*, another son of Ham).

Cantabri. An ancient people who inhabited the N coast of Spain. They were attacked by the Romans (150 B.C.) but were subdued only in a series of campaigns carried out by Augustus (29–19 B.C.).

Canterbury. City located at the foot of the North Downs on the Stour R. in SE Britain. The Mother Church of England, founded before the arrival of Augustine (A.D. 597), is located there.

Capernaum. City on the NW shore of the Sea of Galilee where Jesus performed numerous miracles. Mod. *Tell Hum.* C2—11, 19

Cape Salmone. *See* Salmone, Cape

Capharnaum. *See* Capernaum

Capharsaba. Town 39 miles NW of Jerusalem in a fertile plain. It was rebuilt by Herod the Great and named Antipatris (*q.v.*) after Antipater, his father. The old name continues in use in the village *Kefr Saba*. Ancient Capharsaba, however, is identified with *Ras el-'Ain*. It is identical with the Canaanite royal city of Aphek (Josh. 12:18; I Sam. 4:1; 29:1).

Capharsalama. Location of a battle between Judas the Maccabee and Nicanor (I Macc. 7:31). Mod. *Kh. Selma*, NW of Jerusalem.

Caphtor. A3—2. *See* Crete

Caphtorim. Inhabitants of Crete, Egyptian *Keftiu*. The term probably includes both Crete and adjacent islands and nearby lands (including Caria and Lycia in Asia Minor). According to Genesis 10:14, Caphtor was a descendant of Mizraim (Egypt). The Philistines originated in Caphtor (Amos 9:7; Jer. 47:4).

Capitolias. City of the Decapolis, located S of Abila on an important N-S trade route through Transjordan. Mod. *Beit Ras.* D3—11

Capo della Foresta. *See* Buxentum

Cappadocia. Highland district of E Asia Minor, formed into a Roman province in A.D. 17. C1—6; E2—12; D4—13; D1—15, 16; F2—17; E-F3—18

Capua. Strategic town located on the Appian Way and the Volturno R. in S Italy.

Caralis (Cagliari). Seaport at the head of the Gulf of Cagliari on the S coast of Sardinia. It was founded by the Phoenicians. B2—12

Carchemish. Hittite center on the right bank of the N Euphrates at an important ford of the river. It was situated *ca.* 60 miles W of Haran. Necho of Egypt was decisively defeated by Nebuchadnezzar of Babylon at Carchemish (605 B.C.). Mod. *Jerablus* (*Jerabish*). D2—2; C2—6

Caria. Country in SW Asia Minor. It was taken from Antiochus the Great by the Romans and later incorporated into the province of Asia. B2—7, 15, 16

Cariathaim. *See* Kiriathaim

Cariath-Arbe. *See* Hebron

Cariathiarim. *See* Kirjath-jearim

Cariath-jarim. *See* Kirjath-jearim

Cariath-sepher. *See* Debir

Carmania. SE province of ancient Persia. Mod. *Kerman.* D-E3—7

Carmel. Town in the hill-country of Judah (Josh. 15:55; I Sam. 15:12). Mod. *el-Kirmil*, S of Hebron.

Carmel, Mt. Range of hills *ca.* 15 miles long, terminating in a promontory that juts into the Mediterranean, constituting the S boundary of the Bay of Acco (Acre). The mod. city of Haifa is at the foot of Mt. Carmel. The range is connected with the mountainous region of central Palestine by a chain of lower hills. The Carmel range comprises the SW boundary of the Plain of Esdraelon through which the Kishon R. flows. B2—1, 5; C2—3; B3—4, 11

Carnaim. *See* Karnaim

Carnion. *See* Karnaim

Carpathians. Mt. chain of central Europe that forms an arc *ca.* 900 miles long, enclosing the plain of the Danube to the N and E. D1—12

Carpi. A Dacian tribe located on the lower Danube from the 1st century B.C. They invaded the Roman Empire in the 3rd century A.D. and were later taken under Roman protection. In the time of Theodosius I, they were allies of the Huns.

Carrhae *See* Haran

Cartagena. Latin *Carthago Nova* ("New Carthage"). Port on the Mediterranean, in SE Spain. Founded by the Carthaginian Hasdrubal, *ca*. 225 B.C., it served as the chief Carthaginian base in Spain until captured (209 B.C.) by Scipio Africanus. It continued to flourish under the Romans.

Carthage. N African city on a peninsula in the Bay of Tunis, near mod. *Tunis*, founded in the 9th century B.C. by colonists from Tyre. During the 6th and 5th centuries B.C., Carthage acquired dominance over the W Mediterranean but was defeated by the Romans in a series of Punic (i.e., Phoenician) wars during the 3rd and 2nd centuries B.C. C3—12; B3—18

Carthago Nova. *See* Cartagena

Casaloth. *See* Chesulloth

Caspian Gates. Mt. pass S of the Caspian Sea, E of Rhagae. The Persians, under Darius III, hoped to make a stand against Alexander here. Darius was murdered, however, and Alexander met little opposition as he journeyed E to India.

Caspian Sea (Mare Hyrcanium). Salt lake located between Europe and Asia, bounded by Russia on the N and Iran on the S. The Caucasus Mts. arise from its SW shore, and the Elburz Mts. parallel its S coast. The Caspian receives the Volga, Ural, Kura, and Terek rivers, but it has no outlet. D1—6, 7; F1-2—12

Catabathmus. Town on the Gulf of Salum in Marmarica, E Libya (mod. *as-Sallum* in W Egypt). The Catabathmus Major was the name given in classical times to the descent or slope that separated Egypt from Marmarica.

Caucasus. The mt. system between Europe and Asia. It extends 750 miles from the mouth of the Kuban R. on the Black Sea SE to the Apherson Peninsula on the Caspian. F-G1—2; D1—6; C1—7; F2—12

Cauda. Small island S of Crete (Acts 27:16). It was also known as Clauda. Mod. *Gaudos* or *Gozzo*. C3—17

Cedes. *See* Kedesh

Cedron. City SE of Jamnia, fortified during the Maccabean struggle (I Macc. 15:39, 41). Poss. mod. *Qatra*.

Cedron Valley. *See* Kidron Valley

Celia. *See* Keilah

Celaenae. City of Phrygia, Asia Minor, near the headwaters of the Maeander R. (mod. *Menderes R*.). In Persian times Cyrus the Great had a palace at Celaenae. Alexander conquered the city in 333 B.C. Mod. *Dinar*.

Celesyria. *See* Coele Syria

Celtiberi. An ancient people of Hither Spain who were settled in the area S of the Ebro R.

Celtic Gaul. Area of S-central Gaul inhabited by tribes speaking Celtic languages.

Cenabum. Town on the Loire R., central Gaul. The Romans took Cenabum from the Gauls and re-named it Aurelianum, which became French Orléans.

Cenchrae. *See* Cenchreae

Cenchrea. *See* Cenchreae

Cenchreae. Harbor of Corinth, on the Saronic Gulf *ca*. 7 miles E of the city. Paul visited there (Acts 18:18). A2—15

Cenereth. *See* Chinnereth

Ceneroth. *See* Chinnereth

Central Valley. Valley that once separated the E and W hills of Jerusalem. It is now almost filled with debris as a result of Jerusalem's history of warfare and destruction. B2-3—8; D2-3—9

Cerethi. *See* Cherethites

Cerethites. *See* Cherethites

Cethim. *See* Cyprus

Cetthim. *See* Cyprus

Chalcedon. Ancient Greek city on the Bosporus, on the shore of Asia Minor opposite Byzantium. A church council convened there (A.D. 451). The site is now occupied by the suburbs of Istanbul.

Chalcis (in Euboea). City on the island of Euboea, opposite the Greek mainland. It led the revolt of Euboea against Athens (446 B.C.).

Chalcis (in Syria). City on the Leontes R. in the Beqa'a Valley. It was on the trade route from Antioch to Damascus. B4—13

Chaldea. Term used to designate the S portion of Babylonia, at the head of the Persian Gulf. The Chaldeans founded an empire under Nabopolassar.

Chaldean Empire. *See* Babylonian Empire, New

Chale. *See* Calah

Chanaan. *See* Canaan

Charachmoba. C6—11. *See* Kir-hareseth

Charcamis. *See* Carchemish

Chaseleth. *See* Chesulloth

Chatti. A Germanic people settled E of the Rhine, W of the Hermunduri.

Chauci. A Germanic people settled W of the lower Albis (Elbe), E of the Frisians.

Chenereth. *See* Chinnereth

Chephirah. Gibeonite city (Josh. 9:17) that was assigned to Benjamin (Josh. 18:26). Mod. *Tell Kefireh*, 8 miles NW of Jerusalem.

Cherethites. Nation or tribe inhabiting the S portion of the Philistine country (I Sam. 30:14; Ezek. 25:16; Zeph. 2:5). The name probably means "Cretans," and they are thought to have been related to the Philistines, who also came from the island of Crete.

Cherith, Brook. Wadi, flowing into the Jordan from the E, near which Elijah was fed by ravens (I Kings 17:3–7). Poss. mod. *W. Yabis*, or *W. Qelt*, which enters the Jordan from the W after flowing past Jericho.

Chersonesus. Black Sea port on the S shore of the Crimean Peninsula, known in ancient times as the Chersonese, or Chersonesus, the Greek word for "peninsula." B1—7

Chesalon. Town 10 miles W of Jerusalem on the border between the territories of Judah and Dan. It has been identified with Mt. Jearim (Josh. 15:10). Mod. *Kesla*.

Cheslon. *See* Chesalon

Chesulloth. Town on the border of the territory of Issachar (Josh. 19:18), 3.5 miles SE of Nazareth. Mod. *Iksal*.

Chetthim. *See* Cyprus

Chinnereth. Fortified city of Naphtali (Josh. 19:35; Deut. 3:17), NW of the Lake of Genesareth (Sea of Galilee). Mod. *Tell el-'Oreimeh*. C2—5

Chinnereth, Sea of. C2—1, 5. *See* Galilee, Sea of

Chinneroth. *See* Chinnereth

Chios. Island in the Greek Archipelago, S of Lesbos, at the entrance of the Gulf of Smyrna. B2—16

Chisloth-tabor. *See* Chesulloth

Chittim. *See* Cyprus

Choaspes R. River rising in W Iran, flowing S *ca.* 500 miles to join the Tigris and Euphrates N of the Persian Gulf. Ancient Susa was on its banks. The river is now known as the *Karkheh*.

Chorasmia. Ancient name for the region S of the Aral Sea, including the Oxus Delta. E1—7

Chorasmii. Ancient name of the people settled between the Caspian and Aral seas.

Chorazin. Town NW of the Sea of Galilee. Jesus ministered there, but its inhabitants rejected His message (Matt. 11:21; Luke 10:13). Mod. *Kh. Kerazeh*, 2 miles N of Capernaum. C2—11

Chus. *See* Cush

Cibroth-hatthaava. *See* Kibroth-hattaavah

Cilicia. District in the SE section of Asia Minor separated on the N by the Taurus Mts. from Cappadocia, Lycaonia, and Isauria; and on the E by the Amanus Mts. from Syria. It is bounded on the S by the Mediterranean and on the W by Pamphylia. Tarsus, the birthplace of Paul, was its chief town. B2—7; E3—12, 18; A-B1—13; D5—14; D2—15, 16

Cilician Gates. Mt. pass leading across the Taurus range from Cappadocia to Cilicia. Its ancient name was *Pylae Ciliciae*. Mod. *Gulek Bogaz*, Turkey. D2—15, 16

Cimmerians. A people who entered Asia from beyond the Caucasus, settled in Cappadocia, and for a time threatened the Assyrian Empire. After defeat by Esarhaddon (of Assyria), they overran part of Asia Minor and fought with Gyges of Lydia. Alyattes of Lydia drove them out of Asia Minor.

Cirta. Originally a Carthaginian settlement, Cirta became the capital and commercial center of Numidia, and an important shipping point in the supply of grain to the Romans. It is situated on a plateau on the gorge of the Rhumel R. Mod. *Constantine*, Algeria. B3—12, 18

Cisalpine Gaul. The section of Gaul (*q.v.*) in Italy (literally, "on this side of the Alps"), in contradistinction to Transalpine Gaul ("on the other side of the Alps").

Cison R. *See* Kishon R.

City of Brick Walls. *See* Kir-hareseth

City of David. *See* David, City of

City of Palm Trees. *See* Jericho

Clauda. *See* Cauda

Clonard. Community in central Ireland where a monastery was established (*ca.* A.D. 520) by Welsh Christians. From Clonard the so-called "Twelve Apostles of Ireland" went forth to establish schools throughout Ireland and, later, on the Continent.

Cnidus. City of Caria, SW Asia Minor, mentioned in the account of Paul's voyage to Rome (Acts 27:7). Mod. *Cape Krio*. D3—17

Cnossus. City of ancient Crete, on the N coast, near the sea. The study of the ruins of Cnossus has contributed to our knowledge of Minoan civilization. Near mod. *Candia*. D3—17, 18

Coele Syria. The high plain, also known as the Beqa'a, located between the Lebanon and Anti-Lebanon ranges. It is a fertile area watered by the Leontes R.

Colchis. Ancient land on the E shores of the Black Sea and in the Caucasus region, centered in the fertile Phasis R. valley. Greek trading posts were established there, but it remained independent until conquered (*ca.* 100 B.C.) by Mithridates VI of Pontus. F2—12

Cologne. City on the Rhine in NW Germany. It was established in A.D. 50 as a Roman colony by Claudius. B1—18

Colonia Agrippina. *See* Cologne

Colossae. City of SW Phrygia, Asia Minor, on the R. Lycos E of the point where it joins the Maeander. Ruins near mod. *Khonai*.

Commagene. District on the Euphrates in N Syria, now in SE Turkey. It was part of the Assyrian, and later the Persian, Empire, but revolted under the Seleucid kings of Syria and, early in the 2nd century B.C., became an independent state. Commagene was annexed to the Roman province of Syria by Vespasian (A.D. 72). E2—12

Constanta. *See* Tomi

Constantinople. *See* Byzantium

Coos. *See* Cos

Cophen (Kabul) R. River that flows 300 miles eastward from the Hindu Kush, past Kabul and Jalalabad and through gorges in the Khyber Pass to the Indus R. F2—7

Corcyra. Capital and largest city of the island of the same name off the W coast of Greece. It was established in the 8th century B.C. by colonists from Corinth, but it later made war with the mother city. In 229 B.C. Corcyra passed under Roman rule. Mod. *Corfu*.

Cordoba. *See* Corduba

Cordova. *See* Corduba

Corduba. City in S Spain at the foot of the Sierra de Cordoba on the Guadalquivir R. It is of Iberian origin and flourished under the Romans. Mod. *Cordoba* or *Cordova*. A2—12, 18

Corduene. Ancient name of the region extending S

of Lake Van as far as the Tigris.

Corfinium. Town in central Italy. During the Social War (91–88 B.C.) it served as capital of the republic of Italia.

Corinth. City of Greece on the narrow isthmus between the Peloponnesus and the mainland. It was on a plateau at the foot of an 1,800-foot-high mt.—the Acrocorinthus. Corinth had two harbors: Cenchreae, 8.5 miles E on the Saronic Gulf; and Lecheum, 1.5 miles W on the Corinthian Gulf. D3—12, 18; A2—15, 16; C2—17

Corner Gate. Gate at the NW corner of Jerusalem (*ca.* 445 B.C.). C2—9

Corsica. Mediterranean island, SE of France and N of Sardinia. It was controlled by the Romans from the 3rd century B.C. to the 5th century A.D. *See* Sardinia. B2—12, 18

Cos. Island in the archipelago off the coast of Caria, Asia Minor, in a gulf between Cnidus and Halicarnassus (Acts 21:1). Mod. *Kos*. B2—15, 16; D2—17

Council House. Meeting place of the Sanhedrin, the Jewish governing body charged by the Romans with the general administration of justice.

Court of the Gentiles. *See* Gentiles, Court of the

Creta. D3—12. *See* Crete

Crete (Caphtor). Large island in the Mediterranean, lying SE of Greece. It is traversed by a chain of mts., one of which, Mt. Ida, is 8,065 feet high. Paul sailed along its S coast on his voyage to Rome (Acts 27:7, 12, 13, 21). *See also* Caphtorim. A3—2; A2—6, 7; B2—15, 16; C3—17; D3—18

Crocodilopolis (Arsinoe). Egyptian city, said to have been founded *ca.* 2300 B.C., that served as the chief seat of early Egyptian worship of the crocodile. Near mod. *Al-Faiyum*. A5—3

Croton. City in S Italy on the E coast of Calabria, the Greek colony Magna Graecia, founded at the end of the 8th century B.C. The school of Pythagoras, which was established there, exerted a notable political and moral influence. It was captured by the Romans in 277 B.C. Mod. *Crotone*.

Ctesiphon. City on the left bank of the Tigris, opposite Seleucia, in S Mesopotamia. After 129 B.C. it was the winter residence of Parthian kings. F3—12

Cush. B4—7. *See* Ethiopia

Cutha. *See* Cuthah

Cuthah. City of ancient Mesopotamia, near Babylon. Natives of Cuthah, when settled in Samaria, introduced the worship of Nergal (II Kings 17:24–30). Poss. mod. *Tell Ibrahim*. F4—2

Cyclades. Part of the Greek archipelago in the Aegean Sea. The name originally indicated the islands forming a rough circle (*Kyklades* in Greek) around Delos. They include Andros, Tenos, Naxos, Melos, Paros, and Keos.

Cydonia. City on the Gulf of Canea in W Crete (*q.v.*). Mod. *Khania* or *Canea*.

Cyprus (Alashiya, Kittim), island of. Island in the E Mediterranean, *ca.* 40 miles S of the Cilician coast and 60 W of Syria. Its ancient population

were Kittim or Chetthim (Gen. 10:4), poss. akin to the pre-Hellenic population of Greece. It was subsequently colonized by Phoenicians. The gospel was preached there after Stephen's martyrdom (Acts 11:19–20), and subsequently by Barnabas, Paul, and Mark (Acts 13:4; 15:39). C3—2; A1—4; B2—6, 7; E3—12, 17, 18; A3—13; C5—14; C2—15, 16

Cyprus, town of. Roman fortress S of Jericho captured by the Jews in their first revolt against Rome. C5—11

Cyrenaica (Libya). Region around the ancient city of Cyrene on the N coast of Africa. The Roman province of Cyrene was sometimes called Cyrenaica. D4—12, 18; C4—17

Cyrene. Ancient city in Cyrenaica (*q.v.*) in N Africa. Founded as a Greek colony (*ca.* 631 B.C.), Cyrene submitted to the Persians under Cambyses, but *ca.* 450 B.C. it regained independence. Its subsequent history was closely related to that of the Egyptian Ptolemies, Greece, and (after 96 B.C.) Rome. A2—7; D3—12, 18; C4—17

Cyropolis. City in Sogdiana, on the NE border of the Persian Empire. F2—7

Cyrus R. River that rises in Turkish Armenia, flows NE, then SE, paralleling the Greater Caucasus, a distance of 940 miles to the Caspian Sea. Mod. *Kura R*. F1—2; C2—7

Cyzicus. Ancient city at the neck of the Cyzicus Peninsula in NW Asia Minor. It was founded in 756 B.C. by Greek colonists from Miletus, and for a time it rivaled Byzantium in commercial importance.

Czechs. A W Slavic people related to the Poles, Slovaks, and Moravians. They united politically with the Slovaks to form Czechoslovakia.

D

Dabir. *See* Debir

Dacia. Ancient name of the region corresponding to mod. *Transylvania* and *Romania*. Inhabitants of the area were called Getae by the Greeks, Daci by the Romans. D2—12, 18

Dadan. *See* Dedan

Dahae. An ancient people settled in the region between the Caspian and Aral seas.

Dalmanutha. Place prob. situated on the W shore of the Sea of Galilee. Region to which Jesus went after the 2nd miracle of the loaves and fishes (Mark 8:10). Poss. Magadan (*q.v.*).

Dalmatia. B1—17. *See* Illyricum

Damascus, city of. Syrian city on a plateau watered by the Abana and Pharpar rivers (II Kings 5:12). Important trade routes leading to Egypt, Arabia, and Mesopotamia converge at Damascus, a city mentioned as early as the time of Abraham (Gen. 14:15). Mod. Damascus, on the Barada R. (biblical Abana R. [*q.v.*]), bears the Arabic name *Esh-Sham*. D1—1, 3, 5, 11; D3—2, 15, 16; C3—4; C2—6; B2—7; B4—13; D6—14; F3—17, 18

Damascus, Kingdom of. City-state of S Syria that, after the time of David, was frequently in conflict with Israel (I Kings 11:23–24). It took the lead in resisting the Assyrians and led an alliance against Shalmaneser at Karkar (854– 853 B.C.). Tiglath-pileser captured Damascus (732 B.C.) and carried its inhabitants into exile (II Kings 16:5–9).

Damghan (Hecatompylus). Parthian capital, visited by Alexander the Great during his campaign in the E. Polybius stated that all roads of the Parthian Empire centered there. D2—7

Dan, allotment of. The original allotment of Dan was along the Mediterranean N of the Valley of Sorek (marking the N border of Judah), W of Benjamin, and S and W of Ephraim. It included the towns of Zorah, Eltekeh, and Ekron, and it ended N of Joppa (Num. 1:12, 38, 39; Josh. 19:40–46; 21:5, 23, 24). Cramped for room, the Danites looked for additional territory in the extreme N of the country and conquered the city of Laish and environs, which they named Dan (q.v.).

Dan, town of. Town in the extreme N of Palestine, originally called Laish (Judg. 18) or Leshem (Josh. 19:47). Jeroboam of Israel made Dan a shrine town, placing one of his golden calves there (I Kings 12:28–30). Mod. *Tell el-Qadi*. C1—1, 5, 19; B3—4

Danube (Ister) R. River of central and SE Europe. It rises in the Black Forest in SE Germany and flows E ca. 1,750 miles before entering the Black Sea. A1—6, 7; C1—12, 18

Daphca. *See* Dophkah

David, City of. B2-3—8. *See* Jerusalem

Dead (Salt) Sea. Body of water situated in the deep volcanic fissure that runs through Palestine from N to S. It is fed principally by the Jordan. Its surface is 1,292 feet below sea level. C5—1; C6—11; B6—13; C4-5—19

Debir. City in the hill country of Judah also known as Kirjath-sepher. Poss. mod. *Tell Beit Mirsim*, 12 miles SW of Hebron. C3—3; B5—5, 19

Deblatha. *See* Riblah

Decapolis. District that begins where the Plain of Esdraelon opens into the Jordan Valley and expands eastward. It derives its name from the original association of 10 Hellenistic cities (later expanded to 18). Multitudes from Decapolis followed Jesus early in His ministry (Matt. 4:25). C-D3—11; B5—13

Dedan (descendant of Ham). Arabian tribe that settled W of the Persian Gulf.

Dedan (descendant of Shem). Arabian tribe that settled E of the N sector of the Arabian Gulf (Red Sea).

Dedan, town of. Caravan center ca. 100 miles S of Tema. Jeremiah referred to it (Jer. 25:23; 49:8). Dedan was a descendant of Ham (Gen. 10:7). E6—2; C3—6; B3—7

Dephca. *See* Dophkah

Der'a. *See* Edrei

Derbe. City in SE Lycaonia, Asia Minor, visited by Paul on his First and Second Missionary Journeys (Acts 14:6, 20; 16:1). Prob. the ruins 3 miles NW of mod. *Zosta*, 45 miles S of *Konya* (Iconium), Turkey. C5—14; C2—15

Develtum. Town on the W shore of the Black Sea, ca. 125 miles NW of Byzantium. A church is known to have been there in the 2nd century.

Dhiban. *See* Dibon

Diala R. *See* Diyala R.

Dibon (Dhiban). Town 3 miles N of the Arnon R. in Transjordan. It had been a Moabite town (Num. 21:30; 32:3) but was rebuilt by the tribe of Gad (Num. 32:34) and named Dibongad (Num. 33:45–46). The Moabite Stone, found among its ruins, tells how it was recaptured by the Moabites. Mod. *Dhiban*. D3—3; C5—5; D4—19

Dictones. An ancient people settled along the W coast of Gaul, S of the Liger (Loire).

Dion. City of the Decapolis (q.v.) located on the Yarmuk R. W of the Sea of Galilee. Prob. mod. *Tell el-Ash 'ari*. D3—11

Diospolis. *See* Lod

Diyala R. Tributary of the Tigris. Its source is in the Zagros Mts., from which it flows in a generally SE direction. F3—2

Dnieper R. *See* Borysthenes R.

Dniester R. From its source in the Carpathians, the Dniester flows in a generally SE direction through SE Europe before entering the Black Sea SW of Odessa.

Doch. *See* Dok

Dok. Fortress NW of Jericho (I Macc. 16:15). The spring at the foot of the hill is named *'Ain Duq*.

Don R. River that has its source a short distance SE of Tula, Soviet Russia, and flows 1,232 miles SE, then SW into the Sea of Azov.

Dophkah. Encampment of the Israelites on the route to Sinai between the Red Sea and Rephidim (Num. 33:12–13). Poss. mod. *Serabit el-Khadim*, a mining center in the Sinai Peninsula. B5—3

Dor (Dora), city of. Seaport of ancient Palestine, 8 miles N of Caesarea. Mod. *el-Burj*, N of *Tanturah*. B3—1, 5; D4—2; C2—3; B4—4; B2—19

Dor, district of. Area around the city of Dor (q.v.).

Dora. B3—11. *See* Dor

Dorylaeum. Ancient city of N Phrygia, Asia Minor, used as a trading center by the Romans. Poss. mod. *Eskisehir*, NW Turkey.

Dothain. *See* Dothan

Dothan. City near the Plain of Esdraelon, in central Palestine, N of Samaria. In the vicinity of Dothan, Joseph was sold into slavery (Gen. 37:17–28). Mod. *Tell Dotan*. C3—1, 19; B3—5

Dragon's Well. *See* En-rogel

Drangiana. Ancient country in Asia between Aria to the N and Gedrosia to the S. It was conquered by Alexander the Great. It is now in E Iran and W Afghanistan. E3—7

Druz, J. ed. Mountainous area of the Hauran, in Syria SE of Damascus, inhabited by the Druses, a Moslem sect with a strong element of mystical-pantheistic and ancient pagan concepts.

Duero R. River that rises in the Sierra de Urbion, N-central Spain, and flows 475 miles in a generally SW direction through Spain and Portugal to the Atlantic.

Dumah (in Arabia). Oasis in the NW part of the Arabian Peninsula. Known as *Dumat al-Jandal*, mod. *al-Jauf*. E4—2; C3—6, 7

Dumah (in Judah). Town in the hill-country of Judah, 10 miles SW of Hebron (Josh. 15:52). Mod. *ed-Domeh*.

Dung Gate. Gate on the SW side of Jerusalem (Neh. 2:13; 3:13–14; 12:31).

Dura. Palestinian town, 5 miles SW of Hebron.

Dura-Europos. City founded *ca.* 300 B.C. by a general of Seleucus I, one of Alexander's successors, in the Syrian desert E of Tadmor. F3—18

Durazzo. See Dyrrhachium

Durius R. See Duero R.

Durocotorum. See Reims

Dur Sharrukin. Site of the palace built by Sargon II (713–707 B.C.), NE of Nineveh. Mod. *Khorsabad*.

Du'ru. District around the city of Dor, comprising the Plain of Sharon. See Dor, district of

Dyrrhachium. Adriatic port in W Macedonia founded jointly by Corinth and Corcyra *ca.* 625 B.C. It became part of the kingdom of Epirus and in 229 B.C. was taken by Rome. It was originally called Epidamnus, then Dyrrhachium, then Durazzo. B1—17

E

Eastern Sea. See Dead Sea

East Gate. Gate on the E side of Jerusalem (Neh. 3:29). Poss. corresponds to the mod. Golden Gate.

Ebal, Mt. Mt. separated by a narrow valley from Mt. Gerizim (Deut. 27:12–13), near the oak of Moreh (Deut. 11:30), N of Shechem (Gen. 12:6; 35:4). C3—1; B3—5; C4—11

Ebla. City located *ca.* 18.5 miles S of Haleb (Aleppo). It was the capital of a kingdom in the 3rd century B.C. Excavations there since 1964 have yielded thousands of tablets. Mod. *Tell Mardikh*. D3—2

Eboracum. See York

Ebro R. River in NE Spain. It rises in the Cantabrian Mts., flows *ca.* 575 miles SE between the Pyrenees and Cantabrian mts., and empties into the Mediterranean below Tarraco. Its ancient name was Iberus.

Ecbatana (Achmetha). Capital of ancient Media, summer residence of Achemenian (Persian) and Parthian rulers. Mod. *Hamadan*. G3—2; D2—6, 7

Ecdippa. See Achzib

Edessa. Ancient Mesopotamian city at the site of mod. *Urfa*, Turkey. By the 3rd century it was a center of Syrian Christianity and became a major religious center of the Byzantine Empire. F3—18

Edom. Mountainous territory S of the Dead Sea, extending along the E border of the Arabah Valley to Elath on the Gulf of Aqaba. Known also as Mt. Seir, it was given to Esau and his descendants. C6—1, 5; D4—3; B6—4

Edomites. Descendants of Esau (Edom) who became inhabitants of Edom (*q.v.*). Edomites were enemies of the Israelites until subdued by the Maccabees. In Greco-Roman times they were known as Idumeans, and their land, Idumea.

Edrai. See Edrei

Edrei. Capital city of Bashan, where the Israelites fought with Og (Num. 21:33–35). Mod. *Der'a*, 27 miles E of Gadara. D2—3; C4—4; D3—5

Eglon. City of S Palestine, SW of Lachish. It joined 4 other cities in attacking Gibeon, which had made peace with Joshua (Josh. 10:1–5). The kings were killed and their cities destroyed (Josh. 10:24–27). See Tell el-Hesi. C3—3; B4—19

Egypt. Country occupying the NE portion of Africa. Its Hebrew name is Mizraim (cf. Gen. 10:6 KJV). In ancient times Egypt comprised the area from the 1st cataract of the Nile N to the Mediterranean. Ancient Egypt was the scene of some of man's earliest achievements in literature, art, and architecture. A-B4—3; B3—7; E4—12, 17, 18; A6—19

Egypt, Brook of. C3—3. See 'Arish, W. el

Egypt, Kingdom of. Extended W to Libya in the 6th century B.C. B3—6

Egypt, Lower. The Nile Delta (*q.v.*) area of Egypt. C4—2

Egypt, River of. A5-6—4. See 'Arish, W. el

Egypt, Upper. The area of Egypt S of the Nile Delta (*q.v.*). C5-6—2

Egyptian Empire. Extended to Palestine, Transjordan, and S Syria in the early 2nd millennium B.C. C5-D4—2

Eilat. See Elath

'Ein-gedi. See En-gedi

Eizariya. See Bethany

Ekron. The northernmost of the 5 Philistine cities, located in the territory assigned to Dan, near the border of Judah. Prob. mod. *'Aqir*, 12 miles NW of Ashdod. B4—5

Ela, Valley of. See Elah, Valley of

Elah, Valley of. Valley near Shoco in which the Israelites confronted the Philistines before the combat between David and Goliath (I Sam. 17). Prob. mod. *W. es-Sant*.

Elah R. B4—1. See Elah, Valley of

Elam. Region beyond the Tigris, E of Babylonia, bounded on the N by Assyria and Media, on the S by the Persian Gulf, and on the E and SE by Persia. Seat of the ancient Elamite Empire. See Susiana. G4—2; D3—6

Elasa. Place in N Judea where Judas Maccabeus is said to have camped. Prob. mod. *Kh. Il'asa*, midway between the 2 Beth-horons.

Elath. Town at the head of the Gulf of Aqaba, on the E border of the Wilderness of Paran, through which the Israelites passed on their journey from Sinai to Canaan (Deut. 2:8). It was located E of Ezion-geber, with which it was later identified. Mod. *Eilat*. B3—7

El 'Auja. *See* Auja el-Hafir

Elbe R. C1—12. *See* Albis R.

Elburz Mts. Mt. range of N Iran, S of the Caspian. Mt. Damavand is the highest peak (*ca*. 18,900 feet high).

Eleale. *See* Elealeh

Elealeh. City built by the Reubenites (Num. 32:3) in Transjordan. Later it fell into the hands of the Moabites. It is uniformly mentioned with Heshbon. Mod. *el-Al*, 2 miles NE of Heshbon.

Elephantine. B4—6, 7. *See* Syene

El Ghor. *See* Ghor, El

Elim. Place where Israelites encamped after crossing the Red Sea (Exod. 15:27; 16:1), between Marah and the Wilderness of Sin. Prob. mod. *W. Gharandel*, 63 miles from Suez. B5—3

Elisa. *See* Elishah

Elishah. Descendants of Javan (i.e., Ionians) who inhabited Elishah (Gen. 10:4). Ezekiel 27:7 suggests Carthage, S Italy, and Greece as the land of Elishah.

El Kerak. *See* Kir-haresheth

El Kuntilla. Town in the Sinai Peninsula, NW of Eilat. Numerous trails from SW Sinai and the SE Negeb converge there. It is also known as *Thaimilet es-Suweilmeh*.

Ellip. Region N of Elam in the area between the Zagros Mts. and the Caspian Sea. It was conquered by the Assyrians and subsequently fell to the Medes and Persians.

El Qanawat. *See* Kanatha

El Quneitra. Town in Syria, NE of Lake Hula. It is on a road that ran from Damascus to Palestine, crossing the Jordan midway between Lake Hula and the Sea of Galilee.

El Qusaima. Site in the Wilderness of Paran in the extreme S of Palestine (near the E border of mod. Egypt). It is NW of *'Ain Qadeis*, the probable site of Kadesh-barnea. El Qusaima is closer to the Egyptian road and has been suggested as an alternate site for Kadesh-barnea.

Eltekeh. Town of Dan that was assigned to the Levites (Josh. 19:40, 44; 21:20, 23). Destroyed by Sennacherib (701 B.C.). Prob. mod. *Kh. el-Muqanna'*, 6 miles SE of Ekron.

Elthece. *See* Eltekeh

Eltheco. *See* Eltekeh

Emath. *See* Hamath

Emath, Tower of. *See* Meah, Tower of

Emerita Augusta. A2—12. *See* Merida

Emesa. City on the Orontes R., S of Hamath, in a fertile plain on the trade route between Damascus and Aleppo. Mod. *Homs*. C3—13

Emmaus. Town 7.5 miles (60 furlongs) from Jerusalem, the scene of Christ's revelation of Himself after the resurrection (Luke 24:13). The exact location is not certain. B5—11

Emmaus (Nicopolis). Town 20 miles from Jerusalem on the highway to Joppa. Its distance is such that it cannot be the Emmaus "threescore furlongs" from Jerusalem (Luke 24:13). If textual variants that read 160 furlongs instead of 60 are correct, it

could be the town intended. Mod. *Amwas*. B5—11

Enan. *See* Hazar-enan

En-dor. Town in the territory of Manasseh (Josh. 17:11), on the N shoulder of Little Hermon, 6 miles SE of Nazareth. Mod. *Endor* or *Indur*.

Engaddi. C6—11. *See* En-gedi

En-gannim (Ginae). City in the territory of Issachar (Josh. 19:21) assigned to the Levites (Josh. 21:29). Mod. *Jenin*, 15 miles S of Mt. Tabor.

Engeddi. *See* En-gedi

En-gedi (Engaddi). Fountain and town, also called Hazezon-tamar, near the midpoint of the W shore of the Dead Sea, in Judah *ca*. 30 miles SE of Jerusalem. David took refuge there from Saul (I Sam. 23:29). Mod. *'Ain Jidi*. C5—5

English Channel. Arm of the Atlantic, 350 miles long, between France and England. At the E end, the Strait of Dover connects it with the North Sea.

En-Harod. *See* Harod

En-hasor. *See* En-hazor

En-hazor. Town in the territory of Naphtali (Josh. 19:32, 37). Poss. mod. *Kh. Hasireh*, W of *'Ain Ibl*.

En-mishpat. *See* Kadesh-barnea

Ennom Valley. *See* Hinnom Valley

En-remmon. *See* En-rimmon

En-rimmon. Town in the Judean Negeb (Neh. 11:29), also called Rimmon (Josh. 15:32). Mod. *Kh. Umm er-Rammin*, 9 miles NE of Beersheba.

En-rogel (Dragon's Well). Fountain outside Jerusalem, near the Hinnom Valley, S of the Jebusite fortress (Josh. 15:7; 18:16). It was near the boundary between the territories of Judah and Benjamin. Mod. *Bir Ayyub*. B3—8; D3—9

Ephesus. City in Lydia, W Asia Minor, at the mouth of the Cayster R., midway between Miletus and Smyrna, on an important trade route. In Roman times it was capital of the province of Asia. It was devoted to the goddess Diana. A2—7; D3—12, 18; B2—15, 16; D2—17

Ephra. *See* Ophrah

Ephraim, allotment of. The S boundary of Ephraimite territory was a line W of the Jordan including the cities of Jericho, Ai, Bethel, and Mizpah. Its N boundary (with Manasseh) was irregular, including territory S of Mt. Gerizim and the Kanah R. Ephraim was bounded on the W and SW by the territory of Dan.

Ephraim, city of. City *ca*. 4 miles NE of Bethel (II Sam. 13:23). Mod. *et-Taiyibeh*. C4—11

Ephraim, district of. The hill-country of Ephraim (Mt. Ephraim). The portion of the central mt. range occupied by the tribe of Ephraim.

Ephraim, Gate of. Gate in the NW sector of the wall of Jerusalem. D2—9

Ephron. *See* Ephraim, city of

Epiphania. Name assigned to the city of Hamath (*q.v.*) by Antiochus Epiphanes. C3—13

Epirus. Ancient country on the Ionian Sea, N of the Ambracian Gulf, S of Illyria, and W of

Macedonia and Thessaly. The region is now part of NW Greece and S Albania. B-C2—17

Erech (Uruk). Ancient Sumerian city, on the Euphrates, NE of ancient Ur. Gilgamesh, Babylonian epic hero, was king of Erech. F4—2; D3—6; C3—7

Eridu. Ancient Sumerian city, S of Ur. G4—2

Er Rumman. City of Transjordan, S of the Jabbok R.

Erythraean Sea. The part of the Indian Ocean now known as the Arabian Sea and the Persian Gulf. F4—6; E4—7

Esbus. D5—11. *See* Heshbon

Esdraelon, Plain of. Fertile plain of central Palestine watered by the Kishon R. The Esdraelon extends from the Mediterranean, near Mt. Carmel, SE to the Jordan Valley at Beth-shan. It is the means of access from the coastal plain to the Jordan Valley and beyond. C3—1; B3—5, 11

Eshnunna. Ancient town N of the Diyala R., 50 miles NE of mod. *Baghdad*. An important ancient law code was discovered at Eshnunna, known also as Ashnunnak. Mod. *Tell Asmar*. F3—2

Eshtemoa. Town in the hill-country of Judah 9 miles S of Hebron (Josh. 15:50; I Sam. 30:28). Mod. *es-Semu'*.

Essene Gate. Gate at the SW corner of Jerusalem, leading into the Hinnom Valley.

Esthemo. *See* Eshtemoa

Esztergom. City on the Danube in N Hungary, 25 miles NW of Budapest.

Etam. Town in the hill-country of Judah, fortified by Rehoboam (II Chron. 11:6). Poss. mod. *Kh. el-Khokh*, 2 miles SW of Bethlehem.

Etham. First encampment of the Israelites during the Exodus after having left Succoth. Located on the edge of the wilderness (Exod. 13:20; Num. 33:6).

Etham, Wilderness of. Part of the Wilderness of Shur, apparently reaching as far as Marah. B4—3

Ethiopia (Cush). Country in Africa, S of Egypt (II Kings 19:9; Esther 1:1). The border between Egypt and Ethiopia was Syene, mod. *Aswan*, at the 1st cataract of the Nile (Ezek. 29:10). Cush was a son of Ham (Gen. 10:6–8); in most passages the term *Cush* refers to the land of Ethiopia. B4—6, 7

Etruria. Ancient country of W-central Italy, occupied by the Etruscans.

Euboea. Greek island in the Aegean, separated from Boeotia and Attica on the mainland by a narrow channel. Chalcis is the principal city.

Eulaeus R. *See* Ulai R.

Euphrates R. Rising in the mts. of Armenia (E Turkey), the Euphrates flows *ca.* 1,675 miles before it joins the Tigris to form the *Shatt el-Arab*. The lower Tigris and Euphrates water Mesopotamia (lit., "between the rivers"). E3—2; D1—4; C2—6, 7

Europe. Continent N of Africa, W of Asia. It is separated from Africa by the Mediterranean

Sea, and from Asia by the Ural Mts. and Ural R. in the E, the Caspian Sea and the Caucasus in the SE, and the Black Sea, the Bosporus, and the Dardanelles in the S.

Evora. City of SE Spain (mod. Portugal). Ancient Ebora was renamed Liberalitas Julia, after Julius Caesar.

Ezion-geber. Town at the N end of the Gulf of Aqaba, W of Elath. At the time of Solomon it became an important Red Sea port. Mod. *Tell el-Kheleifeh*. D5—3; B6—4

F

Fair Havens. Harbor on the S coast of Crete, S of Candia, near Lasea (Acts 27:8). It was 5 miles E of Cape Matala. Mod. *Kali Limines*. D3—17

Farah R. This river, or wadi, meets the Jordan R. from the W where the Jabbok meets it from the E. Together they form one of the three crossings through the Jordan Valley. C4—1

Faro. Seaport of SE Spain (mod. Portugal). It was an important Moorish city, retaken A.D. 1249.

Farther Spain. One of two provinces into which Spain was divided by the Romans. Farther Spain (*Hispania Ulterior*) occupied the territory in the S around Gibraltar and the Guadalquivir R. *See also* Hither Spain

Field of Blood. *See* Aceldama

Fish Gate. Gate in the wall on the N side of Jerusalem (II Chron. 33:14; Neh. 3:3; 12:39).

Florence. City of central Italy, on the Arno R. at the foot of the Apennines. Florence was a leading center of the Renaissance.

Fortress Antonia. *See* Antonia, Fortress

Forum of Appius. *See* Appius, Forum of

Fountain Gate. Gate in the wall of the SE sector of Jerusalem. D3—9

Frisians. A Germanic people, closely akin to the Anglo-Saxons, who settled on the coastlands and islands of the North Sea.

Fulda. City on the Fulda R. in W Germany. From the Benedictine abbey of Fulda, founded by St. Boniface, Christianity spread throughout central Germany.

G

Gaba. *See* Geba

Gabaath. *See* Gibeah

Gabae (Aspadana). City in SE Media. Mod. *Isfahan*, midway between Tehran and Shiraz. D3—7

Gabaon. *See* Gibeon

Gabee. *See* Geba

Gabua. *See* Geba, Gibeah, *and* Gibeon

Gad, allotment of. Territory E of the Jordan situated between Reuben (S) and Manasseh (N). Gad occupied most of the territory E of the Jordan from the S end of the Sea of Galilee to the N end of the Dead Sea.

Gadara (in Decapolis). City of the Decapolis, mentioned in the account of the healing of the demoniac (Mark 5:1; Luke 8:26, 37 KJV). It was located opposite Tiberias, *ca*. 6 miles E of the Sea of Galilee. Mod. *Muqeis* or *Umm Qeis*. C3—11

Gadara (in Perea). Chief city of Perea, located *ca*. 15 miles NE of Philadelphia. C4—11

Gaderoth. *See* Gederoth

Gades (Cadiz). City on the Bay of Cadiz, SW Spain. Founded by Phoenicians (*ca*. 1100 B.C.), it fell to the Carthaginians (*ca*. 500 B.C.) and, in the 3rd century B.C., to the Romans. Mod. *Cadiz*.

Gaetulia. Land of the Gaetuli, one of the aboriginal races of N Africa. The area known as Gaetulia was of somewhat uncertain limits.

Galaad. *See* Gilead

Galatia. District in central Asia Minor. Gallic tribes, after having invaded Macedonia and Greece (278–277 B.C.), migrated to Asia Minor and received the territory of Galatia from Nicomedes, king of Bithynia, in return for services rendered him in war. The territory was subsequently enlarged by the Romans. E3—12; C4—14; C-D1—15, 16; E2—17, 18

Galgal. *See* Gilgal

Galgala. *See* Gilgal

Galilee. Hill-country N of the Plain of Esdraelon. Galilee was the northernmost of the 3 provinces into which the Romans divided Palestine W of the Jordan. Because of its mixed population it was known as Galilee of the Nations (Gentiles). B-C2—5; C2—11; B5—13

Galilee, lower. Galilee S of the fault of *Esh-shaghur* (the Plain of *er-Rameh*), which goes from Acco to the region S of Safad. *See* Galilee, upper. C2—1

Galilee (Chinnereth), **Sea of.** Lake in the N part of the Jordan Valley, 12.5 miles long and 7.5 miles wide, variously known as the Sea of Galilee or Chinnereth, or Lake Tiberias. Many of the miracles of Jesus were performed in the communities on the shores of the Sea of Galilee. C2—1, 19; C3—11; B5—13

Galilee, upper. Galilee N of the fault of *Esh-shaghur* to the gorge of the Leontes R., which enters the Mediterranean N of Tyre. *See* Galilee, lower. C2—1

Gallaecia. District in NW Spain occupied by the Gallaeci, a civilized people defeated by the Romans under Brutus (138 B.C.).

Gamala. Fortified city E of the Sea of Galilee. One of the last cities to fall to the Romans in their campaign in Galilee and N Palestine (A.D. 67).

Gandara. Region of NW India, SE of Sogdiana, the E limit of the Persian Empire (*ca*. 500 B.C.). F2—7

Garizim, Mt. *See* Gerizim, Mt.

Gasgas. Region S of the Black Sea in patriarchal times. The people who inhabited the area, known as *Gashgash* in the Hittite language, appear to be related to the Kassite, or Caspian, peoples.

Gate of Ephraim. *See* Ephraim, Gate of

Gath. One of the 5 great Philistine cities, and the home of Goliath (I Sam. 17:4; II Sam. 21:15–

22). Its location is uncertain. Poss. mod. *'Araq el-Menshiyeh*, 8 miles NE of Lachish; or *Tell es-Safi*. B5—4; B4—5

Gath-hepher. Town on the border of the territory of Zebulun, 3 miles NE of Nazareth. Birthplace of Jonah (II Kings 14:25). Prob. mod. *Kh. ez-Zurra'*.

Gath-rimmon. Town in Dan (Josh. 19:45). Poss. mod. *Tell Abu Zeitun*, in the Plain of Joppa.

Gaugamela. Site of a battle in which Alexander the Great defeated Darius III of Persia (331 B.C.). It is 60 miles NW of Arbela, mod. *Erbil*.

Gaul. Ancient name for the land S and W of the Rhine, W of the Alps, and N of the Pyrenees. The name was extended to include N Italy, which was termed Cisalpine Gaul. B1—12, 18

Gaulanitis. Region of Transjordan NE of the Sea of Galilee which took its name from the city of Golan (Gaulan). C-D2—11

Gaulan. *See* Golan

Gaver. *See* Gur

Gaza. Southernmost of the 5 Philistine cities (Gen. 10:19), at the junction of the main road between Mesopotamia and Egypt and a trade route from S Arabia. Mod. *Ghazzeh*. A5—1, 4, 5; D4—2; C3—3; B3—7; A6—11, 13; F4—17; A4—19

Gazara. *See* Gezer

Gaza Strip. Band of territory *ca*. 31 miles long and 4 miles wide stretching along the Mediterranean coast from Gaza to Egypt.

Gazer(a). *See* Gezer

Geba. Town in Benjamin (Josh. 18:24; I Kings 15:22; Ezra 2:26) 6 miles N of Jerusalem. Mod. *Jeba'*. C4—5

Gebal (Byblos). Ancient Phoenician city on the Mediterranean, 25 miles N of Beirut. The port of Gebal was used in exporting cedar wood to Egypt before Sidon, and later Tyre, became the principal Phoenician ports. Byblos was the Greek name given to the city (Josh. 13:5; I Kings 5:18 RSV). D3—2; D1—3; B2—4, 7

Gebbethon. *See* Gibbethon

Gederoth. Town in the lowlands of Judah (Josh. 15:41) captured by the Philistines in the time of Ahaz (II Chron. 28:18). Poss. mod. *Qatra*.

Gedrosia (Maka). Ancient coastal region N of the Arabian Sea and W of India. It was the SE limit of the Persian Empire. Mod. *Makran* in SE Iran and SW Baluchistan. E3—7

Geennom Valley. *See* Hinnom Valley

Gehenna Valley. *See* Hinnom Valley

Gelboe, Mt. *See* Gilboa, Mt.

Genesar, Water of. *See* Galilee, Sea of

Genesareth, Lake of. *See* Galilee, Sea of

Gennath Gate. Gate leading from the N wall of Jerusalem's Upper City to Bethzatha. B5—10

Genoa. City in NW Italy founded in ancient times in the district of Liguria. It flourished under Roman rule and is still an important seaport.

Gentiles, Court of the. Open area in the Jerusalem temple extending from the inner side of the porticoes to the low wall separating this court from the inner courts. Both Jews and Gentiles were free to mingle here, but only Jews could advance to the inner courts. B-C5—10

Gentiles, Isles of the. Islands and coastal regions of the Mediterranean peopled by the "sons of Javan," i.e., Ionian Greeks (Gen. 10:4–5). Some suggest the broader classification of "sons of Japheth" for the inhabitants.

Genua. *See* Genoa

Gerar. Ancient Philistine city on the S border of Palestine, near Gaza (Gen. 10:19). Poss. mod. *Tell Jemmeh*, 8 miles SE of Gaza. A5—4, 5

Gerar, Valley of. Valley extending from a short distance SE of Gerar to the Mediterranean, which it enters S of Gaza.

Gerara. *See* Gerar

Gerar R. A5—1. *See* Gerar, Valley of

Gerasa (Jerash). Ancient city of the Decapolis, 37 miles SE of the Sea of Galilee. The ruins that still remain indicate that it was a flourishing Roman city in the 2nd and 3rd centuries A.D. D4—11; B5—13

Gergesa. Town on the E bank of the Sea of Galilee, opposite Magadan. Mod. *Kursi*.

Gergovia. City of S-central Gaul where Caesar was forced to withdraw his army at the lowest ebb of his campaign.

Gerizim, Mt. Mt. in Samaria near Shechem, S of Mt. Ebal (Deut. 11:29; 27:12; Josh. 8:33). A temple of the Samaritans was located there. Mod. *J. et-Tor*. B4—1, 5, 11

Germania. Country bounded by the Rhine on the SW, the Carpathians on the E, the Baltic on the N, and the Danube on the S. It was inhabited by a branch of the Indo-Germanic race that came to Europe from the Caucasus in prehistoric times. C1—12, 18

Germanicopolis. City in Galatia, central Asia Minor. Located at the foot of a hill, it served as a citadel. In Byzantine times it was known as Gangra. Mod. *Cankiri*, Turkey.

Gerrha. Port on SW coast of the Persian Gulf, mentioned by Strabo and Pliny. Prob. mod. *Oqair*, Saudi Arabia. D3—7

Gesen. *See* Goshen

Geshur. Territory E of the Sea of Galilee, bordering Argob, occupied by an Aramean kingdom at the time of the Israelite monarchy. There David obtained a wife (II Sam. 3:3), and to Geshur his son Absalom fled after having Amnon murdered (II Sam. 13:37). B3—4

Gessen. *See* Goshen

Gessur. *See* Geshur

Getae. An ancient people who lived on the shores of the Danube and in the territory W of the Black Sea. They had an advanced culture and resisted Roman encroachments until A.D. 105, when their country, known as Dacia (*q.v.*), became a Roman colony.

Geth. *See* Gath

Geth-hepher. *See* Gath-hepher

Geth-remmon. *See* Gath-rimmon

Gethsemane. Garden E of Jerusalem, a little beyond the brook Kidron, at or near the foot of the Mt. of Olives. There Jesus agonized in prayer before His arrest (Matt. 26:36–56). C4—10

Gethsemani. *See* Gethsemane

Gezer (Gazara). Ancient Canaanite town on the SE border of Ephraim (Josh. 16:3). It was captured by the pharaoh whose daughter was the wife of Solomon (I Kings 9:16). Mod. *Tell Jezer*. C3—3; B4—4, 5, 19

Gharandal. Site in the W. Arabah known in Roman times as Aridella. It is known to have been occupied in Nabatean and Roman times.

Ghor, El. A name sometimes applied to the entire Jordan rift, which extends 250 miles from Lebanon to the head of the Gulf of Aqaba. Usually, however, it applies to the Jordan Valley from the Sea of Galilee to the Dead Sea, an area entirely below sea level, varying in width from 2 to 15 miles, bounded by mountainous terrain on each side. The term *Zor* ("thicket") is used for the depression, 200 yards to a mile wide, which the Jordan covers during the spring floods. The *Zor* is covered with tropical vegetation and is known as the "Jungle of the Jordan" (KJV, "Pride of the Jordan").

Gibbethon. City in the territory of Dan (Josh. 19:44). Prob. mod. *Tell el-Melat*, E of Ekron. B4—5

Gibeah. Town in the territory of Benjamin *ca.* 4 miles N of Jerusalem. It was the early home of Saul (I Sam. 10:26) and his headquarters in fighting the Philistines (I Sam. 13–14). Mod. *Tell el-Ful*. B4—4; C4—19

Gibeon. Important Hivite city (Josh. 11:19) that, by trickery, made an alliance with Joshua (Josh. 9), thus securing Israelite protection. Mod. *El-Jib*, 6 miles N of Jerusalem. B4—5, 19

Gideroth. *See* Gederoth

Gihon, Spring. Spring E of Jerusalem. Solomon was there anointed king (I Kings 1:33, 38, 45). Mod. *'Ain Sitti-Mariam*. B3—8; D3—9; C6—10

Gilboa, Mt. NE spur of Mt. Ephraim, forming the watershed between the Kishon and the Jordan. The ridge forms an arc E of the Plain of Esdraelon. Here Saul and Jonathan died (I Sam. 28:4; 31:1). C3—1, 5; B4—4

Gilead. Mountainous country E of the Jordan, extending N from the tableland of Moab to the Yarmuk R. It was occupied by the tribes of Reuben and Gad. C4-D3—1, 5

Gilgal. Site between the Jordan and Jericho where the Israelites first encamped after crossing the Jordan. Poss. mod. *Kh. el-Mefjir*. C4—5, 19

Ginae. C3—11. *See* En-gannim

Ginaea. *See* En-gannim

Ginneisar. An Israeli settlement on the W bank of the Sea of Galilee, N of Tiberias. It takes its name from the Valley of Ginossar (Genesareth in the N.T.), the fertile valley that marks the border between lower and upper Galilee.

Gischala. Town in upper Galilee, W of Lake Hula. It was located in fertile territory and was renowned for its olive oil. One of the commanders of the

Jewish revolt against Rome (A.D. 66) was from Gischala. C2—11

Gittah-hepher. *See* Gath-hepher

Gnesen. City *ca*. 30 miles NE of Poznan, Poland. It is the legendary cradle of the Polish nation. Mod. *Gniezno*.

Golan. City in Bashan that belonged to the tribe of Manasseh and served as a city of refuge (Josh. 20:8; 21:27). Mod. *Sahem el-Jolan*.

Golden Gate. C5—10. *See* Beautiful Gate

Golgotha (Calvary). Site of the crucifixion. It has been traditionally located at the Church of the Holy Sepulchre. But Charles G. Gordon, in the nineteenth century, proposed a spot near the Damascus Gate commonly called Gordon's Calvary near the "Garden tomb." A4—10

Gomer. A son of Japheth whose descendants settled in Asia Minor S of the Black Sea.

Gomorrah. City in the Jordan Plain, probably on the SE shore of the Dead Sea. Like Sodom, it was destroyed by fire in a cataclysmic judgment.

Gomorrha. *See* Gomorrah

Gophna. Town N of Jerusalem. In Roman times it was a toparchy, the name given to administrative units in Palestine, each of which was subject to the procurator (governor) who resided at Caesarea. B5—11

Gordion. Ancient capital of Phrygia, located on the Sangarius R., in W-central Asia Minor. B2—7

Gordium. *See* Gordion

Gordon's Calvary. *See* Golgotha

Gortyna. Ancient city in S-central Crete near the foot of Mt. Ida.

Goshen. District in NE Egypt where the Hebrews settled during the time of Joseph (Gen. 46:28–29). A4—3

Goths. A Germanic people who inhabited the neighborhood of the Baltic and the Vistula R. in the 1st century A.D. In the 3rd century they migrated S, where they threatened the power of Rome. Subsequently they divided into 2 groups, Ostrogoths (E Goths) and Visigoths (W Goths). The latter, in A.D. 410, captured and sacked Rome.

Gozam. *See* Gozan

Gozan. Town and district on the Habor R. (*q.v.*) in Mesopotamia. It was one of the places to which people of the Northern Kingdom (Israel) were deported following the fall of Samaria in 722 B.C. (II Kings 17:6; 18:11; 19:12). Mod. *Tell Halaf* and environs.

Great Sea, The. A4—1; A-C3—2; A-C2—3; A-B2—4; A-B3—5. *See* Mediterranean Sea

Great Zab R. One of the principal tributaries to the Tigris. It rises in the mts. between Lakes Van and Urmia and enters the Tigris S of Calah.

Greece. Country that occupies the southernmost part of the Balkan Peninsula and numerous islands of the Ionian and Aegean seas. Ancient Greece was one of the principal contributors to modern W culture. A2—7

Greeks. Indo-Europeans inhabiting the NW corner of the SE Mediterranean peninsula of Europe. *See* Greece. A2—6

Gulf of Aqaba. *See* Aqaba, Gulf of

Gulf of Oman. *See* Oman, Gulf of

Gulf of Suez. *See* Suez, Gulf of

Gur. Ascent near Ibleam (*q.v.*) where Ahaziah of Judah was mortally wounded in battle with Jehu (II Kings 9:27).

Gutium. Area in Zagros Mts. inhabited by Gutians, who destroyed the Akkadian Empire *ca*. 2180 B.C. F-G3—2

H

Habesor R. *See* Besor R.

Habor R. Tributary of the Euphrates, which it enters from the N below Deir, Syria. Along the Habor in Gozan (*q.v.*), Israelite captives from Samaria were settled (II Kings 17:6; 18:11). Mod. *Khabur*.

Haceldama. *See* Aceldama

Hadid. Place in the territory of Benjamin to which many Jews returned following the exile in Babylon (Ezra 2:33; Neh. 7:37; 11:34). Prob. mod. *el-Haditheh*, 3 miles NE of Lydda.

Hadrumetum. Seaport in the Roman province of Africa, founded in the 9th century B.C. by Phoenicians. It was located S of Carthage and became subject to the Carthaginians. Mod. *Sousse* in E Tunisia.

Hai. *See* Ai

Haifa. Mod. Israeli seaport at the foot of Mt. Carmel. It has an excellent harbor and is a major Mediterranean port.

Haleb (Aleppo). City of NW Syria, known also as Beroea, on the main caravan route across Syria to Baghdad. Before 1000 B.C. it was a Hittite center; it was subsequently taken by the conquerors of Syria. D3—2

Halys R. River rising in N-central Asia Minor, flowing 715 miles in a wide arc—SW, N, and NE—into the Black Sea. Mod. *Kizil Irmak*. D1—2, 15, 16; C2—6; B2—7; E1—17

Ham. Town in Transjordan, between Ashtaroth and Moab (Gen. 14:5). Prob. mod. *Ham*, NW of Mt. Gilboa.

Hamath, city of. City on the Orontes R., *ca*. 120 miles N of Damascus. The center of an early Hittite state, it later became an Aramean stronghold. Mod. *Hama*. D3—2; C1—4; B2—7

Hamath, district of (Aramean Kingdom). The district ruled by the city-state of Hamath (*q.v.*). Hamath was allied with Syria and Israel in fighting Shalmaneser III of Assyria at Karkar (853 B.C.). Later Hamath fell to the Assyrians, and some of its inhabitants were settled in Israel after Samaria fell in 722 B.C. (II Kings 17:24–30). Subsequently Hamath became a province of Syria. C1—4

Hamath-zobah. *See* Aram-zobah

Hammath. City in the territory of Naphtali, on W shore of the Sea of Galilee, *ca*. 1 mile S of Tiberias. It is noted for its sulphurous and medicinal waters. Mod. *Hamman-Tabariyeh*. C2—5

Hammon. Village in the territory of Asher (Josh.

19:28), 10 miles S of Tyre. Poss. mod. *Umm el-Awamid*.

Hamon. *See* Hammon

Hananel, Tower of. Tower that formed part of the N wall of Jerusalem in Nehemiah's time (Neh. 3:1; 12:39). It was near the Tower of Meah, between the Sheep and Fish gates.

Hannathon. *See* Asochis

Harad. *See* Harod

Haran (Carrhae). Trading center in N Mesopotamia (Gen. 11:31-32), on the Balikh R. Terah and Abraham sojourned there for a time (Gen. 11:31-32; 12:4-5). Its Roman name was Carrhae. At the Battle of Carrhae (53 B.C.), Parthian artillery routed a Roman army under Marcus Licinius Crassus. E2—2; C2—6, 7

Harmozia. Seaport on the mouth of the R. Anamis, at the NW end of the Gulf of Oman, in mod. Iran. The fleet of Nearchus, Alexander's admiral, stopped there.

Harod. Well near which Gideon pitched camp while the Midianites were at the Hill of Moreh (Judg. 7:1). Prob. mod. *'Ain Jalud* on the NW side of Mt. Gilboa.

Harodi. *See* Harod

Haroseth. *See* Harosheth

Haroseth-Goim. *See* Harosheth

Harosheth. Town on the N bank of the Kishon, 16 miles NW of Megiddo. Home of Sisera (Judg. 4:2, 13, 16). Mod. *Tell 'Amar*, at the foot of Mt. Carmel.

Harosheth-ha-goiim. *See* Harosheth

Harun, J. (Mt. Hor). Mt. in Edom on which Aaron died and was buried (Num. 20:22-29). Traditionally identified with *J. Harun*, E of the Arabah. D4—3

Hasa. Town located at the junction of the W. el-Hasa and the rail line that goes N to Damascus.

Hasa, W. el-. *See* Zered R.

Hasarmoth. *See* Hazarmaveth

Haseroth. *See* Hazeroth

Hasmonean Palace. Constructed by the later Hasmoneans across Jerusalem's Central Valley (*q.v.*), connecting it to the temple area with a bridge. B5—10

Hasor. *See* Hazor

Hatti. D2—2. *See* Hittites

Hattin, Horns of. Twin-peaked hill on the road from Tiberias (on the Sea of Galilee) to Cana and Nazareth. Tradition says that Jesus delivered the Sermon on the Mount there.

Hattusas. City in N-central Asia Minor, E of the Great Bend of the Halys R. It was the capital of an ancient Hittite empire. Monuments and inscriptions from Bogaskoy, ancient Hattusas, have provided valuable information concerning ancient Hittite civilization. D1—2

Hattushash. *See* Hattusas

Hauran. Extremely fertile region S of Damascus, extending to the borders of the territory of Gilead (Ezek. 47:16, 18). It served as the granary for the surrounding area. D2—1

Havilah. District of Arabia peopled in part by Semites, in part by Hamites. It was noted for its gold, aromatic gums, and precious stones (Gen. 2:11-12).

Havoth-jair. *See* Havvoth-jair

Havvoth-jair. Unwalled towns in the region of Argob, NW Bashan, S of the Yarmuk. They are named for Jair the judge (Judg. 10:4). C3—5

Hazar-enan. Village on the N boundary of Palestine (Num. 34:9). Poss. mod. *Qiryatein* on the road from Damascus to Palmyra. C2—4

Hazarmaveth. Joktanite Arabs who peopled a district in S Arabia (Gen. 10:26; I Chron. 1:20). Mod. *Hadhramaut*.

Hazeroth. Stopping place of the Israelites during the Exodus (Num. 11:35; 12:16). Poss. mod. *'Ain Khudra*, 36 miles NE of Mt. Sinai. C5—3

Hazezon-tamar. *See* En-gedi

Hazor. Capital of the Canaanite kingdom in N Palestine ruled by Jabin during the Israelite conquest (Josh. 11:1-13; 12:19). The Israelites captured and burned the city. Mod. *Tell el-Qedah*. D3—2; D2—3; B3—4; C2—5; C1—19

Hebron. Town in the hill-country of Judah (Josh. 15:48, 54), originally named *Kirjath-arba* ("Tetrapolis"). Abraham sojourned there and purchased a burial plot nearby. It later served as a Levitical city and a city of refuge (Josh. 20:7; 21:11). It served as David's 1st capital (II Sam. 2:1-4). Mod. *el-Khalil*. B5—1, 4, 5; D4—2; D3—3; B6—11; B4—19

Hebrus R. Most important river of Thrace. It was closely associated with the worship of Dionysus. On its banks Orpheus was said to have been torn to pieces by the Thracian women. Mod. *Euros R*. C-D1—17

Hecatompylus. *See* Damghan

Helal, J. Mt., 2,926 feet above sea level, in NE Egypt W of the W. el 'Arish. C4—3

Heliopolis (Baalbek). City in the Beqa'a Valley, NW of Damascus, devoted to the worship of Baal, who in later times was identified with the sun god. It became a prominent Roman city and has significant ruins. Baalbek is in mod. Lebanon. B4—13

Heliopolis (On). City of Lower Egypt, 5 miles NE of Cairo. It was a center for worship of the sun god and was called Heliopolis by the Greeks. A4—3; B3—7; E4—17

Hellal, J. *See* Helal, J.

Hellas. Ancient name for Greece (*q.v.*).

Hellespont. Ancient name of the Dardanelles, the strait connecting the Aegean Sea with the Sea of Marmara. It is strategic in that it controls trade between the Black Sea and the Mediterranean. Ancient Troy was near the W entrance to the Hellespont.

Helvetii. A Celtic people that once occupied the area corresponding to mod. Switzerland. They attempted to invade S Gaul but were repulsed by Caesar.

Hemath. *See* Hamath

Hennom Valley. *See* Hinnom Valley

Hepher. Canaanite royal city whose king was defeated by Joshua (Josh. 12:17). Poss. mod. *Tell el-Ifshar*. B4—4

Heraclea. Greek city on the S shore of the Black Sea, founded during the 6th century B.C. by colonists from Megara and Boeotia. It was destroyed by the Romans in wars with Mithridates VI of Pontus. Mod. *Eregli*, Turkey. E1—17

Heraclea Pontica. *See* Heraclea

Heracleopolis. City S of the Faiyum, in N Egypt. Pharaohs of the Ninth and Tenth Dynasties came from Heracleopolis. Subsequently, however, power shifted to Thebes. Sheshonk I (biblical Shishak) was at one time the general of mercenaries at Heracleopolis. C5—2; A5—3

Herat (Alexandria Arion). Ancient walled city on the trade route to India, refounded by Alexander the Great as Alexandria Arion. It is on the Hari Rud R. in mod. Afghanistan.

Herma. *See* Hormah

Hermes R. River of W-central Asia Minor. Its source is in the Taurus Mts., and it flows generally W, N of and parallel to the Maeander. Mod. *Gediz R.* in W Turkey. B2—2

Hermon, Mt. Mt. at the S end of the Anti-Lebanon range, known to the Sidonians as Sirion. It has an elevation of 9,232 feet above sea level and is covered with snow much of the year. D1—1, 11; B3—4; C1—5

Hermopolis. City of Upper Egypt, near mod. *Ashnunein*. In antiquity it was the chief seat of the worship of Thoth. C5—2

Hermunduri. A Germanic people who were settled in central Germany, between the Elbe and the Danube.

Hermus R. *See* Hermes R.

Herod, Kingdom of. The Judean area, governed by Herod the Great from 37 to 4 B.C. Herod rebuilt Caesarea and the Jerusalem temple, but he also attempted to Hellenize the country. E3—12

Herod, Palace of. Palace built by Herod on the W hill of Jerusalem, S of the fortress towers (Hippicus, Phasael, and Mariamne). It became the residence of later Roman rulers of Jerusalem when they visited the city. A5—10

Herodium. One of the mountain-top abodes of Herod the Great, located *ca.* 3 miles SE of Bethlehem. It is the site of Herod's tomb. C5—11; C4—19

Herod's Family Tomb. Mausoleum built of large stones and an adjacent cave, located W of Jerusalem's walls, in which Herod's family (but not Herod) were buried. A5—10

Hesebon. *See* Heshbon

Heshbon. Stronghold of Sihon the Amorite king. It was located on what became the border between the territories of Reuben and Dan. Mod. *Hesban*. D3—3; B4—4; D4—5, 19

Heth. Ancestor of the Hittites (*q.v.*) (Gen. 10:15), whose kingdom centered in Asia Minor, with important settlements also in Syria and Palestine.

Hethite Empire. *See* Hittite Empire

Hevila. *See* Havilah

Hezekiah's Tunnel. The 1,750-feet-long tunnel built by Hezekiah to conduct water from the Spring Gihon (*q.v.*) on the E of Jerusalem to the Pool of Siloam (*q.v.*) in the city, thus assuring a water supply for the city while denying it to any besieging enemy (II Chron. 32:30). D3—9; C6—10

Hezekiah's Wall. Wall built by Hezekiah to enclose the Pool of Siloam (*q.v.*), thereby making it part of the SW quarter of Jerusalem. C3—9

Hibernia. Roman name of Ireland, populated in ancient times by a Celtic people who are, in part, the ancestors of the mod. Irish. Ireland was never incorporated into the Roman Empire.

Hierapolis. City of Phrygia, W Asia Minor, on a plateau above the Lycus Valley, 120 miles NE of Smyrna.

Hill of Moreh. *See* Moreh, Hill of

Hindu Kush. Mt. system of central Asia situated in what is now NE Afghanistan, extending to Pakistan and Kashmir. Passes in the Hindu Kush were used by Alexander the Great in his march to India. F2—7

Hindush (India). The subcontinent of S-central Asia that now comprises primarily the nations of Pakistan and India. Civilization is known to have flourished in the Indus Valley as early as the 3rd millennium B.C. During the 2nd millennium B.C. Aryans entered India through mt. passes in the NW. F3—7

Hinnom Valley. Valley that flanks Jerusalem on the S. It was the scene of the sacrifice of children to Moloch. Mod. *W. er-Rababi*. A3—8; C3—9; A-B6—10

Hippicus. One of three massive towers erected by Herod the Great on Jerusalem's W hill to protect its N approach. This tower was named after a friend of Herod. *See also* Mariamne *and* Phasael. A5—10

Hippodrome (in Jerusalem). Built by Herod the Great in the Tyropoeon Valley. Its exact location is not known. B5—10

Hippo Regius. Mediterranean port founded by the Carthaginians. It later became the Numidian capital and a center of early Christianity. Mod. *Bone*, in NE Algeria.

Hippos (Sussita). City built on a mt. E of the Sea of Galilee. It served as a stronghold during the Jewish revolt against Rome (A.D. 67). C3—11

Hisban. *See* Heshbon

Hispalis (Seville). City on the Guadalquivir R. in SW Spain. As Hispalis it was an important Phoenician settlement. It became the capital of Baetica province under the Romans. Seville is a major port as well as a cultural and industrial center. A2—18

Hispania. A2—12. *See* Spain

Hither Spain. One of two provinces into which Spain was divided by the Romans. Hither Spain (*Hispania Citerior*) occupied the Ebro Valley. *See also* Farther Spain

Hittite Empire. Powerful kingdoms in Asia Minor (*ca.* 1740–1200 B.C.) and important states in Syria and Palestine established by the Hittites (*q.v.*). Carchemish (*q.v.*) on the upper Euphrates was an important Hittite center. C-D2—2

Hittites (Hatti). An Indo-European people who established the Hittite Empire (*q.v.*). C1—4

Holdah Gates. Gates from the Lower City of Jerusalem into the temple area, in N.T. times. C5—10

Holy Sepulchre, Church of the. Church in the old city of Jerusalem that marks the traditional site of the crucifixion and burial of Jesus. It has been regarded as sacred by many Christian groups since the time of Helena, who in the 4th century identified the site. Some Protestant groups identify the site of Jesus' death and burial with Gordon's Calvary and the garden tomb, located outside the present wall of Jerusalem N of the Jaffa Gate. *See* Golgotha (Calvary)

Hor, Mt. *See* Harun, J.

Horeb, Mt. *See* Sinai, Mt.

Horites. E-F2—2. *See* Hurrians

Horma. *See* Hormah

Hormah. Town in the Judean Negeb near the border of Edom. The Israelites suffered a defeat there (Num. 14:45; Deut. 1:44), but subsequently captured the city (Num. 21:3; Josh. 12:14). It was friendly to David (I Sam. 30:30). Poss. mod. *Mishash*, SE of Beer-sheba. D3—3

Horns of Hattin. *See* Hattin, Horns of

Horrites. *See* Hurrians

Horse Gate. Gate in the E wall of Jerusalem, leading into the Kidron Valley, in the time of Nehemiah.

Hucoc. *See* Hukkok

Hukkok. Town in the territory of Naphtali, NE of the Sea of Galilee (Josh. 19:34). Mod. *Yakuk*.

Hula (Semechonitis), **Lake.** Lake on the Jordan, 11 miles N of the Sea of Galilee. The area has been transformed by Israeli drainage and irrigation projects so that much of the area once covered by the lake and its adjacent swamps is now fertile agricultural terrain. C2—1

Huldah Gates. *See* Holdah Gates

Huleh, Lake. *See* Hula, Lake

Hurrians (Horites). A non-Semitic people who entered N and NE Mesopotamia early in the 2nd millennium B.C. They spread W to Syria and S to the borders of Egypt. Biblical Horites inhabited Mt. Seir, or Edom (Gen. 36:20). They were displaced by the descendants of Esau (Deut. 2:12, 22). E-F2—2

Hydaspes (Jhelum) **R.** River that rises in W Kashmir, India, and flows *ca*. 500 miles generally SW to join the Indus (*q.v.*).

Hyphasis (Beas) **R.** The easternmost of the 5 rivers of India's Punjab region. It flows *ca*. 285 miles, generally W, and ultimately joins the Indus. It marked the E limit of Alexander's invasion of India (326 B.C.).

Hyrcania, region of. Province of ancient Persia, SE of the Caspian, now the region around Gorgan, Iran. Parthian kings are said to have had their summer palaces there. E2—6; D2—7

Hyrcania, town of. One of several mountain-top fortresses that Herod the Great spread over his kingdom. It was located *ca*. 15 miles SE of Jerusalem. C5—11; C4—19

I

Iberia. Ancient name of a Transcaucasian country (mod. E Georgia, U.S.S.R.). Long a dependency of Persia, it was subjected in the 1st century B.C. to Mithridates VI of Pontus. F2—12

Ibleam (Bile-am). Town in the territory of Manasseh (Josh. 17:11), identified with mod. *Tell Bel 'ameh ca*. 13 miles NE of Samaria. It was a Levitical city (I Chron. 6:70) and was the place where partisans of Jehu mortally wounded Ahaziah of Judah (II Kings 9:27). C3—5

Iconium. City of Asia Minor, at various times within the territories of Phrygia, Lycaonia, and Cappadocia, and in Paul's time in the Roman province of Galatia. It was visited by the apostle Paul (Acts 13:51-52; 14:19, 21). Mod. *Konya*, Turkey. B2—7; C4—14; C2—15, 16; E2—17; E3—18

Icosium. Town on the Mediterranean coast of Mauretania, NW Africa. Mod. *Algiers* was built during the 10th century A.D. on the site of Roman Icosium.

Idumea. The name used in Greco-Roman times for O.T. Edom (*q.v.*). The Edomites, under pressure from Nabatean Arabs, were forced into territory NW of their earlier settlements. During N.T. times Idumea extended N to the region around Hebron. B6—1, 11

Iim. *See* Ije-abarim

Ije-abarim (Iim, Iyim, Iye-abarim). Place S of Moab where the Israelites stopped during the Exodus (Num. 33:45; cf. 21:11; 33:44). Poss. mod. *Mahay*. D3—3

Ijon. Town in N Palestine captured, along with Dan and Abel, by Ben-hadad of Syria (I Kings 15:20; cf. II Kings 15:29). Prob. mod. *Tell Dibbin*, near *Merjayun*, *ca*. 8 miles NW of Baniyas. C1—5

Ilerda. Town in Hither Spain, between the Pyrenees and the Ebro R. It was the site of a major battle in which Caesar defeated Pompey's legates, Africanus and Petreius.

Ilium. *See* Troy

Illyria. *See* Illyricum

Illyricum (Dalmatia). Region on the E shore of the Adriatic Sea, with adjacent islands. The mountainous portion of the region was subdued by the Romans (A.D. 9) and formed into a province. It was regarded as part of Illyricum, the limit of Paul's missionary journey in that direction (Rom. 15:19). Titus also preached in Dalmatia (II Tim. 4:10). C2—12, 18; B1—17

India. F3—7. *See* Hindush

Indo-Iranians (Aryans). The name used to describe peoples who speak Indo-Iranian and Indo-European languages, as distinguished from those who speak Semitic languages and those of other families.

Indus R. The river that rises in the Himalayas in W Tibet and flows 1,800 miles through Tibet, Kashmir, W Pakistan, and India to the Arabian Sea. The lower Indus Valley was one of the earliest centers of civilization. F3—7

Ionian. *See* Javan

Ipsus. Small town in ancient Phrygia, Asia Minor. It was the site of an important battle (301 B.C.) in which Antigonus I was defeated and slain by Seleucus and Lysimachus. Mod. *Ipsili Hissar*, Turkey.

Irbid. C2—19. *See* Arbela (in Palestine)

Ireland. Mod. name of the island W of Britain, from which it is separated by the North Channel, Irish Sea, and St. George's Channel. Celtic tribes occupied the island in the centuries immediately preceding the Christian era. Anc. *Hibernia* (*q.v.*).

Iris R. River that arises in N Asia Minor, flows 260 miles NW to enter the Black Sea near mod. *Samsun*, Turkey. Mod. *Yesil Irmak*.

Iron (Yiron). Fortified city in the territory of Naphtali (Josh. 19:38). Poss. mod. *Yarun*, 10 miles W of Lake Hula.

Irshemesh. *See* Beth-shemesh

Isbeita. Nabatean and Byzantine town in the Negeb, NE of Avdat. B6—19

Isca. *See* Caerleon

Isin. City 50 miles NW of Erech that supplanted Ur as the leading city of Sumer in the early 2nd millennium B.C. G4—2

Isles of the Gentiles. *See* Gentiles, Isles of the

Israel. As a nation, *Israel* may refer to the entire body of descendants of Jacob (Israel)—the 12 tribes and the land they occupied. The term *Israel* is also used of the mod. Jewish state in Palestine. B4—4, 19

Israel, Kingdom of. During the period of the divided kingdom (following the death of Solomon), *Israel* was the name given to the 10 tribes that acted independently of Judah. The N and E tribes (Israel, the Northern Kingdom) separated from Judah (the Southern Kingdom). B-C3—5

Israel, Pool of. Pool just outside the NE corner of the Jerusalem temple enclosure. C4—10

Issachar, allotment of. Territory of Issachar was bounded on the N by that of Zebulun and Naphtali, on the E by the Jordan, and on the S and W by the territory of Manasseh. Mt. Tabor was on its N border, and Jezreel was near its S border.

Issin. City of ancient Mesopotamia, SE of Babylon. It was a rival of Larsa (*ca.* 2000 B.C.), subsequently conquered by Hammurabi of Babylon. Mod. *Ishan Bahriyat*.

Issus. Town in SE Asia Minor on a strip of land backed by high mts. It is near the Cilician Gates, the famed pass into Syria. In 333 B.C. Alexander the Great defeated Darius III of Persia there. Mod. *Iskanderun*, or *Alexandretta*. B2—7

Istanbul. *See* Byzantium

Ister R. A1—6, 7; D2—12. *See* Danube R.

Italy. Boot-shaped peninsula in S Europe, W of Greece. The Alps form the N boundary, dividing Italy from France (in the NW) and from Switzerland and Austria (in the N). Ancient inhabitants of Italy included Ligurians and Iberians, who were in part supplanted by the Etruscans from Asia Minor (*ca.* 800 B.C.). The S of Italy was colonized by Greeks. C2—12, 18; A1—17

Itil. Town at the head of the delta of the Volga R., NW of the Caspian Sea, near mod. *Astrakhan*, U.S.S.R.

Iturea. Country on the N boundary of Syria, occupied by Arabian tribes. It was conquered by Aristobulus (105 B.C.) and later, after a brief period of independence, taken by Pompey. It was united to the Roman province of Syria in A.D. 50. C-D1—11

Iye-abarim. *See* Ije-abarim

Iyim. *See* Ije-abarim

Izalla. Area E of Kue (*q.v.*) that was a province in both the Assyrian and New Babylonian empires. C2—6

J

Jaazer. *See* Jazer

Jabbok (Zarqa) **R.** An E tributary to the Jordan, which it enters *ca.* 43 miles S of the Sea of Galilee and 23 miles N of the Dead Sea. It marked the S boundary of Gilead. Before the Israelite conquest, the area S of the Jabbok was ruled by Sihon, an Amorite king. D3—1; D2—3; C4—5, 11

Jabes-Galaad. *See* Jabesh-gilead

Jabesh-gilead. City in Transjordan, in ancient Gilead. Saul began his career as king by lifting the siege of Jabesh-gilead (I Sam. 11:1–11). Poss. mod. *Tell el-Maqlub*, SE of Beth-shan. C3—5

Jabneel (Jamnia, Jabneh, Jabnia; in Judah). Town on the N border of Judah (Josh. 15:5, 11), occupied by Philistines in the time of Uzziah (II Chron. 26:6). It was known as Jamnia in Maccabean times (I Macc. 4:15) and became a center of Jewish life following the destruction of Jerusalem. Mod. *Yebna*, or *Yavne Yam*, 9 miles NE of Ashdod, 4 miles inland from the Mediterranean. A4—5

Jabneel (in Naphtali). Frontier town in the territory of Naphtali (Josh. 19:33). Poss. mod. *Kh. Yamma*, 7 miles SW of Tiberias.

Jabneh. *See* Jabneel (Jamnia)

Jabnia. *See* Jabneel (Jamnia)

Jaboc R. *See* Jabbok R.

Jacob's Well. Ancient well near Shechem (John 4:6). Mod. *Bir Ja'qub*.

Jaffa. *See* Joppa

Jahas. *See* Jahaz

Jahaz. Town in the Plain of Moab (Jer. 48:34) that was the site of Sihon's battle against Israel (Josh. 13:18; Num. 21:23). It was subsequently assigned to Reuben (Josh. 13:18) and made a Levitical city (Josh. 21:36). Mod. *Kh. Umm el-Idham*. D5—5

Jahaza(h). *See* Jahaz

Jahzah. *See* Jahaz

Jamnia. A5—11. *See* Jabneel

Janoe. *See* Janohah

Janoah. Town on E boundary of Ephraim (Josh. 16:6–7).

Japho. *See* Joppa

Jarash. *See* Gerasa

Jarmo. Ancient village in the hills of Iraqi Kurdistan, E of mod. Kirkuk. It is one of the earliest-known food-producing settlements. F3—2

Jarmuth. Town in the lowlands of Judah (Josh. 15:35). A Canaanite royal city before the Israelite occupation (Josh. 10:3, 5, 23), it was repopulated after the exile (Neh. 11:29). Mod. *Kh. Yarmuk.*

Jassa. *See* Jazer

Jattir. City SE of Hebron in the hill-country of Judah (Josh. 15:48), to which David sent spoil (I Sam. 30:27). It was a Levitical city (Josh. 21: 14). Mod. *Kh. 'Attir.*

Javan (Ionian). Name applying to Greek-speaking islands of the Mediterranean, the Greek area of Asia Minor, and later Greece itself (Gen. 10:2– 4).

Jaxartes R. River that flows 1,300 miles NW from the mts. of Bactria to the Aral Sea. It served as the boundary between Sogdiana and Scythia in ancient times and was thought to flow into the Caspian. Mod. *Syr Darya.* F1—6; E1—7

Jazer. City in Gilead, in the territory of Gad (Josh. 13:25). It was a Levitical city (Josh. 21:39) and later passed into Moabite control. Prob. mod. *Kh. Jazzri* near mod. *es-Salt.* C4—5

Jeabarim. *See* Ije-abarim

Jearim, Mt. *See* Chesalon

Jeb. *See* Syene

J. ed Druz. *See* Druz, J. ed

Jeblaan. *See* Ibleam

Jebneel. *See* Jabneel

Jeboc R. *See* Jabbok R.

Jebus. *See* Jerusalem

Jecmaam. *See* Jokneam

Jecnaam. *See* Jokneam

Jecnam. *See* Jokneam

Jeconam. *See* Jokneam

Jectan. *See* Joktan

Jegbaa. *See* Jogbehah

Jerash. D3—19. *See* Gerasa

Jericho (City of Palm Trees). Important city in the Jordan Valley NE of the Jordan's entrance into the Dead Sea. The city was destroyed by Joshua (Josh. 6) but rebuilt by Ahab (I Kings 16:34). The mod. *Tell es-Sultan,* 1 mile NW of *Riha,* is the site of O.T. Jericho. Ruins of Herodian Jericho lie a little farther S. C4—1, 5, 19; D4—2; D3—3; B4—4; C5—11; B6—13

Jerimoth. *See* Jarmuth

Jeron. *See* Iron

Jerusalem. City in the hill-country between Judah and Benjamin, occupied by the Jebusites until the time of David and subsequently made the capital of the kingdom of David and his successors. The old city of Jerusalem is mod. *El-Kuds.* B4—1, 4, 5; D4—2; D3—3, 15, 16; C3—6; B3—7; B5—11; E3—12; A6—13; D6—14; F4—17; F3—18; C4—19

Jeshanah. Town in the hill-country of Ephraim, N of Jerusalem. Prob. mod. *Burj el-Isaneh.*

Jeshua. Village of S Judah (Neh. 11:26). Poss. mod. *Tell es-Sa'wi,* E of Beer-sheba.

Jesrael. *See* Jezreel

Jesus, tomb of. The location of Jesus' tomb is unknown, but a tradition that is at least as old as the 4th century places it at a site now covered by the Church of the Holy Sepulchre. *See* Golgotha. A4—10

Jeta. *See* Juttah

Jether. *See* Jattir

Jetta. *See* Juttah

Jezrael. *See* Jezreel

Jezrahel. *See* Jezreel

Jezreel. Town in the territory of Issachar (Josh. 19:18), frequently mentioned as the country residence of the kings of Israel (II Sam. 2:9). Naboth's vineyard was nearby (I Kings 21:1– 24). Mod. *Zer'in.* B4—4; B3—5

Jezreel, Plain of. *See* Esdraelon, Plain of

Jezreel, Valley of. Three-mile-wide, ten-mile-long valley joining the Plain of Esdraelon with the Jordan Valley. C3—1

Jhelum R. *See* Hydaspes R.

Jogbehah. Town in the territory of Gad (Num. 32:35). Mod. *Jubeihat,* 6 miles NW of Amman on the road from es-Salt to the Jordan

Jokneam. Town in the territory of Zebulun (Josh. 19:11). It was a Levitical city (Josh. 21:34). Mod. *Tell Qeimun,* 12 miles SW of Nazareth.

Joktan. Descendant of Shem whose posterity, the Joktanite Arabs, settled in the S sector of the Arabian Peninsula.

Joppa. City on the Mediterranean coast in the territory of Dan. It was the Mediterranean seaport of ancient Israel. It became the mod. city of Jaffa, a predominantly Arab city that in 1949 was joined with Tel Aviv (originally settled by Jews as a suburb of Jaffa) to form the municipality of Tel Aviv–Jaffa. B4—1; D4—2; C3—3; A4—4, 11; A5—5; A6—13; B3—19

Joppe. *See* Joppa

Jordan. Arab state that comprises the territory formerly known as Transjordan. C-D3—19

Jordan R. The largest river of Palestine. It rises at the foot of Mt. Hermon, flows through Lake Hula and the Sea of Galilee, and ends at the Dead Sea. From Baniyas to the Dead Sea is a distance of 104 miles. C3—1, 5, 19; D2—3; B4—4; C4—11; B5—13

Jotapata (Jotbah). Town in Galilee that was the home of King Amon's mother (II Kings 21:19). Prob. mod. *Kh. Jefat,* 7 miles N of Sepphoris.

Jotbah. *See* Jotapata

J. Serbal. *See* Serbal, J.

Juda. *See* Judah

Judah. The tribe, and later the district, that occupied the highland region between Samaria and the Negeb. *Judea* is the Greek and Latin form of *Judah.* B5—4; B3—6, 7

Judah, allotment of. Judah was assigned territory W

of the Dead Sea and S of Dan and Benjamin. A portion of the territory was in Philistine control.

Judah, Kingdom of. The S portion of the divided kingdom that followed Solomon's death. *See* Israel, Kingdom of. B-C5—5

Judah, Wilderness of. Region between the hill-country of Judah *(q.v.)* and the Dead Sea. C5-6—5

Judea. B5—1, 11; A6—13; D6—14; D3—15; F4—17. *See* Judah

Judea, Wilderness of. C5—1. *See* Judah, Wilderness of

Judgment Gate. *See* Miphkad Gate

Julias. *See* Bethsaida-Julias

Julias (Livias). C5—11. *See* Betharamphtha

Juttah. Town in the hill-country of Judah, S of Hebron (Josh. 15:55). It was a Levitical city (Josh. 21:16). Mod. *Yatta*.

J. Yusha'. *See* Yusha', J.

K

Kabul R. F2—7. *See* Cophen R.

Kadesh. City on the Orontes R. It was the site of a battle between Ramses II of Egypt and the Hittites. Mod. *Tell Nebi-Mend*. D3—2; C2—4

Kadesh-barnea. City in the Judean Negeb in the extreme S of Palestine (Gen. 14:7; Num. 13:26). The Israelites encamped there during the Exodus (Num. 34:4; Deut. 1:2). Prob. mod. *'Ain Qadeis*. *See also* El Qusaima. D4—2; C4—3; A5—4; A6—19

Kafr Bir'im. One of several sites in Galilee where the ruins of synagogues have been discovered. C1—19

Kamon. *See* Camon

Kanah. Town in the territory of Asher, 6 miles SE of Tyre. Mod. *Qana*.

Kanah R. Stream forming the boundary between the territories of Manasseh and Ephraim. It enters the Mediterranean N of Tel Aviv. Mod. *Yarkon* (Josh. 16:8; 17:9). Mod. *W. Qanah*. B4—1, 5

Kanatha (El Qanawat). City of the Decapolis in N Transjordan on the W slope of J. Hauran. Called Kenath in the O.T. (I Chron. 2:23), it was 16 miles NE of Bostra.

Kanish. Hittite town of W Asia Minor. Mod. *Kultepe*. D2—2

Karabel. Mt. near mod. *Izmir* on which are some Hittite rock carvings. B2—2

Karkar. City on the Orontes R., NW of Hamath. Site of a battle (854 B.C.) between Shalmaneser III of Assyria and an alliance of kings from Syria and Palestine.

Karnaim, district of. Region E of the Sea of Galilee.

Karnaim, town of. Place in Bashan, N of Ashtaroth *(q.v.)*. D2—5

Karnub. Nabatean and Byzantine town in the Negeb. B6—19

Kashka. Ancient district of NE Asia Minor. D-E1—2

Kassites. Indo-European tribes from the Zagros Mts. who overran Babylonia (*ca*. 1650 B.C.). G3—2

Kazalla. City of S Babylonia.

Kedar. Nomadic tribe of the N Arabian Desert, W of Syria. E4—2

Kedesh (in Naphtali). Town NW of Lake Hula in the territory of Naphtali. It was the home of Barak (Judg. 4:6) and the rallying place for the Israelites in their battles with the Canaanites (Judg. 4:10). B3—4; C2—5

Kedesh (in Negeb). *See* Kadesh-barnea

Kedron. *See* Cedron

Kefar 'Eqran. *See* Ekron

Keilah. Town in the lowlands of Judah (Josh. 15:44) *ca*. 8.5 miles NW of Hebron. David relieved Keilah from a siege by the Philistines (I Sam. 23:1–13). Mod. *Kh. Qila*.

Kenites. Nomadic tribe that entered Palestine with the Israelites and settled in the S (Gen. 15:19; Num. 24:21).

Khalab. *See* Haleb

Khalasa. Town *ca*. 15 miles SW of Beer-sheba and on the Besor. B5—19

Kh. 'Ar'ir. D5—19. *See* Aroer (in Moab)

Kh. el-Kerak. D5—19. *See* Kir-haresheth

Kh. el-Mefjir. C4—19. *See* Gilgal

Kh. et-Tannur. Ruin of a Nabatean city on the Zered R., *ca*. 20 miles E of the S end of the Dead Sea. D6—19

Kh. Qumran. *See* Qumran

Kibroth-hattaavah. Stopping place during the Exodus (Num. 11:34–35). Prob. mod. *Ruweis el-Ebeirig*, NE of Sinai. C5—3

Kidron Valley. Deep valley or ravine E of Jerusalem, between the city and the Mt. of Olives. B2-3—8; D2-3—9; C4-6—10

Kiev. City on the Dnieper R. in the Russian Ukraine. In the Middle Ages it served as a Slavic settlement on the great trade route between Scandinavia and Constantinople.

Kingdom of Damascus. *See* Damascus, Kingdom of

Kingdom of Egypt. *See* Egypt, Kingdom of

Kingdom of Og. *See* Og, Kingdom of

Kingdom of Sihon. *See* Sihon, Kingdom of

King's Garden. Garden at the S end of Jerusalem (II Kings 25:4). D3—9

King's Highway. Road extending from Damascus to the Gulf of Aqaba, passing through Bashan, Gilead, Ammon, Moab, and Edom. D4—3

Kir-haresheth (Kir-moab). Capital city of Moab (II Kings 3:25), also known as *Kirheres* (Isa. 16:11), or *Kir*. Mod. *el-Kerak*. C6—1, 5; D3—3; B5—4

Kiriathaim (Shaveh-kiriathaim). Ancient city of the Emim (Gen. 14:5), rebuilt by the Reubenites (Num. 32:37). According to the Moabite Stone (line 10), it subsequently fell to Moab. Poss. mod. *Kh. el-Qureiyat*, NW of Dibon.

Kiriath-jearim. Gibeonite city (Josh. 9:17) on the boundary between Judah and Benjamin (Josh. 18:15). Also called Kiriath-baal (Josh. 15:60). Mod. *Tell el-Azhar, ca*. 8 miles W of Jerusalem.

Kirjathaim. *See* Kiriathaim

Kirjath-arba. *See* Hebron

Kirjath-sepher. *See* Debir

Kir-moab. *See* Kir-haresheth

Kish. Ancient city of the Euphrates Valley, *ca.* 8 miles E of Babylon. It contained a palace built by Sargon of Akkad and a temple built by Nebuchadnezzar and Nabonidus. F4—2

Kishon R. River of Palestine that rises below Mt. Gilboa, flows NW through the Valley of Esdraelon, and empties into the Mediterranean near Haifa. B2—1; B3—5

Kition. Ancient Phoenician colony in SE Cyprus. Mod. *Larnaca*.

Kittim. C3—2; A1—4. *See* Cyprus, island of

Kizzuwadna. *See* Kizzuwatna

Kizzuwatna. District of SE Asia Minor. Its people were allies of the Hittites in the battles between Hittites and Egyptians. D2—2

Kue. Country in Asia Minor mentioned in I Kings 10:28 (RSV) and II Chron. 1:16 (RSV). It was located in the area that later became Cilicia. C2—6

Kurun Hattin. *See* Hattin, Horns of

Kushshar (Alisar Huyuk). Important city of the Old Hittite Kingdom in central Asia Minor. It was occupied as early as the 4th millennium B.C. by a Hattic people who preceded the Hittites in Asia Minor. A group of Hittites who used hieroglyphic writing founded their first capital at Kushshar. After the cuneiform Hittites dominated the area, Kushshar lost its primacy.

L

Laabim. *See* Lehabim

Labana. *See* Libnah

Labyrinth. Intricate building of chambers and passages built to confuse the person inside. It was located near Lake Moeris in Egypt and was built by Amenemhet IV of the Twelfth Dynasty.

Lachis. *See* Lachish

Lachish. Fortified city in the lowlands of Judah whose king was defeated and slain by Joshua (Josh. 10:3–35). It was besieged by Sennacherib (701 B.C.) and destroyed by Nebuchadnezzar (597 B.C. and 587 B.C.). Mod. *Tell ed-Duweir*, 30 miles SW of Jerusalem on the main road from central Palestine to Egypt. D3—3; B5—4, 5; B4—19

Ladder of Tyre. Steep mt. on the Mediterranean coast *ca.* 12 miles N of Acco (Ptolemais). It forms the traditional S end of the Lebanon (cf. I Macc. 11:59). Mod. *Naqura*. B2—11

Lagash. Ancient Sumerian city-state, *ca.* 50 miles N of Ur, in S Mesopotamia. Under the *ensi* ("governor") Gudea, Lagash led a Sumerian revival following the rule of Sargon of Akkad. Mod. *Tello*. G4—2

Lais. *See* Dan, town of

Laisa. *See* Elasa

Laish. *See* Dan, town of

Lake Ballah. *See* Ballah, Lake

Lake Hula. *See* Hula, Lake

Lake Moeris. *See* Moeris, Lake

Lake Sevan. *See* Sevan, Lake

Lake Tatta. *See* Tatta, Lake

Lake Timsah. *See* Timsah, Lake

Lake Tuz. *See* Tuz, Lake

Lake Urmia. *See* Urmia, Lake

Lake Van. *See* Van, Lake

Lakhish R. Wadi that flows from the hill-country SW of Hebron, past Lachish, then generally NW to the Mediterranean, which it enters N of Ashdod.

Lambaesis. Site of the permanent camp built by the Roman emperor Trajan in Numidia, N Africa, for the Third Augustan Legion.

Laodicea. Chief city of Phrygia Pacatiana in Asia Minor, situated a little S of Colossae and Hierapolis, on the Lycos R., a tributary of the Maeander. Mod. *es-Eskihisar*, 56 miles SE of Izmir (Smyrna), Turkey. D2—17; E3—18

Laodicea ad Mare. Hellenized city on the Phoenician coast. Mod. *Latakia*. B2—13

Larisa. *See* Larissa

Larissa. City on the Pinios R. in N Greeçe. It was the chief city of ancient Thessaly and was annexed (4th century B.C.) by Philip of Macedon. It became a Roman colony in 196 B.C. D3—18

Larsa. Ancient city-state of S Mesopotamia, *ca.* 30 miles NE of Eridu. It was conquered by Elamites who established a dynasty there (*ca.* 1770 B.C.). G4—2

Lasea. Seaport of Crete, *ca.* 5 miles E of Fair Havens. The vessel that carried Paul passed there (Acts 27:8). D3—17

Lebanon. Arab republic bounded on the W by the Mediterranean, N and E by Syria, and S by Israel. Its capital is Beirut. The name *Lebanon* is derived from the mt. chain that occupies most of the country's land area. C1—19

Lebanon Mts. Mt. chain running parallel to the coast of N Palestine (mod. *Lebanon*). It is a continuation of the Taurus Mts. (*q.v.*) and is separated from a parallel range to the E, the Anti-Lebanon Mts. (*q.v.*), by the Beqa'a Valley. Its peaks rise to heights of 10,000 feet. C1—1, 11; D1—3; B3—4, 13

Lebna. *See* Libnah

Lebo-hamath. City that marked the N border of the land promised by God to Israel in Numbers 34:8 ("the entrance of Hamath" is Lebo-hamath). C2—4

Lebona. *See* Lebonah

Lebonah. Town situated 3 miles NW of Shiloh (Judg. 21:19). Mod. *Lubban* on the road between Shechem and Jerusalem.

Lehabim. Tribe related to the Egyptians (Gen. 10:13), prob. to be identified with the Libyans, or Lubim. The Egyptian pharaoh Sheshonk (biblical Shishak) was of Libyan extraction.

Lemovii. Germanic tribe that was settled in N Germany W of the Oder R.

Leon. City in NW Spain that dates back to Roman times. In A.D. 882 it was taken from the Moors, and subsequently it became capital of the kingdom of Leon.

Leontes (Litani) **R.** River that flows through the Beqa'a Valley, between the Lebanon and Anti-Lebanon ranges S toward the Jordan Valley. It makes a sharp westward turn, however, and flows into the Mediterranean N of Tyre. C1—1, 5, 11; B4—13

Leptis Magna. Ancient city on the Mediterranean coast of N Africa. Founded by Phoenicians (*ca.* 600 B.C.), it subsequently became an important Roman port. Mod. *Lebda*, E of Tripoli in Libya. C3—12

Lesbos. Greek island in the Aegean. The home of Sappho the poet and Theophrastus the philosopher. B1—15, 16; D2—17

Lesem. *See* Dan, town of

Leshem. *See* Dan, town of

Libnah. Canaanite city, near Lachish, captured by Joshua (Josh. 10:29–32). It became a Levitical city in Judah (Josh 21:13) and was besieged by Sennacherib (II Kings 19:8–36). Prob. mod. *Tell es-Safi*.

Libya. The term *Libya* was first applied by the Greeks to all Africa W of Egypt. Subsequently the term was restricted to the area between Egypt and the Roman province of Africa. Under Rome, Libya was divided into 2 parts: Libya Inferior, or Marmarica (*q.v.*), and Libya Superior, or Cyrenaica (*q.v.*). A3—7; C4—17

Libyan Desert. Desert W of Egypt that comprises most of Libya (*q.v.*). A-B5—2; A3-4—7

Libyans. Inhabitants of Libya (*q.v.*) prob. to be identified with the Lehabim or Lubim of the Bible. A3—6

Liger R. *See* Loire R.

Lincoln. City of E-central Britain famed for its cathedral and medieval churches. In Roman times it was the colony of Lindum, inhabited by the Coritani.

Lisan. Peninsula S of the Arnon R., Transjordan, that projects into the Dead Sea from the E.

Lisht. City in Upper Egypt, S of Memphis, where the pyramid of the Twelfth Dynasty pharaoh Amenemhet I was discovered. His capital is thought to have been nearby.

Litani R. *See* Leontes R.

Lithuanians. Tribe that spoke a Baltic language and formed a unified state in the 13th century A.D. Lithuania, one of the largest states of medieval Europe, is now part of the U.S.S.R.

Livias (Julias). C5—11. *See* Betharamphtha

Lixus. Town in NW Africa on the Atlantic coast, S of the Strait of Tangier. Phoenicians sailed beyond Gibraltar and colonized Lixus, which later became part of Roman Mauretania (*q.v.*).

Lod (Lydda). Town 11 miles SE of Joppa, situated in the Valley of Aijalon as it enters the Plain of Sharon. Mod. *Ludd*. B4—5

Loire R. Longest river in Gaul (France). Rising in the mts. in SE France, it flows NW, then W for 625 miles before flowing into the Atlantic at Saint-Nazaire, the port of Nantes.

Lombards. An ancient Germanic people who were settled along the lower Albis (Elbe) during the 1st century A.D. They migrated southward, and in A.D. 547 Justinian allowed them to settle in Pannonia and Noricum. They invaded N Italy (A.D. 568), however, and established a kingdom there.

Londinium. *See* London

London. British city that became the capital of the Roman province. In A.D. 141 the London Wall was built. The system of Roman roads built throughout Britain converged on London.

Lower City (in Jerusalem). That part of Jerusalem S of the temple, bounded on the E by the Kidron Valley and on the W by the Tyropoeon Valley. B6—10

Lower Egypt. *See* Egypt, Lower

Lower Galilee. *See* Galilee, lower

Lower (Old) **Pool.** Pool or reservoir SE of the Pool of Siloam. From this pool the water flows in a small rill across the road and irrigates gardens in the Kidron Valley.

Lower Sea. G5—2; D3—7. *See* Persian Gulf

Lubim. *See* Lehabim

Luca. City in NW Italy. It marked the S boundary of Caesar's province (Cisalpine Gaul) and was the site of a meeting of the First Triumvirate (Caesar, Pompey, and Crassus) in 56 B.C.

Lud. A people believed to be identical with the Lydians of W Asia Minor. Genesis 10:22 classes them as Semites. According to Herodotus their first king was of Assyrian descent.

Lugdunensis. Roman province in central Gaul, the major cities of which were Lutetia (*q.v.*) in the N and Lugdunum (*q.v.*) in the S. B1—12

Lugdunum (Lyons). City at the confluence of the Rhone and Saone rivers. Founded in 43 B.C. as a Roman colony, it became the principal city of Gaul and capital of the province of Lugdunensis. B2—12

Lugii. A Germanic tribe that settled in central Germany in the Oder Valley.

Lukka. Country in SW Asia Minor inhabited by Sea People by the same name. This area became Lycia. B-C2—2

Lulu. Mountainous region NE of Babylon. Cuneiform tablets from Nuzi speak of Lullians as slaves to the Mesopotamians.

Lusitani. Warlike tribes of the Iberian Peninsula (cf. Lusitania) who resisted Roman domination until their leader was killed by treachery (139 B.C.).

Lusitania. Roman province in the Iberian Peninsula, constituted *ca.* A.D. 5 by Augustus. It included what is now central Portugal and W Spain. A2—12

Lutetia (Paris). Fishing hamlet before Caesar's conquest of Gaul. It subsequently expanded beyond the Ile de la Cité (an island in the Seine R., 90 miles from the English Channel) and became the town Lutetia Parisiorum. Legend says that St. Genevieve, patroness of Paris, through her prayers preserved the city from destruction by the Huns in the 5th century. The city subsequently became a political and cultural center for France. B1—12

Lutetia Parisiorum. *See* Lutetia

Luxeuil. Site of an abbey, established *ca.* A.D. 590, at Luxovium in E Gaul.

Lycaonia. Elevated, inland district of Asia Minor that contained 3 cities visited by Paul: Iconium, Derbe, and Lystra. The land of Lycaonia was suitable for pasturage, and the people spoke a dialect peculiar to the region (cf. Acts 13:51– 14:23). C4—14; C2—15

Lycia. Province of Asia Minor that juts S into the Mediterranean. It is bounded on the N by Caria, Phrygia, Pisidia, and Pamphylia. During his voyages Paul stopped at 2 of its port cities, Patara and Myra (Acts 21:1–2; 27:5–6). B2—6; D3—12; C2—15, 16; E2—17

Lycopolis. *See* Siut

Lydda. B5—11; A6—13. *See* Lod

Lydia. Ancient district of W Asia Minor bounded on the N by Mysia, on the E by Phrygia, on the S by Caria, and on the W by the Aegean. The dynasty of Gyges, which seized the throne about 700 B.C., lasted 150 years, during which time the Lydian Empire became wealthy and extended its territory to the Halys R. The wealth of King Croesus became proverbial. In 546 B.C. Cyrus absorbed the Lydian Empire into the Persian. A-B2—7; B2—15, 16

Lydia, Kingdom of. B2—6. *See* Lydia

Lyons. B2—18. *See* Lugdunum

Lystra. City of Lycaonia and a Roman colony. There Paul healed a crippled man and would have been worshiped as a god had he not refused (Acts 14:6–21). Mod. *Zoldera, ca.* 25 miles SW of Iconium on the Imperial Road to Pisidian Antioch. C5—14; C2—15; E3—18

M

Maacah. City and Aramean city-state at the foot of Mt. Hermon, near Geshur (Josh. 13:13; II Sam. 10:6, 8). Its king joined an Aramean alliance against David (II Sam. 10:6–8). B3—4

Maacha. *See* Maacah

Maachah. *See* Maacah

Ma'an. Administrative center of the S district of Jordan. It is situated on the edge of the desert and serves as the shopping center for nomadic tribes in the neighborhood.

Maceda. *See* Makkedah

Macedonia. Country of SE Europe bounded on the S by Thessaly and the Aegean, on the E by Thrace, and on the W by Illyria. Under Alexander the Great, Macedonia ruled an empire that reached E as far as the Punjab region of India. A1—7, 15, 16; D2—12, 18; B1—17

Machaerus. Hasmonean fortress on the E shore of the Dead Sea, rebuilt by Herod the Great. When John the Baptist, preaching in Perea, antagonized Herod, the prophet was placed in one of the dungeons beneath the palace at Machaerus. C5—11

Machmes. *See* Michmash

Madaba. D4—19. *See* Medeba

Madai. *See* Medes

Madaura. City in N Africa *ca.* 50 miles S of Hippo Regius. According to tradition, 4 Christians were martyred there (A.D. 180), the first Africans to die for their faith.

Madian. *See* Midian

Madmannah. Town in the S part of Judah (Josh. 15:31), thought to be the mod. *Umm Deimneh, ca.* 13 miles NE of Beer-sheba.

Madon. Town in N Canaan whose king joined with Hazor against Israel (Josh. 11:1–12). Thought to have been located near the Horns of Hattin (*q.v.*). D2—3

Maeander R. River of Asia Minor, rising in Phrygia and flowing W *ca.* 250 miles to enter the Aegean Sea S of Samos. Its winding course gave rise to the term *meander*. Mod. *Ruyuk Menderes*. B2—2, 7

Magadan (Magdala). Town *ca.* 3 miles N of Tiberias on the W shore of the Sea of Galilee. It was the home of Mary Magdalene. As Tarichea it served as a Jewish stronghold during the struggle with Rome. Mod. *Kh. Mejdel*. C2—11

Magdala. *See* Magadan

Magdeburg. City on the Albis (Elbe) R., E-central Germany. It is first mentioned A.D. 805, and by A.D. 968 it became an archiepiscopal see.

Mageddo. *See* Megiddo

Mageth (Maked). Town in Gilead in which the Jews were besieged during the time of the Maccabees (I Macc. 5:26). Mod. *Tell Miqdad*.

Magog. A people (and country) listed among the sons of Japheth (Gen. 10:2). They are thought to have lived at the N extremity of the Bible world. Josephus identified them with the Scythians.

Magyars. A nomadic people who migrated (*ca.* A.D. 460) from the Urals to the N Caucasus region. In the 9th century they were forced W into (present) Romania, and then N into Hungary, where they settled permanently.

Mahanaim. Town in Gilead associated with a crucial experience in the life of Jacob (Gen. 32:2). It became a Levitical town (Josh. 21:38) and was Ish-bosheth's capital (II Sam. 2:8, 12, 29). Poss. mod. *Kh. Mahneh*. B4—4; D4—5

Mainz. City in W Germany, on the left bank of the Rhine, opposite the mouth of the Main. It was the Roman city Maguntiacum, or Mogontiacum. In the 8th century, St. Boniface became its first archbishop.

Maka. E3—7. *See* Gedrosia

Maked. *See* Mageth

Makkedah. Town in the lowlands of Judah, *ca.* 15 miles W of Bethlehem. It was taken by Joshua (Josh. 15:41). Poss. mod. *Kh. el-Kheishum*.

Malaca. Coastal town of Farther Spain, founded by the Phoenicians.

Malataya. E2—2. *See* Melitene

Malatha. B6—11. *See* Arad

Malta (Melita). Island in the Mediterranean, S of Sicily. It was controlled, successively, by the

Phoenicians, Greeks, Carthaginians, and Romans. Paul was shipwrecked there (Acts 28:1). A3—17

Mamre. A plain near or in what later became the city of Hebron (*q.v.*) in S Palestine. Abraham pitched his tents there (Gen. 13:18). Mod. *Ramet el-khalil*.

Manasse. *See* Manasseh

Manasseh, allotment of. Half the tribe of Manasseh chose as its inheritance part of Gilead and all of Bashan (Deut. 3:13–15), E of the Jordan. The other half of the tribe chose its inheritance in central Palestine, W of the Jordan. It was bounded on the S by Dan and Ephraim; on the N by Asher, Zebulun, and Issachar; and on the W by the Mediterranean.

Manasseh's Wall. Wall on the E side of Jerusalem built by Manasseh (II Chron. 33:14). D2—9

Manasses. *See* Manasseh

Maon. Town in the hill-country of Judah (Josh. 15:55), *ca.* 8.5 miles S of Hebron. It was the home of Nabal (I Sam. 25:2) in an area in which David took refuge from his enemies (I Sam. 23:24–25). Mod. *Tell Ma'in*.

Mara. *See* Marah

Maracanda. *See* Samarkand

Marah. Fountain of bitter water in the Wilderness of Shur, at which the Israelites stopped, following the Exodus. Mod. *'Ain Hawara*. B5—3

Marathon. Site of a famous battle between the Greeks and the Persians (490 B.C.). It is on the NE coast of Attica, *ca.* 22 miles N of Athens. A2—7

Marcomanni. A Germanic people who lived between the Rhine and Danube rivers. Subsequently they migrated to Bohemia and parts of Bavaria and joined other tribes in the harassment of Rome. Peace was made by Commodus (A.D. 180).

Mare Hyrcanium. *See* Caspian Sea

Mare Internum. B-D3—12. *See* Mediterranean Sea

Maresa. *See* Mareshah

Mareshah (Marisa). Town in the lowlands of Judah (Josh. 15:44) that was fortified by Rehoboam (II Chron. 11:8). A battle between King Asa of Judah and Zerah the Ethiopian (of Egypt) was fought nearby (II Chron. 14:9–10). In Maccabean times it was known as Marisa. Mod. *Tell Sandahanna*, 1 mile SE of Beth-gubrin. B5—5; B4—19

Margiana. Chief city of Margus (*q.v.*). E2—7

Margus. N border province of ancient Persia, E of the SE shore of the Caspian Sea. E2—7

Mari, city of. Ancient city-state on the middle Euphrates S of its junction with the Habor. Amorites from Mari brought disaster to the Sumerian cities of S Mesopotamia. Mari, however, after a period of cultural brilliance, fell to Hammurabi of Babylon. Mod. *Tell Hariri*. E3—2

Mari, Kingdom of. Area ruled by the city-state of Mari (*q.v.*), which extended over a wide area in the middle Euphrates basin. Zimri-Lim was the last king of Mari before its conquest by Hammurabi. His palace archives, discovered since 1935, help us reconstruct life during patriarchal times.

Mariamne. One of three massive towers erected by Herod the Great on Jerusalem's W hill to protect its N approach. This tower was named after Herod's wife. *See also* Hippicus *and* Phasael. A5—10

Marienburg. Town on the Nogat R., SE of Danzig. It was originally a castle, founded A.D. 1274 by the Teutonic knights, and subsequently sold to Poland.

Marisa. B5—11. *See* Mareshah

Market of Appius. *See* Appius, Forum of

Marmarica. District of N Africa between Libya and Cyrenaica. It is a desert plateau, now a part of NE Cyrenaica.

Marqash. Town in the Anti-Taurus Mts. of N Syria. It was once the capital of a Hittite kingdom and later the center of the Aramean kingdom of Gurgum. Roman *Germanicea*. Mod. *Maras*.

Marseille. Chief Mediterranean port of France, founded by Phocaean Greeks from Asia Minor *ca.* 600 B.C. Ancient Massilia became an ally of Rome, which annexed it (49 B.C.) after it supported Pompey against Caesar in the civil war.

Masada. Mt. stronghold overlooking the Dead Sea, *ca.* 11 miles S of En-gedi. It was the last fortress to hold out against the Romans during the Jewish revolt. After withstanding siege for 3 years, the defenders put themselves to death rather than fall to the enemy (A.D. 73). The fall of Masada marked the end of Jewish independence. C6—11; C5—19

Masepha. *See* Mizpah

Mash. A name in the table of nations (Gen. 10), thought to refer to an Aramean people.

Maspha. *See* Mizpah

Masrephoth-maim. *See* Misrephoth-maim

Massagetae. A people of central Asia who lived E of the Aral Sea. Cyrus the Great was defeated and slain by them. E1—7

Massilia. *See* Marseille

Mauretania. Roman province of NW Africa corresponding to Morocco and W Algeria. It was bounded on the E by the province of Numidia. It was formed into a Roman province by Claudius. A3—12, 18

Mazaca. *See* Caesarea Mazaca

Meah, Tower of. Tower of ancient Jerusalem located between the Tower of Hananel and the Sheep Gate (Neh. 3:1; 12:39 KJV).

Medeba. Ancient Moabite town located *ca.* 16 miles SE of the mouth of the Jordan, 6 miles S of Heshbon. It was allotted to Reuben (Josh. 13:9, 16) but reverted to Moab (Isa. 15:2). B4—4; C5—5; D5—11

Medemena. *See* Madmannah

Medes (Madai). An ancient people who invaded the mt. country S of the Caspian and, by 700 B.C., had built a prosperous nation. *See* Median Empire

Media. The mt. country S of the Caspian inhabited by the Medes (*q.v.*). G3—2; D2—6; C2—7

Median Empire. At its peak this empire extended from India to the Black Sea. The Medes (*q.v.*) dominated the relatively small nation of Persia until Cyrus the Great mastered Media (*ca.* 549 B.C.) and began his career of conquest. D-E2—6

Mediolanum. *See* Milan

Mediterranean (Great, Upper) **Sea** (Mare Internum). Sea comprising an area of 1,145,000 square miles, with a maximum length of 2,300 miles and a maximum width of 1,200 miles. It is surrounded by Europe, Asia, and Africa, connecting with the Atlantic Ocean through the Strait of Gibraltar. A4—1; A3—2, 5, 11, 17, 19; A2—3, 4, 6; B3—12, 15, 16, 18; A5—13

Megiddo, city of. Important city of N-central Palestine, overlooking the Plain of Esdraelon. It dominated the intersection of important trade routes and served as the key to the defense of the Jordan Valley (from the S) and the coastal plain (from the N). Mod. *Tell el-Mutesellim*. B3—1, 5; D4—2; D2—3; B4—4; C3—6; B2—19

Megiddo, district of. The Plain of Esdraelon is called "the valley of Megiddo(n)" (Zech. 12:11). The city of Megiddo gave its name to the surrounding district.

Meiron. Town 5 miles NW of Safad revered by orthodox Jews as the burial place of Rabbis Simeon ben Yochai, Hillel, Shammai, and others. C1—19

Melita. *See* Malta

Melitene. City at the E foot of the Taurus Mts. in Armenia. It was an important city in Cappadocia and an early Christian center. Mod. *Malataya*, Turkey. C2—7

Mello. *See* Millo

Memphis (Noph). Ancient capital of Lower Egypt, 14 miles S of Cairo. Tradition states that it was built by Menes, the king who united Upper and Lower Egypt into one kingdom. C4—2; A4—3; B3—6, 7; E4—12, 18

Mephaath. Town in Transjordan that belonged to the tribe of Reuben (Josh. 13:18). It became a Levitical city (Josh. 21:37) and later was taken by Moab (Jer. 48:21). Prob. mod. *Tell Jawah*, near *Kh. Nefa'a*, 6 miles S of Amman.

Merida. City of SW Spain. Founded by the Romans as Emerita Augusta in the 1st century B.C., it became the capital of Lusitania. A2—18

Merom. Site of a battle in which Joshua defeated a coalition of kings from N Canaan (Josh. 11:5, 7). The "waters of Merom" are probably the spring and wadi near the village of Meiron, at the base of J. Yarmuk, W of Safad. C2—5

Meron, Mt. Highest mt. in lower Galilee, rising 3,963 feet. Mod. *J. Jermaq*. C2—1

Mersin. Seaport in SE Asia Minor, *ca*. 20 miles W of Tarsus. Its history predated that of the Hittites in Anatolia. D2—2

Mes. *See* Mash

Mesembria. Town of Thrace, on the Black Sea at the foot of Mt. Haemus. It was founded by the people of Chalcedon and Byzantium in the days of Darius Hystaspis. D1—17

Meshech. A people mentioned in the table of nations (Gen. 10:2) as descendants of Japheth. Assyrian records mention *Mushki* as a people in the mts. on the N borders of Assyria. Herodotus placed the *Moschi* SE of the Black Sea.

Mesopotamia. District of W Asia between the Tigris and Euphrates. The region extends from the Persian Gulf to the mts. of Armenia, from the Iranian Plateau to the Syrian Desert. The term *Mesopotamia* was first used by the Greeks in Seleucid times. F3—18

Mesraim. *See* Egypt

Messina. Coastal city of NE Sicily on the Straits of Messina. It was founded by Greek colonists in the 8th century B.C. The 1st Punic war resulted from the request of the Mamertines of Messina for help from Rome against Syracuse.

Michmash. Town in the territory of Benjamin, E of Bethel, 7 miles N of Jerusalem. Jonathan defeated the Philistines there (I Sam. 13– 14). Mod. *Mukhmas*.

Midian. Territory S of Edom, E of the Gulf of Aqaba, in which the nomadic Midianites lived. D5—2, 3

Migdal Ashqelon. Town in mod. Israel consisting of an Old Quarter with narrow crooked lanes and a New Quarter with new dwellings among olive groves. Migdal ("tower of") Ashqelon is a short distance NE of Ashkelon (*q.v.*), the ancient Philistine city.

Milan. City on the Lombard Plain in N Italy. It was of Celtic origin, but Rome conquered the city and in late Roman times it became the seat of the Western Empire.

Miletus. Ancient seaport near the mouth of the Maeander R. in Caria, W Asia Minor. It was occupied *ca*. 1000 B.C. by Greeks and sacked by the Persians (499 B.C.). It fell to Alexander the Great and was successively subject to Pergamum and Rome. A2—7; B2—15, 16; D2—17; E3—18

Millo (in Jerusalem). Prob. the great terraced fill on the E side of the ridge above the Spring Gihon, first built by the Jebusites. After occupying Jerusalem, David "built the city round about from the Millo [i.e., 'filling'] inward" (II Sam. 5:9 RSV). B2—8; C2—9

Minoan-Mycenaean Domain. Islands subject to the Minoan rulers of Crete. According to some traditions, Minos was an able ruler who made Crete a great sea power. A2-C3—2

Miphkad (Muster) **Gate.** Easternmost gate into the city of Jerusalem from the N (*ca.* 445 B.C.).

Mishneh Gate. Gate from the W into the Mishneh quarter of Jerusalem (*ca.* 445 B.C.).

Misphat. *See* En-mishpat

Misrephoth-maim. Place to which Joshua pursued the Canaanite kings defeated at the "waters of Merom" (Josh. 11:8; 13:6). Poss. mod. *Kh. el-Musheirefeh*.

Mitanni. Powerful kingdom from *ca.* 1500 to 1350 B.C., located between the Assyrians and Hittites. The ruling class was Indo-Aryan, the population predominantly Hurrian. E2—2

Mitylene. Capital of Lesbos (*q.v.*), located on the E

of the island. It was colonized by Aeolians and subsequently became an important naval power. Paul stopped there on his journey from Assos to Chios (Acts 20:13–15). B1—16

Mizpah (in Ephraim). Town on the border between Israel and Judah (during the time of the divided kingdom), fortified by Asa of Judah (I Kings 15:22). The Babylonian governor fixed his residence there after the destruction of Jerusalem (II Kings 25:23–25). Prob. mod. *Tell en-Nasbeh*, 7 miles N of Jerusalem. B4—5, 19

Mizpah (in Gilead). Site on the frontier between Israel and Aram where Jacob and Laban made a covenant (Gen. 31:44–49). Poss. mod. *Kh. Jel'ad*, S of the Yarmuk.

Mizpeh. *See* Mizpah

Mizraim. *See* Egypt

M'lefaat. City of ancient Assyria, located on the Great Zab R., a tributary of the Tigris.

Moabites. A people closely related to the Ammonites (Gen. 19:37–38). Their land was, ideally, bounded on the N by the Arnon and on the S by the Zered in the territory E of the Dead Sea. During times of Israelite weakness, they occupied territory N of the Arnon, but when Israel was strong, Moab was forced to pay tribute. C-D5—1; D3—3; B5—4; C-D6—5

Moab, Plains of. Moab is largely a rolling plateau, *ca.* 3,200 feet above sea level, and is well adapted for pasturage. The Plains of Moab were those parts of the level Jordan Valley that once belonged to Moab. They lie E of the Jordan, opposite Jericho, and E of the Dead Sea. C4—1

Modin. Town that gave birth to the Maccabean revolt. It was located *ca.* 7 miles E of Lydda and *ca.* 16 miles from the Mediterranean on the edge of the Philistine plain. Mod. *el-'Arba'in*, near *El-Midyah*.

Moeris, Lake. Ancient name of Lake Karun, in the Faiyum, 50 miles SW of Cairo. Crocodilopolis (Arsinoe) was the chief town on the lake. A5—3

Moesi. Ancient tribal people who gave their name to Moesia (*q.v.*).

Moesia. Ancient name for the region of SE Europe S of the lower Danube. It was organized as a Roman province (A.D. 44). The territory included mod. Serbia and Bulgaria. D2—12, 18; C-D1—17

Molada. *See* Moladah

Moladah. Town in S Judah (Josh. 15:26), assigned to Simeon (Josh. 19:2). Poss. mod. *Tell el-Milh*, 14 miles SE of Beer-sheba, 22 miles SW of Hebron.

Moreh, Hill of. Hill in the Plain of Esdraelon, N of the spring of Harod. Prob. *J. Dahy*, or Little Hermon, 8 miles NW of Mt. Gilboa, 1 mile S of Nain. C3—1

Moresheth-gath. Town in Judah (Micah 1:14), thought to be the home of the prophet Micah (cf. 1:1). Prob. mod. *Tell el-Judeideh*.

Moschi. C2—7. *See* Meshech

Mosoch. *See* Meshech

Mt. Ararat. *See* Ararat, Mt.

Mt. Carmel. *See* Carmel, Mt.

Mt. Gerizim. *See* Gerizim, Mt.

Mt. Gilboa. *See* Gilboa, Mt.

Mt. Meron. *See* Meron, Mt.

Mt. Nebo. *See* Nebo, Mt.

Mt. Nisir. *See* Nisir, Mt.

Mt. of Olives. *See* Olives, Mt. of

Mt. Pisgah. *See* Pisgah, Mt.

Mt. Sinai. *See* Sinai, Mt.

Mt. Tabor. *See* Tabor, Mt.

Mughara, W. el-. Located on the lower W slope of Mt. Carmel, *ca.* 11 miles S of the N promontory of the mt. and 2 miles E of the Mediterranean. Several caves there have yielded significant Stone Age remains. B2—19

Mujib, W. el-. *See* Aron R.

Munda. Roman colony and town in Farther Spain. Scene of Scipio's victory over the Carthaginians (216 B.C.) and of Julius Caesar's over Pompey's sons (45 B.C.).

Murabba'at Caves. Caves on the W shore of the Dead Sea where Bar Kokhba and his followers hid during the second revolt (A.D. 132–134). C4—19

Musa, W. *See* W. Musa

Musasir. Town on the border between ancient Urartu and Assyria, located in the mountainous district SE of Lake Urmia. It was conquered by the Assyrian ruler Shalmaneser III.

Muster Gate. *See* Miphkad Gate

Mycenaean-Minoan Domain. *See* Minoan-Mycenaean Domain.

Myra. City of Lycia, S Asia Minor, *ca.* 2 miles from the Mediterranean built on and about a cliff at the mouth of a gorge leading into the interior mt. region. Paul changed ships there (Acts 27:5–6). Mod. *Dembre*. E3—17, 18

Mysia. Province in the extreme NW of Asia Minor bounded on the N by the Propontis (mod. Sea of Marmara), on the S by Lydia, on the E by Bithynia, and on the W by the Aegean Sea. Paul passed through Mysia to Troas, one of its cities (Acts 16:7–8). Assos (Acts 20:13) and Pergamum (Rev. 1:11) are also in Mysia. B1—15, 16; E2—18

N

Naarah. Town in Ephraim, N of Jericho (Josh. 16:7). It is prob. identical with Naaran (I Chron. 7:28).

Naarath(a). *See* Naarah

Naare. *See* Nazareth

Naasson. *See* Hazor

Nabatea. Country in the land of Edom and Moab from *ca.* 200 B.C. to A.D. 100. Petra (*q.v.*) was its capital. C6-D5—11; E3-4—12

Nabateans. Arabian people who developed a remarkable civilization during the 1st and 2nd centuries B.C. and the 1st century A.D. Their capital, Petra, was on important trade routes between S Arabia and Syria. Nabateans built irrigation systems and farmed the land. B6-C5—13

Nablus. Roman name for a town near the site of ancient Shechem (*q.v.*). *See* Neapolis (in Palestine).

Nabo. *See* Nebo, Mt.

Nabutheans. *See* Nabateans

Nahariyah. Site on the Mediterranean coast, N of Acco *ca.* 7 miles, where remains of Canaanite habitation have been discovered. B1—19

Naim. *See* Nain

Nain. Town 6 miles SE of Nazareth in the NW corner of J. ed-Duhy (Little Hermon). Here Jesus restored to life the only son of a widow (Luke 7:11). Mod. *Nain.* C3—11

Nantes. Town on the Loire R., W France. It was of pre-Roman origin and was ravaged by Norsemen in the 9th century.

Naphtali, allotment of. Land in N Palestine, bounded on the E by the upper Jordan and the Sea of Galilee, and on the S by Issachar and Zebulun.

Naples. City in S Italy, built at the base of a ridge of hills rising from the Bay of Naples. It was a Greek colony, conquered (4th century B.C.) by the Romans.

Narbata. Town *ca.* 8 miles E of Caesarea that, according to Josephus, was conquered by Cestius during the first revolt. Mod. *Kh. Beidus.* B3—11

Narbo. City in S France near the Mediterranean coast. As Narbo Martius it was the 1st Roman colony established (118 B.C.) in Transalpine Gaul. B2—12

Narbonensis. Roman province in S Gaul, located W and S of the Alpine provinces. Its capital was Narbo. A2—12

Narbonne. *See* Narbo

Narona. Roman colony in Illyricum, on the Naro R. and the road to Dyrrhachium.

Naucratis. City on the E bank of the Canopic branch of the Nile in the Delta. It was colonized by Milesians and remained a Greek city. Aphrodite was its principal goddess.

Nawa. Syrian city *ca.* 25 miles W of the Sea of Galilee.

Nazareth. Town in a secluded valley of lower Galilee, N of the Plain of Esdraelon. It was the boyhood home of Jesus (Luke 2:39; 4:16). C2—1; B3—11

Neapolis (in Italy). *See* Naples

Neapolis (in Macedonia). Seaport of Philippi, situated on the Strymonic Gulf, 10 miles SE of the city. Mod. *Kavalla.* B1—15, 16

Neapolis (in Palestine). City built by the Romans in A.D. 72 just W of the site of ancient Shechem (*q.v.*). Mod. *Nablus* (a corruption of *Neapolis*, "new city"). B4—11

Neballat. Town in Benjamin, *ca.* 4 miles NE of Lydda. It was inhabited after the exile (Neh. 11:34). Mod. *Beit Naballa.*

Nebo, Mt. Peak in the Abarim Mts. opposite Jericho (Num. 33:47; Deut. 32:49). Mod. *J. en-Neba*, 12 miles E of the mouth of the Jordan. D4—1; D3—3

Negba. Town in Israel, E of Ashkelon. It is situated in an area of fertile fields and plantations.

Negeb. The dry southland of Judea, beginning a few miles S of Hebron and extending to Kadesh-barnea. Beer-sheba is an oasis in the N Negeb. A-B6—1, 5; C-D3—3

Negev. *See* Negeb

Nemrod. *See* Nimrod

Nephtahli, allotment of. *See* Naphtali, allotment of

Nervii. A warlike people of Gallia Belgica, decisively defeated by Caesar in 58 B.C.

New Babylonian Empire. *See* Babylonian Empire, New

Nicaea. City built on the E side of Lake Ascania, in Bithynia, Asia Minor. It was a royal residence of Bithynian kings and sometimes served as its capital. Constantine convened a great ecclesiastical council there in A.D. 325.

Nicephorium. Fortified town built on the Euphrates, S of Edessa, at the command of Alexander the Great.

Nicomedia. City of Bithynia, Asia Minor, located at the head of the Gulf of Astacus on the Propontis. Founded by Nicomedes I (264 B.C.), it became a chief city of the Roman Empire. *See* Astacus. E2—18

Nicopolis (in Asia Minor). City in Pontus. Site of a Byzantine victory over Arab invaders. Ancient *Acroinum*, mod. *Afyonkarahisar*, Turkey.

Nicopolis (in Greece). City in NW Greece, founded by Octavian (Augustus) to celebrate his victory at nearby Actium (31 B.C.). C2—17; D3—18

Nicopolis (in Palestine). B5—11. *See* Emmaus

Nile Delta. Delta that begins where the Nile R. branches out and is 120 miles wide on the Mediterranean coast. The two principal branches, each *ca.* 146 miles long, enter the sea at Rosetta (on the W) and Damietta (on the E). A3—3

Nile R. River that flows *ca.* 4,050 miles through NE Africa from its ultimate headstream, the Kagera, N to the Mediterranean. Ancient Egypt was the land along the Nile and its Delta from the 1st cataract at Aswan to the Mediterranean. C5—2; A5—3; B3—6; B4—7; E4—12, 18

Nimrah. *See* Beth-nimrah

Nimrod. Dominion of a son of Cush (Gen. 10:8–12), in S Mesopotamia.

Nimrud. F3—2. *See* Calah

Nineve. *See* Nineveh

Nineveh. Ancient capital of Assyria, located on the E bank of the Tigris opposite the site of mod. *Mosul*. An alliance of Medes, Babylonians, and Scythians destroyed the city in 612 B.C. F2—2; C2—6

Ninus. *See* Nineveh

Nippur. Sumerian center on the Euphrates in central Babylonia. It was the seat of the worship of the goddess En-lil. F4—2; D3—6; C3—7

Nisibis. City of N Mesopotamia. Site of battles between the Parthians and Romans. C2—6; F3—18

Nisir, Mt. Mt. E of Mosul and the Tigris near the Little Zab R. According to the Gilgamesh Epic, the ark rested there following the flood.

No (Thebes). Biblical No-Amon (Nahum 3:8). It was the capital of Upper Egypt. Ruins are at mod. *Luxor* and *Karnak*. C6—2

No-Amon. *See* No

Nob. Town in the territory of Benjamin, N of Jerusalem (Isa. 10:32). The tabernacle was there for a time, and Nob was known as "the city of the priests" (I Sam. 22:19). Prob. mod. *Ras Umm et-Tala'* on the E slope of Mt. Scopus.

Nobah. Town in Transjordan along a road leading to the country of the nomads (Judg. 8:11).

Nobe. *See* Nob

Noph. C4—2; A4—3. *See* Memphis

Noreia. Capital city of the Norici, the people of Noricum (*q.v.*), situated S of the Murius R.

Noricum. Province of the Roman Empire that corresponds to mod. Austria S of the Danube and W of Vienna. C2—12

North Sea. Portion of the Atlantic Ocean NW of central Europe. It touches the shores of Scotland, England, Norway, Denmark, Germany, the Netherlands, and N France.

North Wall, First (in Jerusalem). The N wall running E from Herod's towers (Hippicus, in particular) to the temple-enclosure walls. B5—10

North Wall, Second (in Jerusalem). A wall that, according to Josephus, began near the Gennath Gate of the First North Wall and enclosed the N quarter of the city, ending at the Fortress Antonia. B4—10

Nubia. Region in Upper Egypt, extending N to Aswan and the 1st cataract of the Nile. Its boundaries were indefinite, but it did include the Nubian Desert. C6—2

Numidia. Country in NW Africa, occupying territory corresponding to mod. Algeria. After being under control of Carthage, Numidia enjoyed a period of independence before being subjugated by Rome. B3—18

Nuzi. Ancient city of Mesopotamia, near mod. *Kirkuk*. Archaeological discoveries there have illuminated life during patriarchal times. Mod. *Yorghan Tepe*. F3—2

O

Oboth. Place where the Israelites stopped en route from Kedesh to the plains of Moab. Poss. mod. *'Ain el-Weiba*, S of the Dead Sea.

Oceanus Germanicus. *See* North Sea

Odollam. *See* Adullam

Og, Kingdom of. Territory in the Transjordanian district of Bashan, from the Yarmuk R. to Mt. Hermon (Deut. 3:8–10).

Olbia. Colony of Greek Miletus, founded *ca.* 645 B.C. near mod. *Nikolayev*, Ukraine. It served as a center for the export of wheat from the S Ukraine.

Old Babylonian Empire. *See* Babylonian Empire, Old

Old Pool. *See* Lower Pool

Olives, Mt. of. Hill E of Jerusalem, from which it is separated by the Kidron Valley. It was the site of Jesus' Olivet discourse and His ascension. C4—1; D4—10

Olivet, Mt. *See* Olives, Mt. of

Oman, Gulf of. Gulf that connects the Persian Gulf with the Indian Ocean, bounded on the N by Iran and on the S by Oman in SE Arabia.

'Omer. Town *ca.* 3 miles NE of Beer-sheba on the road that formerly connected Beer-sheba with Hebron and Jerusalem.

On. C4—2; A4—3. *See* Heliopolis

Ono. Town in Benjamin, 7 miles SE of Joppa. It was reoccupied following the Babylonian captivity (Ezra 2:33; Neh. 7:37). Mod. *Kafr 'Ana*.

Ophel. S sector of the E hill of Jerusalem. It was originally a tower or projection in the fortification. B2-3—8; D2-3—9

Ophera. *See* Ophrah

Ophir. Territory of a tribe descended from Joktan (Gen. 10:29). It was famed for its gold (Ps. 45:9). It was prob. located in SW Arabia.

Ophrah (in Benjamin). Town N of Michmash (I Sam. 13:17). It was identical with Ephron (II Chron. 13:19) and Ephraim (II Sam. 13:23; John 11:54). *See* Ephraim, city of

Ophrah (in Issachar). Town of Gideon known as "Ophrah of the Abiezrites" (Judg. 8:27, 32). Location uncertain. Poss. mod. *et-Taiyibeh*, NW of Beth-shan.

Opis. One of the principal cities of N Babylonia (Akkad). It was situated on the Tigris. D2—6; C2—7

Ornan, threshing floor of. *See* Araunah, threshing floor of

Orontes R. River in Syria formed from sources in the Lebanon and Anti-Lebanon Mts. It flows N through the Beqa'a Valley, then SW past Syrian Antioch to the Mediterranean. C1—4; C2—13

Ortona. Town in S-central Italy that was once a major Adriatic port.

Ostia. Town at the mouth of the Tiber R. that served as the port of Rome. A1—17

Oxus R. River that rises in the Hindu Kush (*q.v.*) and flows 1,450 miles in a generally NW direction to the Aral Sea. Mod. *Amu Darya*. F1—6; E1—7

Oxyrrhynchus. Town in Upper Egypt, W of the Nile, near the Faiyum. Significant finds of papyri have been made there.

P

Pactyans. Ancient people of Arachosia (*q.v.*).

Padan-aram. *See* Paddan-aram

Paddan-aram. Region in upper Mesopotamia (Gen. 25:20; 28:2) where relatives of the biblical patriarchs settled. It was also known as Aram-naharaim (Gen. 25:20). E2—2

Palestine. Strictly speaking, "the land of the Philistines," the coastal plain E of the Mediterranean and S of Joppa. *Palestine* came to be used of the whole land of Israel, both E and W of the Jordan.

Palm Trees, City of. *See* Jericho

Palmyra. *See* Tadmor

Palus Maeotis. *See* Azov, Sea of

Pamphylia. Country in S Asia Minor, bounded on the N by Pisidia, on the S by a gulf of the Mediterranean called the Sea of Pamphylia, on the E by Cilicia, and on the W by Lycia. D–E3—12; C5—14; C2—15, 16; E2—17

Paneas. Region in Syria between Iturea (to the N) and Ulatha (to the S). Its main city, Caesarea Philippi (*q.v.*), sometimes went by the name *Paneas* (or *Baniyas*). C-D1—11

Panias. *See* Paneas

Pannonia. Country of a mixed Illyrian-Celtic people, S of the Danube R. and extending to the Save Valley. Conquered by Rome 12–9 B.C. C2—12

Panticapaeum. Town in the E sector of the Crimean Peninsula of the Black Sea. It was founded by Milesians *ca.* 541 B.C. B1—7

Paphlagonia. District in N Asia Minor between Bithynia and Pontus.

Paphos. Port city on the W coast of Cyprus. Old Paphos was of Phoenician origin and was a center for the worship of Venus. The Romans built New Paphos, which was the capital of 1 of the 4 districts into which Cyprus was divided. C5—14; E3—18

Paraetonium. Important town on the N coast of Africa, near Cape Artos. It was an important center for the worship of Isis. The town was restored by Justinian.

Paran, Wilderness of. Wilderness between Sinai (or Hazeroth) and Canaan (Num. 10:12; 12:16). It was S of Judah and included Kadesh (Num. 13:26), or Kadesh-barnea. C4—3

Paran R. Brook that flows from the Wilderness of Paran NE to the W. ʿAraba.

Parathon. *See* Pirathon

Pardes Hanna. Mod. Israeli settlement in a region of citrus groves on the road from Hadera to ʿAfula.

Paricanians. Ancient people who inhabited Gedrosia (*q.v.*).

Paris. *See* Lutetia

Parsa (Persepolis). One of the capitals of ancient Persia, located 35 miles SE of mod. *Shiraz*. Mod. *Takht-i-Jamshid*. D3—7

Parthia. Country in W Asia, SE of the Caspian, adjoining Media. E2—6, 7

Parthian Empire. *Ca.* 250 B.C. Arcases I threw off the yoke of the Seleucid Syrian kings. Under Mithridates I the Parthian Empire extended from the N Euphrates to beyond the Indus. Ctesiphon was its capital. F3—12

Pasargadae. Capital of ancient Persia and site of the tomb of Cyrus the Great. Its ruins are 54 miles by road NE of Persepolis on the Murgab Plain on both sides of the Pulvar R. D3—7

Patara. Chief seaport of Lycia, Asia Minor. It was colonized by Dorians from Crete and boasted an Apollo oracle. Restored by Ptolemy Philadelphus, it was renamed Arsinoe. Mod. *Gelemish*. C2—16; D3—17

Pathros. Ancient name for Upper Egypt, the land S of the Delta. It is located between Egypt (i.e., the Delta) and Cush in Isaiah 11:11.

Pathrusim. Inhabitants of Pathros (*q.v.*), who were descendants of Mizraim (Gen. 10:14).

Patmos. Aegean island 28 miles S of Samos (*q.v.*) to which Domitian exiled the apostle John *ca.* A.D. 95. Patmos was part of the Roman province of Asia. D3—18

Pattala. Ancient city in India at the head of the Indus R. delta. Alexander the Great took Pattala without battle. There he planned the naval expedition that would sail from the mouth of the Indus to the Persian Gulf. F3—7

Pella (in Gilead). City in Transjordan to which Christians fled before the Romans captured Jerusalem (A.D. 70). Mod. *Tabaqat Fahl*. C3—11; B5—13

Pella (in Macedonia). Macedonian town that Philip made his capital. Birthplace of Alexander the Great.

Pelusium (Sin). Ancient Egyptian city on the easternmost branch of the Nile, *ca.* 20 miles E of mod. *Port Said*. It was known as Sin in the Bible (Ezek. 30:15–16). B3—3, 7

Peniel. *See* Penuel

Penuel (Peniel). Encampment E of the Jordan where Jacob had his historic encounter with God (Gen. 32:30–31). It was a fortified place at the time of Gideon (Judg. 8:8, 9, 17) and Jeroboam (I Kings 12:25). C4—5

Perea. Region in Transjordan between the Jabbok and the Arnon. The term is sometimes used of the entire country E of the Jordan. C4—11

Perga. City in ancient Pamphylia, Asia Minor, NE of Attalia. It was located *ca.* 7 miles from the mouth of the Kestros R. and served as a center for the worship of Artemis (Diana). Paul ministered there during his First Missionary Journey (Acts 13:13–14). Mod. *Murtana*, Turkey. C5—14

Pergamum. Most important city of ancient Mysia, W Asia Minor, situated 3 miles N of the R. Caicus and *ca.* 15 miles from the Aegean Sea. Eumenes II of Pergamum (190 B.C.) identified himself with the Romans and, with their aid, ruled a powerful kingdom. Mod. *Bergama*. D2—12, 17; B1—15, 16; E3—18

Perge. *See* Perga

Persepolis. D3—7. *See* Parsa

Persia. E3—6. *See* Persis

Persian Empire. Empire extending to (but not including) Greece in the W and India in the E. It included both Egypt and Babylonia. It was established by Cyrus in the mid-6th century B.C. and lasted until defeat by Alexander the Great in 331 B.C. B–F2—7

Persian Gulf (Lower Sea). Arm of the Arabian Sea between Persia (mod. *Iran*) and Arabia. It extends *ca.* 600 miles from the mouth of the Tigris-Euphrates to the Strait of Hormuz, which connects it with the Gulf of Oman. G5—2; D–E3—6

Persis. Country N of the Persian Gulf inhabited by an Indo-European people known as Persians.

Persis, or Persia, seems to have been early inhabited by Sumerian peoples, but following the fall of Assyria, the Medes became heirs to its political power and civilization. D3—7

Pessinus. Ancient city in SW Galatia, Asia Minor. Under Constantine it became capital of Galatia Salutaris, a Roman province.

Petra. *See* Sela

Phaddan-aram. *See* Paddan-aram

Phanuel. *See* Penuel

Phara. *See* Pirathon

Pharathon. *See* Pirathon

Pharos. W extremity of Alexandria, Egypt. It is an island that in ancient times was the location of a famous lighthouse and that is now connected to Alexandria by a causeway.

Pharpar R. River of Damascus (II Kings 5:12). Prob. mod. *Awaj*, which is also S of mod. Damascus and flows E into swamps. D1—1

Pharsalus. Town in Pharsalia, Thessaly, near the Enipeus R. It was the scene of fighting in the war between Rome and Macedonia (197 B.C.).

Phasael. One of three massive towers erected by Herod the Great on Jerusalem's W hill to protect its N approach. The tower was named after Herod's brother. *See also* Hippicus *and* Mariamne. A5—10

Phasaelis. Town in the Jordan Valley, laid out by Herod the Great in honor of his brother Phasael. The town was artificially irrigated. Mod. *Fasa-'il.* C4—11

Phaselis. Seaport of Lycia on the boundary of Pamphylia, S Asia Minor (I Macc. 15:23). It was a center of pirate activity in ancient times. Mod. *Tekirova,* Turkey.

Phasga, Mt. *See* Pisgah, Mt.

Phasis. City on the E shore of the Black Sea in ancient Colchis. It was founded by the Greeks at the mouth of the Phasis R. (mod. *Rioni*). Mod. *Poti,* in W Georgian S.S.R. C1—7

Phatures. *See* Pathros

Phenice. *See* Phoenix

Phetrusium. *See* Pathrusim

Philadelphia (in Asia Minor). City of Lydia, W Asia Minor, *ca.* 28 miles SE of Sardis. It was the seat of 1 of the 7 churches of Revelation (Rev. 1:11). Mod. *Alasheher,* Turkey. D2—17

Philadelphia (in Transjordan). D4—11; B6—13. *See* Amman

Philippi. City in NE Macedonia named after Philip II, who annexed it and exploited the gold and silver mines nearby. Paul visited it and made several converts there, including his jailor (Acts 16:12–40). Philippi is *ca.* 10 miles NW of its seaport, Neapolis. A1—15, 16; C1—17; D2—18

Philistia. Land of the Philistines. It was that part of the maritime plain of Canaan that lies between Joppa and Gaza. This area is *ca.* 50 miles long and 15 miles wide. A5-B4—4; A-B5—5

Philistia, Plain of. Fertile plain of SW Canaan that produced grain, figs, olives, and other fruit. *See* Philistia. A-B5—1

Philistim. *See* Philistines

Philistines. An ancient non-Semitic people who lived along the S coast of Palestine (*see* Philistia). They appear to have come from Crete and poss. from the coasts of Asia Minor. They possessed a high culture and used iron before it was known in Israel (I Sam. 13:19–21).

Philoteria. *See* Beth-yerah

Phinon. *See* Punon

Phithom. *See* Pithom

Phoenicia. Ancient country on the Mediterranean coast N of Palestine. It occupied the area between the Lebanon Mts. and the sea. Mod. *Lebanon.* B2-C1—1, 5, 11; B2-3—4; B4-5—13

Phoenicians. Semitic inhabitants of Phoenicia (*q.v.*) who developed important maritime cities (e.g., Tyre, Sidon) and engaged in extensive colonization of the Mediterranean islands and coastlands. Because Sidon was the earliest of the Phoenician city-states, the term *Sidonian* (or *Zidonian*) is frequently synonymous with *Phoenician.*

Phoenix. Harbor in Crete (Acts 27:12). Because it opened toward the NE and NW, it was safe throughout the year. Mod. *Loutro.* C3—17

Phrygia. Ancient country of central Asia Minor inhabited by a warlike people who entered the region from Europe (*ca.* 1200 B.C.). C2—15, 16; E3—18

Phrygian Kingdom. Prior to the 7th century B.C. Phrygia ruled much of W Asia Minor. Subsequently the Lydians became the dominant power in that region.

Phunon. *See* Punon

Phut (Put). A people related to the Egyptians (Gen. 10:6). Phut is closely associated with the Lubim (Nah. 3:9).

Pibeseth (Bubastis). Ancient city of NE Egypt. Mod. *Tell Basta.* A4—3

Pirathon (Pharathon). Town N of the Kanah R., *ca.* 7.5 miles SW of Shechem. Pirathonites are mentioned in the O.T. (Judg. 12:13–15; II Sam. 23:30), and the city was fortified in Maccabean times (I Macc. 9:50).

Pisa. City of ancient Etruria, NW Italy. It was founded around the 6th century B.C. and subsequently fell to Rome. Political freedom was preserved, however.

Pisgah, Mt. Part of the Abarim Mts. E of the NE corner of the Dead Sea. Prob. mod. *Ras es-Siagha,* slightly NW of *J. en-Neba* (*see* Mt. Nebo).

Pisidia. District in Asia Minor bounded on the N by Phrygia, on the S by Lycia and Pamphylia, on the E by Lycaonia, and on the W by Caria. It formed part of the Roman province of Galatia. Its chief town was Antioch of Pisidia (Acts 13:14). C5—14; C2—15, 16

Pithom. One of two store cities built by Israelites while in Egyptian bondage (Exod. 1:11). Poss. mod. *Tell el-Maskhuta,* in the E Nile Delta. A4—3

Pityus. Town founded by Ionian Greek colonists on the NE shore of the Black Sea.

311

Plain, Sea of the. *See* Dead Sea

Plain of Esdraelon. *See* Esdraelon, Plain of

Plain of Philistia. *See* Philistia, Plain of

Plain of Sharon. *See* Sharon, Plain of

Plains of Moab. *See* Moab, Plains of

Poles. Early in the 9th century A.D. a Slavic people known as Polians, or Poles, gained hegemony over other Slavic tribes in the area that became known as Poland.

Pomeranians. Slavic peoples who settled in the N European plains S of the Baltic Sea. The land was sandy and marshy, but it had large forests and numerous lakes.

Pompeiopolis (Soli). Town on the Mediterranean coast of Cilicia, SE Asia Minor. It was founded *ca.* 700 B.C. by colonists from Rhodes and later colonized by Athenians, who named it Soli. It was destroyed by the Armenian king Tigranes (91 B.C.) but rebuilt by Pompey, for whom it was renamed Pompeiopolis.

Pontus. Ancient district of Asia Minor along the Black Sea. It was a strong monarchy (*ca.* 400 B.C.) until its king, Mithridates, was defeated by Pompey (63 B.C.). Thereafter it was joined to the Roman province of Galatia-Cappadocia. E2—12, 18; C-D1—16; D-F1—17

Pontus Euxinus. *See* Black Sea

Pool of Amygdalon. *See* Amygdalon, Pool of

Pool of Bethzatha. *See* Bethzatha, Pool of

Pool of Siloam. *See* Siloam, Pool of

Pozzuoli. *See* Puteoli

Preslav. City W of the Black Sea and S of the Danube. It was the ancient capital of Bulgaria.

Prophthasia. City built by Alexander the Great in Drangiana, S of Alexandria Arion.

Propontis. Ancient name for the Sea of Marmara, which connects on the E with the Black Sea through the Bosporus, and on the W with the Aegean Sea through the Dardanelles. Constantinople (Byzantium, mod. *Istanbul*) is situated on the entrance of the Bosporus into the Sea of Marmara.

Prussians. A Baltic people, conquered and largely exterminated by Teutonic knights during the 13th century. Medieval Prussia was the section of NE Germany subsequently known as E Prussia.

Pteria. Town in Cappadocia, Asia Minor, on the Persian royal road that connected Susa with Sardis. It had earlier been known as Hattusas (*q.v.*) and served as a great Hittite center. B2—7

Ptolemais (in Egypt). Hellenistic city of Upper Egypt, located on the Nile, S of Abydos. It was founded by Ptolemy Soter on the site of a small village, and it replaced Thebes as the capital. Mod. *Menchah*.

Ptolemais (in Palestine). B2—11, 19; A5—13; D3—16. *See* Acco

Punon. Town in Edom at which the Israelites stopped during their journey to Canaan (Num. 33:42). Copper was mined there in ancient times. Poss. mod. *Feinan*, 25 miles S of the Dead Sea. D4—3; B5—4

Pura. Ancient town in Gedrosia (*q.v.*) through which Alexander passed on his return journey from India. E3—7

Put. *See* Phut

Puteoli (Pozzuoli). Important port on the Bay of Naples, Italy, founded in the 6th century B.C. as Dicearchia. It was the usual port of debarkation for travelers from Egypt and the East. Paul's vessel landed there, and he enjoyed the hospitality of Christians from the town (Acts 28:13). A1—17; C2—18

Pyramids, Great. Pyramids near Giza, including those built for Khufu (Cheops), Khafre (Chephren), and Menkure. They were built to serve as massive tombs for these pharaohs of the 3rd century B.C. A4—3

Pyramus R. River of SE Asia Minor. From its source in the Anti-Taurus range, it flows generally SW and enters the Mediterranean at Antioch-on-the-Pyramus, W of the Gulf of Issus. Mod. *Ceyhan*.

Pyrenees Mts. Mt. chain of SW Europe between France and Spain, separating the Iberian Peninsula from the European mainland. It extends *ca.* 280 miles from the Bay of Biscay on the W to the Mediterranean on the E.

Q

Qarnini. Assyrian name for the provinces of N Palestine E of the Jordan. It is the same as the district of Karnaim.

Qarqar. *See* Karkar

Qasile. City near where the Kanah R. empties into the Mediterranean. It might have been the port through which Phoenician building materials reached Jerusalem (II Chron. 2:16; Ezra 3:7). Mod. *Tel Qasila*. B3—19

Qatna. Ancient city a short distance S of Hamath on the Orontes, E of Arvad. During the 2nd millennium B.C. it came under Hittite, Hurrian, and Amorite influences, successively. Mod. *Tell el-Mishrifeh*. D3—2

Qumran. Site on the NW shore of the Dead Sea where an ancient sectarian group (thought to have been Essenes) maintained an ascetic settlement. The Dead Sea Scrolls were found in caves in the vicinity, and ruins of a community center have provided information concerning life in a pre-Christian Jewish community. C5—11; C4—19

R

Raamah. A region and people of SE Arabia. It is mentioned with Sheba as trading with Tyre (Ezek. 27:22). Raamah was a Cushite tribe (Gen. 10:7).

Raamses. *See* Ramses

Rabba. *See* Amman

Rabbah. D4—1, 5; D3—3; C4—4. *See* Amman

Rabbah. *See* Areopolis

Rabbath-ammon. *See* Amman

Rabbath-Moab. *See* Areopolis

Raetia. Country conquered by Rome *ca*. 15 B.C. and made a Roman province. Its S boundary was the Alps, and it went as far N as the Danube. C2—12

Raetii. Germanic peoples who inhabited the region S of the Danube R. in an area corresponding to the greater part of the Tirol.

Rafiah. *See* Raphia

Ragaba. Town in Gilead, N of the Jabbok. Alexander Jannaeus died there.

Rages. *See* Rhagae

Rama. *See* Ramah

Ramah (in Benjamin). Town located on a hill 5 miles N of Jerusalem. It was fortified by Baasha of Israel to keep the Southern Kingdom from invading (I Kings 15:17, 21, 22). It was on the route of the Assyrian army (Isa. 10:29) and was repopulated after the exile (Neh. 7:30; 11:33). Mod. *er-Ram*. B4—5

Ramah (in Naphtali). Walled city located *ca.* ·17 miles E of Acco (Josh 19:36). Poss. mod. *er-Rameh*.

Ramallah. Town *ca*. 3 miles SW of Bethel in Jordan. It is on the ridge running N and S from Jerusalem.

Ramat Gan. Town E of Tel Aviv. Founded in 1921, it soon developed into a major industrial center. Numerous public gardens and a national park give evidence of its cultural interests.

Ramatha. *See* Arimathea

Ramathaim. *See* Arimathea

Ramat Rahel. Iron Age fortress honoring Rachel, wife of Jacob. This was a suburb of O.T. Jerusalem. C4—19

Rameses. *See* Ramses

Ramle. Town in Israel, SW of Lydda. It was founded by the Arabs (A.D. 717) and soon became their capital in Palestine. Subsequently it was occupied by Seljuk Turks, Crusaders, Mamelukes, and the Turkish Empire. It is now an important Israeli city on the road to Jerusalem.

Ramoth-galaad. *See* Ramoth-gilead

Ramoth-gilead. Town in Gilead, E of the Jordan, in the territory of Gad, near the border with the tribe of Manasseh. It was a Levitical city (Josh. 21:38) and a city of refuge (Deut. 4:43). C4—4; D3—5

Ramses (Tanis, Zoan). City in the E Nile Delta, in the district of Goshen. The Israelites built it ("Raamses," Exod. 1:11) as a store city for the pharaoh. At the Exodus, the Israelites marched from there ("Rameses," Exod. 12:37). Prob. mod. *Qantir*. A3—3

Raphana. D2—11. *See* Raphon

Raphia (Rafiah). Town in SW Palestine, S of Gaza. It was the site of Ptolemy Philopator's decisive victory over Antiochus the Great of Syria. A5—1, 4, 5; C3—3

Raphon. City of S Syria, NE of Karnaim. Pliny mentioned it as one of the cities of the Decapolis. Some mod. scholars identify it with Ashtaroth (*q.v.*).

Ravenna. City of Cisalpine Gaul, N of the Rubicon. It was founded by colonists from Thessaly and served as 1 of 2 chief stations of the fleet of Augustus.

Rebla. *See* Riblah

Reblatha. *See* Riblah

Red Sea (Arabian Gulf). Narrow sea, *ca*. 1,500 miles long between Africa and Arabia, lying in the Great Rift Valley. The Red Sea has 2 N arms between which the Sinai Peninsula is located. The left arm is the Gulf of Suez; the right arm, the Gulf of Aqaba. D6—2; C6—3; C4—6; B3—7; E4—12; F4—18

Regensburg. Ancient city on the Danube, in E Bavaria. As Castra Regina it was an important Roman frontier station. It is also known as Ratisbon.

Regma. *See* Raamah

Rehoboth. A well dug by Isaac in the Valley of Gerar (Gen. 26:22). Prob. mod. *er-Ruheibeh*, 18 miles SW of Beer-sheba.

Reims (Rheims, Durocotorum). City of NE France, ancient Durocotorum, the city of the Remi (*q.v.*). It was one of the most important cities of Roman Gaul. It became the see of an archbishopric in the 8th century.

Remi. People of ancient Gaul who lived in the territory traversed by the Axona R. They joined forces with Caesar (57 B.C.) when the other Belgae made war against him.

Remmon. *See* Rimmon

Rephidim. Last place the Israelites stopped during the Exodus before Mt. Sinai (Exod. 17:1, 5, 6). There they battled the Bedouin Amalekites (Exod. 17:8–16). Poss. mod. *W. Refayid*. C5—3

Reuben, allotment of. Territory assigned to the tribe of Reuben. The E boundary was Ammon; the S boundary, the Arnon R.; the W boundary, the Jordan and the Dead Sea; and the N boundary, a line from the Jordan S of Beth-nimrah to Heshbon.

Rha (Volga) **R.** Largest river of Europe, which runs a course of 2,290 miles through central and E Europe, creating a delta at its mouth at the Caspian Sea. F1—12

Rhagae (Rages). Principal city of Media, SW of mod. *Tehran*. It was destroyed by an earthquake and restored by Seleucus Nicator, who renamed it Europus. It was the scene of some of the principal events in the apocryphal book of Tobit. D2—7

Rhegium. Ancient Greek town on the Strait of Messina, S Italy. It was one of few Greek towns to preserve its language and customs under Roman rule. Paul's vessel touched it after having made a circuit from Syracuse (Acts 28:13). Mod. *Reggio di Calabria*. A2—17

Rheims. *See* Reims

Rhine R. River of mod. Germany that in ancient times formed the boundary between Gaul and Germany. It extends *ca*. 850 miles in a generally NW direction, emptying into the North Sea. B1—12; C1—18

Rhodes. Most easterly of the Aegean islands, off the

S coast of Caria, Asia Minor. It lost its independence to Alexander the Great but regained it after his death. Under the Romans it enjoyed a semiindependent status. The vessel in which Paul sailed from Assos to Palestine touched upon Rhodes (Acts 21:1). B3—2; B2—7, 15, 16; D3—17

Riblah. Town on the Orontes R., in the state of Hamath, 36 miles NW of Baalbek. It was the military headquarters of Necho (II Kings 23:33) and Nebuchadnezzar, who caused Hezekiah to be blinded there (II Kings 25:6–21). C2—6

Riga. City on the Gulf of Riga at the mouth of the W Dvina R., in mod. *Latvia*, U.S.S.R. It was founded A.D. 1201 and became a center for Christianity in the Baltic region.

Rimmon. Town in the territory of Zebulun (Josh. 19:13), 6 miles NE of Nazareth. It was assigned to the Levites (Josh. 21:35, "Dimnah"). Mod. *Rummaneh*.

Riphath. A people descended from Gomer (Gen. 10:3), thought to have lived on the S shore of the Black Sea. The name is similar to that of the Riphean Mts., supposed by the ancients to skirt the N shores of the world.

River of Egypt. *See* Egypt, River of

Rohoboth. *See* Rehoboth

Rome. City on the left bank of the Tiber, 16 miles from the Tyrrhenian Sea, in W-central Italy. The traditional date of its founding is 753 B.C. After an early period of incessant warfare, Rome became a republic and, later, the capital of a world empire. C2—12, 18; A1—17

Rouen. Ancient capital of Normandy, located near the mouth of the Seine, in N France. It has been an archiepiscopal see since the 5th century A.D.

Roxolani. Warlike people of European Sarmatia, settled on the banks of the Palus Maeotis (*q.v.*). They are thought to have been the ancestors of the Russians.

Royal Portico. Three-aisled colonnade at the S wall of the temple in Jerusalem. Its name was perhaps in remembrance of Solomon's royal quarters, which once occupied this area. B-C5—10

Ruben, allotment of. *See* Reuben, allotment of

Rubicon. Stream that formed the boundary between Italy and Cisalpine Gaul. When he crossed it (49 B.C.), Julius Caesar began the civil war. C2—12

Rugians. A Germanic people who lived along the Baltic coast between the Viadua and Vistula rivers.

Rumah. Town in Galilee that was the home of Pedaiah, grandfather of King Jehoiakim (II Kings 23:36). Poss. mod. *Kh. er-Rumeh*. C2—5

Russians. A Slavic people who settled in the area now known as Russia, beginning *ca.* the 9th century A.D.

S

Saba. *See* Sheba

Sabastiya. *See* Samaria

Sabratha. City of Africa Nova (Numidia) *ca.* 110 miles W of Leptis Magna.

Safad. Town in NE Israel, *ca.* 12 miles NW of the Sea of Galilee, at an elevation of 2,700 feet. During the 16th century it became a center for Jewish cabalistic studies.

Sagartians. Ancient inhabitants of Drangiana, one of the E districts of Media and Persia.

Sahara. Desert area of N Africa that extends from the Atlantic Ocean to the Nile, and from the Mediterranean to the Sudan, an area of 3,000,000 square miles.

Saida. *See* Sidon

Saint Albans. *See* Verulamium

Sais. Ancient Egyptian city in the W-central Nile Delta. It was the royal residence of pharaohs of the Twenty-sixth Dynasty and a shrine center for Neith and Osiris. B3—6, 7

Saka. F1—7. *See* Scythians

Salamina. *See* Salamis

Salamis. Ancient seaport on the E coast of Cyprus, visited by Paul on his First Missionary Journey (Acts 13:5). It was N of mod. *Famagusta*. A2—13; D5—14; E3—18

Saleah. *See* Salecah

Salecah. City of Bashan, on the boundary of the kingdom of Og and, later, the N boundary of the territory of Gad (I Chron. 5:11). It is 66 miles E of the Jordan, opposite Beth-shan. Mod. *Salkhad*. C4—4

Salecha. *See* Salecah

Salem. *See* Jerusalem

Salim. Town near which John the Baptist ministered (John 3:23). Eusebius located it 8 miles S of Scythopolis at mod. *Tell Radgah*. Others suggest the site of mod. *Salim*, 3.5 miles E of Nablus, near the springs of *W. Far'ah*. C4—11

Salkhad. *See* Salecah

Salmone, Cape. Cape that constitutes the NE extremity of Crete (Acts 27:7). Mod. *Cape Sidero*. D3—17

Salona. Capital of ancient Dalmatia. It was strongly fortified by the Romans and became a Roman colony. C2—18

Salonae. C2—12. *See* Salona

Salonika. *See* Thessalonica

Salt, Valley of. S continuation of the Jordan–Dead Sea Valley, now known as the *W. 'Araba*. It was the scene of victories of David (II Sam. 8:13–14) and Amaziah (II Kings 14:7) over the Edomites.

Salt Sea. C5—1, 5; D3—3; B5—4. *See* Dead Sea

Samaga. Town in Transjordan, *ca.* 4 miles W of Heshbon. After taking Medeba following a 6-month siege of the city, John Hyrcanus took Samaga for the Jews.

Samal. Aramean city-state in N Syria. It was also known as Ya'udi, mod. *Senjirli*, Turkey. Samal and other Aramean states flourished between 1000 and 700 B.C., after which they were absorbed into the Assyrian Empire.

Samaria (Sebaste), city of. Capital city of Israel (the Northern Kingdom), built by Omri (I Kings 16:24) on a hill 5.5 miles NW of Shechem in a fertile valley. It was rebuilt by Herod the Great and renamed Sebaste. Mod. *Sebastiyeh*. B3—1, 5, 19; B4—11

Samaria, district of. Area around Samaria (Sebaste) in the hill-country between Galilee (to the N) and Judea (to the S). Samaria was the geographical center of N.T. Palestine. B-C3—1; B-C4—11; B5—13

Samarkand (Maracanda). Oldest city of central Asia and chief city of Sogdiana (*q.v.*). Samarkand was on the ancient trade route between the Near East and China. It was conquered by Alexander and became a meeting place of W and Chinese culture.

Samos. Island of the Aegean Sea, off Ionia. Polycrates, tyrant of Samos, was put to death by the Persians during the reign of Cyrus. Subsequently, however, Samos regained its independence and remained Greek in culture. B2—16; D2—17

Samothrace. Small island opposite the mouth of the Hebrus R. in Thrace, inhabited by Pelasgians. It fought on the side of the Persians at Salamis (480 B.C.). Paul stopped there en route to Philippi during his Second Missionary Journey (Acts 16:11). B1—15

Sangarius R. River that flows from the highlands of NW Asia Minor in a generally E, then N direction, emptying into the Black Sea. Mod. *Sakarya*. C1—2

Sanhedrin. *See* Council House

Saphir (Shaphir). Town of Judah (Micah 1:11), tentatively located at mod. *es-Suwafir*, 3.5 miles SE of Ashdod.

Saphon. *See* Zaphon

Saraa. *See* Zorah

Sarafand. *See* Sarepta

Saragossa. *See* Caesarea Augusta

Sarangians. Ancient inhabitants of E Drangiana (*q.v.*).

Sarath-sahar. *See* Zareth-shahar

Sardica. City of Moesia (*q.v.*) on a plain watered by the Oescus R. A church council met there (A.D. 343). Mod. *Sofia*.

Sardinia. Large Mediterranean island S of Corsica and W of Italy. It was early known to the Greeks and colonized by Carthaginians. About 228 B.C. it, with Corsica, became a Roman province. B2—12, 18

Sardis. City of W Asia Minor at the foot of Mt. Tmolus on the E bank of the Hermes R., *ca*. 50 miles E of Smyrna. It was the capital of Croesus, the rich Lydian king, and was conquered (546 B.C.) by Cyrus of Persia. Later it fell successively to Alexander, Antiochus, and the Romans, who incorporated it into their province of Asia. It was 1 of 7 cities to which letters were addressed in the Revelation (Rev. 1:11). Mod. *Sart*, Turkey. B2—6, 15, 16; A2—7; D2—17; E3—18

Sarea. *See* Zorah

Sarepta (Zarephath). Town on the Mediterranean coast of Phoenicia 8 miles S of Sidon, 14 miles N of Tyre. Elijah spent time there (I Kings 17:8—24). C1—11

Sarid. Village on the S frontier of the territory of

Zebulun (Josh. 19:10, 12), in the N part of the Plain of Esdraelon, 5 miles SW of Nazareth. Mod. *Tell Shadud*.

Sarmatia. Name given by the Romans to the country in Europe and Asia between the Vistula R. and the Caspian Sea. Its people were called Sarmatians, or Sauromatae. D-E1—12

Sarohen. *See* Sharuhen

Saron, Plain of. *See* Sharon, Plain of

Sarus R. River that rises in the Anti-Taurus Mts. of E Turkey and flows 320 miles in a generally SW direction. It passes Adana before entering the Mediterranean. Mod. *Seyhan*, or *Sihun*.

Saxons. A Germanic people who, according to Ptolemy, inhabited the S portion of the Cimbrian Peninsula, the area now known as Schleswig, in the 2nd century. In A.D. 286 they appeared as pirates in the North Sea and the English Channel. They were associated with Angles and Jutes in the conquest of Britain. The Saxons who remained on the Continent, known as the Old Saxons, occupied NW Germany.

Scodra. Town on the Barbana R. in Illyricum. It was the strongly fortified capital of Gentius, the king of Illyricum who in 168 B.C. withstood Rome.

Scorpion Pass. *See* Akrabbim, Ascent of

Scythians (Saka). A people who inhabited the region N and NE of the Black Sea in the 7th century B.C., and who later invaded Assyria and Palestine. They spoke an Indo-European language, lived a nomadic life, and were skilled horsemen. They invaded the Balkan Peninsula and were attacked there both by Darius I and Alexander the Great, with no decisive results. In the 3rd century B.C. they were replaced by the Sarmatians, to whom they appear to have been related. D1—6; F1—7

Scythopolis. C3—11; B5—13; C2—19. *See* Bethshan

Sea of Adria. *See* Adria, Sea of

Sea of Azov. *See* Azov, Sea of

Sea of Galilee. *See* Galilee, Sea of

Sebaste. B4—11; B5—13; B3—19. *See* Samaria, city of

Sebastia. Important trading center in W Asia Minor. It was at the junction of important commercial roads during Roman times and was situated near copper mines. Mod. *Sivas*, Turkey.

Second Quarter (in Jerusalem). Quarter bounded by the First North Wall (*q.v.*) on the S, the temple on the E, and the Second North Wall on the N and W. B4-5—10

Sedada. *See* Zedad

Segor. *See* Zoar

Sehon, Kingdom of. *See* Sihon, Kingdom of

Seir. *See* Edom

Seir, Mt. *See* Edom

Sela (Petra). Ancient Nabatean city in the W. Musa (*q.v.*), noted for its buildings carved in the rocks. Ancient caravan routes passed through it, bringing it considerable wealth. D4—3; B6—4

Selcha. *See* Salecah

Seleucia (in Gaulanitis). Village NW of the Sea of

Galilee. It is reputed to have been built by Herod the Tetrarch.

Seleucia (Opis; in Mesopotamia). City on the Tigris, opposite Ctesiphon, N of Babylon. Built by Seleucus I of Syria (312–302 B.C.), it was captured by the Romans under Severus (A.D. 198) and fell into decay.

Seleucia (in Syria). See Seleucia Pieria

Seleucia Pieria. City located 5 miles from the mouth of the Orontes R. It was built on the site of an earlier town by Seleucus I and served as the seaport of Syrian Antioch (q.v.), which was 16 miles farther upstream. B2—13; D5—14

Seleucia Tracheotis. Town on the banks of the Kalykadnos R. in SE Asia Minor. It was founded by Seleucus I early in the 3rd century B.C. A1—13

Seleucid Empire. One of the empires that arose when, following the death of Alexander the Great, his kingdom was divided among his generals. Seleucus I was able to gain control of a large part of Asia Minor, all of Syria, and the E extremities of Alexander's conquest—as far as the Oxus and the Indus rivers.

Selinus. City in SW Cilicia, Asia Minor. Here Trajan died (A.D. 117) following his campaigns in the E. Near mod. Alanya, Turkey.

Semechonitis, Lake. C2—1. See Hula, Lake

Semeron. See Shimron

Semnones. A Germanic people that settled along the Albis (Elbe) in N-central Germany during the 1st century B.C.

Semron. See Shimron

Sepphoris. Town in Galilee, 4 miles by road NW of Nazareth. It is the traditional birthplace of Mary. It was the capital of Galilee during the early part of the reign of Herod Antipas (4 B.C.–A.D. 39). Although a Roman city (like Tiberias) during the time of Jesus, it became a Jewish center of Talmudic study following the destruction of Jerusalem. Mod. Saffuriyeh. C3—11; C2—19

Sequani. A Celtic people who, in the days of Caesar, occupied E Gaul (mod. Franche-Comte and most of Alsace).

Serbal, J. Mt. in the Sinai Peninsula, NW of J. Musa, the traditional Mt. Sinai. Certain ancient writers, including Eusebius and Jerome, identified J. Serbal with Sinai, regarding it as more in accord with the biblical description than J. Musa.

Serpent's Pool. Pool, or reservoir, W of the Upper City of Jerusalem in N.T. times. A6—10

Sevan, Lake. Lake in Armenia, S of the Cyrus R. and about midway between the Black and Caspian seas. It covers an area of ca. 546 square miles and is fed by about 30 streams. Its only outlet is the Zanga R., a tributary to the Araxes (q.v.).

Seville. See Hispalis

Shaphir. See Saphir

Sharon, Plain of. Palestinian coastal plain between Joppa and Mt. Carmel, extending E to the hills of Samaria. It was ca. 50 miles long and 10 miles

wide, and it was noted for its fertility. B3—1, 5; B4—11

Sharuhen. Town in S Palestine, in the territory of Simeon (Josh. 19:6). It was on the main N-S route between Palestine and Egypt. Prob. mod. Tell el-Far'ah on the Besor S of Gaza and W of Beer-sheba. A5—5

Shaveh-kiriathaim. See Kiriathaim

Sheba (descendant of Ham). Cushite Sheba (Gen. 10:7) may be located on the W side of the Persian Gulf.

Sheba (descendant of Shem). Semitic Sheba (Gen. 10:28) may have been one of the early settlers in SW Arabia. This was the home of a Semitic merchant people known as Sabeans, who operated camel caravans throughout the Middle East. The Queen of Sheba was one of their rulers (I Kings 10:1–13).

Shechem. Walled town in the hill-country of Ephraim (Josh. 20:7), near which Abraham camped (Gen. 12:6). It continued to be important in subsequent biblical history. Shechem lies in the upland valley bounded on the N by Mt. Ebal and on the S by Mt. Gerizim. It was a city of refuge (Josh. 20:7) and a Levitical city (Josh. 21:21). Mod. Tell Balata, SE of the later Roman city Nablus. C4—1, 5; D4—2; D2—3; B4—4; C3—19

Sheep Gate. Gate from the N suburb of Bethesda into the temple area of Jerusalem in N.T. times. It may be traced back to the 5th century B.C. when a Sheep Gate, at approximately the same location, was a means of access into the Mishneh quarter of Jerusalem.

Shephelah. Name given to the S part of the district between the hill-country of Palestine and the coastal plain. It was a region of low hills and included such strategic cities as Lachish, Debir, Libnah, and Beth-shemesh. B5—1

Shihor-libnath R. River that formed the S boundary of the territory of Asher (Josh. 19:26). Prob. mod. Nahr ez-Zerqa, 6 miles S of Dor and just N of Caesarea. It is not to be confused with the Jabbok, E of the Jordan, which has a similar Arabic name in contemporary use.

Shiloh. Town in Ephraim on the E side of the highway connecting Bethel with Shechem (Judg. 21:19). There the Israelites, under Joshua, set up the tabernacle. It served as the spiritual center of Israel before Jerusalem was occupied. It was evidently destroyed by the Philistines (Jer. 26:6) but subsequently rebuilt. Mod. Kh. Seilun. C4—1, 5; D3—3; C3—19

Shimron. Town in the territory of Zebulun (Josh. 19:15), which earlier had joined Jabin of Hazor in seeking to defeat Joshua (Josh. 11:1–5). Poss. mod. Kh. Sammuniyeh, 5 miles W of Nazareth.

Shinar. Alluvial plain of Babylonia, including the cities of Babel, Erech, and Akkad (Gen. 10:10; 11:2; Dan. 1:2). Amraphel was king of at least a large part of the region (Gen. 14:1, 9).

Shittim. C4—5. See Abel-shittim

Shocho(h). See Shoco

Shoco (Socoh). City in the low-country of Judah (Josh. 15:35). It was the site of a major battle with the Philistines (I Sam. 17:1) and was later fortified by Rehoboam (II Chron. 11:7). Mod. *Kh. Abbad*.

Shunat Nimrin. *See* Beth-nimrah

Shunem. Town in the territory of Issachar, 5 miles N of Mt. Gilboa, 3.5 miles NE of Jezreel. Elisha restored to life the son of a Shunammite woman (II Kings 4:8, 12). C3—5

Shur, Wilderness of. Region E of the Nile Delta and S of Palestine. After crossing the Red Sea the Israelites journeyed through this wilderness for 3 days (Exod. 15:22) before turning S into the Sinai Peninsula. B-C4—3

Shuruppak. Ancient Sumerian city, N of Erech in S Mesopotamia. It is mentioned as an old city at the time of the flood described in the Gilgamesh Epic.

Shushan. *See* Susa

Sicelag. *See* Ziklag

Sichem. *See* Shechem

Sicilia (Sicily). Largest island of the Mediterranean, occupying 9,928 square miles, separated from the mainland of Italy by the Straits of Messina. It was early colonized by Phoenicians, Carthaginians, and Greeks. Following the 1st Punic war it became a Roman colony (241 B.C.). C3—12

Sicily. A2—17; C3—18. *See* Sicilia

Siddim, Valley of. Valley where the kings from the area S of the Dead Sea fought against a coalition of kings from Mesopotamia (Gen. 14:3, 8). It is thought to have been the shallow part of the Dead Sea S of the Lisan Peninsula.

Sidon. Ancient Phoenician, or Canaanite, seaport (Gen. 10:15) on the Mediterranean coast, 22 miles N of Tyre. Sidon is mentioned in Scripture as the "firstborn" of Canaan (Gen. 10:15). Mod. *Saida*. C1—1, 11; D3—2, 15, 16; D1—3; B3—4; B1—5; B4—13; F3—17; E3—18

Sidonians. *See* Phoenicians

Sihon, Kingdom of. Sihon, the Amorite king, ruled the territory from the Arnon N to the Jabbok, and from the Jordan to the borders of Ammon. This territory was subsequently assigned to the tribes of Reuben and Gad, who desired it because of its excellent pastureland (Num. 21:21–34; 32:33).

Sihor Labanath R. *See* Shihor-libnath R.

Silo. *See* Shiloh

Siloah, Pool of. *See* Siloam, Pool of

Siloam, Pool of. Conduit on the SE side of Jerusalem that brought water from the Spring Gihon to a pool within the city. The pool was really a reservoir—58 feet long, 18 feet wide, and 19 feet deep—built of masonry. An inscription in the tunnel that leads to the pool was discovered in 1880. Written in pure Hebrew, it is known as the Siloam Inscription. C3—9; B6—10

Siloe, Pool of. *See* Siloam, Pool of

Simeon, allotment of. The tribe of Simeon was assigned land in the extreme S of Canaan in the midst of the inheritance of the children of Judah (Josh. 19:1–9). The 2 tribes made common cause against the Canaanites (Judg. 1:1, 3, 17).

Sin, city of. B3—3. *See* Pelusium

Sin, Wilderness of. Desert region through which the Israelites passed on their way from Elim to Mt. Sinai (Exod. 16:1; 17:1). Poss. mod. *Debbet er-Ramleh*. C5—3

Sinai, district of. C-D5—2. *See* Sinai Peninsula

Sinai, Mt. (Mt. Horeb). Mt. at the foot of which Israel encamped while Moses received the law (Exod. 20:1–24:8). Tradition suggests the mt. range in the S part of the peninsula, including J. Musa. Others, however, suggest J. Serbal (*q.v.*). C5—3

Sinai Peninsula. Peninsula between the Gulfs of Suez and Aqaba, the W and E arms of the Red Sea. C5—3

Singidunum. Town in upper Moesia at the junction of the Danube and Savas rivers. It served as headquarters for the Roman legion stationed in Moesia.

Sinope. Ancient city and seaport on the N coast of Asia Minor. It was founded by Milesian colonists during the 8th century B.C. and subsequently destroyed and rebuilt by the Cimmerians. During the 2nd century B.C. the city fell to Pontus. It was later taken by Rome and made a free city. C1—6; B1—7; E2—12; F1—17; E2—18

Sinus Arabicus. *See* Red Sea

Sippar. Ancient city in N Babylonia on the Euphrates. It is mentioned in the Sumerian King List as 1 of 5 cities existing before the flood. It was devoted to Shamash, the sun god, whose temple was located there. F3—2; D2—6; C2—7

Siraces. People of S Sarmatia, settled in the region N of the Caucasus Mts., between the Black and Caspian seas.

Sirmium. Ancient city of lower Pannonia. It was founded by the Taurisci and became the capital of Pannonia under the Romans. It also served as headquarters for the Romans in their wars with the Daci.

Siscia. Fortified town in upper Pannonia. It was captured by Tiberius, who is thought to have made it a colony. Later it was colonized by Septimus Severus.

Siut. Town of Egypt, *ca*. 250 miles S of mod. *Cairo*. Siut was known to the Greeks as Lycopolis ("wolf city") because it was the center of the worship of Anubis, a jackal-headed god. Tombs from the Thirteenth Dynasty are located in the hills W of Siut. Mod. *Asyut*.

Siwa. A3—7. *See* Amon, Temple of

Smyrna. Ancient city on the W coast of Asia Minor. After occupation by Aeolian Greeks and, later, Ionian Greeks, it was destroyed by Alyattes of Lydia (*ca*. 580 B.C.). Rebuilt by Alexander the Great, it became a flourishing commercial center and then part of the Roman province of Asia. It had 1 of the 7 churches addressed in the Revelation (Rev. 1:11). Mod. *Izmir*, Turkey. B2—15, 16; D2—17; D3—18

Soan. *See* Ramses

Soba. *See* Aram-zobah

Socchoth. *See* Succoth

Sochoh (in Sharon). *See* Socoh

Socoh (in Judah). *See* Shoco

Socoh (in Sharon). Town on the edge of the Plain of Sharon, NW of Samaria. It was in Solomon's 3rd district (I Kings 4:10). Mod. *Tell er-Ras*. B3—5

Sodom. One of the cities of the Plain of Jordan (Gen. 13:10). Lot chose it for a permanent settlement (Gen. 13:11–13) despite its evil reputation. Subsequently it was plundered by Chedorlaomer (Gen. 14:11) and destroyed in a cataclysmic judgment (Gen. 19:1–29). The ruins of Sodom are thought to lie beneath the S part of the Dead Sea. A mt. on the SE shore, *J. Usdum*, suggests the name of Sodom.

Sogdiana. NE sector of the Iranian Plateau, between the Oxus and Jaxartes rivers. It was invaded by Alexander the Great (*ca*. 327 B.C.). E-F2—7

Soli. *See* Pompeiopolis

Solomon's Porch. Colonnade at the E wall of the temple in Jerusalem. Jesus taught there (John 10:23) and Peter preached from there (Acts 3:11). C4-5—10

Sophene. Name of a district in the Armenian Mts., W of Lake Van, drained by the upper Tigris.

Sorec. *See* Sorek

Sorek, Valley of. Valley that begins *ca*. 13 miles SW of Jerusalem and extends in a generally NW direction to the Mediterranean, which it enters *ca*. 8.5 miles S of Joppa. Much of Samson's life was centered there. Mod. *W. es-Sarar* between Zorah and Timnah.

Sorek R. B4—1. *See* Sorek, Valley of

Spain (Hispania). Mod. name of the Iberian Peninsula in SW Europe (comprising Spain and Portugal). Its early inhabitants included Basques and Iberians. The peninsula was colonized by Phoenicians, Carthaginians, and Greeks. Roman victory over Carthage in the 2nd Punic war (218–201 B.C.) brought about the beginning of the Romanization of the peninsula, which continued until the 1st century A.D. A2—18

Sparta. Major city-state of S Greece, founded *ca*. 1100 B.C. Noted for its military efficiency, Sparta for a time (405–379 B.C.) exercised control over all Greece. Athens and Sparta were bitter rivals. A2—6, 7, 15, 16; C2—17

Spring Gihon. *See* Gihon, Spring

Strato's Tower. *See* Caesarea (in Palestine)

Subartu. Portion of Mesopotamia N of the Diyala R. inhabited by non-Semitic Subarians. About 1500 B.C. the Hurrians established their kingdom, Mitanni, in the same region. It was known to the Egyptians as Naharin. Arrapakha (*q.v.*) was their principal settlement, and Nuzi, its suburb, has provided significant archaeological materials.

Succoth (in Egypt). The first stopping place of the Israelites after leaving Ramses during the Exodus (Exod. 12:37; 13:20). *Succoth* means "booths," and it may have been a temporary encampment between Ramses and Etham. B4—3

Succoth (in Gad). Town E of the Jordan, 1.3 miles N of the Jabbok in the territory of Gad. Jacob sojourned there when returning from Mesopotamia (Gen. 33:17–22). It was on the

route of Gideon's army (Judg. 8:5–16). Near mod. *Tell Deir 'alla*. B4—4; C4—5; C3—19

Suez, Gulf of. W arm of the Red Sea (*q.v.*) separating Egypt from the Sinai Peninsula. The Suez Canal now connects this gulf with the Mediterranean. B5—3

Sumer. Ancient name of S Mesopotamia, the area N of the Persian Gulf. Non-Semitic Sumerians built city-states there during the 2nd and 3rd millenniums B.C. They were displaced by Semitic Amorites, who occupied the region after 2000 B.C. F4—2

Sunem. *See* Shunem

Sur. *See* Tyre

Sur, Desert of. *See* Shur, Wilderness of

Susa (Shushan). Ancient Persian city and the capital of Susiana. It was located along the Coaspes R. and served as the winter residence of the Persian kings. There Nehemiah served as cupbearer to Artaxerxes Longimanus (Neh. 1:1), and Esther was brought to Ahasuerus (Xerxes?) (Esther 2:5–7). G4—2; D3—6, 7

Susan. *See* Susa

Susiana. Province of the ancient Persian Empire, corresponding to mod. *Khuzistan*. Susa was the capital. *See also* Elam. D3—7

Sussita. *See* Hippos

Sychar. Town in Samaria in the vicinity of the land given by Jacob to Joseph (John 4:5; cf. Gen. 48:22). Poss. mod. *'Askar* on the E slope of Mt. Ebal, 1.8 miles NE of Nablus (Shechem) and .5 mile N of Jacob's Well. C4—11

Syene (Elephantine). Island near the 1st cataract of the Nile, opposite Aswan. In Persian times a Jewish military colony was settled there. B4—6; B3—7

Syracuse. Seaport of E Sicily. It was founded *ca*. 734 B.C. and became the chief Greek city of the island. It was captured and sacked by the Romans (214–212 B.C.). C3—12, 18; A2—17

Syria (Aram). The Greek term *Syria* is thought to be an abbreviation of *Assur(ia)*, applied to the territories of the Arameans, hence the English translation of "Syria" for *Aram*. The country of the Arameans extended W from the Lebanons to the area E of the Euphrates, S from the Taurus Mts. to Damascus and beyond. During the period of the Israelite monarchy, Syria consisted of a number of independent states. In N.T. times Syria was a Roman province, with Antioch serving as its capital. D1—5, 11, 19; C2—6; E3—12; C3—13; D5—14; D2—15, 16; F3—17, 18

Syrian Desert. N portion of the Arabian Desert, comprising the steppe country between Mesopotamia and Syria-Palestine. D3—4

Syrians (Arameans). A people whose ancestry is traced to Shem (Gen. 10:22–23). They are thought to have left Arabia shortly before the time of Abraham and to have settled in Aram. They established a number of states (cf. Aram-Damascus, Aram-zobah, Aram-Maacah, Geshur), some of which played an important part in O.T. history.

Syrtus Major. One of two gulfs on the N coast of

Africa, comprising parts of the Mediterranean. Syrtus Major was the E gulf.

Syrtus Minor. Gulf on the Mediterranean coast of Africa (cf. Syrtus Major). Syrtus Minor was the W gulf.

T

Taanach. Canaanite city (Josh. 17:11) in the Plain of Esdraelon 5 miles SE of Megiddo. Its king was defeated and slain by Joshua (Josh. 12:21). The battle between Barak and Sisera was fought near there (Judg. 5:19). Mod. *Tell Ta'annak*. D2—3; B4—4; B3—5; B2—19

Taanath-shiloh. Town on the border between Ephraim and Manasseh (Josh. 16:6), 7 miles SE of Shechem. Mod. *Kh. Ta'nah*.

Tabaqat Fahl. *See* Pella (in Gilead)

Taberah. Place in the wilderness where the Israelites murmured and were burned by fire from the Lord (Num. 11:1–3). C5—3

Tabgha. Town on the NW bank of the Sea of Galilee, bordered to the E by the Mt. of the Beatitudes. It is the traditional site of Jesus' multiplication of the loaves and fishes. C2—19

Tabigha. *See* Tabgha

Tabor, Mt. Mt. on the boundary of the territory of Issachar, 12 miles N of Mt. Gilboa, 5.5 miles SE of Nazareth. Forces of Zebulun and Issachar assembled there before battle with Sisera (Judg. 4:6, 12, 14). Mod. *J. et-Tur*. C2—1; C3—5, 11

Tadmor (Palmyra). Oasis 140 miles NE of Damascus and 120 miles S of the Euphrates. It was fortified by Solomon (II Chron. 8:4) to control the caravan routes. Under Queen Zenobia, Palmyra (the Roman name for Tadmor) became an independent state that temporarily defied Rome (A.D. 251–273). E3—2; D2—4; C2—7

Tagus R. Important river of Spain, rising in the territory of the Celtiberi (*q.v.*) and flowing W to the Atlantic. Lisbon (ancient Olisipo) stands at its mouth.

Tahpanhes. City in the Nile Delta on the Pelusiac branch. The Jews fled there following the murder of Gedaliah (Jer. 43:7–9). Poss. mod. *Tell Dafna*, 12 miles N of Pithom.

Tamar. Town at the E end of the S frontier of Palestine (Ezek. 47:19; 48:28). It was S of the Dead Sea. Poss. mod. *Thamara*, located on the road between Hebron and Elath. B5—4; B6—5

Tanais R. *See* Don R.

Tanis. A3—3. *See* Ramses

Taphnes. *See* Tahpanhes

Taphnis. *See* Tahpanhes

Tappuah. Town in the lowlands of Judah (Josh. 15:34). Prob. mod. *Beit Nettif*.

Tarentum. Ancient Greek city located in a fertile district of S Italy, founded (8th century B.C.) as a Spartan colony. It was taken by Rome (272 B.C.) but fell to Hannibal in the 2nd Punic war (212 B.C.). C2—12; B1—17

Tarichea. *See* Magadan

Tarraco. Ancient town on a high rock on the E coast of Spain, between the Iberus (Ebro) R. and the

Pyrenees. It was founded by colonists from Massilia and served as headquarters for Scipio during the 2nd Punic war (218 B.C.). B2—12

Tarraconensis. Roman province in N and E Spain. Its leading city was Tarraco (*q.v.*). A2—12

Tarragona. *See* Tarraco

Tarshish. Phoenician word meaning "smelting plant" or "refinery." One such Tarshish was Tartessus in S Spain, near Gibraltar. Another was in Cilicia, the later Tarsus (*q.v.*).

Tarsus. Chief city of Cilicia, SE Asia Minor, on the Cydnus R. 10 miles from the sea. It was a provincial capital during Roman times and was famed for its schools. Its most illustrious son was "Saul of Tarsus," later known as the apostle Paul (Acts 13:9). B2—6, 7; E3—12, 18; A1—13; D5—14; D2—15, 16; F2—17

Tatta, Lake. Salt lake in central Asia Minor that serves as the salt supply for the adjacent country. Mod. *Tuzgulu*.

Taurus Mts. Mt. chain paralleling the coast of S Asia Minor. It was crossed N of the Tarsus by means of the Cilician Gates (*q.v.*). An extension of the Taurus, across the Sarus R., is known as the Anti-Taurus. C-D2—19

Tavium. Important town in N Galatia, Asia Minor. The church there is known to have been founded before the Diocletian persecution (A.D. 304). Mod. *Bojuk Nefeskoi*, Turkey.

Taxila. Town in Gandara, in the Punjab of India. It was the E limit of the Persian Empire (*ca.* 500 B.C.). Alexander the Great passed through it (326 B.C.). F2—7

Tekoa. Town in Judah, 6 miles S of Bethlehem. It was fortified by Rehoboam (II Chron. 11:6) and was the home of Amos (Amos 1:1). Mod. *Taqu'a*. B5—5

Tel Aviv–Jaffa. *See* Joppa

Teleilat el-Ghassul. Site in the Transjordan, N of the Dead Sea and SE of Jericho. It has yielded artifacts from the Ghassulian culture (*ca.* 4500–3000 B.C.). C4—19

Tell Abu Matar. Chalcolithic site in the Negeb, near Beer-sheba. A5—19

Tell Ajjul. Mound S of mod. *Gaza* that was once a Hyksos stronghold. It has been tentatively identified as Beth-eglaim. A5—19

Tell 'Arad. B5—19. *See* Arad

Tell Asur. *See* Tell Azur

Tell Azur. One of the highest spots of Samaria, *ca.* 3,333 feet above sea level. It is located in the central mt. range *ca.* 20 miles S of Shechem. C4—1

Tell Beit Mirsim. B5—19. *See* Debir

Tell Brak. Site on Habor R. (*q.v.*) of the ancient town Brak, which was destroyed in 1400 B.C. Deported Israelites were settled in this region by several Assyrian kings (I Chron. 5:26; II Kings 17:6; 18:11). E2—2

Tell Deir 'alla. C3—19. *See* Succoth (in Gad)

Tell el-Amarna. C5—2; A6—3. *See* Akhetaton

Tell el-Far'a. A5—19. *See* Sharuhen

Tell el-Hesi. B4—19. *See* Eglon

Tell el-Judeideh. B4—19. *See* Moresheth-gath

Tell en-Nasbeh. B4—19. *See* Mizpah (in Ephraim)

Tell es-Safi. Mound 10 miles SE of Ekron and 10 miles E of Ashdod. It is one of several possible locations for Gath (*q.v.*). B4—19

Tell es-Saidiyeh. C3—19. *See* Zarethan

Tell es-Seba. Site of ancient Beer-sheba (*q.v.*). B5—19

Tell Halaf. E2—2. *See* Gozan

Tell Jemmeh. A5—19. *See* Gerar

Tema. Important caravan center in NW Arabia. Nabonidus, king of the New Babylonian Empire (555–539 B.C.), chose to live there rather than in Babylon for 10 years of his reign. E5—2; C3—6; B3—7

Temple (in Jerusalem). Temple built by Solomon in the 10th century B.C., destroyed by the Babylonians in 587 B.C., rebuilt by Zerubbabel in the 6th century B.C., torn down and rebuilt by Herod the Great late in the 1st century B.C., and destroyed by the Romans in A.D. 70. B2—8; D2—9; B5—10. pinnacle of the, C5—10

Tepe Gaura. *See* Tepe Gawra

Tepe Gawra. Mound NW of Nineveh that is the site of one of the earliest known village settlements. Excavations revealed a pre-Sumerian type of painted pottery. F2—2

Tepe Giyan. Mound in the Zagros Mts., S of the Choaspes R. It was the center of a highly developed Chalcolithic culture characterized by fine painted pottery. Near mod. *Nihavend*. G3—2

Tepe Siyalk. Mound in N Persia, S of the Caspian. Excavations there show a transition from a seminomadic way of life to a settled agricultural community. It produced painted pottery and had trade connections with the Persian Gulf area (*ca*. 3000 B.C.).

Thaanach. *See* Taanach

Thaanath-silo. *See* Taanath-shiloh

Thabera. *See* Taberah

Thabor, Mt. *See* Tabor, Mt.

Thalassa. *See* Lasea

Thamna. *See* Timnath-serah

Thamnata. *See* Timnah

Thamnath-sare. *See* Timnath-serah

Thaphsa. *See* Tiphsah

Thapphua. *See* Tappuah

Thapsacus. B2—7. *See* Tiphsah

Thapsus. Seaport in the Roman province of Africa, *ca*. 100 miles SE of Carthage. Caesar defeated Pompey there (46 B.C.), ending opposition in Africa.

Tharsis. *See* Tarshish

Thasos. Greek island in the N Aegean off the coast of Macedonia. Gold of Thasos was exploited by the Phoenicians.

Theater (in Jerusalem). Built by Herod the Great. It might have been located in the Tyropoeon Valley, though no remains of it have been discovered. B5—10

Thebes. C6—2; B3—6, 7; E4—12. *See* No

Thebez. Fortified town on the road to Beth-shan, 10 miles NE of Shechem. Abimelech, Gideon's son, was killed while besieging the town (Judg. 9:50).

Thecua. *See* Tekoa

Thecue. *See* Tekoa

Thermopylae. Pass in Greece, 9 miles SE of Lamia between the cliffs of Mt. Oeta and the morass on the shore of the Malic Gulf. It was the only gate for ingress into Greece from the N.

Thersa. *See* Tirzah

Thessalonica (Salonika). Ancient city of Macedonia first known as Therma. It was captured by the Athenians shortly before the Peloponnesian War (432 B.C.). Paul preached in a synagogue there (Acts 17:1–13). D2—12, 18; A1—15, 16; C1—17

Thiras. *See* Tiras

Thogorma. *See* Togarmah

Thrace. Region comprising the SE tip of the Balkan Peninsula in SE Europe. It was bounded by the Black Sea to the NE and the Sea of Marmara and Aegean Sea to the S. A1—7; D2—12, 18; B1—16; C1—17

Thracians. A group of tribes occupying Thrace. They spoke an Indo-European language; formed separate, petty kingdoms; and did not absorb Greek culture. A-B1—6

Three Taverns. Small station on the Appian Way, *ca*. 10 miles from the Forum of Appius and 30 miles from Rome. A1—17

Thuringians. Germanic tribe that occupied central Germany between the Elbe and Danube. It was conquered by the Franks in the 6th to 8th centuries A.D.

Thyatira. City of Lydia, Asia Minor. It was on the road from Pergamum to Sardis. Its inhabitants were known for skill in dyeing (cf. Acts 16:14). One of the 7 churches of Revelation was located there (Rev. 1:11). Mod. *Ackisar*. B1—15

Tiberias. City on the W shore of the Sea of Galilee. It is *ca*. 12 miles S of the entrance of the Jordan into the sea and 6 miles N of the Jordan's exit. It was established by Herod Antipas. C3—11; B5—13; C2—19

Tiberias, Lake. *See* Galilee, Sea of

Tieum. Greek colony on the S shore of the Black Sea, in ancient Phrygia.

Tigranocerta. Town in Armenia, S of Lake Van. The site of an Armenian defeat by the Romans in the 3rd Mithridatic war (74–64 B.C.).

Tigris R. River in SW Asia that rises in the Taurus Mts. and flows 1,150 miles SE before joining the Euphrates. The combined stream empties into the Persian Gulf. Biblical *Hiddekel*. F2—2; D2—6; C2—7

Til Barsip. Town on the Euphrates SE of Carchemish. It was capital of the state of Adini until captured by Shalmaneser and made an Assyrian provincial capital.

Timnah. Town in the Valley of Sorek on the N boundary of Judah, W of Beth-shemesh. It was occupied by the Philistines in the days of Samson (Judg. 14:2).

Timnath-serah. Village in the hill-country of Ephraim, given to Joshua as an inheritance (Josh. 19:50; 24:30). Poss. mod. *Tibnah*, 12 miles NE of Lod (Lydda).

Timsah, Lake. Lake in E Egypt N of the Gulf of Suez and the Bitter Lakes. The Suez Canal now passes through this part of Egypt.

Tingis. Town on the Strait of Gibraltar in Mauretania, NW Africa. A3—12

Tiphsah (Thapsacus). Town at the limit of Solomon's dominion toward the Euphrates (I Kings 4:24). Identified with Thapsacus on the right bank of the Euphrates above its junction with the Balikh. D1—4

Tiras. Land and its inhabitants, associated with the line of Japheth (Gen. 10:2). Traditionally associated with Thrace or the islands and coastlands of the Aegean.

Tirzah. Ancient Canaanite town captured by Joshua (Josh. 12:24). In the days of Jeroboam I it became capital of the Northern Kingdom (I Kings 14:17; 15:21, 33). Prob. *Tell el-Far'ah*, 7 miles NE of Shechem. C3—5, 19

Tishbe. Town in Gilead, mentioned as the home of Elijah (I Kings 17:1). Its location is uncertain. C3—5

Tob. Region E of the Jordan to which Jephthah fled when rejected by his brethren (Judg. 11:3, 5). B4—4

Togarmah (Beth-togarmah). N country (Ezek. 38:6) inhabited by a people descended from Japheth (Gen. 10:3). Poss. *Til-qarimmu* in E Cappadocia.

Toledo. City in central Spain on a granite hill surrounded on 3 sides by a gorge of the Tagus R. Known in ancient times as Toletum, it fell to the Romans in 193 B.C. It served later as a capital of the Visigoths and was the scene of several important church councils.

Toletum. *See* Toledo

Tolosa. *See* Toulouse

Tomb of Jesus. A4—10. *See* Holy Sepulchre, Church of the

Tomi (Constanta). Town on the W bank of the Black Sea. Constantine I founded Constanta near the site of ancient Tomi. It early became an episcopal see and is now the major Black Sea port of Romania.

Toulouse. City on the Garonne R. in S France. It was an important city before the Roman conquest of Gaul and became an episcopal see in the 4th century A.D.

Tours. City on the Loire R. in N-central France. An old Gallo-Roman town, it grew rapidly after the death of its bishop St. Martin (A.D. 397). It was a center of Christian culture during the Middle Ages.

Tower of Meah. *See* Meah, Tower of

Tower's Pool. Pool in NW Jerusalem—near Herod the Great's three towers (Hippicus, Mariamne, and Phasael)—that was fed by an aqueduct from the W. A5—10

Trachonitis. District in ancient Palestine beginning *ca*. 20 miles SE of Damascus and extending to Batanea and Auranitis. The region is rough and barren.

Transalpine Gaul. *See* Cisalpine Gaul

Trapezus (Trebizond). Port on the Black Sea, NE Asia Minor, founded in the 8th century by colonists from Sinope. C1—7; E2—12

Trebizond. *See* Trapezus

Treveri. A people of ancient Belgica. Allies of the Romans, the Treveri were noted for their cavalry. Their country extended from the Rhine to the Seine.

Trèves. *See* Trier

Trier (Trèves). Founded by Augustus, Trier was capital of the Roman province of Belgica. It was situated on the Moselle and was known in Roman times as Augusta Treverorum. C1—18

Tripolis. Ancient Phoenician city on the Mediterranean coast N of Byblos. In the 7th century B.C. it was the capital of a federation of Tyre, Sidon, and Aradus (Arvad). It flourished under the Seleucids and the Romans. B3—13

Troas. Seaport of Mysia in W Asia Minor. Paul saw a vision there of a man of Macedonia inviting him to Europe (Acts 16:8– 10). Located S of Homeric Troy. B1—15, 16; D2—17; D3—18

Trogyllium. Town on the W coast of Asia Minor opposite the island of Samos.

Troy. Ancient city of NW Asia Minor, also called Ilium or Ilion. It has been identified as the mound of Hissarlik, located *ca*. 4 miles from the mouth of the Dardanelles. It was made famous by Homer in the *Iliad*. B1—2

Tubal. Tribe descended from Japheth and settled near Meshech.

Turdetani. Ancient inhabitants of S Spain.

Turushpa (Tushpa). Town at the E end of Lake Van. It served as capital of the kingdom of Van (Urartu) and was frequently attacked by the Assyrian kings.

Tushpa. *See* Turushpa

Tuz, Lake. Salt lake that occupies a vast depression in the center of the Anatolian plateau, central Asia Minor. C2—2

Tyana. Town of ancient Cappadocia, Asia Minor, at the N foot of the Taurus Mts.

Tyras. City on the NW shore of the Black Sea at the mouth of the Tyras R.

Tyras R. River that rises in the Carpathians in E Europe and flows SE to the Black Sea.

Tyre (Sur). Phoenician maritime city 22 miles S of Sidon on the Mediterranean coast. Hiram, king of the city-state of Tyre, provided David and Solomon with materials for the palace and temple (II Sam. 5:11; I Kings 5:1). B1—1, 5, 11; D3—2, 15, 16; D2—3; B3—4; B2—6, 7; B4—13; F3—17; C1—19

Tyre, Ladder of. *See* Ladder of Tyre

Tyropoeon Valley. B2—8; B6—10. *See* Central Valley

Tyrrhenian Sea. Part of the W Mediterranean, bounded by the W coast of Italy, the N coast of Sicily, and the E coast of Sardinia and Corsica. A2—17

U

Ubi. Name given to the region of Damascus (*q.v.*) in the Amarna Age (14th century B.C.).

Ugarit. Ancient city-state on the Mediterranean coast in N Syria. It was an important center of Minoan trade in Syria. The period of its greatest prosperity was the 15th and 14th centuries B.C. Mod. *Ras Shamra.* D3—2; B1—4

Ulai (Eulaeus) R. Artificial canal near Susa. On its banks Daniel saw his vision (Dan. 8:2, 16). D3—7

Ulatha. Name used by Josephus to designate the marshlands around Lake Hula (*q.v.*). C-D2—11

Umma. Ancient Sumerian city of S Mesopotamia. It was NW of, and at times subject to, Lagash (*q.v.*). Mod. *Yokha.*

Upper City (in Jerusalem). SW Jerusalem, built on the Western Hill and bounded on the E by the Central Valley and on the N by the First North Wall. B5—10

Upper Egypt. *See* Egypt, Upper

Upper Galilee. *See* Galilee, upper

Upper Room (in Jerusalem). Room in which Jesus and the apostles ate the Last Supper (Mark 14:15; Luke 22:12). Its location has not been identified. The traditional site—located above the Tomb of King David and next to a Benedictine monastery—was not identified until the 14th century A.D. B6—10

Upper Sea. A-C3—2; A-B2—7. *See* Mediterranean Sea

Ur. Important Sumerian city on the Euphrates in S Mesopotamia. It is identified with the home of Abraham, known in the Bible as "Ur of the Chaldees." Mod. *el-Muqaiyar.* G4—2; D3—6

Urartu. Ancient kingdom of Armenia, located E of Asia Minor in the region of Lake Van. It was in the mts. of Urartu or Ararat that the ark settled following the flood. E-F2—2; C-D2—6

Urmia, Lake. Shallow salt lake in NW Iran. G2—2; C2—7

Uruk. *See* Erech

Utians. Ancient inhabitants of Carmania, the country E of Persia and NE of the Arabian Sea.

Utica. African city *ca.* 15 miles N of Carthage. It became the capital of the Roman province of Africa following the 3rd Punic war.

Utrecht. City in the Netherlands, on a branch of the lower Rhine. It dates back to Roman times and became (7th century A.D.) an episcopal see for Willibrord, apostle to the Frisians.

Uxellodunum. Town of the Cadurci tribes in S Gaul.

Uzal. District of SW Arabia settled by the clan of Uzal, a descendant of Shem.

V

Vaccaei. A people of Hither Spain, living W of the Celtiberi and S of the Cantabri.

Vagarshapat. Town of central Armenia, located between the Black and Caspian seas. It dates from the 6th century B.C. and was capital of Armenia

from the 2nd to the 4th century A.D. Mod. *Echmiadzin.*

Valencia. Former kingdom on the Mediterranean coast in E Spain. It was a mountainous country with fertile coastal plain. The capital of the kingdom, later a Roman province, was also named Valencia (or Valentia).

Valentia. *See* Valencia

Valley Gate. (1) Gate into the City of David (*ca.* 1000 B.C.) from the NW. (2) Gate into Jerusalem (*ca.* 445 B.C.) from the Hinnom Valley into the SW sector of the city.

Valley of Aijalon. *See* Aijalon, Valley of

Valley of Elah. *See* Elah, Valley of

Valley of Gerar. *See* Gerar, Valley of

Valley of Hinnom. *See* Hinnom Valley

Valley of Salt. *See* Salt, Valley of

Valley of Siddim. *See* Siddim, Valley of

Valley of Sorek. *See* Sorek, Valley of

Van, Lake. Salt lake in the Armenian mt. territory SE of the Black Sea. It covers 1,454 square miles and has no apparent outlet. F2—2; C2—7

Veneti. A Celtic people of ancient Gaul who settled in NW France.

Verona. City on the Adige R. in NE Italy, on the Brenner Road to central Europe.

Verulamium (Saint Albans). City on the slope and summit of a hill above the Ver R. NW of London.

Vesontio. City of the Sequani in E Gaul.

Vienne. City on the Rhone, S of Lyons, in SE France. B2—18

Vistula R. Principal waterway of Poland. It rises in the Carpathians and flows 667 miles N to the Baltic. In ancient times it formed the boundary between Germany and Sarmatia.

Volga R. F1—12. *See* Rha R.

W

Washuk-kanni. Capital of Mitanni (*q.v.*). Its precise location is still in question, but it was prob. near Gozan in the upper Habor area. Poss. mod. *Tell Fakhariyah.* E2—2

Water Gate. Gate into the old City of David W of Spring Gihon in the Kidron Valley (*ca.* 445 B.C.). C3—9; C6—10

Water shaft (in Jerusalem). Jebusite tunnel system designed to bring water from Spring Gihon into the city. David used it to enter the city and defeat the Jebusites (II Sam. 5:8 RSV). B2—8

Way of the Sea, The. Most lucrative trade route between Egypt and Mesopotamia. It followed the coastal plain (Philistia) through Palestine. B-C3—3

Way to Shur, The. Road from the Judean highlands to Egypt, passing through Beer-sheba and the Wilderness of Shur. B-C4—3

W. el-Hasa. *See* Zered R.

W. el-Mughara. Site N of Dor where remains of Stone Age men have been discovered. B2—19

Western Hill (in Jerusalem). The most commanding

of the several hills on which Jerusalem was built. It is bounded on the W and S by the Hinnom Valley and on the E by the Central Valley. In post-Roman times it was known as Mt. Zion. A2—8; C2—9

Wilderness of Etham. *See* Etham, Wilderness of

Wilderness of Paran. *See* Paran, Wilderness of

Wilderness of Shur. *See* Shur, Wilderness of

Wilderness of Sin. *See* Sin, Wilderness of

Wilderness of Zin. *See* Zin, Wilderness of

W. Musa. River bed that extends E from the Petra region of S Jordan. It is dry most of the year.

X

Xanthus. City in Lycia, W Asia Minor, on the Xanthus (Scamander) R. B2—7

Xois. City in the Nile Delta on an island. It was the seat of a dynasty of Egyptian pharaohs but fell into decay during Roman times.

Xystus. Market place in the NE section of Jerusalem's Upper City (20 B.C.–A.D. 70).

Y

Yarmuk R. River that rises in the Hauran, SE of Mt. Hermon. It flows SW and enters the Jordan S of the Sea of Galilee. C2—1; C3—5, 11

Yavne Yam. B4—19. *See* Jabneel

Yazd. Ancient Persian city *ca.* 165 miles SE of Gabae. D3—7

Yiron. *See* Iron

York. City at the confluence of the Ouse and Foss rivers in N England. As Eboracum, it was a chief station of the Roman province of Britannia.

Yusha', J. Mt. in Gilead, S of the Jabbok R. It reaches a height of 3,652 feet. D4—1

Z

Zabulon. *See* Zebulun

Zadrakarta. Important city in the Persian province of Hyrcania (*q.v.*). D2—7

Zagros Mts. Range in W Iran E of the Tigris, extending from NW to SE in several parallel ridges. F-G3—2

Zanoah. Town in S Palestine (Josh. 15:34; Neh. 3:13; 11:30), located 15 miles W of Bethlehem.

Zaphon. City E of the Jordan in the territory of Gad (Josh. 13:27).

Zareah. *See* Zorah

Zared R. *See* Zered R.

Zarephath. *See* Sarepta

Zarethan. Town in Transjordan that was one source

of metal vessels for the Jerusalem temple (I Kings 7:46). Poss. mod. *Tell es-Saidiyeh* or *Tell Umm Hamad.* C3—19

Zareth-shahar. *See* Zereth-shahar

Zarqa R. D4—1. *See* Jabbok R.

Zebulun, allotment of. Territory in N Palestine bounded on the S by Manasseh and Issachar; on the N and W by Naphtali; and on the E by Asher. The Kishon R. and the Plain of Jezreel touched its S border.

Zedad. City on the N boundary of Palestine (Num. 34:8). It has been identified with Sadad, SE of Hamath. C2—4

Zela. Ancient city of Pontus, NE Asia Minor. It was the site of Caesar's defeat of Pharnaces, king of Pontus (47 B.C.).

Zelea. Ancient city of Mysia, NE Asia Minor. It was the headquarters of the Persian army during Alexander's invasion.

Zemaraim. Town in the territory of Benjamin (Josh. 18:22). Prob. mod. *Ras ez-Zeimara*, N of Jerusalem. C4—5

Zered R. (W. el-Hasa). Brook (and valley) that the Israelites crossed en route to Canaan through E Palestine (Num. 21:12; Deut. 2:13–14). It served as the border between Edom and Moab, SE of the Dead Sea. C6—1, 5; D3—3

Zereth-shahar. Town on the E bank of the Dead Sea in the territory of Reuben (Josh. 13:19).

Ziklag. Town in S Judah (Josh. 15:31), at one time ruled by David as a vassal of the Philistine king Achish (I Sam. 27:6). Prob. mod. *Tell el-Khuweilifeh*, between Debir and Beer-sheba. B5—4, 5

Zilu. Town on the NW edge of the Nile Delta and on The Way of the Sea. Mod. *Tell Abu Seifah.* B4—3

Zin, Wilderness of. Wilderness SW of the Dead Sea, close to the S border of Canaan (Num. 13:21). It was part of the Wilderness of Paran (*q.v.*) and included the city of Kadesh-barnea. C3-D4—3

Zion. *See* Jerusalem

Ziph. Town 4 miles SE of Hebron in the hill-country of Judah (Josh. 15:55). It was fortified by Rehoboam (II Chron. 11:8). Mod. *Kh. ez-Zif.* B5—5

Zoan (Avaris). C4—2. *See* Ramses

Zoar. One of the cities of the plain (Gen. 19:20, 22). It was associated with Sodom and Gomorrah. Lot fled there after Sodom's destruction (Gen. 19:20–22). It was located S of the Dead Sea. D3—3; C6—5

Zobah. *See* Aram-zobah

Zorah. Town in Dan on a hillside overlooking the Sorek (*q.v.*). It was the birthplace of Samson (Judg. 13:2, 25) and was later fortified by Rehoboam (II Chron. 11:10). B4—5

INDEX
OF MODERN PLACE NAMES

The modern place names found in this index are mentioned in the gazetteer descriptions, but do not appear as separate entries in the gazetteer. This index is a guide to the specific gazetteer entries in which the modern place names are mentioned.

A

'Abarah. *See* Bethabara

Ackisar. *See* Thyatira

Adalia. *See* Attalia

Afyonkarahisar. *See* Nicopolis (in Asia Minor)

Aghri Dagh. *See* Ararat, Mt.

'Ain Duq. *See* Dok

'Ain el-Weiba. *See* Oboth

'Ain Hajlah. *See* Beth-hoglah

'Ain Hawara. *See* Marah

'Ain Ibl. *See* En-hazor

'Ain Jalud. *See* Harod

'Ain Jidi. *See* En-gedi

'Ain Khudra. *See* Hazeroth

'Ain Qadeis. *See* El Qusaima *and* Kadesh-barnea

'Ain Sitti-Mariam. *See* Gihon, Spring

Alanya. *See* Selinus

Alasheher. *See* Philadelphia (in Asia Minor)

Alexandretta. *See Issus*

Al-Faiyum. *See* Crocodilopolis

Algiers. *See* Icosium

Alisar. *See* Ankuwa

Al-Iskandariya. *See* Alexandria (in Egypt)

Al-Jauf. *See* Dumah (in Arabia)

Alsace. *See* Sequani

'Amman. *See* Amman

Amu Darya. *See* Oxus R.

'Amwas. *See* Emmaus

'Anata. *See* Anathoth

Ancheylo. *See* Anchialus

Antakya. *See* Antioch (in Syria)

Appio, Foro. *See* Appius, Forum of

'Aqir. *See* Ekon

'Araq el-Menshiyeh. *See* Gath

Ararah. *See* Aroer (in Judah)
Aras R. *See* Araxes R.
Ashnunein. *See* Hermopolis
'Askalon. *See* Ashkelon
'Askar. *See* Sychar
As-Sallum. *See* Catabathmus
Astrakhan. *See* Itil
Aswan. *See* Ethiopia
Asyut. *See* Siut
Azerbaijan. *See* Albania

B

Baghdad. *See* Eshnunna
Balkh. *See* Bactra
Barce. *See* Barca
Beirut. *See* Berytus
Beit-hakerem. *See* Beth-haccherem
Beitin. *See* Bethel
Beit Lahm. *See* Bethlehem
Beit Naballa. *See* Neballat
Beit Nettif. *See* Tappuah
Beit Ras. *See* Capitolias
Beit 'Ur el-Foqa. *See* Beth-horon
Beit 'Ur et-Tahta. *See* Beth-horon
Bengasi. *See* Berenice (in Cyrenaica)
Bereitan. *See* Berothai
Bergama. *See* Pergamum
Beyrouth. *See* Berytus
Bir Ayyub. *See* En-rogel
Bir Ja'qub. *See* Jacob's Well
Bojuk Nefeskoi. *See* Tavium
Bone. *See* Hippo Regius
Brindisi. *See* Brundisium
Brittany. *See* Armorica
Burgas. *See* Apollonia (in Thrace)
Burj el-Isaneh. *See* Jeshanah
Burjes-Sur. *See* Beth-zur
Buseira. *See* Bozrah
Busr el-Hariri. *See* Bosor

C

Cadiz. *See* Gades
Candia. *See* Cnossus
Canea. *See* Cydonia
Cankiri. *See* Germanicopolis
Cape Krio. *See* Cnidus
Ceyhan R. *See* Pyramus R.
Chodjend. *See* Alexandria Eschate
Constantine. *See* Cirta

Cordoba. *See* Corduba
Cordova. *See* Corduba
Corfu. *See* Corcyra
Crotone. *See* Croton

D

Debbet er-Ramleh. *See* Sin, Wilderness of
Dembre. *See* Myra
Der'a. *See* Edrei
Dinar. *See* Celaenae
Dura. *See* Adoraim

E

Echmiadzin. *See* Vagarshapat
Ed-Domeh. *See* Dumah (in Judah)
Eilat. *See* Elath
El-Al. *See* Elealeh
El-'Arba'in. *See* Modin
El-'Azariyeh. *See* Bethany
El-Bire. *See* Beeroth
El-Burj. *See* Dor, city of
El-Haditheh. *See* Hadid
El-Jib. *See* Gibeon
El-Kerak. *See* Kir-hareseth
El-Khalil. *See* Hebron
El-Kirmil. *See* Carmel
El-Kuds. *See* Jerusalem
El-Midyah. *See* Modin
El-Muqaiyar. *See* Ur
Endor. *See* En-dor
Erbil. *See* Arbela (in Assyria) *and* Gaugamela
Eregli. *See* Heraclea
Er-Ram. *See* Ramah (in Benjamin)
Er-Rameh. *See* Ramah (in Naphtali)
Er-Rameh, Plain of. *See* Galilee, lower
Er-Ruheibeh. *See* Rehoboth
Esdud. *See* Ashdod, city of
Es-Eskihisar. *See* Laodicea
Esh-shaghur. *See* Galilee, lower
Esh-Sham. *See* Damascus, city of
Eskisehir. *See* Dorylaeum
Es-Salt. *See* Jazer
Es-Semu'. *See* Eshtemoa
Es-Suwafir. *See* Saphir
Et-Taiyibeh. *See* Ephraim, city of, *and* Ophrah (in Issachar)
Et-Tell. *See* Achshaph, Ai, *and* Bethsaida-Julias
Euros R. *See* Hebrus R.
Ez-Zib. *See* Achzib

F

Famagusta. *See* Salamis
Fasa'il. *See* Phasaelis
Feinan. *See* Punon
Fiq. *See* Aphek (in Transjordan)
Franche-Comte. *See* Sequani

G

Gallilpoli. *See* Anxa
Gaudos. *See* Cauda
Gediz R. *See* Hermes R.
Gelemish. *See* Patara
Ghazzeh. *See* Gaza
Gniezno. *See* Gnesen
Gozzo. *See* Cauda
Gulek Bogaz. *See* Cilician Gates

H

Hadhramaut. *See* Hazarmaveth
Hama. *See* Hamath, city of
Hamadan. *See* Ecbatana
Hamman-Tabariyeh. *See* Hammath
Hari R. *See* Aria
Hesban. *See* Heshbon
Homs. *See* Emesa

I

Ibn Ibraq. *See* Bene-berak
'Id el-Ma. *See* Adullam
Iksal. *See* Chesulloth
Indur. *See* En-dor
Ipsili Hissar. *See* Ipsus
Isfahan. *See* Gabae
Ishan Bahriyat. *See* Issin
Iskanderun. *See* Alexandria (in Syria) *and* Issus
Izmir. *See* Smyrna
Izmit. *See* Astacus

J

Jeba'. *See* Geba
J. Dahy. *See* Moreh, Hill of
J. en-Neba. *See* Nebo, Mt., *and* Pisgah, Mt.
J. et-Tor. *See* Gerizim, Mt.
J. et-Tur. *See* Tabor, Mt.
J. Hauran. *See* Auranitis
J. Jermaq. *See* Meron, Mt.
J. Murr. *See* Baal-zephon
J. Usdum. *See* Sodom

Jenin. *See* En-gannim
Jerabish. *See* Carchemish
Jerablus. *See* Carchemish

K

Kabul. *See* Cabul
Kafr 'Ana. *See* Ono
Kafr Kenna. *See* Cana
Kali Limines. *See* Fair Havens
Karkheh R. *See* Choaspes R.
Karnak. *See* No
Kaukab el-Hawa. *See* Agrippina
Kavalla. *See* Neapolis (in Macedonia)
Kayseri. *See* Caesarea Mazaca
Kefr Saba. *See* Capharsaba
Keissariyeh. *See* Caesarea (in Palestine)
Kerman. *See* Carmania
Kesla. *See* Chesalon
Khabur R. *See* Habor R.
Khania. *See* Cydonia
Kh. Abbad. *See* Shoco
Kh. 'Abde. *See* Abdon
Kh. 'Addaseh. *See* Adasa
Kh. 'Anab. *See* Anab
Kh. 'Ar 'ir. *See* Aroer (in Moab)
Kh. Attarus. *see* Ataroth (in Moab)
Kh. 'Attir. *See* Jattir
Kh. Batneh. *See* Betonim
Kh. Beidus. *See* Narbata
Kh. Beit Sakaria. *See* Beth-zacharias
Kh. Dajun. *See* Beth-dagon
Kh. el-Kheishum. *See* Makkedah
Kh. el-Khokh. *See* Etam
Kh. el-Mefjir. *See* Gilgal
Kh. el-Muqanna'. *See* Eltekeh
Kh. el-Musheirefeh. *See* Misrephoth-maim
Kh. el-Qureiyat. *See* Kiriathaim
Kh. er-Rumeh. *See* Rumah
Kh. et-Tubeiqeh. *See* Beth-zur
Kh. ez-Zif. *See* Ziph
Kh. ez-Zurra'. *See* Gath-hepher
Kh. Hasireh. *See* En-hazor
Kh. Ibziq. *See* Bezek
Kh. Il'asa. *See* Elasa
Kh. Irbid. *See* Arbela (in Palestine)
Kh. Jazzri. *See* Jazer
Kh. Jefat. *See* Jotapata
Kh. Jel'ad. *See* Mizpah (in Gilead)
Kh. Kerazeh. *See* Chorazin

Kh. Mahneh. *See* Mahanaim
Kh. Mejdel. *See* Magadan
Kh. Nefa'a. *See* Mephaath
Kh. Qana. *See* Cana
Kh. Qila. *See* Keilah
Kh. Sammuniyeh. *See* Shimron
Kh. Seilun. *See* Shiloh
Kh. Selma. *See* Capharsalama
Kh. Ta'nah. *See* Taanath-shiloh
Kh. Umm el-Idham. *See* Jahaz
Kh. Umm er-Rammin. *See* En-rimmon
Kh. Yamma. *See* Jabneel (in Naphtali)
Kh. Yarmuk. *See* Jarmuth
Khonai. *See* Colossae
Khorsa-bad. *See* Dur Sharrukin
Khuzistan. *See* Susiana
Kirkuk. *See* Jarmo
Kizil Irmak. *See* Halys R.
Konya. *See* Iconium
Kos. *See* Cos
Kultepe. *See* Kanish
Kura R. *See* Cyrus R.
Kursi. *See* Gergesa

L

La Coruna. *See* Brigantium
Larnaca. *See* Kition
Latakia. *See* Laodicea ad Mare
Latvia. *See* Riga
Lebda. *See* Leptis Magna
Loutro. *See* Phoenix
Lubban *See* Lebonah
Ludd. *See* Lod
Luxor. *See* No

M

Mahay. *See* Ije-abarim
Ma'in. *See* Baal-meon
Makran. *See* Gedrosia
Malataya. *See* Melitene
Maras. *See* Marqash
Menchah. *See* Ptolemais (in Egypt)
Merjayun. *See* Ijon
Mishash. *See* Hormah
Mosul. *See* Nineveh
Mukhmas. *See* Michmash
Muqeis. *See* Gadara (in Decapolis)
Murtana. *See* Perga

N

Nablus. *See* Neapolis (in Palestine)
Nahr Barada. *See* Abana R.
Nahr ez-Zerqa. *See* Shihor-libnath R.
Naqb es-Safa. *See* Akrabbim, Ascent of
Naqura. *See* Ladder of Tyre
Neochori. *See* Amphipolis
Nihavend. *See* Tepe Giyan
Nikolayev. *See* Olbia

O

Oqair. *See* Gerrha

P

Pollina. *See* Apollonia (in E Macedonia)
Port Said. *See* Pelusium
Poti. *See* Phasis

Q

Qala'at el-Mudiq. *See* Apamea
Qala'ah Sherqat. *See* Ashur
Qamm. *See* Camon
Qana. *See* Kanah
Qantir. *See* Ramses
Qarn Sartabeh. *See* Alexandrium
Qatra. *See* Cedron *and* Gederoth
Qiryatein. *See* Hazar-enan

R

Rabbah. *See* Areopolis
Ramet el-Khalil. *See* Mamre
Ras el-'Ain. *See* Antipatris *and* Capharsaba
Ras el-Kharrubeh. *See* Anathoth
Ras es-Siagha. *See* Pisgah, Mt.
Ras ez-Zeimara. *See* Zemariam
Ras Shamra. *See* Ugarit
Ras Umm et-Tala'. *See* Nob
Reggio di Calabria. *See* Rhegium
Rentis. *See* Arimathea
Riha. *See* Jericho
Rioni. *See* Phasis
Romania. *See* Dacia
Ruad. *See* Arvad
Rummaneh. *See* Rimmon
Ruweis el-Ebeirig. *See* Kibroth-hattaavah
Ruyuk Menderes. *See* Maeander R.

S

Saffuriyeh. *See* Sepphoris
Sahem el-Jolan. *See* Golan
Saida. *See* Sidon
Sakarya R. *See* Sangarius R.
Salkhad. *See* Salecah
Samsun. *See* Iris R.
Sart. *See* Sardis
Sebastiyeh. *See* Samaria, city of
Senjirli. *See* Samal
Serabit el-Khadim. *See* Dophkah
Seyhan R. *See* Sarus R.
Sidero, Cape. *See* Salmone, Cape
Sihun R. *See* Sarus R.
Sivas. *See* Sebastia
Sofia. *See* Sardica
Sousse. *See* Hadrumetum
Syr Darya. *See* Jaxartes R.

T

Tabaqat Fahl. *See* Pella (in Gilead)
Takht-i-Jamshid. *See* Parsa
Tanturah. *See* Dor, city of
Taqu'a. *See* Tekoa
Tehran. *See* Rhagae
Tekirova. *See* Phaselis
Tell Abil. *See* Abel *and* Abila (in Batanea)
Tell Abu Zeitun. *See* Gath-rimmon
Tell 'Amar. *See* Harosheth
Tell 'Ana. *See* Anat
Tell 'Arad. *See* Arad
Tell 'Ashtara. *See* Ashtaroth
Tell Asmar. *See* Eshnunna
Tell 'Atshaneh. *See* Alalakh
Tell Balata. *See* Shechem
Tell Basta. *See* Pibeseth
Tell Beit Mirsim. *See* Debir
Tell Bel 'ameh. *See* Ibleam
Tell Bileibil. *See* Beth-nimrah
Tell Dafna. *See* Tahpanhes
Tell Deir 'alla. *See* Succoth (in Gad)
Tell Dibbin. *See* Ijon
Tell Dotan. *See* Dothan
Tell ed-Damieh. *See* Adam
Tell ed-Der. *See* Agade *and* Akkad
Tell ed-Duweir. *See* Lachish
Tell el-Amarna. *See* Akhetaton
Tell el-Ash'ari. *See* Dion
Tell el-'Azeimeh. *See* Beth-jeshimoth
Tell el-Azhar. *See* Kiriath-jearim

Tell el-Bedeiwiyeh. *See* Asochis
Tell el-Far'ah. *See* Sharuhen *and* Tirzah
Tell el-Ful. *See* Gibeah
Tell el-Hosn. *See* Beth-shan
Tell el-Ifshar. *See* Hepher
Tell el-Judeideh. *See* Moresheth-gath
Tell el-Kheleifeh. *See* Ezion-geber
Tell el-Khuweilifeh. *See* Ziklag
Tell el-Maqlub. *See* Jabesh-gilead
Tell el-Maskhuta. *See* Pithom
Tell el-Melat. *See* Gibbethon
Tell el-Milh. *See* Moladah
Tell el-Mishrifeh. *See* Qatna
Tell el-Mutesellim. *See* See Megiddo, city of
Tell el-'Oreimeh. *See* Chinnereth
Tell el-Qadi. *See* Dan, town of
Tell el-Qedah. *See* Hazor
Tell en-Nasbeh. *See* Mizpah (in Ephraim)
Tell Erfad. *See* Arpad
Tell er-Rameh. *See* Betharamphtha
Tell er-Ras. *See* Socoh (in Sharon)
Tell el-Rumeileh. *See* Beth-shemesh
Tell esh-Sheikh-Madhkur. *See* Adullam
Tell es-Safi. *See* Gath *and* Libnah
Tell es-Saidiyeh. *See* Zarethan
Tell es-Sa'wi. *See* Jeshua
Tell es-Sultan. *See* Jericho
Tell Fakhariyah. *See* Washuk-kanni
Tell Halaf. *See* Gozan
Tell Hariri. *See* Mari, city of
Tell Hum. *See* Capernaum
Tell Ibrahim. *See* Cuthah
Tell Iqtanu. *See* Bethramphtha
Tell Jawah. *See* Maphaath
Tell Jemmeh. *See* Gerar
Tell Jezer. *See* Gezer
Tell Kefireh. *See* Chephirah
Tell Kefrein. *See* Abel-shittim
Tell Kurdaneh. *See* Aphek (in Asher)
Tell Ma'in. *See* Maon
Tell Mimas. *See* Beth-emek
Tell Miqdad. *See* Mageth
Tell Nebi-Mend. *See* Kadesh
Tell Nimrim. *See* Beth-nimrah
Tello. *See* Lagash
Tell Qeimun. *See* Jokneam
Tell Radgah. *See* Salim
Tell Sandahanna. *See* Mareshah
Tell Shadud. *See* Sarid
Tell Sheikh edh-Dhiab. *See* Ataroth (in Ephraim)

Tell Shesubar. *See* Agade
Tell Ta'annak. *See* Taanach
Tell Umm Hamad. *See* Zarethan
Tell Zakari-yeh. *See* Azekah
Tel Qasila. *See* Qasile
Thaimilet es-Suweilmeh. *See* El Kuntilla
Thamara. *See* Tamar
Tibnah. *See* Timnath-serah
Til-qarimmu. *See* Togarmah
Transylvania. *See* Dacia
Tunis. *See* Carthage
Tuzgulu. *See* Tatta, Lake

U

Umm Deimneh. *See* Madmannah
Umm el-Awamid. *See* Hammon
Umm Qeis. *See* Gadara (in Decapolis)
Urfa. *See* Edessa

V

Verria. *See* Beroea

W

W. 'Araba. *See* Arabah, Paran R., *and* Salt, Valley of
W. el-'Eshsh. *See* Alush
W. er-Rababi. *See* Hinnom Valley

W. es-Sant. *See* Elah, Valley of
W. es-Sarar. *See* Sorek, Valley of
W. Far'ah. *See* Salim
W. Gharandel. *See* Elim
W. Qanah. *See* Kanah R.
W. Qelt. *See* Cherith, Brook
W. Refayid. *See* Rephidim
W. Yabis. *See* Cherith, Brook

Y

Yakuk. *See* Hukkok
Yalo. *See* Aijalon
Yalovatch. *See* Antioch (in Pisidia)
Yarkon R. *See* Kanah R.
Yarun. *See* Iron
Yatta. *See* Juttah
Yavne Yam. *See* Jabneel (in Judah)
Yebna. *See* Jabneel (in Judah)
Yesil Irmak. *See* Iris R.
Yokha. *See* Umma
Yorghan Tepe. *See* Nuzi

Z

Zer'in. *See* Jezreel
Zoldera. *See* Lystra
Zosta. *See* Derbe

Index

A

Aaron, 74, 75, 87
Abana R., 133, 149
Abarim Mts., 76
Abbas, 234
Abdullah, 243
Abel-meholah, 103
Abel-mizraim, 62
Abgar, 232
Abigail, 127
Abilene, 186, 187
Abimelech, 58
Abner, 131
Abraham, 37, 42, 43, 44, 50, 55, 56, 57, 58, 59, 60, 61, 69, 79, 82, 131, 142
Absalom, 56, 60, 134
Accho (see also Acre), 136, 184, 220, 239, 265
Accho, Plain of, 25, 102
Aceldama, 145
Achaia, 215, 219
Achan, 89
Achsah, 90
Achshaph, 136
Ackisar, 226
Acra, 142
Acre, 235, 239
Acre, Bay of, 220, 239
Acropolis, 215
Actium, Battle of, 178, 186
Adab, 266
Adalia, 212
Adam, 55
Adamah, 136
Aden, Gulf of, 14
Admah, 56
Adon, 265
Adoni-bezek, 90
Adonijah, 135
Adoni-zedek, 89
Adriatic Sea, 214, 219
Adullam, 126, 127
Aegean Sea, 40, 80, 82, 167, 207, 214, 218, 219, 220
Aegina Gulf, 216
Aelia Capitolina, 141, 231
Aelius Hadrianus, 141
Aeneas, 204
Aeolic Greeks, 225
Aesculapium, 268
Aesculapius, 220
Afghanistan, 234
Africa, 13, 14, 16, 41, 65, 136, 178
Agabus, 220
Agag, 125
Aggada, 41

Agri Dagh, 17
Ahab, 58, 150, 151, 152, 254
Ahasuerus, 167
Ahaz, 50, 149, 157
Ahimelech, 126
Ai, 89, 258
'Ain Hawara, 74
'Ain Khudra, 75
'Ain Qadeis, 75
'Ain Sitti Mariam, 141
Ajalon, 30, 89
Akhenaten, 265, 266
Akkad, Akkadian, 47, 48, 82
Alalakh, 262
Alashehir, 227
Albright, W. F., 80, 255, 256, 261
Albright Institute, 260
Aleppo, 244, 245
Alexander Jannaeus, 174
Alexander (of Macedon), 52, 67, 73, 82, 167, 171, 208, 215, 219, 220, 225, 254
Alexandria (Egypt), 67, 73, 171, 172, 218, 232, 234, 247
Alexandria (Syria), Alexandrette, 212
'Alma, 133
Alps, 177
Alyattes, 38
Amalek, 69
Amalekites, 44, 57, 69, 74, 75, 101, 102, 125, 128
Amanus Mts., 17, 212
Amarna Tablets, 42, 43, 131
Amasis II, 164
Amaziah, 154
Amenhotep III, 258
Amenhotep IV (Akhenaten), 265
American School of Classical Studies, 216, 269
American Schools of Oriental Research, 255, 256, 260, 262, 266
Amman, 79, 260
Ammon, Ammonites, 79, 84, 87, 88, 101, 103, 104, 124, 125, 133, 158
Amnon, 134
Amon, 158, 159
Amon, Temple of, 67
Amon-Re, 171
Amorites, 37, 42, 48, 49, 62, 75, 82, 83, 87, 131
Amos, 154
Amphipolis, 213, 214
Anabasis, 167
Anakim, 80

Anamim, 41
Anatolia, 268
Anaximander, 220
Ancyra, 212, 248
Andrew, 197
Angista R., 214
Ankara, 248
Anna, 98, 191
Anshan, 20, 52, 164
Antakya, 245
Antigonus I (Cyclops), 172
Antigonus, son of Aristobulus, 178, 185
Anti-Lebanon Range, 16, 17, 31, 125
Antioch (in Pisidia), 209, 211, 212
Antioch (in Syria), 202, 204, 210, 212, 218
Antiochus III, 177, 202, 225
Antiochus IV (Epiphanes), 172, 174
Antiochus VII, 173
Antipas (see also Antipater), 184
Antipater, 151, 174, 178
Antipatris (Aphek), 221
Anti-Taurus Range, 20
Antonia, Tower of, 220
Antony, 178, 185, 213, 214
Aphek (in Ephraim), 104, 128, 221
Aphek (in Geshur), 151
Aphrodite, 210, 269
Apollo, 220
Appian Way, 222
Appii Forum, 222
Aqaba, Gulf of, 15, 43, 57, 67, 68, 69, 70, 75, 87, 136, 152, 157
Aquila, 207, 216, 218
Arab, Arabia, 13, 15, 41, 56, 59, 80, 87, 136, 203, 260, 261
Arabah, 68, 127, 136
Arabia Petraea, 179, 188
Arabian Desert, 149, 179
Arabian Peninsula, 14, 16
Arad, 33, 96
Aram, Aramaeans, 14, 20, 43, 44, 101, 125, 149, 153
Aram-maachah, 133
Aram Naharaim, 20, 56
Aram-zobah, 133
Ararat, 13, 17
Araunah, 134, 142, 145
Archelaus, 186
Archias, 222
Arculf, 61
Areopagus, 216

Aretas, 186, 188
Ariel, 141
Arimathaea, 123
Aristarchus, 221
Aristobulus II, 174, 178, 185
Arkite, 42, 43
Armenia, 13, 15, 17, 19, 38, 167, 179, 207
Arnon R., 29, 42, 75, 87, 101, 103, 154, 184
Aroer, 103
Arphaxad, 43
Arqa, 43
Artaxerxes I, 52, 167
Artaxerxes II, 167
Artaxerxes III, 221
Artemis, 210, 218, 226, 268
Arvad, Arvadite, 42, 43, 158
Asa, 149
Asahel, 131
Ascanios, 38
Ascension, Mt. of, 142, 145
Ashdod, 31, 80, 104, 158
Asher, 98, 136
Ashkelon, 82, 254, 265
Ashkenaz, 38
Ash-Shara Mts., 70
Ashtaroth, 57
Ashur, 15, 49, 263
Ashurbanipal, 40, 50, 67, 158, 159
Asia, 14, 40, 44, 178, 208, 216, 225
Asia Minor, 13, 15, 17, 20, 37, 38, 42, 44, 49, 50, 52, 82, 178, 210, 267, 268
'Askar, 196
Asshur (see also Assyria), 43
Assos, 219
Assyria, Assyrians, 14, 15, 17, 19, 37, 38, 40, 41, 43, 44, 47, 50, 52, 67, 80, 149, 150, 154, 157, 158, 209, 263
Astarte, 218
Astyages, 164
Aswan, 16, 41, 247
Atbara, 16
Athaliah, 152, 153
Athena, 222
Athens, 167, 214, 215, 216, 269
Athlit, 235
Atossa, 167
Attalia, 210, 212
Attalus I, 178, 225
Attalus III, 225
Atys, 44
Augustus, 178, 186, 211, 213, 214
Aurelian, 135, 180
Avaris, 66, 73
Avim, 80
Awil-Marduk, 164
Azekah, 126, 254, 258
Azotus (see also Ashdod), 202

B

Baal, 56, 58, 73, 151, 152, 153
Baalbek, 186
Baal-peor, 76
Baal-zephon, 73
Baasha, 150
Babel, Tower of, 41
Babylon, Babylonia, 14, 16, 19, 38, 41, 43, 47, 48, 49, 52, 67, 70, 150, 154, 157, 158, 160, 163, 164, 172, 263
Bactria, 168, 171, 232
Badè, F. W., 255
Baghdad, 15, 48, 234, 235, 245, 264
Balaam, 75, 76, 87
Baldwin, 234
Balfour Declaration, 236, 241
Balikh R., 55
Bana-yamina, 262
Banias, 26, 28
Banks, E., 263
Barak, 97, 98, 102
Barnabas, 203, 204, 210, 212
Bartholomew, 193, 232
Bashan, 20, 33, 75, 79, 87, 95, 149
Basra, 245
Bath-sheba, 135
Beatitudes, Mt. of, 32
Beeroth, 89
Beer-sheba, 31, 58, 59, 75, 96, 133
Behistun Inscription, 267
Beirut, 245
Beisan (Beth-shan), 235
Beitin, 61, 256
Beit Jibrin, 126
Belshazzar, 52, 164
Ben-hadad, 149, 151, 152
Benjamin, 62, 96, 101, 104, 132, 150, 183
Beqa'a Valley, 16, 18, 31
Berea, 214, 215, 219
Bered, 59
Bermius, Mt., 214
Bethabara, 193
Bethany, 197, 198
Bethany (beyond Jordan), 193
Beth-bara, 103, 104
Bethel, 56, 60, 61, 89, 96, 104, 150, 256
Bethesda, 142
Beth-horon, 89
Bethlehem, 61, 79, 82, 132, 191, 239, 244
Beth-palet, 256
Bethphage, 142
Beth-rehob, 133
Bethsaida, 186, 194, 196
Beth-shan, 79, 80, 97, 103, 128, 184, 192, 235, 255
Beth-shemesh, 104, 154, 255

Beth Yerah, 258
Beth-zur, 256
Bezer, 98
Bezetha, 142
Bîr Ayyûb, 141
Birs Nimrûd, 41
Bismaya, 263
Bithynia, 38, 178, 207, 210, 212, 288
Bitter Lakes, 68, 73, 74
Black Sea, 167, 207
Bliss, F. J., 146, 251, 254
Bogaskoy, 267
Bokhàra, 234
Botta, P. E., 263
Bozrah, 70
Braidwood, R., 262
Breasted, J. H., 13, 261
Britain, British, 179, 180, 232, 236, 239, 246, 254
British Museum, 239
Brutus, 213, 214
Buseirah, 70
Byblos (Gebal), 80, 158, 245, 265
Byzantium, Byzantine Empire, 180, 233, 235, 248

C

Cabul, 136
Caesar, Julius, 151
Caesarea (Philippi), 26, 186, 197
Caesarea (Stratonis), 14, 186, 187, 201, 204, 218, 221, 231
Cairo, 17, 67, 234, 239, 247
Caleb, 80, 90
Caligula, 179, 187
Callaway, Joseph, 258
Callias, 167
Calneh, 17
Calvary, 198
Cambyses, 19, 52, 165
Cana, 193
Canaan, 13–34, 42, 50, 56, 59, 60, 79–84, 87–92 *et passim*
Canaanites, 14, 37, 42, 47, 75, 80, 82, 102, 131, 197
Canopic Branch (Nile), 17, 65, 67
Capernaum, 192, 194
Caphtor, Caphtorim (Crete), 41, 42, 80, 221
Cappadocia, 37, 42, 179, 209
Car, 44
Carchemish, 13, 20, 50, 52, 75, 82, 160, 163, 261
Caria, 44, 207, 212
Carmel, Mt., 14, 25, 32, 79, 104, 183, 192, 201
Carter, Howard, 266

Carthage, 20, 38, 80, 177
Casluhim, 41, 42
Caspian Sea, 13, 14, 17, 245
Cassandra, 214
Cassius, 184, 185, 213, 214
Castor and Pollux, Temple of, 222
Caucasus Mts., 37, 80, 158
Cauda, 222
Cenchrea, 216, 218
Chaldeans, Chaldean Empire, 50, 52, 158
Champollion, J. F., 264
Chebar R., 163
Chedorlaomer, 19, 79
Chemosh, 84
Chephirah, 89
Cherethites, 134
Chiera, E., 263
Chinnereth, 29
Chios, 219
Chittim, 40
Christ, Christianity, 40, 55, 231
Church of the Holy Sepulchre, 146, 198
Cicero, 210, 220
Cilicia, 40, 138, 204, 209, 220
Cilician Gates, 17, 202, 209, 212, 218
Cimmerians, 158
Cities of Refuge, 95, 98
Clauda (Cauda), 222
Claudius, 179, 187, 216
Cleopatra, 178
Cnidus, 209, 221
Coastal Plain, 79, 80, 131, 132
Coele Syria, 17
Coenaculum, 198
Cogamus R., 227
Colossae, 210
Constantine, 141, 208, 232
Constantinople (see also Byzantium, Istanbul), 180, 235
Coos (Cos), 220
Corinth, 215, 216, 218
Cornelius, 201, 204
Corsica, 177
Cos (Coos), 220
Crete, Cretans, 42, 80, 134, 221
Crimaean War, 240
Crispus, 216
Crocodile R., 30
Croesus, 44, 164, 208, 227, 268
Crowfoot, J. M., 258
Crusaders, 234, 235, 239
Cumae, 222
Cumont, F., 261
Cunaxa, 167
Cush, Cushites, 40, 41, 75, 151
Cushan-rishathaim, 101
Cyaxeres, 50, 158
Cybele, 226
Cydnus R., 202
Cynoscephalae, 177

Cyprus, 40, 158, 167, 210, 212, 234
Cyrus, 19, 38, 44, 52, 154, 164, 166, 208
Cyrus the Younger, 167

D

Dacia, 179
Dagon, 104
Dalmatia, 218
Damascus, 20, 44, 50, 57, 61, 95, 98, 133, 136, 138, 149, 151, 192, 202, 203, 233, 234, 244
Dan, 26, 28, 57, 92, 96, 104, 150, 183
Danel, 15
Daniel, 15, 40, 79, 160, 163
Danites, 57, 104
Danube, 178, 232
Danunim, 40
Dardanelles, 208
Dardanians, 40
Darius the Great, 52, 166, 167
Darius III, 168, 169
Daroma, 183
David, 14, 42, 43, 56, 58, 60, 70, 80, 82, 87, 88, 96, 98, 102, 126, 127, 128, 150, 191
David's Tower, 146
Dead Sea, 15, 26, 29, 30, 42, 57, 62, 68, 69, 70, 79, 84, 103, 127, 133, 134
Debir, 89, 90, 92, 255
Deborah, 97, 102
Decapolis, 184, 192, 197, 198
Dedan, 41
Demeter, 268
Demetrius, 219
Demetrius II, 173
Demetrius III, 168, 171, 174
de Morgan, J., 266
Der'a, 87
Deuteronomy, 16
de Vaux, R., 259
Diala R., 264
Diana, 218, 219, 268
Dibon, 150, 152
Diodorus, 40
Dion, 184
Dionysius, 219
Diospolis, 227
Djoser, 67, 265
Dodanim, 38, 40
Dome of the Rock, 15
Dophkah, Oasis of, 68
Dorcas, 201, 204
Dothan, 61, 260
Dung Gate, 151
Dura Europus, 232, 261
Dussaud R., 261

E

Ebal, Mt., 32, 56, 60, 89, 97, 196
Ecbatana, 124, 171
Ecole Biblique, 240, 259
Eden, 44
Edessa, 232
Edom, Edomites, 57, 68, 69, 70, 75, 79, 101, 125, 133, 135, 150, 151, 157, 188, 258
Edrei, 75, 87
Eglon, 89, 101, 102, 136, 254
Egnatian Way, 214
Egypt, Egyptians, 13, 14, 16, 17, 22, 40, 41, 43, 50, 52, 56, 59, 62, 65–67, 68, 70, 73, 75, 80, 133, 136, 138, 157, 167, 171, 191, 192, 221, 233, 239, 247, 264–266
Egypt, River of (see also *Wadi el-'Arish*), 134
Ehud, 102
Eilat, 242
Ekron, 82, 104, 158
Elah, Valley of, 31, 126
El Alamein, 247
Elam, Elamites, 17, 19, 43, 49, 154, 157
Elasa, 173
Elat, Elath, 26, 57, 70, 154, 242
el-'Azarîyeh, 197
El-berith, 256
Elephantine, 16, 41
Eleutheropolis, 126
Eli, 126
Eliakim, 255
Elijah, 58, 151
Elim, 68, 74
Elimelech, 84
Elisha, 98
Elishah, 38
el-Jîb, 131, 260
el Kuds, 141
el-Muqaiyar, 263
El-Paran, 57
el-Qadi, 92
Eltekeh, 158
Elymas, 210
Emim, 79
En-dor, 98, 128
En-gedi, 57, 127
En-mishpat, 57
Ephes-dammim, 126
Ephesus, 209, 218, 219, 220, 225, 228, 268
Ephraim, Ephraimites, 69, 96, 103, 104, 128, 138, 198
Ephraim, Mt., 26, 97, 123
Ephrath (see also Bethlehem), 61
Ephron, 42, 56, 59, 82
Erastus, 216
Eridu, 47
er-Râha, 74

er-Râm, 123
Esarhaddon, 37, 50, 67, 158, 261
Esau, 56, 59, 69, 70, 79, 82
Esdraelon, Valley and Plain of, 18, 25, 26, 33, 34, 96, 98, 131, 184, 186, 192, 220
Eshnunna, 47
Eshtaol, 92, 104
Essenes, 259
Etham, Wilderness of, 68, 73
Ethbaal, 261
Ethiopia, Ethiopians, 16, 40, 75, 151, 202
Etruscans, 40, 177
et-Taiyibeh, 102, 198
et-Tell, 196, 258
Eumenes II, 225
Euphrates R., 14, 15, 16, 47, 48, 50, 55, 67, 70, 82, 135, 149, 179
Euraquilo, 221
Euroclydon, 221
Europe, 13, 14, 52
Eusebius, 126
Eutychus, 219
Evil Counsel, Hill of, 145
Evil Merodach, 164
Exile, 133, 163–165
Exodus, 73–76
Ezekiel, 163
Ezion-geber, 135, 136, 152, 154, 157, 258–259
Ezra, 167

F

Fair Havens, 221, 222
Fatimids, 234
Felix, 221
Fertile Crescent, 14, 16, 19, 43, 47, 49, 50, 52, 55, 101
Fisher, Clarence S., 255
Fitzgerald, G. H., 255
Flavian Emperors, 179
Forest of Ephraim, 134
France, 240, 244
Frankfort, Henri, 264
Free, Joseph P., 260
Fuad I, 247
Fustat, 234

G

Gad, 76, 89, 95, 126
Gadara, 184, 196
Gagia, 38
Galatia, 178, 207, 209, 210, 212
Galilee, 136, 149, 151, 184, 188, 231
Galilee, Sea of, 15, 29, 57, 82, 90, 103
Gallio, 216, 218

Gamaliel, 203
Gangites R., 213
Garstang, John, 254, 258, 261
Gath, 82, 104, 126, 132, 153
Gaugamela, 168, 171
Gaul, 178, 180, 232
Gaza, 25, 59, 69, 80, 82, 104, 151, 171, 202, 239, 254, 256
Gaza Strip, 247
Geba, 104, 125
Gebal (see also Byblos), 43
Gedaliah, 160
Gehenna, 30, 145
Ge-Hinnom (see also Gehenna), 145
Genesareth, 196
Georgia, 232
Gephissus, 215
Gerar, 59, 80, 96, 255, 256
Gerasa (see also Jarash), 125, 184, 196
Gergesa, 196
Gerizim, 32, 56, 60, 89, 174, 183
German Palestine Society, 240
Germany, 179
Gesenius, W., 261
Geshur, 44, 134
Gethsemane, 198
Gezer, 80, 88, 254, 260, 265
Gibeah, 123, 126, 255
Gibeon, Gibeonites, 82, 89, 96, 131, 260
Gibraltar, 40
Gideon, 102, 103
Gihon, Spring, 135
Gilboa, Mt., 32, 102, 128, 183, 192
Gilead, Gileadites, 29, 57, 79, 87, 103, 153, 192
Gilead, Mt., 32
Gilgal, 88, 89, 123, 124
Gimirrai, 37
Girgasite, 37, 42, 82
Giza, 265
Glueck, Nelson, 70, 125, 258
Golan, 98
Golan Heights, 242
Goliath, 80, 126
Gomer, 37
Gomorrah, 56
Gordius, 210
Gordon's Calvary, 198
Goshen, 62, 65, 67, 68, 73
Gospel of Thomas, 266
Gospel of Truth, 266
Granicus R., 171
Grant, Elihu, 255
Greece, Greeks, 17, 37, 38, 40, 42, 44, 49, 52, 166, 171, 188, 215, 216, 219, 268, 269
Greek Orthodox Church, 240
Gulloth-illith, 90
Gulloth-mayim, 90
Gulloth-tachtith, 90

Guy, P. L. O., 255
Gyges, 38

H

Habakkuk, 40
Habor R. (Khabur), 48, 154, 263
Hadad, 138
Hadadezer, 133
Hadassah Hospital, 142
Hadramaut, 41, 44
Hagar, 59, 68
Haifa, 14, 32, 240
Haik, 38
Halicarnassus, 171, 209
Hall, H. R., 263
Halys R., 42, 167, 207, 209
Ham, 37, 44, 57, 65, 79
Hama, 244
Haman, 167
Hamath, 16, 42, 43, 80, 149, 244
Hamathite, 42, 43
Hammurabi, 19, 20, 42, 43, 48, 49, 50, 83, 163, 262
Hannibal, 177
Hanukkah, 173
Haran, 13, 50, 55, 56, 60, 159
Harding, G. Lankester, 258, 259
Hareth, Forest of, 126, 127
Harosheth, 102
Harper, R., 263
Hasmonaeans, 151, 173
Hattin, Horns of, 32, 196, 234
Hattushash, 49, 267
Hauran, 33
Havilah, 40, 41, 44
Hazael, 153
Hazarmaveth, 44
Hazeroth, 75
Hazezon-tamar, 57, 127
Hazor, 79, 89, 90, 102, 136, 260
Hebrew, 38, 48
Hebrew Union College, 260
Hebrew University, 142, 260
Hebron, 26, 42, 57, 58, 59, 60, 61, 62, 69, 75, 80, 82, 89, 98, 127, 128, 131, 134, 151, 153, 239, 244
Helam, 133
Helena, 141, 198
Heliopolis, 67
Hellenism, 171–174
Hellespont, 167, 171, 208
Hercules, Pillars of, 40
Hermon, Mt., 17, 57, 96, 133, 149, 196, 201, 202
Hermus R., 226
Herod Agrippa I, 187
Herod Agrippa II, 187, 188, 221
Herod Antipas, 186

Herod Archelaus, 260
Herod the Great, 146, 151, 174, 178, 184, 185, 186, 197, 254
Herodotus, 40, 67
Hesban R., 95
Heshbon, 82, 87, 95, 104, 260
Hetep-heres, 266
Hezekiah, 157, 158
Hiddekel, 15
Hierapolis, 210
Hinnom, Valley of, 30, 142, 145, 157
Hippicus, 146
Hippocrates, 220
Hippos, 184
Hiram, 98, 135, 136, 261
Hittites, 16, 20, 42, 49, 50, 80, 82, 89, 210, 261, 267
Hivites, 42, 43, 82, 89
Hobah, 57
Homer, 37, 38, 40, 67, 219
Homs, 244
Hor, Mt., 75
Horeb, Mt., 69, 74
Horites (Hurrians), 43, 69, 82, 89, 263
Hormah, 75, 90, 96
Horn, Sigfried, 260
Horus, Way of, 73
Hosea, 154
Hula Lake, 29, 89, 133, 183
Hur, 74
Hurrians (Horites), 50, 70, 79, 80, 82, 89, 263
Hyksos, 50, 66, 67, 255
Hyrcanus, John, 151, 173, 174, 186
Hyrcanus II, 174, 178

I

Ibleam, 97
Iconium, 209, 211, 218
Idumaea, Idumaeans, 69, 70, 151
Iliad, 40
Ilissus, 215
Ilium, 208
Illyria, Illyricum, 171, 178, 219
Imhotep, 67
India, 14, 232, 234
Indian Ocean, 14
Indus R., 166, 234
Inge, Charles, 258
Ionians, 38, 219
Ipsus, 172
Iran, 13, 14, 43, 245, 246, 266, 267
Iraq, 15, 16, 245
Isaac, 55, 56, 59, 60, 61, 70
Isaiah, 50, 157
Ish-bosheth, 60, 128, 131
Ishmael, 160
Ishtar, 262

Islam, 233, 235
Israel, Israelites, 14, 38, 40, 42, 43, 44, 55–61, 149, *et passim*
Israel Exploration Society, 259, 260
Issachar, 97, 98, 102
Issus, 167, 171, 212
Istanbul (see also Constantinople, Byzantium), 248
Italy, 40, 216
Izmir, 225

J

Jabbok R., 29, 61, 87, 103
Jabesh-gilead, 125, 128
Jabin, 89, 102
Jacob, 29, 42, 56, 59, 60, 61, 62, 70, 82, 97, 103
Jael, 102
Jaffa (see also Joppa), 14, 25, 240
Jahaz, 75, 83, 87
James, 187, 203
Japheth, 37, 40
Jarash (see also Gerasa), 125, 196
Jarmo, 263
Jarmuth, 89
Javan, 37, 38
Jaxartes R., 166
Jeba', 125
Jebeil (see Byblos)
Jebel ed-Druz, 244
Jebel en-Neba, 33, 76
Jebel Makmal, 18, 37
Jebel Musa, 69, 74
Jebel Yarmuk, 26, 32
Jebus, Jebusites, 37, 42, 82, 131, 142
Jehoahaz, 160
Jehoiachin, 160, 164, 255
Jehoiada, 153
Jehoiakim, 160
Jehoram (Joram), 151, 183
Jehoshaphat, 70, 152
Jehu, 151, 153
Jephthah, 95, 103, 133
Jeremiah, 38, 160, 163
Jericho, 26, 30, 33, 62, 79, 88, 89, 96, 101, 102, 150, 254, 260
Jeroboam I, 60, 138, 151, 256
Jeroboam II, 43, 154, 254
Jerome, 126
Jerusalem, 41, 42, 43, 50, 52, 58, 59, 61, 70, 79, 80, 82, 87, 88, 89, 96, 104, 131, 132, 133, 135, 141–146, 153, 178, 184, 185, 191, 192, 218, 219, 220, 221, 231, 233, 239, 242
Jeshimon, 127
Jesus, 142, 146, 191–198
Jewish Agency, 242

Jezebel, 58, 98, 151
Jezreel (see also Esdraelon), 96, 98, 102, 103, 128, 136
Jiljiliyeh, 124
Joab, 14, 131, 134, 141
Joash, 151, 153
Job, 141
John the Baptist, 186, 193
Jonathan, 128
Jonathan (the Maccabee), 173
Joppa (Tel Aviv—Jaffa), 14, 80, 104, 136, 150, 201, 204, 231, 239
Jordan, Hashemite Kingdom, 243–244
Jordan River and Valley, 26, 28, 29, 60, 69, 75, 82, 83, 84, 87, 88, 101, 197, 242
Joseph, 61, 97, 138, 260
Joseph (N.T.), 191
Josephus, 38, 187, 192
Joshua, 42, 73, 74, 82, 88, 89, 90, 95, 101, 102, 125
Josiah, 159
Jotapata, 194
Jotham, 157
Judaea, Judaeans, 75, 80, 151, 163, 166, 178, 183, 231
Judah, 41, 47, 60, 67, 70, 96, 104, 127, 131, 149, 150, 157–160
Judah, Wilderness of, 193
Judaism, 231
Judas (Iscariot), 145
Judas (the Maccabee), 173
Judges, 90, 101–103, 123
Julias (Bethsaida), 196, 197
Julius Caesar, 178, 184, 216, 220
Julius (centurion), 221
Justus, 216

K

Kadesh (Naphtali), 98
Kadesh-barnea, 57, 59, 68, 69, 74, 75
Kadesh-on-the-Orontes, 16
Kagera R., 16
Kanah R., 30
Kanatha, 184
Karim Shahir, 262
Karkar (on Jabbok), 103
Karkar (on Orontes), 151
Karnaim, 57
Karnak, 67, 151
Kavalla, 213
Kefr et-Tur, 142
Kefr Kennā, 193
Kefr Nahum (Capernaum), 194
Kefr Thilth, 124
Keftiu, 42
Keilah, 127
Keisâriyeh, 201

Kelso, J. L., 260
Kenyon, Kathleen, 258
Kestros R., 210
Khartoum, 16
Khirbet el-Etheleh, 88
Khirbet el-Mird, 260
Khirbet en-Nitla, 88
Khirbet et-Tubeiqeh, 256
Khirbet ez-Zîf, 127
Khirbet Fahil, 125
Khirbet Hamzeh, 104
Khirbet Ibzîq, 90, 125
Khirbet Kerak, 260
Khirbet Mahne, 134
Khirbet Qâna, 194
Khirbet Qîla, 127
Khirbet Qumrân, 259
Khirbet Tequ'a, 134
Khirbet Terrameh, 92
Khirbet Umm el-Idhâm, 87
Kibroth-hattaavah, 75
Kidron Valley, 30, 141, 145, 198
Kiel, Erich, 196
Kimmerioi, 37, 38
King's Highway, 57, 70
King's Pool, 146
Kirjath-arba, 80
Kirjath-jearim, 89, 104, 132
Kirjath-sepher, 90, 255
Kirkuk, 263
Kish, 47, 267
Kishon R., 30, 102
Kition, 40
Kittim, 38, 40
Knossus, 262
Koldewey, R., 263
Koppel, R., 256
Kraeling, E. G., 197
Krio, Cape, 220, 221
Kue, 138
Kurnat es-Sauda, 32
Kursî, 196
Kyle, Melvin Grove, 255

L

Laban, 44, 56, 60, 103
Labashi-Marduk, 164
Lachish, 89, 126, 251, 258
Lagash, 47
Laish (Leshem), 92, 96, 104
Laodice, 227
Laodicea, 211, 227, 228
Latin Church, 240
Latin Kingdom, 234
Lawrence, T. E., 236, 261
Layard, A. H., 263
Lazarus, 197
League of Nations, 245
Leah, 56, 60
Lebanon, Lebanons, 16, 17, 31, 43, 242, 244, 245, 261, 262
Lechaeum, 216

Lehabim, 41
Leontes R., 30
Lepanto, Gulf of, 216
Lepsius, R., 265
Lesbos, 219
Leshem, 104
Lesser Armenia, 179
Levi, 61, 98
Libnah, 89, 254
Libya, Libyans, 42, 52, 166, 247
Lipit Ishtar, 47
Lisan, 57
Litani R. (Leontes), 30
Little Hermon, 196
Lod, 124
Lot, 56, 57, 59, 83, 84
Lubim, 41
Lud, 43
Luden, 44
Luke, 212, 219, 221
Lutro, 221
Lycanus, 186, 188
Lycaonia, 178, 207, 209, 210, 212
Lycia, 179, 209
Lycus R., 227
Lydda, 124, 204, 231
Lydia, Lydian Empire, 19, 41, 44, 52, 164, 207, 210, 212, 226
Lydia (woman), 214
Lydus, 44
Lysias, 173
Lysimachus, 172
Lystra, 209, 211, 218

M

Maachah Zobah, 44, 133
Ma'an, 41
Macalister, R. A. S., 254
Maccabees, 40, 172–174
Macedon, Macedonians, 40, 169, 171, 177, 208, 213, 214, 215, 219
Mackenzie, Duncan, 255
Madai (Medes), 19, 37, 38
Magnesia, 225
Magog, 37, 38
Mahanaim, 60, 134
Mahaneh-Dan, 92
Maisler, B., 260
Makkedah, 89
Malichus, 184
Mallon, A., 256
Malta, 222
Manasseh (king), 146, 158, 159
Manasseh (tribe), 76, 87, 95, 96, 138, 153
Maon, 127
Marah, 74
Marathon, 166
Mardonius, 167
Marduk, 167

Mareshah, 151
Mari, 48, 82, 262
Mariamne, 186
Mariette, A. E., 265
Mark, John, 210, 212
Marmara, Sea of, 207
Marquet-Krause, Judith, 258
Mars Hill, 216
Martel, Charles, 234
Martha, 197
Mary, 191, 197
Masada, 127
Massah, 74
Matapan, Cape, 221
Mattathias, 173
Matthew, 194
Mauretania, 179
Media, Medes, 17, 19, 38, 50, 52, 158
Mediterranean Sea, 13, 14, 16, 25, 41, 43, 48, 50, 65, 67, 79, 209
Megiddo, 25, 30, 34, 80, 97, 102, 136, 146, 152, 192, 254, 255
Meiron, 26, 29, 32, 90
Melchizedek, 58, 131
Melita (Malta), 222
Memphis, 67, 165, 247
Menahem, 154
Menes, 65, 66
Meribah, 74
Merneptah, 69
Merodach-baladan, 157
Merom, Waters of, 29, 89, 90
Mesha, 150, 152
Meshech, 37, 40
Mesopotamia, 14, 16, 20, 41, 42, 43, 44, 47, 48, 49, 55, 56, 79, 82, 101, 133, 154, 179, 232, 233
Messana, 177
Messina, Straits of, 222
Micah, 92, 157
Michmash, 125
Midas, 210
Midian, Midianites, 69, 87, 102, 103
Milcom, 134
Miletus, 171, 209, 219, 220
Minaean, 261
Minnith, 103
Minoan Crete, 221
Miriam, 75
Mitanni, 49, 50, 80, 101
Mithridates, 178, 207
Mizpeh (in Benjamin), 123, 160, 255
Mizpeh (in Gilead), 103
Mizpeh (in Moab), 126
Mizraim, 40, 41, 65
Moab, Moabites, 28, 33, 57, 62, 75, 76, 79, 82, 84, 125, 126, 133, 135, 150, 152, 183, 258
Moawiya, 234

Modin, 173
Moesia, 178
Mohammed, 233, 234
Molech (Milcom), 84, 145
Mongols, 235
Montet, M., 261
Moreh, Hill of, 32, 103, 196
Moresheth-gath, 254
Moriah, 58, 142, 145
Morocco, 179, 234
Moschi, 40
Moses, 70, 73, 74, 75, 76, 87, 88
Moslem, 245
Mosul, 15, 245
Muqeis, 196
Mushki, 40
Musri, 138
Mycenaeans, 221
Myra, 209, 221
Mysia, Mysians, 38, 44, 207, 208, 210, 212
Mysus, 44

N

Nabal, 127
Nabataeans, 69, 70, 150, 151, 258
Nablus, 186
Nabonidus, 52, 164
Nabopolassar, 38, 50, 52, 158, 160, 163
Nag Hammadi, 266
Nahash, 125
Nahor, 56, 262
Nahr Bâniyâs, 28
Nahr Baradâ, 133
Nahr Bereigheth, 29
Nahr el-Liddânî, 29
Nahr ez-Zarqâ, 29, 30
Nahr Hasbânî, 29
Nain, 192
Naomi, 84
Naphtali, 102, 154
Naphtuhim, 41
Napoleon, 239
Na Ptah, 41
Nar-Mer, 65
Naroth, 126
Nathan, 102
Nathaniel, 193
Nazareth, 98, 191, 192, 240
Neapolis, 213
Nebo, Mt., 28, 33
Nebuchadnezzar, 52, 67, 70, 150, 151, 157, 160, 163–164, 220, 255, 256, 258–265
Necho, 50, 52, 160, 163, 265
Negeb, 26, 31, 32, 58, 59, 70, 75, 90, 183, 188, 242
Negev (see Negeb)
Nehemiah, 146, 167
Nein, 196
Nelson, H. N., 239

Neo-Babylonian Empire, 158, 163–169
Neriglissar, 164
Nicaea, 208, 210
Nicholas, St., 221
Nicomedia, 208
Nile, Battle of the, 239
Nile Delta, 41, 42, 66
Nile R., 13, 16, 40, 56, 62, 65, 66, 73, 247
Nimrod, 37, 40, 41, 47
Nimrûd, 47
Nineveh, 15, 19, 20, 38, 43, 49, 50, 55, 158, 159, 263
No, 67, 158
Noah, 19, 47
No-Amon, 67, 158
Nob, 126
Noricum, 178
Nubia, 40, 65, 158
Nuzi, 80, 263

O

Obadiah, 70
Obed-edom, 133
Octavian, 178, 185, 186
Offense, Mount of, 145
Og, 42, 75, 79, 87, 95
Olives, Mount of, 38, 142, 145, 198
Olivet (see Mount of Olives)
Omar, 233
Omayads, 234
Omri, 150, 152, 153, 254
On, 67
Ophel, 142
Ophir, 44, 136
Ophrah, 102
Oppenheim, Max von, 262
Oreb, 103
Ornan, 134
Orontes R., 16, 30, 43, 149, 151, 202, 210, 244
Osorkon, 151
Othniel, 90, 101

P

Padan-aram, 13, 20, 55
Padi, 158
Palatine Hill, 177, 222
Palestine, 25–33, 79–84, 183–188, *et passim*
Palestine Exploration Fund, 145, 240, 258
Palmerston, H. J. T., 239
Palmyra (Tadmor), 135, 180
Pamphylia, 209
Pangaean Mts., 213
Panias, 186, 197
Panium, Battle of, 172
Pannonia, 178

Paphlagonia, 38
Paphos, 210
Paran, 68, 75
Parrot, A., 48, 262
Parthenon, 216
Parthia, Parthians, 178, 179, 185, 232
Pas-dammim, 126
Patara, 209, 220
Pathros, Pathrusim, 41
Patmos, 225
Paul, 40, 203, 207–222
Pausanius, 215, 218
Pekah, 149
Pelagonia, 213
Peleg, 262
Pelethites, 134
Pella (Macedonia), 213
Pella (Palestine), 184
Peloponnesian War, 214, 215
Peloponnesus, 216
Pelusiac Branch (Nile), 16, 65
Pelusium, 165
Peniel (Penuel), 60, 95, 103, 150
Pentecost, 209
Peraea, 183, 188, 198
Perez-uzzah, 132
Perga, 209, 210
Pergamum (or Pergamos), 225, 228
Perizzites, 82
Per-Rameses, 73
Persepolis, 166, 171
Persia, Persian Empire, 13, 14, 19, 38, 52, 67, 164–167, 171, 172, 210, 232, 233, 234
Persian Gulf, 13, 14, 41, 43, 47, 50, 245
Peshitta, 232
Pessinus, 212
Peter, 187, 194, 197, 201, 203, 204, 269
Pethor *(Pitru)*, 75
Petra (see also Sela), 69, 70, 133, 154
Petrie, Sir Flinders, 240, 251, 256, 265
Pfeiffer, R. H., 263
Pharisees, 174, 187
Pharos, 247
Pharpar, 149
Pharsalus, 178
Phasael, 146, 185
Phenice, 221
Philadelphia (Asia Minor), 209, 227, 228
Philadelphia (Rabbath-ammon), 184
Philip (the Apostle), 197
Philip of Macedon, 171, 215
Philip the Tetrarch, 186, 187, 196, 197
Philippi, 185, 213, 214, 219, 269

Philistia, Philistines, 14, 20, 25, 42, 73, 80, 82, 104, 125, 126, 132, 154, 221
Phillips, Wendell, 261
Philostratus, 215
Phinehas, 87
Phoenicia, Phoenicians, 14, 17, 20, 38, 42, 80, 177, 197, 220
Phoenix (Phenice), 221
Phrygia, 38, 40, 172, 207, 210, 212, 218
Phut, 40, 42
Phythian-Adams, W. J., 254
Pieria, Mt., 210
Pi-hahireth, 73
Pilate, 187
Pion, Mt., 219
Piraeus, 215
Pishon R., 44
Pisidia, 178, 207, 209, 210
Plataea, 167
Pliny, 41, 167, 184, 208, 216
Po Valley, 177
Polycarp, 225
Pompey, 174, 178, 209
Pontifical Biblical Institute, 256
Pontus, 178, 207, 209
Portuguese, 236
Posidon, 268
Pozzuoli, 222
Priam, 210
Priscilla, 216, 218
Pritchard, J. B., 260
Propontis, 207, 208
Psamtik, 165
Ptah, 41
Ptolemaïs, 184, 220, 239
Ptolemy (Maccabean), 173
Ptolemy I (Soter), 172
Ptolemy II (Philadelphus), 226, 247
Ptolemy IV (Philopator), 172
Punic Wars, 177
Punjab, 171
Punt, 42
Purim, 167
Put, 42
Puteoli (Pozzuoli), 222

Q

Qal'aah Sherqât, 263
Qataban, 261
Qumran, 30, 40, 127, 259

R

Raamah, 40, 41
Raamses (Rameses), 67, 73
Rabbah (Rabbath-ammon), 84, 134, 243, 244
Rachel, 56, 60, 61, 97
Raetia, 178
Rahab, 55, 80

Ramah, 123, 126
Ramathaim (Ramathaim-zophim), 123
Rameses II, 16, 67, 255, 258, 267
Rameses III, 80
Ramle, 254
Ramoth-gilead, 152
Ramsay, William M., 212, 267, 268
Raphana, 184
Râs el-'Ain, 104
Râs es-Safsafeh, 74
Râs Shamra (see also Ugarit), 79, 262
Rawlinson, H., 267
Re, 67
Red Sea, 13, 14, 41, 44, 67, 70, 73, 74
Reeds, Sea of (see also Red Sea), 73, 74
Reggio di Calabria, 222
Rehoboam, 41, 149, 151, 254
Rehoboth, 59
Renaissance, 235
Rentis, 123
Repha, 79
Rephaim, 79
Rephaim, Valley of, 79, 132, 145
Rephidim, 74, 87, 125
Reuben, 76, 87, 95
Rezin, 149
Rezon, 138
Rhegium, 222
Rhine R., 178
Rhodes, 40, 220, 225
Riblah, 16, 133
Richard the Lionhearted, 234
Riphaean Mts., 38
Riphath, 38
Robinson, Edward, 240
Rodanim, 40
Roediger, E., 261
Roman Catholic Church, 240
Rome, Roman Empire, 40, 67, 173, 177–180, 188, 220, 222, 233, 268, 269
Romulus and Remus, 177
Rosetta Stone, 239, 264
Rostovtzeff, M. I., 261
Rothschild, Edmund, 240
Rowe, A., 255
Roxanna, 172
Rubicon, 178
Rubuta, 59
Russia, 240, 247
Ruth, 55, 84, 191

S

Saad, Zaki, 265
Saba, Sabaeans, 41, 136, 261

Sabatah, 41
Sabtah, 40, 41
Sabtechah, 40, 41
Sadducees, 174
Safad, 239
Saguntum, 177
Saint Paul's Bay, 222
Sa'îr, 153
Sakkarah, 67, 265
Saladin, 234
Salah-ed-Din, 234
Salamis (Cyprus), 210
Salamis (Greece), 167
Salem, 58, 131
Salmone, Cape, 221
Salome, Alexandra, 174
Saloniki, 214
Salt, Valley of, 133
Salt Sea, see Dead Sea
Samal, 261
Samaria, Samaritans, 32, 50, 56, 59, 60, 61, 67, 97, 151, 152, 154, 165, 166, 174, 183, 188, 192, 202, 231, 258
Samarkand, 234
Samos, 167, 219
Samothrace, 213
Samson, 104
Samuel, 104, 123, 124, 125, 126
Sappho, 219
Sarah (Sarai), 56, 59, 68
Sardinia, 40, 177
Sardis, 171, 209, 226, 227, 228, 268
Sargon (II), 50, 82, 149, 154, 157, 261
Sargon of Akkad, 43, 48, 101
Saron (see also Sharon), 183
Saronic Gulf, 215
Saturn, Temple of, 222
Saudi Arabia, 13
Saul, 60, 70, 98, 104, 123–128
Schaeffer, F. A., 262
Scipio, 177
Scopus, Mt., 126, 142
Scylla, 222
Scythians, 38, 158
Seba, 40, 41, 44
Sebaste (see also Samaria), 186
Sebastiyeh (Samaria), 254
Sechu, 126
Seil ed-Dilbeh, 90
Seir, Mt., 57, 69, 70, 75, 79
Sela (see also Petra), 133, 154, 188
Seleucia (Pieria), 16, 204, 210
Seleucids, 172–174
Seleucus I, 172, 202, 226
Seleucus II, 227
Seljuks, 234
Sellers, O. R., 256
Semechonitis, Lake (see also Hula), 183
Semites, 43, 49, 65
Seneca, 216

Sennacherib, 19, 43, 50, 150, 157, 158
Septuagint, 67, 172
Serabit el-Khadim, 68
Sergius Paulus, 210
Serug, 262
Seti I, 255
Shabwat, 41
Shalisha, 124
Shalmaneser III, 38, 50, 151, 152
Shalmaneser V, 50, 154
Shamgar, 102
Sharon, Plain of, 25, 183, 204
Sharuhen, 256
Shatt al Arab, 15, 16
Sheba, 41, 44, 134, 136, 261
Shechem, 32, 42, 56, 59, 60, 61, 82, 89, 96, 98, 149, 256
Shem, 41, 43
Shephelah, 25, 31, 80, 89, 127, 131, 132, 254
Sheshbazzar, 165
Sheshonk I (Shishak), 41, 151, 255, 266
Sheveh Kiriathaim, 57
Shibboleth, 104
Shiloh, 95, 96
Shishak, 41, 151, 255, 266
Shobach, 133
Shual, 124
Shunem, 98
Shur, Wilderness of, 65, 68, 74
Shushan (Susa), 167, 171, 266
Siannu, 43
Sicily, 40, 177, 222
Siddim, Valley of, 57
Sidon, 37, 42, 197, 204, 221, 245, 265
Sihon, 42, 75, 83, 84, 87, 95
Silas, 212, 214
Siloam, 145
Silwân, 145
Simeon, 61, 96, 150, 183, 191
Simirra, 43
Simon (Maccabee), 173, 184
Simon the Leper, 197
Simons, J., 73, 92, 125
Sin, Wilderness of, 68, 74
Sinai, Mt., 13, 15, 67, 68, 69, 73, 74
Sinai Peninsula, 242, 247
Sinites, 42, 43
Sinjirli, 261
Sinuhe, 66
Sisera, 98, 102
Smyrna, 225, 228, 268
Socoh, 31, 126
Sodom, 56, 57, 58
Solomon, 14, 42, 43, 44, 70, 82, 88, 98, 131, 135–138, 142, 149, 150
Somaliland, 42
Sorek, Valley of, 31, 104
Spain, 40, 177, 178

Sparta, 167, 173, 178
Starkey, J. L., 258
Starr, Richard, 263
Stekelis, M., 260
Stephen, 201
Strabo, 10, 40, 220, 254
Strato's Tower (see also Caesarea, Stratonis), 186
Strymon R., 214
Succoth, 60, 73, 103, 136
Sudan, 16
Suez, Gulf of, 15, 17, 67
Suez Canal, 73, 239, 247
Sukenik, E., 258
Suleiman I, 145
Sumer, Sumerians, 14, 19, 47, 48, 65, 154, 245
Susa (Shushan), 20, 43, 167, 171, 266
Sychar, 196
Syene, 16
Syracuse, 222
Syr Darya, 166
Syria, 13, 16, 17, 20, 40, 42, 43, 48, 49, 50, 52, 67, 80, 82, 101, 133, 149, 172, 178, 209, 234, 242, 244, 261–263
Syrian Gates, 212

T

Taanach, 97
Taberah, 75
Tabigha, 194, 196, 197
Tabor, Mt., 32, 98, 102, 128, 192
Tabriz, 246
Tadmor, 135
Talmud, 192
Tamar, 134
Tamerlane, 227
Tanis, 73, 266
Tarentines, 177
Tarq, 234
Tarshish, 38, 40
Tarsus, 202, 203, 204, 209
Tartars, 235
Tartessus, 40
Tattenai, 166
Taurus Mts., 17, 40, 202, 209
Tavium, 212
Taylor, J. E., 263
Teheran, 246
Tekoa, 134
Tel-abib, 163, 202
Tel Arad, 260
Tel Aviv, 242, 259
Tel Beer Sheva, 260
Teleilât el-Ghassûl, 256
Tell Abū Kharaz, 125
Tell 'Amar, 102
Tell Araq-Menshîyeh, 126
Tell 'Atshâneh, 262
Tell-Balatah, 60, 256

Tell Beit Mirsim, 90, 92, 255, 258
Tell Deir 'Allā, 60, 136
Tell Dotan, 260
Tell ed-Duweir, 254, 258
Tell el-'Ajjūl, 256
Tell el-Amarna, 256, 265
Tell el-Azhar, 104
Tell el-Fâr'ah, 256, 259
Tell el-Fûl, 123, 255
Tell el-Hesī, 253, 254
Tell el-Judeideh, 254
Tell el-Kheleifeh, 258
Tell el-Khuweilifeh, 128
Tell el-Maqlûb, 125
Tell el-Meqbereh, 125
Tell el-Mutesellim, 255
Tell el-Qâdī, 29
Tell el-Qedah, 260
Tell esh-Sheckh Madhkûr, 126
Tell es-Sâfī, 126, 254
Tell es-Sa'īdiyeh, 136
Tell Halâf, 262
Tell Hariri, 262
Tell Hûm, 194
Tell Jemmeh, 254, 256
Tell Jezer, 136, 254
Tell Ma'în, 127
Tell Qasileh, 259
Tell Zakariyeh, 254
Terah, 37, 43, 56, 245
Tertullian, 232
Teutons, 233
Thales, 220
Thebes, 67, 158
Therma, 214
Thermaic Gulf, 214
Thermopylae, 167
Thessalonica, 214, 219
Thessaloniki, 214
Thrace, 166, 171, 179
Three Taverns, 222
Thutmose III, 25, 204, 256
Thyatira, 209, 226, 228
Tiberias (City), 196, 231, 239
Tiberius (Caesar), 179, 197
Tiglath-pileser I, 50
Tiglath-pileser III, 43, 95, 96, 98, 149, 150, 154, 157, 260, 261
Tigris R., 14, 15, 16, 43, 47, 50, 80, 167, 244
Til-garimmu, 38
Timna (South Arabia), 261
Timnah (Timnath), 104
Timothy, 212
Timsah, Lake, 62, 68
Tiras, 37, 40
Tirhakah, 50
Tirzah, 150, 259
Titus, 142, 219
Tob, 103, 133
Togarmah, 38
Tours, 234
Tower of Furnaces, 146
Trabizond (Trapezus), 167

Trajan, 179, 208, 210
Trans-Jordan, 79, 243, 258
Trapezus, 167
Tripolis (Tripoli), 43, 245
Troas, 208, 212, 213, 219
Trogyllium, 219
Troy, 40, 212
Trypho, 173
Tubal, 37, 40
Tula Abū el-'Alâyiq, 260
Turkestan, 234
Turkey, Turks, 16, 235, 236,
    239, 241, 244, 246, 247, 248,
    267, 268
Turusha, 40
Tutankhamun, 266
Tyre, 14, 37, 38, 40, 41, 42, 43,
    135, 136, 158, 171, 177, 204,
    220, 240, 245, 251, 254, 265
Tyropoeon Valley, 141, 142,
    145
Tyrsenoi, 40

U

Ugarit, 79, 262
Umm Qeis, 196
United Arab Republic, 247
University of Pennsylvania
    Museum, 255
University of Tel Aviv, 260
Ur, 14, 47, 55, 56, 131, 245, 263
Urartu, 19, 50
Uriah, 82, 134, 244
Ur-Nammu, 47
Uruk, 47
Urusalim, 58
Uzzah, 133
Uzziah, 154

V

Valley Gate, 146
Vashti, 167
Verria, 214
"Via Maris," 34
Vienna, 235
Viri Galiloei, 142

W

Wadi 'Araba, 133
Wadi el-'Arish, 31, 65, 68
Wadi el-Hasā, 28, 30
Wadi el-Milh, 133
Wadi el-Mughârah, 79
Wadi el-Mûjib, 29
Wadi en-Nâr, 145
Wadi es-Sant, 31
Wadi Far'ā, 30
Wadi Gharandel, 74
Wadi Ghazzeh, 31
Wadi Murabbâ'at, 30, 259–260
Wadi-Qelt, 30, 88
Wadi-Qumrân, 30
Wadi-Sayyal, 30
Wadi-Tumilat, 62
Wadi Yâbis, 125
Warka, 47
Wilhelm II, Kaiser, 241
Winkler, Hugo, 267
Woolley, Sir L., 261, 262
Wright, G. Ernest, 256

X

Xanthus R., 209
Xenophon, 167
Xerxes I, 52, 166

Y

Yadin, Yigael, 260
Yam Suph, 73
Yarkon R., 30
Yarmuk R., 28, 29, 87, 95, 233
Yemen, 41, 43, 136, 261
Yorghan Tepe, 263, 264

Z

Zab R., 19, 43
Zagros Mts., 17, 38, 80, 245
Zalmunna, 103
Zama, 177
Zarethan, 136
Zebah, 103
Zeboiim, 56
Zebulun, 98, 102
Zedekiah, 67, 160, 164, 255
Zeeb, 103
Zemarite, 42, 43
Zenobia, 135
Zephath, 90
Zephathah, Valley of, 31
Zerah, 151
Zered R., 30, 69, 75, 87
Zerubbabel, 165, 186
Zeus, 173, 226, 268
Ziklag, 96, 127, 128, 131
Zimri-Lim, 48, 262
Zin, Wilderness of, 68
Zion, Mt., 32, 141, 144
Zoan, 73
Zoar, 56
Zobah, 44, 125, 133
Zorah, 92, 104
Zuph, 124
Zuzim (Zamzummim), 79